THE EUROPEAN CONVENTION ON HUMAN RIGHTS AS AN INSTRUMENT OF TORT LAW

THE EUROPEAN CONVENTION ON HUMAN RIGHTS AS AN INSTRUMENT OF TORT LAW

Stefan Somers

intersentia
Cambridge – Antwerp – Chicago

Intersentia Ltd
Sheraton House | Castle Park
Cambridge | CB3 0AX | United Kingdom
Tel.: +44 1223 370 170 | Fax: +44 1223 370 169
Email: mail@intersentia.co.uk
www.intersentia.com | www.intersentia.co.uk

Distribution for the UK and Ireland:
NBN International
Airport Business Centre, 10 Thornbury Road
Plymouth, PL6 7PP
United Kingdom
Tel.: +44 1752 202 301 | Fax: +44 1752 202 331
Email: orders@nbninternational.com

Distribution for Europe and all other countries:
Intersentia Publishing nv
Groenstraat 31
2640 Mortsel
Belgium
Tel.: +32 3 680 15 50 | Fax: +32 3 658 71 21
Email: mail@intersentia.be

Distribution for the USA and Canada:
Independent Publishers Group
Order Department
814 North Franklin Street
Chicago, IL 60610
USA
Tel.: +1 800 888 4741 (toll free) | Fax: +1 312 337 5985
Email: orders@ipgbook.com

The European Convention on Human Rights as an Instrument of Tort Law

ISBN 978-1-78068-683-7
D/2018/7849/87
NUR 822

British Library Cataloguing in Publication Data. A catalogue record for this book is available from the British Library.

For Sanne

CONTENTS

LIST OF CASES

EUROPEAN COURT OF HUMAN RIGHTS

1968

1971

1972

1974

1975

1976

1978

1979

1980

1981

1982

1983

1984

1985

1986

1987

1988

1989

1990

1991

1992

1993

1994

1995

1996

1997

1998

1999

2000

2001

2002

2003

2004

2005

2006

2007

2008

2009

2010

2011

2012

2013

2014

2015

2016

2017

EUROPEAN COMMISSION OF HUMAN RIGHTS

INTRODUCTION

In 2011, Elisabeth Lambert Abdelgawad wrote that Art. 41 of the ECHR had not yet gained much attention in legal scholarship.[1] At that time, the topic had been touched upon in several articles and had been the main topic of the PhD of Michiel Van Emmerik.[2] But the topic had not yet been the subject of a vividly academic debate. Publications regarding tort law and human rights stood as lone rocks in the vibrant sea of human rights doctrine. When I began to do research on the relationship between human rights and Belgian tort law in 2011, I had the impression that I was digging into a topic that fell between the field of interest of human rights scholars and tort lawyers. It seemed as if none of them were really interested in the topic. Human rights scholars seldom paid much attention to topics like damages and compensation. They were more interested in substantial topics, the major societal issues that come to the surface when human rights are at stake. Tort lawyers on the other hand, are often unaware of the possible influence of the European Convention on Human Rights. Since one of the main purposes of tort law is the reparation of damages, it seemed likely that scholars in tort law would be interested in the jurisprudence of the ECtHR on restitution. But this did not seem to be true. At least in Belgium, it looked as if tort lawyers were almost unaware of the fact that the ECtHR has the ability to award damages, let alone that this ability can potentially influence national tort law.

This disregard of tort law and human rights for one another is reasonable if one takes into account that for a long time both fields of law were perceived as part of two different spheres of the law. Human rights are traditionally part of public law, that is the law that regulates the vertical relations between the state and private persons. Tort law is a

1 E. Lambert Abdelgawad, 'Introduction générale' in J.-F. Flauss and E. Lambert Abdelgawad (eds.), *La pratique d'indemnisation par la Cour européenne des droits de l'homme*, Brussels, Bruylant, 2011, p1 at 1.

2 M.L. Van Emmerik, *Schadevergoeding bij schending van mensenrechten. De rechtspraktijk onder het EVRM vergeleken met die in Nederland*, Stichting NJCM-Boekerij, Leiden, 1997.

part of private law, that is the law that applies in the horizontal relations between private persons inter se. Both spheres of the law were perceived as different in nature. This is mainly so because of the monopoly over violence of the state. This monopoly enables the state to exercise coercion on its citizens, whereas it disables citizens from using coercion towards one another. Consequently, the power of the state in its relations towards citizens has no counterpart in the relations between citizens. As a result, the rules that apply in both spheres of the law have to be different in nature, since they target two very different types of relations. Indeed, human rights are the conditions that the state has to abide by according to the social contract. They are the legal limitations on the state's sovereign power, and do not apply in horizontal relations.

During the last decades, this traditional approach has been challenged on several occasions. Judges and lawyers refer more and more to human rights when dealing with conflicts between private persons.[3] It has even become common sense to talk about the so-called horizontal effect of human rights, by which we mean the influence of human rights on the relations among citizens. From a theoretical perspective, two arguments are often invoked to support the horizontal effect of human rights. First, the rise of multinationals and other large companies results in the existence of private legal persons that, just as states, have a powerful position within society.[4] It is said that these actors, when they have a relationship with normal private persons, need to abide by the same or similar rules as states have to do. Secondly it is noted that states often try to avoid their human rights obligations by delegating some of their competences to private institutions that are not subject to human rights obligations.[5]

---

3 T. Barkhuysen and M. Van Emmerik, 'Constitutionalization of Private Law: The European Convention on Human Rights Perspective' in T. Barkhuysen and S. D. Lindenbergh (eds.), *Constitutionalization of Private Law*, Leiden, Martinus Nijhoff Publishers, 2006, p.43 at 44–45; A. Mowbray, *The Development of Positive Obligations Under the European Convention on Human Rights by the European Court of Human Rights*, Oxford, Hart Publishing, 2004; N. Van Leuven, *Contracten en mensenrechten. Een mensenrechtelijke lezing van het contractenrecht*, Leuven, Intersentia, 2009, at 17–182; and J. Wright, *Tort Law and Human Rights*, Oxford, Hart Publishing, 2017, at 18ff.

4 A. Clapham, *Human Rights in the Private Sphere*, Oxford, Clarendon, 1993, at 137–138; O. Gerstenberg, 'What constitutions do (but courts sometimes don't): property, speech, and the influence of constitutional norms on private law', *Can JL & Jur* 2004, p61 at 70; and C. van Dam, 'Tort Law and Human Rights: Brothers in Arms. On the Role of Tort Law in the Area of Business and Human Right', *JETL* 2011, p221–254.

5 K. Gray and S. Gray, 'Civil Rights, Civil Wrongs and Quasi-Public Space', *EHRLR* 1999, p46 at 48f; H. Thorgeirsdottir, 'Journalism worthy of the name: an affirmative reading of Article 10 of the ECHR', *NQHR* 2004, p601 at 617; R.-J. Uhl,

Because the line between private and public law institutions becomes blurred, proponents of this argument argue that it is necessary that the human rights of citizens are also protected against unlawful infringements by private persons. A third argument for the horizontal effect of human rights can be found in the fundamental nature of human rights and the horizontal dimension of the social contract. According to this line of reasoning, the primordial function of the state is to protect human rights in horizontal relations. The horizontal application of human rights is the reason for the state's existence.[6] The vertical application of human rights is the only condition that the state has to abide by when it exercises its prerogatives. Indeed, a state cannot act legitimately if it harms the same rights as it, according to its reason of being, has to protect.[7]

On the basis of this last argument, it becomes clear that states have a positive obligation to protect human rights in horizontal relations. Consequently, human rights have a horizontal dimension and can be relevant for private law. This book starts from this premise and discusses how the European Convention on Human Rights can influence the field of tort law. It starts to do so by analyzing the instruments via which the Convention can influence national tort law. The first aspect of which is the theory of positive obligations of states to protect human rights in general and the notion of positive obligations to protect human rights in horizontal relations more specifically. The first chapter will deal with these theories and will elaborate on the criteria that the ECtHR developed in its jurisprudence. With this in mind, the question will be asked whether the Court applies a different set of criteria when it is confronted with an infringement of a positive obligation, or a positive obligation to protect human rights in horizontal relations, as to when it is confronted with a violation of a negative obligation. The elaboration on this theory is important, since it is the basis in positive law for the influence of human rights on private law in general.

'Vrijheid van meningsuiting en eigendomsrecht', *NJCM-Bulletin* 2005, p416 at 424; A. Williams, 'Public authorities: what is a hybrid public authority under the HRA?' in D. Hoffman (ed.), *The impact of the UK Human Rights Act on Private Law*, Cambridge, Cambridge University Press, pp48–65.

6 Which is why human rights often conflict, as was observed by Besson: S. Besson, 'Human Rights in Relation. A Critical Reading of the ECtHR's Approach to Conflicts of Rights' in S. Smet and E. Brems, *When Human Rights Clash at the European Court of Human Rights*, Oxford, Oxford University Press, 2017, p24 at 29ff.

7 S. Somers, 'Protecting human rights in horizontal relationships by tort law or elaborating tort law from a human rights perspective', *EHRLR* 2015, p149 at 153.

In order to understand the possible impact of the Convention on national tort or liability law, it is important to look at Art. 13 of the Convention, especially when read in conjunction with Art. 41 of the Convention. This is done in the second and third chapters. Chapter 2 illustrates that the Convention sometimes requires an instrument of state liability in national law in order to provide an effective remedy to a human rights victim (or an injured party) as is required under Art. 13 of the Convention. Moreover, by reading this requirement in conjunction with Art. 41 of the Convention, on the basis of which the Court can award compensations to the victims of human rights violations, it becomes clear that national tort law needs to take into account the compensatory practice that the Court develops under Art. 41 of the Convention. The third chapter will then illustrate that these principles are not only relevant for state liability, but also for the application of tort law in pure private law relations.

A third instrument via which the European Convention on Human Rights might be relevant for national tort law is developed in the fourth chapter. This short chapter discusses how a tortfeasor can appeal to his Convention rights. Thus, whereas the second and third chapters discuss mechanisms of human rights protection of the injured party in national tort law, the fourth chapter discusses the protection of the rights of the tortfeasor.

The fifth chapter then discusses how Art. 41 of the Convention on its own can be seen as a correction on national tort law in the sense that it empowers the Court to award additional compensations to human rights victims if they received only partial compensation under national law. This is the mechanism via which the Court can enforce the principles that were developed in Chapters 2 and 3 on the member states. Indeed, whereas these chapters illustrated that a state sometimes has to provide liability schemes via which compensation is provided that are in line with those that the Court awards under Art. 41, this chapter illustrates that a person who received a more limited compensation can appeal to the Court and can claim an additional compensation under Art. 41 of the Convention.

In the five first chapters, it becomes apparent that Art. 41 of the Convention can have an impact on national tort law. Because of this, it is important to know how this provision is applied and how one can read this provision from a tort law perspective. This will be done in the following chapters. Chapter 6 starts with a general outline of Art. 41 of the Convention. Chapter 7 then discusses the concept of damages as applied in the context of this provision; Chapter 8 examines the concepts of fault and blameworthiness; Chapter 9 causality; and Chapter 10 restitution. Throughout these chapters, the question always arises of how the ECtHR perceives these elements of tort law and how this approach can influence national law. The results of these chapters must thus always be read with the first five chapters in mind. Throughout these chapters, a lot of topics of national tort law will be discussed, ranging from matters such as moral damages, punitive damages or the estimation of damages, towards contributory negligence.

Although it would lead us too far to discuss all these issues in the introduction of this book, one topic needs special attention: the question of whether Art. 41 of the Convention grants human rights victims a right to compensation. In other words: is the Court obliged to award compensation to human rights victims when it finds a violation of the Convention, or is it up to the discretion of the Court to do so? This question is important, for it somehow determines whether the interpretation of the jurisprudence on Art. 41 of the Convention from a tort law perspective makes sense. If the Court is not bound by any rules when ruling on this provision, then why would we try to explain its jurisprudence on the basis of rules of tort law? By asking this question, one questions the purpose of this project. As a consequence, this is a preliminary question that needs an answer at the beginning of this book, and not at the end. This question will however be answered towards the end of the book. In order to understand the discretion of the Court on the basis of Art. 41, it is important to understand the explicit and implicit rules that are applied by the Court. This book will argue that human rights victims under Art. 41 of the Convention have a right to compensation that is similar to the right of compensation that tort victims have under national tort law. This means that the Court is not bound to award a compensation every time it finds a violation of an applicant's substantive Convention rights. Nevertheless, when it refuses to award compensation, it will have to rely on reasons that are familiar in national tort law. For example, if the Court does not award compensation, it can be because there is no causal link between the human rights violation and the claimed damages, because it finds that the damages should be attributed to the fault of the applicant himself, because there was not enough evidence, because it finds that the damages are so small so that they fall under the *de mimimis* rule, and so on. It is only by interpreting the jurisprudence of the Court from a tort law perspective that one can understand how the Court can be bound by principles when awarding compensation. Moreover, this book will also argue that the Court must be bound by these principles for two reasons. The first reason is rather theoretical, but quite fundamental: that not even the Court stands above the law. The second reason is more practical. It starts from the observation made in the first chapters that the Court under Art. 13 of the Convention often requires member states to provide national remedies that can provide compensation that are more or less in line with those that the Court awards under Art. 41 of the Convention. Thus, if the Court requires national legal systems to take its jurisprudence into account under Art. 41, it must adhere to some principles. Otherwise it is impossible for the member states to do so.

There are two interesting aspects, or points of view, on the influence of human rights on tort law that are not discussed in this book. First, this book does not elaborate on the substantial impact of the Convention rights on tort law. This can be regretted. It is indeed interesting to look at how the ECtHR interprets several rights such as the right to privacy or the right to life and how this might affect national tort law. Such an approach has for example been used by J. Wright who, in her outstanding book, looked amongst other things at the impact of the Convention and the English Human Rights Act on the law of defamation.[8] Secondly, this book does not approach the relationship between human rights and tort law from a national perspective. Such an approach requires a case-by-case analysis for every European legal system, as has been done for several legal systems in an interesting monograph edited by E. Baginska.[9]

To conclude this introduction, some practical remarks must be made. First, in the back of the book you can find a long list of all the jurisprudence of the Court and the Commission that is used. The list contains the full references. In the footnotes, only short references are made. With regard to doctrine, the footnotes only contain the full reference the first time a publication is referred to. From the second time onwards, only a short reference is used. Thirdly, some terms are always abbreviated. So, instead of the European Court of Human Rights and the European Convention on Human Rights, the text simply refers to the ECtHR or the Court and the ECHR or the Convention.

---

8 J. Wright, *Tort Law and Human Rights*, Oxford, Hart Publishing, 2017, at 233ff.

9 E. Baginska (ed.), *Damages for Violations of Human Rights. A comparative Study of Domestic Legal Systems*, Heidelberg, Springer, 2016, 486p.

CHAPTER 1

HUMAN RIGHTS IN HORIZONTAL RELATIONS

1. THE HORIZONTAL DIMENSION OF HUMAN RIGHTS IN THE CONVENTION TEXT

The most common understanding of human rights or fundamental rights is based on negative obligations. Negative obligations impose obligations on states to restrain from interfering in the fundamental rights of its citizens. From this perspective, the state cannot kill its citizens or interfere in the privacy of its citizens, etc. Positive obligations, on the other hand, are obligations that oblige states to act to protect human rights. Within the field of positive obligations, there are obligations for the state to protect the human rights of private persons against the interference of other private persons. These obligations are called the positive obligation to protect human rights in horizontal relations. To grasp a better understanding of these types of obligations, the right to life can be illustrative. Seen from the perspective of negative obligations, the right to life stipulates that the state cannot kill its citizens. If the state actively kills persons, it violates its human rights obligations. But the right to life can be threatened by factors other than the state. The right to life can be threatened by shortages of food or by disease. Thus, from the perspective of positive obligations, the right to life imposes an obligation on states to provide basic health and food supplies to its citizens. Moreover, the right to life can also be threatened by private persons. People can violently or negligently kill one another. From the perspective of positive obligations of the state to protect human rights in horizontal relations, this has the consequence that the state must provide instruments of criminal and private law to prevent and cure violations of the right to life in order to fulfil its human rights obligations.

Although one might say that the protection of human rights in horizontal relations is the primary function of the state, it has never been self-evident. Indeed, the primary focus of the ECHR has always been on negative obligations and not on positive obligations, let alone on positive obligations to protect human rights in horizontal relations. Nevertheless, there are some indications in the Convention that human rights have a horizontal dimension. A clear indication can be found in the limitation clauses in Arts 8, 9 and 10 ECHR. These clauses stipulate that Convention rights can be restricted in order to protect the rights and freedom of other persons. Thus, it is clear that these limitation clauses relate to the horizontal relations between private persons.[1] They give permission to states to limit the protection of someone's human rights in order to protect the rights of another. The same can be said of Art. 2 ECHR. The first paragraph of this provision stipulates that 'everyone's right to life shall be protected' and that 'no one shall be deprived of his life intentionally save in the execution of a sentence of a court following his conviction of a crime for which this penalty is provided by law.' By using these words, the Convention does not describe a general human right to life. Not one that only applies to the relationship between states and citizens. The same can be said of Art. 4. This provision prohibits slavery and servitude in general and does not refer to the vertical relationship between the state and its citizens at all. Furthermore, Art. 2, §2 stipulates that the right to life shall not be regarded as inflicted if it results from the use of force which is no more than is absolutely necessary in defense of any person from unlawful violence. Thus, just as with Arts 8, 9 and 10, states are permitted to infringe someone's right to life if this is necessary to protect the right to life of another.[2]

Another provision in the Convention that somehow refers to the horizontal dimension of human rights is Art. 17. This provision reads as follows:

> Nothing in this Convention may be interpreted as implying for any State, group or person any right to engage in any activity or perform any act aimed at the destruction of any of the rights and freedoms set forth herein or at their limitation to a greater extent than is provided for in the Convention.

---

1 A. Clapham, 'The "Drittwirkung" of the Convention' in R. Macdonald, F. Matscher and H. Petzold (eds.), *The European System for the Protection of Human Rights*, Dordrecht, Martinus Nijhoff Publishers, 1993, p163 at 169.

2 Cremer is of the opinion that the fact that the right to life is protected directly by the law itself proves that human rights must find application in horizontal relationships: H.-J. Cremer, *Human Rights and the Protection of Privacy in Tort Law. A Comparison between English and German law*, London, Routledge, 2001, at 117.

The aim of this provision is to prevent states, individuals and groups from appealing to the Convention to abolish it. It has been perceived as an instrument of continuous strife against anti-democratic persons and groups. The provision is interpreted as an all or nothing mechanism. An applicant loses his right to appeal to the ECtHR if it seems that he is appealing to the Court to challenge an alleged violation of the Convention that has been caused by an act of the applicant that was intended to limit or annul someone's Convention rights.[3] However, if one reads Art. 17 closely, it seems possible that the provision may have a more significant function. First, the provision does not only target states, but also groups and persons. Secondly, the provision targets these actors when they aim to destruct any of the Convention rights or when they aim to limit the rights to a greater extent than allowed by the Convention. Since all holders of Convention rights are private persons, it seems as if the provision can be applied in cases where private persons try to destroy or limit the Convention rights and freedom of other persons. From this perspective, Art. 17 can be used as a tool to control the behavior of private persons in horizontal relations by subjecting their Convention rights to human rights obligations.

This broader reading of Art. 17 finds support in the jurisprudence of the Court where it uses the provision as an interpretative tool for the limitation clauses in the Convention.[4] In these judgments, the Court does not rule that applicants lose their rights. Instead it rules that the limitation of the exercise of the applicant's rights is necessary in a democratic society and is proportionate if the applicant exercises his rights with the aim of limiting or destroying the Convention rights and freedom of others.[5] This illustrates that acts of private persons can violate the Convention rights of other private persons, and that such acts are not protected by the Convention. Accordingly, when the Court applies this broad interpretation of Art. 17 in conjunction with other treaty provisions, it seems as if Art. 17 brings acts of private persons within the scope of application of

---

3 J. Vande Lanotte and Y. Haeck, *Handboek EVRM*. Part 2, *Artikelsgewijze Commentaar. Vol. II*, Antwerp, Intersentia, 1995, at 246–251.

4 F. Jacobs, R. White and C. Ovey, *The European Convention on Human Rights*, Oxford, Oxford University Press, 2010, at 124.

5 In *Garaudy*, where the claimant argued that his rights under Art. 10 of the Convention had been violated, the Court found that a criminal prosecution of a person who had denied the Holocaust in a book was legitimate because the denial of the Holocaust infringes Art. 17 of the Convention: *Garaudy v. France*, 24 June 2003 (decision), appl. no. 65831/01.

human rights in the sense that it takes away the human rights of persons who limit the rights of others.

But although the text of Art. 17 provides reasons to believe in this approach, it does contradict the intentions of the founding states of the Convention.[6] According to the intentions of the founding states and the jurisprudence of the Court, Art. 17 is only applicable to anti-democratic movements that appeal to their Convention rights in order to spread Nazi, racist or negationist ideologies. Thus, although the text of Art. 17 does not exclude a broad interpretation so that the provision might support a horizontal application of the Convention, this viewpoint is not supported in positive law.[7]

We can therefore conclude that a lot of provisions in the Convention somehow indicate that human rights have a horizontal dimension, but they do not oblige states to regulate horizontal relationships in order to protect human rights from infringements of other private persons as such.[8] On the other hand, they do not exclude it either.[9] Moreover, they do not grant the right to citizens to invoke human rights directly against other citizens. Indeed, it must be stressed that only states can be sued by the ECtHR, individuals cannot.[10]

---

6 H. Cannie and D. Voorhoof, 'The abuse clause and freedom of expression in the European Human Rights Convention', *NQHR* 2011, p54 at 58ff; and D. Keane, 'Attacking hate speech under Article 17 of the European Convention on Human Rights', *NQHR* 2007, p641 at 641–651.

7 F. Jacobs, R. White and C. Ovey, *The European Convention*, 2010, above n. 4, at 125; and S. Van Drooghenbroeck, 'L'Article 17 de la convention européenne des droits de l'homme. Est-il indispensable?', *Rev.trim.D.H.* 2001, p540 at 544ff.

8 J. Krzeminska-Vamvaka and P. O'Callaghan, 'Mapping out a right of privacy in tort law' in G. Brüggemeier, A. Colombi Ciacchi and G. Comandé (eds.), *Fundamental Rights and Private Law in the European Union*, Part II, *Comparative Analyses of Selected Case Patterns*, Cambridge, Cambridge University Press, 2010, p111 at 128.

9 A. Drzemczewski, 'The European Human Rights Convention and Relations between private parties', *Nethl Int'l L Rev* 1979, 163, 176; L. Garlicki, 'Relations between Private Actors and the European Convention on Human Rights' in A. Sajo and R. Uitz (eds.), *The Constitution in Private Relations: Expanding Constitutionalism*, Utrecht, Eleven, 2005, p129 at 131; D. Spielmann, 'The European Convention on Human Rights' in D. Oliver and J. Fëdtke (eds.), *Human Rights and the Private Sphere – A Comparative Study*, London, Routledge, 2007, p427 at 430.

10 L. Zwaak, 'General Survey of the European Convention' in P. Van Dijk, F. Van Hoof, A. Van Rijn and L. Zwaak (eds.), *Theory and Practice of the European Convention on Human Rights*, Antwerp, Intersentia, 2006, (1) at 29; and D. Harris, M. O'Boyle, E. Bates and C. Buckley, *Law of the European Convention on Human Rights*, Oxford, Oxford University Press, 2009, at 20 and 787.

2. THE HORIZONTAL DIMENSION OF HUMAN RIGHTS IN THE JURISPRUDENCE OF THE COURT

There is no provision in the Convention that provides a solid ground for the application of human rights in horizontal relations. But the Convention provides a starting point for the jurisprudence. In this regard, the Court looked at Art. 1 of the Convention. This provision proclaims the principle of effectivity. Based on this principle, one can argue that a member state can be held accountable under the Convention if it neglects to take reasonable and appropriate measures to protect the Convention rights in an effective manner, whether they are infringed in horizontal or vertical relations.[11] It is from this line of reasoning that the Court developed the notion of positive obligations in general, and in horizontal relations more specifically.

2.1. THE THEORY OF POSITIVE OBLIGATIONS IN GENERAL

2.1.1. Foundation

The ECtHR applied the theory of positive obligations for the first time implicitly in the *Belgian linguistic* case.[12] The question arose as to whether Belgium violated the right to free education by not providing education in French in Flanders. In its judgment, the Court referred to the obligation of states to provide and regulate access to education for minors. By doing so, the Court implicitly made clear that the right to education does not only consist of negative obligations (an obligation for states not to interfere in human rights), but also of positive obligations. Unfortunately, the Court did not explicitly elaborate on this topic. It was only in 1979, in the cases of *Marckx*[13] and *Airey*,[14] that the Court explicitly referred to the notion

---

11 J. Merills, *The Development of International Law by the European Court of Human Rights*, Manchester, Manchester University Press, 1988, at 103; and D. Xenos, *The Positive Obligations of the State under the European Convention of Human Rights*, New York, Routledge, 2012, at 11.

12 Case relating to certain aspects of the laws on use of languages in education in Belgium, 23 July 1968, appl. no. 1474/62 et al.

13 *Marckx v. Belgium*, 13 June 1979 (Plenary), appl. no. 6833/74.

14 *Airey v. Ireland*, 9 October 1979, appl. no. 6289/73.

of positive obligations of states to protect human rights. Even then the Court did not elaborate a theoretical framework of these obligations. The Court nevertheless referred to the requirement of an effective treaty protection in order to legitimize the positive obligations. This connection between an effective treaty protection and the positive obligations of states has been confirmed often since then.[15] This occurs in the context of all Convention rights.[16] Indeed, positive obligations can be found not only in socio-economic and/or cultural rights, but also in civil and political rights.[17] Up until now, this broad field of application has not moved the Court to develop a general theory on positive obligations. The Court even explicitly refused to elaborate such a theory.[18] Moreover, the Court has refused to define the notion of positive obligations. The only definitions of positive obligations to be found in the jurisprudence of the Court are those that have been made in dissenting or concurring opinions such as the dissenting opinion of Judge Martens in the *Gül* case: 'Negative obligations require member States to refrain from action, positive to take action.'[19]

2.1.2. *Specific Criteria in the Application of Positive Obligations*

The absence of a general theory of positive obligations is not particularly problematic in the jurisprudence of the Court, because the Court seems to use the same criteria for both sets of human rights obligations.[20]

---

15 E.g.: *Keegan v. Ireland*, 26 May 1994, appl. no. 16969/90, §49; *Kroon et al. v. the Netherlands*, 27 October 1994, appl. no. 18535/91, §31; *Odièvre v. France*, 13 February 2003 (Grand Chamber), appl. no. 42326/98, §40; *Evans v. the United Kingdom*, 10 April 2007 (Grand Chamber), appl. no. 6339/05, §75; and *S.H. et al. v. Austria*, 3 November 2011 (Grand Chamber), appl. no. 57813/00, §87. See also: A. Mowbray, *The Development of Positive Obligations*, Oxford, Hart Publishing, 2004, at 221.

16 F. Jacobs, R. White and C. Ovey, *The European Convention*, 2010, above n. 4, at 30–100.

17 Indeed, as one observer noticed: 'To be effective, even civil and political rights have to be protected – and protection has a price. The right of access to the courts would be meaningless if there were no courts, or if they were not properly financed, or if only a few people could get to them owing a lack of money.' R. Sing, *The Future of Human Rights in the United Kingdom: Essays on Law and Practice*, Oxford, Hart Publishing, 1997, at 54.

18 *Ärzte 'für das Leben' v. Austria*, 21 June 1988, appl. no. 10126/82, §31; and *VgT Verein gegen Tierfabriken v. Switzerland*, 28 June 2001, appl. no. 24699/94, §46.

19 Dissenting opinion of Judge Martens on *Gül v. Switzerland*, 19 February 1996, appl. no. 23218/94, §7.

20 Y. Haeck, *Procederen voor het Europees Hof voor de Rechten van de Mens*, Antwerp, Intersentia, 2009, 42–43.

The only clear exception stems from the fact that the Court does not require a legal base for a violation of a positive obligation.[21] However, this cannot be seen as a real departure from the criteria that the Court uses in the context of negative obligations, for the reason that the exception stems from the nature of positive obligations. Indeed, since a violation of positive obligations is a negligence, it is senseless to speak of an active interference, let alone of a legal basis for such an interference. Consequently, the Court will be more inclined to apply the legitimacy and proportionality assessment regarding positive obligations.[22]

From a historical perspective, it is far from self-evident that the Court uses the same criteria for both positive and negative obligations. In *Abdulaziz, Cabales and Balkandali*, one of the earliest judgments that referred to positive obligations, the Court considered:

> as far as those positive obligations are concerned, the notion of 'respect' is not clear-cut: having regard to the diversity of the practices followed and the situations obtaining in the Contracting States, the notion's requirements will vary considerably from case to case. Accordingly, this is an area in which the Contracting Parties enjoy a wide margin of appreciation in determining the steps to be taken to ensure compliance with the Convention with due regard to the needs and resources of the community and of individuals.[23]

This wording clearly suggest that the member states have a wider margin of appreciation in cases of positive obligations than in cases of negative obligations. However, in the later jurisprudence of the Court, the reference

---

21 J. Velaers, 'De proliferatie van de zgn. Klassieke "liberale" grondrechten in de XXste en de XXIste eeuw' in B. Peeters and J. Velaers (eds.), *De grondwet in groothoekperspectief. Liber amicorum discipulorumque Karel Rimanque*, Antwerp, Intersentia, 2007, p99 at 125–126.

22 It has to be noted that some grounds to restrict human rights in the Treaty cannot be applied in cases of positive obligation; which forces the Court in such situations to use a proportionality assessment: N. Moreham, 'The Right to Respect for Private Life in the European Convention on Human Rights: A Re-examination', *EHRLR* 2008, p44 at 48.

23 *Abdulaziz, Cabales and Balkandali v. the United Kingdom*, 28 May 1985 (Plenary session), appl. nos. 9214/80, 9473/81 and 9474/81, §67. See also: D. Spielman, 'Obligations Positives et Effet Horizontal des Dispositions de la Convention' in F. Sudre (ed.), *L'interprétation de la Convention des droits de l'homme*, Brussels, Bruylant, 1998, p133 at 142–151. It was soon obvious that in both situations the courts must balance the violation of a fundamental right and the legitimate goal that can be pursued, with the fact that the government has a margin of appreciation: *Rees v. the United Kingdom*, 17 October 1986 (Plenary), appl. no. 9532/81, §35 and *X, Y and Z v. the United Kingdom*, 22 April 1997 (Grand Chamber), appl. no. 21830/93, §41.

to the wider margin of appreciation disappeared.[24] In the *Powell and Rayner* judgment, the Court decided that:

> Whether the present case be analysed in terms of a positive duty on the State to take reasonable and appropriate measures to secure the applicants' rights under paragraph 1 of Article 8 (Art. 8-1) or in terms of an "interference by a public authority" to be justified in accordance with paragraph 2 (Art. 8-2), the applicable principles are broadly similar.[25]

By using the term 'broadly', the Court still seemed to be uncertain as to whether it had to grant states a wider margin of appreciation regarding positive obligations. However, in 1994[26] the term 'broadly' completely disappeared from the wording that the Court used. Accordingly, the criteria of positive and negative obligations became identical.[27] This can only be applauded, as there are situations in which the same complaint can be categorized under negative as well as positive obligations.[28]

Nevertheless, the hesitation of the Court in the case law cited above makes it likely that it considers elements in the assessment of positive obligations that are not taken into account in cases where it has to assess presumed violations of negative obligations.[29] This can be explained by the fact that positive obligations, as was mentioned before, are quite specific in their nature. Consequently, the deviating treatment of positive obligations

---

24 Dissenting opinion of Judge Martens in *Gül v. Switzerland*, 19 February 1996, appl. no. 23218/94, §8.

25 *Powell and Raynar v. the United Kingdom*, 21 February 1990, appl. no. 9310/81, §41. See also: *Lopez Ostra v. Spain*, 9 December 1994, appl. no. 16798/90, §51.

26 See: R. Lawson, 'Positieve verplichtingen onder het EVRM: opkomst en ondergang van de "fair balance" test – Deel 2', *NJCM-Bulletin* 1995, p727 at 739ff.

27 *Keegan v. Ireland*, 26 May 1994, appl. no. 16969/90, §49; *Kroon et al. v. the Netherlands*, 27 October 1994, appl. no. 18535/91, §31; *Stjerna v. Finland*, 25 November 1994, appl. no. 18131/91, §38; *X, Y and Z v. the United Kingdom*, 22 April 1997 (Grand Chamber), appl. no. 21830/93, §41; *Hatton et al. v. the United Kingdom*, 8 July 2003 (Grand Chamber), appl. no. 36022/97, §98; *Odièvre v. France*, 13 February 2003 (Grand Chamber), appl. no. 42326/98, §40; *Broniowski v. Poland*, 22 June 2004 (Grand Chamber), appl. no. 31443/96, §144; *A., B. and C. v. Ireland*, 16 December 2010 (Grand Chamber), appl. no. 25579/05, §247; and *S.H. et al. v. Austria*, 3 November 2011 (Grand Chamber), appl. no. 57813/00, §87.

28 R. Lawson, 'Positieve verplichtingen onder het EVRM', 1995, p727 at 732–736.

29 This can also explain why the Court sometimes does not accept that the existence of negative obligations does not always imply additional positive obligations. Consequently, it is not acceptable that the prohibition to discriminate people because of their sexual orientation implies that the State has the positive obligation to protect transsexuals and to help them integrate into society: *Rees v. the United Kingdom*, 17 October 1986 (Plenary), appl. no. 9532/81, §38ff.

by the Court can be explained by the fact that the Court in general does not apply uniform criteria in assessing the margin of appreciation and decides on a case-by-case basis.[30]

This is illustrated by the *Botta* case. In this case, a handicapped man believed his right to privacy – also implying the right to develop social contacts – was violated because the Italian government did not ensure the accessibility of (amongst other things) private beaches. The Court decided that there was no direct link between the violation of the right of a family life in Art. 8 of the Convention and the measures that were asked by the applicant – the right to easy access of public beaches by handicapped persons – because the beaches were not in the proximity of the place of residence of the applicant.[31] Even though the Court does not grant a wider margin of appreciation in cases of positive obligations, the *Botta* case seems to take into account the impact or weight of the measures that were required by the positive obligations demanded.[32] Indeed, one cannot expect that a state renders each beach accessible.[33] In other cases the Court has been more explicit that positive obligations may not be interpreted in a way that requires impossible actions by governments: 'the scope of the positive obligation must be interpreted in a way which does not impose an impossible or disproportionate burden on the authorities.'[34] A violation

30 R. Macdonald, 'The Margin of Appreciation' in R. Macdonald, F. Matscher and H. Petzold (eds.), *The European System for the Protection of Human Rights*, Dordrecht, Martinus Nijhoff Publishers, 1993, p83 at 122–123.

31 *Botta v. Italy*, 24 February 1998, appl. no. 21439/93, §35.

32 This can be about the weight/burden of the administrative or financial measures (*Christine Goodwin v. the United Kingdom*, 11 July 2002, appl. no. 28957/98, §86–88) and about the magnitude of legislative work (*Botta v. Italy*, 24 February 1998, appl. no. 21439/93, §44) necessary to meet to positive obligation.

33 See similarly: P. De Hert, *Art. 8 E.V.R.M. en het Belgisch recht. De bescherming van privacy, gezin, woonst en communicatie*, C.D.P.K. – libri – 4, Ghent, Mys en Breesch, 1998, 49.

34 *Osman v. the United Kingdom*, 28 October 1998, appl. no. 23452/94, §116; *Özgür Gündem v. Turkey*, 16 March 2000, appl. no. 23144/93, §43; *Mahmut Kaya v. Turkey*, 28 March 2000, appl. no. 22535/93, §86; *Akkoc v. Turkey*, 10 October 2000, appl. nos. 22947/93 and 22948/93, §78; *Keenan v. the United Kingdom*, 3 April 2001, appl. no. 27229/95, §90; *Paul and Audrey Edwards v. the United Kingdom*, 14 March 2002, appl. no. 46477/99, §55; *Appleby et al. v. the United Kingdom*, 6 May 2003, appl. no. 44306/98, §40; *Novoseletskiy v. Russia*, 22 February 2005, appl. no. 47148/99, §70; *Bone v. France*, 1 March 2005 (decision), appl. no. 69869/01; *Koku v. Turkey*, 31 May 2005, appl. no. 27305/95, §127; *Erikan Bulut v. Turkey*, 2 March 2006, appl. no. 51480/99, §32; *Kontrová v. Slovakia*, 31 May 2007, appl. no. 7510/04, §50; *Renolde v. France*, 16 October 2008, appl. no. 5608/05, §82; *K.U. v. Finland*, 2 December 2008, appl. no. 2872/02, §48; *Opuz v. Turkey*, 9 June 2009, appl. no. 33401/02, §129; *Verein gegen Tierfabriken Schweiz (VgT) v. Switzerland (no.2)*, 30 June 2009

of a positive obligation can only be assumed if the government 'failed to take measures within the scope of their powers which, judged reasonably, might have been expected to avoid the risk.'[35] Furthermore, in the *Botta* case the Court seemed to consider the foreseeability of a violation. Indeed, it cannot be expected that the state knows which beaches Botta wishes to visit.

The criterion of foreseeability was also explicitly mentioned in *Öneryildiz*.[36] Because of the accumulation of toxic gases in the waste on a dump, the dump exploded, causing the death of several persons who lived in their dwellings on the periphery of the dump. The victims were of the opinion that the local authorities had violated the right to life because experts had warned the municipal authorities of the dangerous situation. The Court in this case decided:

> Where it is established that the negligence attributable to State officials or bodies on that account goes beyond an error of judgment or carelessness, in that the authorities in question, fully realising the likely consequences and disregarding the powers vested in them, failed to take measures that were necessary and sufficient to avert the risks inherent in a dangerous activity.[37]

By using the words 'fully realising the likely consequences', the Court contends that if the state was not aware of the potential danger, it would not have found a violation of the Convention. Thus, awareness or foreseeability of the potential violation is an essential element in the assessment of positive obligations. This does not however mean that this element is not also of vital importance to the assessment of negative obligations.

(Grand Chamber), appl. no. 32772/02, §81; *Rantsev v. Cyprus and Russia*, 7 January 2010, appl. no. 25965/04, §219; *Fedina v. Ukraine*, 2 September 2010, appl. no. 17185/02, §53; *Georgel and Georgeta Stoicescu v. Romania*, 26 July 2011, appl. no. 9718/03, §51; *C.N. v. the United Kingdom*, 13 November 2012, appl. no. 4239/08, §68; *Remuszko v. Poland*, 16 July 2013, appl. no. 1562/10, §63; and ECtHR, *Tikhonova v. Russia*, 30 April 2014, appl. no. 3596/05, §68.

35 *Mahmut Kaya v. Turkey*, 28 March 2000, appl. no. 22535/93, §86; *Akkoc v. Turkey*, 10 October 2000, appl. nos. 22947/93 and 22948/93, §78; *Keenan v. the United Kingdom*, 3 April 2001, appl. no. 27229/95, §90; *Paul and Audrey Edwards v. the United Kingdom*, 14 March 2002, appl. no. 46477/99, §55; *Koku v. Turkey*, 31 May 2005, appl. no. 27305/95, §128; *Erikan Bulut v. Turkey*, 2 March 2006, appl. no. 51480/99, §32; *Kontrová v. Slovakia*, 31 May 2007, appl. no. 7510/04, §50; *Opuz v. Turkey*, 9 June 2009, appl. no. 33401/02, §129; *Rantsev v. Cyprus and Russia*, 7 January 2010, appl. no. 25965/04, §219; *Fedina v. Ukraine*, 2 September 2010, appl. no. 17185/02, §53; *Georgel and Georgeta Stoicescu v. Romania*, 26 July 2011, appl. no. 9718/03, §51; and *Tikhonova v. Russia*, 30 April 2014, appl. no. 3596/05, §69.

36 *Öneryildiz v. Turkey*, 30 November 2004 (Grand Chamber), appl. no. 48939/99.

37 *Ibid.*, §93.

Indeed, when assessing negative obligations it is also necessary to check whether the consequences of an act could be foreseen at the moment that the act is posed. In the context of positive obligations, however, it has a more important function.

2.2. THE THEORY OF POSITIVE OBLIGATIONS TO PROTECT HUMAN RIGHTS IN HORIZONTAL RELATIONS

2.2.1. Legal Basis

If one recognizes positive obligations to protect human rights in general, it is only a small step further to recognize the positive obligation to protect human rights in horizontal relations. Indeed, the protection of human rights in horizontal relations is, as Jan Velaers contends, only a specific application of the theory of positive obligations.[38] It is thus not surprising that the Court – like the Inter American Court of Human Rights[39] – reads positive obligations to intervene in horizontal relations into several human rights.[40]

This theory does not imply that a citizen can sue another citizen before the Court because of a violation of his human rights. Only states can be referred to the Court. But this theory enables private parties to complain about the legislator's, the executive's and/or the judiciary's attitude towards violations of the Convention in relations between private persons.[41] In other words: human rights in horizontal relations cannot be

38 J. Velaers, 'De proliferatie', 2007, p99 at 131.

39 The Inter American Court of Human Rights recognized this principle quite soon with regard to the right to life: A. Clapham, 'Opinion: The Privatisation of Human Rights', *EHRLR* 1996, p20 at 25–26.

40 E.g. *Otto-Preminger-Institut v. Austria*, 20 September 1994, appl. no. 13470/87, §47; *Ignaccolo-Zenide v. Romania*, 25 January 2000, appl. no. 31679/96, §95; *Özgür Gündem v. Turkey*, 16 March 2000, appl. no. 23144/93, §42–43; *Lunari v. Italy*, 11 January 2001, appl. no. 11463/93, §34; *Sovtransavto Holding v. Ukraine*, 25 July 2002, appl. no. 48553/99, §96; *Appleby et al. v. the United Kingdom*, 6 May 2003, appl. no. 44306/98, §§39–50; *M.C. v. Bulgaria*, 4 December 2003, appl. no. 39272/98, §§150–153; *Pla and Puncernau v. Andorra*, 13 July 2004, appl. no. 69498/01, §§59–60; and *Moreno Gomez v. Spain*, 16 November 2004, appl. no. 4143/02.

41 J.M. Emaus, *Handhaving van EVRM-rechten via het aansprakelijkheidsrecht. Over de inpassing van de fundamentele rechtsschending in het Nederlands burgerlijk recht*, The Hague, Boom juridische uitgevers, 2013, 7; and H. Thorgeisdottir, 'Journalism worthy of the name: an affirmative reading of Article 10 of the ECtHR', *NQHR* 2004, p601 at 617.

referred directly to the Court, but human rights have an indirect effect on horizontal relations because the state can be held responsible when it neglects its duties to intervene in horizontal relations in order to protect the Convention rights.[42]

The first case in which the Court has read positive obligations of the state to intervene in horizontal relations is *X and Y v. the Netherlands*.[43] The applicants were a disabled Dutch girl who had been raped, and her father. They were, under the Dutch legal system, both unable to launch criminal procedures against the perpetrator. The girl was unable to launch criminal law remedy because she was mentally disabled. The father could not launch a criminal complaint for his disabled daughter because she had already reached the age of majority. Dutch law did not provide for any criminal sanction in this particular situation. Accordingly, the Court was of the opinion that the Dutch government did not sufficiently protect their private life (Art. 8).[44] This case, which this book shall return to later, bears of course upon criminal law. This is a legal branch belonging to public law. But inferring from this fact that the Court's considerations in *X and Y v. the Netherlands* only apply to vertical, and not horizontal relations, seems artificial.[45] Criminal provisions often bear upon relations between private individuals. This also appears from the civil consequences of a criminal conviction in the form of damages. Therefore, the necessity to provide a criminal law instrument has consequences in tort law.[46] Moreover, the ECtHR is not bound by national law and its division in legal branches, and does not have to take them into account if it mentions the duty to protect human rights in private relations.

---

42 B. Girard, *Responsabilité civile extracontractuelle et droits fondamentaux*, Paris, LGDJ, 2015, at 151; and R. Kay, 'The European Convention on Human Rights and the Control of Private Law', *EHRLR* 2005, (466) 475–476.

43 *X and Y v. the Netherlands*, 26 March 1985 (Grand Chamber), appl. no. 8978/80. Also: *Young, James and Webster v. the United Kingdom*, 13 August 1981, appl. nos. 7601/76 and 7806/77.

44 *X and Y v. the Netherlands*, 26 March 1985 (Grand Chamber), appl. no. 8978/80, §30. The ECtHR did not proceed to the balancing of Art. 13 ECHR because the assessment of Art. 8 is identical and thus sufficient (§36). See also with regard to the possibility of taking action against a rapist: *Stubbings et al. v. the United Kingdom*, 22 October 1996, appl. nos. 22083/93 and 22095/93; *M.C. v. Bulgaria*, 4 December 2003, appl. no. 39272/98 and *D.J. v. Croatia*, 24 July 2012, appl. no. 42418/10.

45 See similarly: H.-J. Cremer, *Human Rights and the Protection of Privacy in Tort Law*, 2001, above n. 2, at 123–125.

46 See similarly: S. Jansen, 'The Defect of Consent Deceit, Information Duties and Discrimination Legislation: The Thor Steinar Cases Applied in Belgian Law', *European Review of Private Law*, 2011, p371 at 392.

Another early example is *Costello-Roberts*. In this case the ECtHR decided that the prohibition of torture had been violated because of the application of corporal punishment in a private school.[47] The Court did not explicitly mention the positive obligation to protect human rights in horizontal relations but decided upon a violation of the Convention after mentioning the right to education and the principle that a state cannot avoid its duties by delegating it to private entities. That the Court does not refer explicitly to the theory of positive obligations is not exceptional – in further cases the Court has applied the horizontal effect of human rights without mentioning the theory of positive obligations, as illustrated by the following observation:

> [o]wing to the absolute character of the right guaranteed, the Court does not rule out the possibility that Article 3 of the Convention (Art. 3) may also apply where the danger emanates from persons or groups of persons who are not public officials.[48]

These observations illustrate that the absolute character of the prohibition of torture makes it applicable in horizontal relations as well. Similarly, the prohibition of slavery and forced labor (Art. 4) has a horizontal effect. The member states must criminalize slavery and forced labor and detect infringements on an effective basis.[49] This is very reasonable from a historical perspective, as slavery was an institution that was mainly used in private relations and was based on contract.

But the other Convention rights also have to be protected in horizontal relations.[50] In *Ärtze fur das Leben* the Court read such a duty in the freedom

---

47 *Costello-Roberts v. the United Kingdom*, 25 March 1993, appl. no. 13134/87.

48 *H.L.R. v. France*, 29 April 1997, appl. no. 24573/94, §40. This case concerned the question whether the extradition of a drug trafficker to Colombia violated Art. 3 for the prospect of a decease or inhumane treatment. It is comparable to the well-known *Soering* case: *Soering v. the United Kingdom*, 7 July 1989 (Plenary session), appl. no. 4038/88. However, in *H.L.R.* the threat came from private persons, whereas in *Soering* the threat came from the death penalty in the United States. See also: *Z. et al. v. the United Kingdom*, 10 May 2005 (Grand Chamber), appl. no. 29392/95, §73; and A. Clapham, 'The "Drittwirkung"', 1993, above n. 1, p163 at 171–176.

49 *Siliadin v. France*, 26 July 2005, appl. no. 73316/01, §89; *Rantsev v. Cyprus and Russia*, 7 January 2010, appl. no. 25965/04, §285; *C.N. and V. v. France*, 11 October 2012, appl. no. 67724/09, §69; and F. Jacobs, R. White and C. Ovey, *The European Convention*, 2010, above n. 4, at 198.

50 With regard to Arts 6 and 8 and Art. 1 of the first Protocol, see: P. Kenna, 'Housing Rights: Positive Duties and Enforceable Rights at the European Court of Human Rights', *EHRLR* 2008, (193) 197 et seq.

of association and assembly.[51] The case concerned a complaint by a group of Austrian doctors campaigning against the legalization of abortion. In 1980 and 1982 this group organized two demonstrations that were interrupted by their opponents, even though police agents were present. The group of doctors started an action before the ECtHR and requested to determine the infringements of their freedom of religion (Art. 9 of the Convention), their freedom of expression (Art. 10 of the Convention) and their freedom of assembly (Art. 11 of the Convention) because of the passive demeanor of the police during the demonstrations and the lack of effective remedies to challenge it afterwards (Art. 13 of the Convention). In its judgment, the Court only touched upon the right to assembly (Art. 11 of the Convention). When the Austrian government invoked that the right to assembly only imposes negative obligations and no positive obligations to protect demonstrations, the Court responded as follow:

> A demonstration may annoy or give offence to persons opposed to the ideas or claims that it is seeking to promote. The participants must, however, be able to hold the demonstration without having to fear that they will be subjected to physical violence by their opponents; such a fear would be liable to deter associations or other groups supporting common ideas or interests from openly expressing their opinions on highly controversial issues affecting the community. In a democracy the right to counter-demonstrate cannot extend to inhibiting the exercise of the right to demonstrate. Genuine, effective freedom of peaceful assembly cannot, therefore, be reduced to a mere duty on the part of the State not to interfere: a purely negative conception would not be compatible with the object and purpose of Article 11. Like Article 8, Article 11 sometimes requires positive measures to be taken, even in the sphere of relations between individuals, if need be (see, mutatis mutandis, the X and Y v. the Netherlands judgment of 26 March 1985, Series A no. 91, p. 11, §23).[52]

Consequently, the Court explicitly holds that governments sometimes have to take positive measures 'even in the sphere of relations between individuals.'[53] The reference in this case to *X and Y v. the Netherlands*, which related to criminal law,[54] indicates that the Court does not attach

---

51 *Ärzte 'für das Leben' v. Austria*, 21 June 1988, appl. no. 10126/82.

52 *Ärzte 'für das Leben' v. Austria*, 21 June 1988, appl. no. 10126/82, §32.

53 See also: *Schmidt and Dahlström v. Sweden*, 6 February 1976, appl. no. 5589/72, §33; *Khurshid Mustafa and Tarzibachi v. Sweden*, 16 December 2008, appl. no. 23883/06, §32; and D. Harris, M. O'Boyle, E. Bates and C. Buckley, *Law of the European Convention*, 2009, above n. 10, at 537.

54 *X and Y v. the Netherlands*, 26 March 1985 (Grand Chamber), appl. no. 8978/80.

much importance to formal divisions between public, criminal and private law, but looks at the substantial requirements of an effective protection of human rights.

2.2.2. Specific Criteria of Positive Obligations to Interfere in Horizontal Relations

2.2.2.1. General Outline

At first sight, there does not seem to be a limit on the positive obligations to interfere in horizontal relations. Since the state has a monopoly on the use of force and citizens are prohibited to act themselves in private conflicts, every horizontal relation has a vertical element.[55] In every relationship between private parties the possibility exists that there will be a conflict and that one of the parties will turn to the state for protection. Because of this, the field of application of positive obligations to protect human rights in horizontal relations seems to be infinite. The question then arises whether the Court should develop specific criteria to limit these positive obligations.

In the famous *Pla and Puncernau* judgment, where the Court found that the execution of a will violated the Convention because the will excluded children born outside of marriage, the Court seemed to limit the positive obligations to intervene in horizontal relations:

> Admittedly, the Court is not in theory required to settle disputes of a purely private nature. That being said, in exercising the European supervision incumbent on it, it cannot remain passive where a national court's interpretation of a legal act, be it a testamentary disposition, a private contract, a public document, a statutory provision or an administrative practice appears unreasonable, arbitrary or, as in the present case, blatantly inconsistent with the prohibition of discrimination established by Article 14 and more broadly with the principles underlying the Convention.[56]

Although the Court points out that in theory it is not competent to adjudicate private disputes, it considers itself competent to assess the compatibility of a judgment of a national judge with the Convention. Nevertheless, the Court seems to show restraint to require that a judgment

[55] K. Rimanque and P. Peeters, 'De toepasselijkheid van grondrechten', 1982, p1 at 13.

[56] *Pla and Puncernau v. Andorra*, 13 July 2004, appl. no. 69498/01, §59.

must be unreasonable, arbitrary or blatantly in violation of the Convention. Luc Verhey is of the opinion that in reality the Court does not show much restraint. He remarks that the Court in *Pla and Puncernau* easily interpreted the will in a different way to the national judges. Moreover, the Court has continued to do so.[57] Verhey refers to *Khurshid Mustafa and Tarzibachi*. The question arose as to whether a prohibition imposed by a private landlord on his tenants to use a satellite dish violated the tenants' freedom of expression.[58] The Court repeated the passage cited above from *Pla and Puncernau* (without mentioning the term 'blatantly') and decided that the current case did not concern a pure private dispute because of three reasons. It ruled first that the Swedish judge did not only interpret the tenancy contract but also the Swedish tenancy legislation. Secondly, the Court found that the right to information of the applicants (Art. 10 of the Convention) was at stake. Finally, the Court noticed that the applicants moved to a different home because of the judgment of the Swedish judge. Verhey infers from this that these criteria render the incompetence of the Court to adjudicate private disputes purely theoretical. He correctly points out that tenancy contracts are always concluded in a statutory context, that in such a dispute, before reaching the ECtHR, a national judge must be seized and that an applicant is almost always someone who has lost a national case.[59] Since the Court, if these conditions are met, assesses whether a national judge has sufficiently safeguarded human rights in a private dispute, the Court in fact imposes surveillance on the civil judge. Indeed, the Court increasingly assesses whether the civil judge has balanced the human rights interests adequately.[60]

In other cases, however, the Court showed some restraint by emphasizing the importance of the state's margin of appreciation.[61] In addition, since the Court only refers to the general criteria of Art. 8 and does not refer to the specific requirements that are applicable after the

---

57 L. Verhey, 'Zweedse schotelantennes en de horizontale werking van artikel 10 EVRM' (case-note under *Khurshid Mustafa and Tarzibachi v. Sweden*, 16 December 2008, appl. no. 23883/06), *NJCM-Bulletin* 2009, p893 at 899ff. See also: R. Kay, 'The European Convention', p466 at 468 et seq.

58 *Khurshid Mustafa and Tarzibachi v. Sweden*, 16 December 2008, appl. no. 23883/06.

59 L. Verhey, 'Zweedse schotelantennes en de horizontale werking van artikel 10 EVRM', 2009, above n. 57, p893 at 900.

60 L. Verhey, 'Horizontale werking van grondrechten: de stille Straatsburgse revolutie' in T. Barkhuysen, M. Van Emmerik and J. Loof (eds.), *Geschakeld recht. Verdere studies over Europese grondrechten ter gelegenheid van de 70'ste verjaardag van prof. mr. E.A. Alkema*, Deventer, Kluwer, 2009, p517 at 525–526.

61 *Mosley v. the United Kingdom*, 10 May 2011, appl. no. 48009/08, §107.

assessment of positive obligations of the government to protect the right to private life in horizontal relations, it does not seem willing to deviate from the normal criteria.[62] The same was clear in the *Von Hannover* case, where the Court (with reference to *X and Y v. the Netherlands*) read positive obligations of the government to protect the right to privacy in horizontal relations in Art. 8.[63] The Court pointed out that it was difficult to draw the line between positive and negative obligations of the government, but didn't seem to find it very problematic because in both cases there must be a balance between the interests of the state and those of the individual. In both situations the state has a wide margin of appreciation.[64]

Concluding, it seems that just as in the case of positive obligations in general, no specific criteria exist for the positive obligation to protect human rights in horizontal relations. But the specific characteristics of the situations in which positive obligations to protect human rights in horizontal relations apply, imply that the general test takes a particular turn.

2.2.2.2. A Wider Scope of Application When Human Rights Conflict?

One might disagree that positive obligations in horizontal relations do not require specific criteria since the Court in some cases ruled that states have a wider margin of appreciation if two rights of the Convention conflict with each other and have to be reconciled.[65] Because states have no human

---

62 See also *Evans v. the United Kingdom*, 10 April 2007 (Grand Chamber), appl. no. 6339/05, §74ff.

63 *Von Hannover v. Germany*, 24 June 2004, appl. no. 59320/00, §57. See also: *Stubbings et al. v. the United Kingdom*, 22 October 1996, appl. nos. 22083/93 and 22095/93, §62; *N. v. Sweden*, 16 October 1986 (decision), appl. no. 11366/85; *Cumpana and Mazare v. Romania*, 17 December 2004 (Grand Chamber), appl. no. 33348/96, §91; *Dickson v. the United Kingdom*, 4 December 2007, appl. no. 44362/04, §70 and *Armonienė v. Lithuania*, 25 November 2008, appl. no. 36919/02, §36.

64 See also: *Mikulic v. Croatia*, 7 February 2002, appl. no. 53176/99, §58; *Odièvre v. France*, 13 February 2003 (Grand Chamber), appl. no. 42326/98, §40; *Moreno Gomez v. Spain*, 16 November 2004, appl. no. 4143/02 §55; *Mizzi v. Malta*, 12 January 2006, appl. no. 26111/02, §106; *Pfeifer v. Austria*, 15 November 2007, appl. no. 12556/03, §37; *Armonienė v. Lithuania*, 25 November 2008, appl. no. 36919/02, §37; *Biriuk v. Lithuania*, 25 November 2008, appl. no. 23373/03, §36; *S.H. et al. v. Austria*, 3 November 2011 (Grand Chamber), appl. no. 57813/00, §87; *Von Hannover v. Germany (no.2)*, 7 February 2012, appl. nos. 40660/08 and 60641/08, §99 and *Knecht v. Romania*, 2 October 2012, appl. no. 10048/10, §55.

65 *Frette v. France*, 26 February 2002, appl. no. 36515/97, §42; *Odièvre v. France*, 13 February 2003 (Grand Chamber), appl. no. 42326/98, §44–49 and *Evans v. the United Kingdom*, 10 April 2007 (Grand Chamber), appl. no. 6339/05, §77.

rights, a conflict between two human rights can only arise if human rights of private persons violate one another.[66] In cases regarding obligations to intervene in horizontal relations (in cases where human rights of different persons conflict), one could contend that states dispose of a wider margin of appreciation than in cases of negative obligations. However, this assumption is premature for several reasons.

First, the Court only invokes the wider margin of appreciation in very specific cases, namely when the right of a child to know its parents conflicts with the right of the father to remain anonymous. This problem is very delicate in the legal systems of many member states and is approached in different ways. Thus, the wider margin of appreciation might also flow from the divergent approaches of the member states and not from a different test for conflicting rights.[67]

Second, such an interpretation seems incompatible with the text of the Convention. As already mentioned, some restriction clauses stipulate that Convention rights can be restricted by the 'rights and freedoms of others'. Since these grounds for restriction are enumerated between other interests that can serve as limitation grounds, they must be weighted at equal value. Karel Rimanque and Bruno Peeters note that although the restrictions on Convention rights are almost exclusively oriented towards the formulation of collective objects of legal protection, it would not be reasonable to infer from this that – *a contrario* – any private interest must give in to the fundamental rights of another person.[68]

Third, one must take into account the *Arhrens* case, in which the Court made a similar consideration.[69] After it determined the presence of a wide margin of appreciation, the Court indicated that it uses the criteria in

---

It is sometimes said in doctrine that a wider margin of appreciation should be applied when human rights conflict, for the reason that such a conflict indicates that there are high interests at stake on both sides of the conflict. One can however wonder whether this is a good approach, and whether the Court might only accept a wider margin of appreciation when national judicial bodies already took the conflicting rights into account: E. Brems, 'Evans v. UK. Three Grounds for Ruling Differently'; S. Besson, 'Human Rights in Relation. A Critical Reading of the ECtHR's Approach to Conflicts of Rights' in S. Smet and E. Brems (eds.), *When Human Rights Clash at the European Court of Human Rights*, Oxford, Oxford University Press, 2017, p75 at 77.

66 A. Clapham, 'The "Drittwirkung"', 1993, above n.1, p163 at 187.

67 A similar approach can be found in the jurisprudence concerning positive obligations for transsexuals: G. Cohen-Jonathan, 'Respect for Private and Family Life' in R. Macdonald, F. Matscher and H. Petzold (eds.), *The European System for the Protection of Human Rights*, Dordrecht, Martinus Nijhoff Publishers, 1993, p405 at 411.

68 K. Rimanque and P. Peeters, 'De toepasselijkheid van grondrechten', 1982, p1 at 15.

69 *Ahrens v. Germany*, 22 March 2012, appl. no. 45071/09, §65.

'any case under Article 8 of the Convention'. Therefore, the fact that there is a conflict between human rights does not seem to imply that the Court uses different criteria. By stressing that positive obligations depend on the nature of the interests of the concerned and the nature of the element of private life, the Court does not seem to indicate that the difference between positive and negative obligations is relevant to determine whether a state has a wide margin of appreciation, but only the circumstances of the case.

Fourth, it must be noted that the Court in *Von Hannover*, for example, found a violation of the Convention, although German judges had already balanced the conflicting human rights in this case.[70]

Fifth, there are some theoretical arguments. When the Court has to review a claimed violation of the Convention, it has to balance the impact of the restriction of the human right on the one hand with the legitimate aim on the other.[71] If a human right is restricted in horizontal relations, the behavior of a private person by whom this human right is restricted has to fall at least within a normative framework, and this legal framework has to be inspired by a legitimate aim. In this context it must be noted that the existence of a legitimate aim is hardly ever contested in the jurisprudence of the Court.[72] Accordingly, it seems difficult to accept that a state has a wider margin of appreciation when legislating situations where two parties can invoke Convention rights, than when only one of the parties can do so. Even more problematic from this perspective is that the principle of subsidiarity, according to which states are in principle better placed to protect the Convention rights,[73] has as a consequence that states are permitted to attribute a higher degree of protection to these rights.[74] Accordingly, it would be problematic that if a private party

---

[70] C. Warbrick, 'The European Convention on Human Rights and the Human Rights Act: the view from outside' in H. Fenwick, G. Philippson and R. Masterman (eds.), *Judicial reasoning under the UK Human Rights Act*, Cambridge, Cambridge University Press, 2007, (25) 38.

[71] On the topic of the restrictions of human rights see: Y. Arai, 'The System of Restrictions' in P. Van Dijk, F. Van Hoof, A. Van Rijn and L. Zwaak (eds.), *Theory and Practice of the European Convention on Human Rights*, Antwerp, Intersentia, 2006, (333) at 343–346.

[72] D. Harris, M. O'Boyle, E. Bates and C. Buckley, *Law of the European Convention*, 2009, above n. 10, at 397.

[73] *Handyside v. the United Kingdom*, 7 December 1976 (Grand Chamber), appl. no. 5493/72, §48.

[74] D. Harris, M. O'Boyle, E. Bates and C. Buckley, *Law of the European Convention*, 2009, above n. 10, at 13; and H. Petzold, 'The Convention and the Principle of Subsidiarity' in R. Macdonald, F. Matscher and H. Petzold (eds.), *The European System for the Protection of Human Rights*, Dordrecht, Martinus Nijhoff Publishers, 1993, p41 at 43–44.

infringes a Convention right when invoking a human right of the internal legal order, the state would have a stricter margin of appreciation than if this party could also invoke a Convention right. This would be at odds with the principle of subsidiarity because it would imply that the review under the Convention would be stricter if a state has developed a (constitutional) statutory regulation than in a case where a state did not do so.[75]

Finally, the Court requires states to consider possible conflicts between two human rights. For example, the Court attaches importance to the question of whether or not national judges take into account the existence of a conflict with the right to privacy and the freedom of expression in its case law about press liability.[76] When a national judge does so, the Court will be less inclined to decide upon a violation of the treaty.[77] This does not, however, imply that the Court grants states a broader margin of appreciation. It is only a procedural interpretation of the principle of subsidiarity. According to which the Court will show more restraint if a national judge has already decided upon certain matters.[78]

Because of the numerous arguments above, the Court cannot grant states a wider margin of appreciation when assessing claimed violations of positive obligations to protect human rights in horizontal relations than when it has to assess a vertical application of those same human rights.[79] If the Court in a certain case rules that a state disposes of a wider margin of appreciation, this must be so because the Court – also in cases of negative obligations – takes into account the nature and the circumstances of each and every specific situation.[80]

---

75 A similar line of argument can be found in: H.-J. Papier, 'Execution and Effects of the Judgments of the European Court of Human Rights from the Perspective of German National Courts', *HRLJ* 2006, p1 at 3.

76 *Dyundin v. Russia*, 14 October 2008, appl. no. 37406/03, §33; *OOO IVPress et al. v. Russia*, 22 January 2013, appl. no. 33501/04 et al., §71. See also: *Schüth v. Germany*, 28 June 2012 (Art. 41), appl. no. 1620/03, §23.

77 The Court in this case intended to grant the member states a wider scope of appreciation; it did not however develop a global approach in this way: N. Lavender, 'The Problem of the Margin of Appreciation', *EHRLR* 1997, pp380–390.

78 See also H. Petzold, 'The Convention and the Principle of Subsidiarity', 1993, p41 at 62.

79 This does not contradict the finding that the Court is more reluctant to recognize positive obligations. See on this theme: L. Lavrysen, 'Human Rights in a Positive State: Rethinking the Relationship between Positive and Negative Obligations Under the European Convention on Human Rights', Ghent University Dissertation, 2016, at 188ff.

80 See also about the difference in the margin of appreciation that the Court grants in disputes about horizontal relations in *Pla and Puncernau* on the one hand, and in *Khurshid Mustafa and Tarzibachi* on the other: L. Verhey, 'Zweedse schotelantennes en de horizontale werking', 2009, above n. 57, p893 at 902.

2.2.2.3. Uniqueness of Positive Obligations to Protect Human Rights in Horizontal Relations

Although the ECtHR does not grant states a wider margin of appreciation when it has to assess positive obligations to interfere in horizontal relations than in cases that concern negative obligations, the Court seems (just as in cases of positive obligations in general) to take into account the magnitude of the measures that a state has to take to fulfill its positive obligations in horizontal relations. The existence of positive obligations to interfere in horizontal relations cannot have the effect that a state can be held responsible for each horizontal violation of the Convention. The state cannot be blamed for the fact that private persons violate each other's Convention rights (think about manslaughter as a violation of the right to life), but only if it does not provide effective measures and mechanisms to prevent and sanction such behavior (by, e.g. criminalizing certain violations of the treaty and by punishing the violators of these crimes). It is impossible for the state, regardless of its organization, to prevent every violation of the Convention from occurring.[81] For example, in *Osman* the Court decided:

> For the Court, and bearing in mind the difficulties involved in policing modern societies, the unpredictability of human conduct and the operational choices which must be made in terms of priorities and resources, such an obligation must be interpreted in a way which does not impose an impossible or disproportionate burden on the authorities. Accordingly, not every claimed risk to life can entail for the authorities a Convention requirement to take operational measures to prevent that risk from materialising.[82]

In addition, the Court also applies the criterion of foreseeability:

> For the Court, and having regard to the nature of the right protected by Article 2, a right fundamental in the scheme of the Convention, it is sufficient for an applicant to show that the authorities did not do all that could be reasonably expected of them to avoid a real and immediate risk to life of which they have or ought to have knowledge.[83]

---

81 F. Bydlinski, 'Methodological Approaches to the Tort Law of the ECtHR' in A. Fenyves et al. (eds.), *Tort Law in the Jurisprudence of the European Court of Human Rights*, Göttingen, De Gruyter, 2011, p29 at 60–61.

82 *Osman v. the United Kingdom*, 28 October 1998, appl. no. 23452/94, §116. See also: *Botta v. Italy*, 24 February 1998, appl. no. 21439/93, §35.

83 *Osman v. the United Kingdom*, 28 October 1998, appl. no. 23452/94, §116. This principle does not only apply with regard to the police that have to prevent crimes, but

Regarding the right to life, the Court for example had to decide whether or not the police remained at fault by not acting in a situation in which the family of the applicants were threatened by another person. The Court decided that the state could not foresee, in this specific case, the urgency and the threat of the situation. In other judgments the Court formalized the foreseeability and the material possibility explicitly by considering a case in which the violation of the right to life was invoked:[84]

> For a positive obligation to arise, it must be established that the authorities knew or ought to have known at the time of the existence of a real and immediate risk to the life of an identified individual from the criminal acts of a third party and that they failed to take measures within the scope of their powers which, judged reasonably, might have been expected to avoid that risk.[85]

Also interesting is *Fedina*.[86] During a walk, two men noticed that an electricity cable was broken and had fallen into a river. One of them stepped into the river and tried to fetch the cable. While doing so, he was electrocuted. His companion reached out for help, but in vain. The bereaved of the deceased sued the electricity company in criminal and tort law. As a result, the company had to indemnify the bereaved because of the application of a statutory faultless liability scheme, but the criminal complaint was rejected. The bereaved found that this violated the right to life. The ECtHR did not follow this line of reasoning. Since the cable had been broken by a storm and the authorities could not have been aware of the fact that the cable had fallen into the river, the Court decided that the government could not be criticized and could not be held responsible.

This illustrates that positive obligations to protect human rights in horizontal relations are limited by the material impossibility to prevent violations of human rights to occur and by their foreseeability.[87] As a result, positive obligations to protect human rights in horizontal relationships

---

also with regard to the role of the government to ensure that buildings should be of a decent quality: *Banel v. Lithuania*, 18 June 2013, appl. no. 14326/11, §65.

84 See extensively: D. Xenos, *The Positive Obligations of the State*, above n. 11, 2012, at 76ff.

85 *Keenan v. the United Kingdom*, 3 April 2001, appl. no. 27229/95, §90.

86 *Fedina v. Ukraine*, 2 September 2010, appl. no. 17185/02.

87 Which can also be described as the principles of knowledge and proximity: L. Lavrysen, 'Human Rights in a Positive State: Rethinking the Relationship between Positive and Negative Obligations Under the European Convention on Human Rights', 2016, above n. 80, 121ff.

are almost always obligations of effort and not of result.[88] Of course, the specification of the criteria differs according to which positive obligation is assessed.[89] It is important to understand that the responsibility of states in the context of positive obligations to intervene in horizontal relations matches what Paul De Hert describes as 'systemic responsibility'.[90] This means that governments are not directly responsible for every human rights violation that occurs in the framework of horizontal relations, but that they have to provide for an effective allocation of responsibilities between private entities.[91] In contrast, the ECtHR can hold a state responsible for violating positive obligations to protect human rights in horizontal relations if it would appear that there is no rigorous allocation or distribution of responsibilities.

If we think about this criterion, it can be argued that the Court must take into account the difference between interpersonal relations between private persons on the one hand and the relationship between the state and its citizens on the other hand. Indeed, the state that is the first addressee of the ECHR is obliged to protect the human rights of all persons that are located in its jurisdiction. The reason for this can probably be found in the fact that the government has a relationship with all these individuals. For private persons this is not true. Private persons do not have other private persons under their jurisdiction for the simple reason that they cannot take unilateral measures (since the government holds the monopoly over violence). Private persons can rely on their human rights. For instance, they can rely on their right to a family life, their right to a private life and their right to freedom of association to choose with whom they engage in interpersonal relations. Private persons do not have a direct relationship with all other private citizens. Consequently, they cannot be held responsible for protecting the human rights of all other private citizens.

---

88 In one case the Court found, without referring explicitly to the applicability in horizontal relations, that the obligations of states to secure the right to assembly is not an obligation of results but an obligation as to measures to be taken: *Frumkin v. Russia*, 5 January 2016, appl. no. 74568/12, §36.

89 Xenos notes that the criterion of foreseeability and material impossibility are less important when a legal framework has been drafted than when the executive power has been negligent in protecting and enforcing human rights in a concrete situation: D. Xenos, *The Positive Obligations of the State*, 2012, above n. 11, at 100–105.

90 P. De Hert, 'Systeemverantwoordelijkheid voor de informatiemaatschappij als positieve mensenrechtenverplichting' in D. Broeders, C. Cuijpers and C. Prins (eds.), *De staat van informatie*, Amsterdam, Amsterdam University Press, 2011, p33 at 44.

91 An illustrative case in this regard is: *Lopes De Sousa Fernandes v. Portugal*, 19 December 2017 (Grand Chamber), appl. no. 56080/13.

Their obligation to protect human rights in private relationships depends on the nature and the character of the relationship and the human right in question. If infringements of human rights are perfectly foreseeable and very far-reaching, such as an infringement on someone's right to life, the interpersonal relationship can quite easily be established.

One can compare this principle with the neighborhood-principle, or the requirement of proximity, as is sometimes used in the English *tort of negligence*.[92] This principle was used for the first time in *Donoghue v. Stevenson*.[93] At the center of this case lay the fact that Donoghue had drunk a bottle of beer brewed by Stevenson, which contained a decomposed snail. Donoghue only discovered this after he had drunk a part of the beer. Upon discovery he went into shock and then developed intestinal problems. This raised the question of whether Stevenson could be sued for negligence. From a more abstract position the question arose of to whom one can have an obligation to protect. In this context Lord Atkin reasoned:

> The rule that you are to love your neighbour becomes in law you must not injure your neighbour; and the lawyer's question "Who is my neighbour?" receives a restricted reply. You must take reasonable care to avoid acts or omission which you can reasonably foresee would be likely to injure your neighbour. Who then is my neighbour? The answer seems to be persons who are so closely and directly affected by my act that I ought reasonably to have them in contemplation as being so affected when I am directing my mind to the acts or omissions which are called in question.

With this reasoning, Lord Atkin developed the idea that the tort of negligence is only applicable in cases where there is a certain proximity between the tortfeasor and the damaged person. The fact that he used the term 'neighbour' in this context, does not mean that persons have to be in physical proximity:

> I think that this sufficiently states the truth if proximity be not confined to mere physical proximity; but be used, as I think it was intended, to extend to such close and direct relations that the act complained of directly affects a person whom the person alleged to be bound to take care would know would be directly affected by his careless act.

---

92 On this topic, see: V. Harpwood, 'Negligence: breach of duty' in K. Oliphant (ed.), *The Law of Tort*, Suffolk, LexisNexis Butterworths, 2007, (731) 732.

93 House of Lords 26 May 1932, *Donoghue v. Stevenson* UKHL 1932, 100.

It occurs that this approach is – at least implicitly – always used if a judge must determine someone's responsibility for negligence.[94] According to this approach, people have a duty to take care of each other because of the special relationship they have and the balance between the gravity of the potential harm and the efforts that must be made to prevent the potential harm from occurring. It is interesting here that Helmut Koziol indicates that a special relationship cannot only be based on a law or a contract, but that the relationship can also have a special nature as such.[95] He gives the example of two friends who decide to climb the Matterhorn. These two friends probably do not have a specific contract and are not obligated by law to help each other. Nevertheless, it remains that they undertake a joint venture in climbing the mountain. This fact in itself gives rise to strong mutual obligations. Indeed, one expects that people who climb a mountain together will look out for each other's safety.

What this illustrates is that the type of relationship can be decisive in determining whether private persons have an obligation (both under tort law as under human rights law) to protect one another. The size of this obligation increases in intensity if the relationship becomes stronger. However, more specific criteria cannot be provided. The intensity and character of relationships must be judged on a case-by-case basis. Certain, is the fact that in a situation where two people have a relationship with one another and where one has the possibility to easily prevent the harm of the other person from occurring, he is obliged to do so.[96] This option is not only preferential from a moral point of view but is also preferable from a legal and economic perspective.[97]

With regard to the horizontal application of human rights, this criterion also has to be applied to active violations and not only on negligences, as is the case with the 'neighbourhood principle' in English law. This might not be surprising, since most tort law systems do not clearly differentiate active torts and a negligence.[98] Moreover, from a theoretical point of view it is

94 A similar principle is also included in the Principles of European Tort Law. This stems from the discussion of Art. 3:102 of the PETL: C. Von Bar, *Principles of European Law*, München, European Law Publishers, 2009, at 585ff.

95 H. Koziol, 'Liability for Omissions. Basic Questions', *JETL* 2011, p127 at 132.

96 An analogous legitimation of the duty of care has been developed in English tort law: E. Quill, 'Affirmitive Duties of Care in the Common Law', *JETL* 2011, p151 at 168.

97 See: M. Faure, 'Liability for Omissions in Tort Law: Economic Analysis', *JETL* 2011, 184–208.

98 The fact that involuntary and voluntary acts are treated similarly in tort law must be approved because both situations often cannot be clearly distinguished: H. Koziol, 'Liability for Omissions. Basic Questions', *JETL* 2011, p127 at 129.

important to stress that negligences can be as voluntary (or involuntary) as active behaviors. Where a voluntary act can be seen both as the result of a personal assessment in a given situation to reach a goal or the lack of any assessment at all, a negligence can also be the result of the lack of assessments or of the assessment that it is better not to act in a given situation at all.[99]

---

99 This topic has been discussed thoroughly in: H.M. Smith, 'Non-Tracing Cases of Culpable Ignorance', *Criminal Law and Philosophy* 2011, 115–146.

CHAPTER 2

ARTICLES 13 AND 41 ECHR AND STATE LIABILITY

Now that this book has shown that human rights are relevant for the relations between private persons, and thus for private law, attention must be paid to the fact that the Convention contains provisions that can be used in the more specific sphere of damages. It is an established practice of the Court to provide compensation for the victims of human rights violations under Art. 41. Thus, it must be investigated whether this provision can have an influence on national tort law. Based on this line of reasoning, this chapter will argue that the Convention is not only relevant for private law in general, but also for national tort law specifically, mainly by reading Art. 41 in conjunction with Art. 13.

1. ARTICLE 13 AND THE REASONABLE TIME REQUIREMENT

Article 13 requires states to provide effective remedies in national law in order to prevent violations of the Convention from occurring or to compensate for the violations that have already occurred. The idea of this provision is clear: if the national law provides such instruments, human rights victims no longer need to go to Strasbourg. Thanks to this provision, people are not only entitled to the substantive rights of the Convention, but they are also entitled to protection of these rights under the national legal order. Nevertheless, Art. 13 is not the most notable provision of the Convention. This is so because it is a subsidiary or parasitic provision: one can only invoke this provision in conjunction with a substantial treaty provision.[1] It is, however, not a requirement that the other treaty

[1] Y. Arai, 'Right to an effective Remedy before a National Authority (Article 13)' in P. Van Dijk, F. Van Hoof, A. Van Rijn and L. Zwaak (eds.), *Theory and Practice of the European Convention on Human Rights*, Antwerp, Intersentia, 2006, p997 at 998–999.

provision is violated.[2] Article 13 is already applicable if someone proves he has an 'arguable claim' that a substantial treaty provision is violated.[3] Concerning the application of Art. 13, the question arises as to what the Court considers to be an effective remedy. The Court has not developed a blueprint as to how it approaches this question. Instead it applies the provision in a casuistic way.[4] The basis of this jurisprudence is that a remedy must be effective not only in a theoretical way, but also in a practical way.[5]

With regard to the relationship between the Convention and tort law, the question is raised as to whether a claim in tort law can provide an effective remedy. An important case in this regard is *Kudla*. In this case the Court ruled that Art. 13 (read in conjunction with Art. 6) creates the positive obligation to provide a remedy against the state if the requirement to provide a judgment within a reasonable time is not respected.[6] The Court does not however indicate what such a national remedy must look like.[7] It argues that the member states have a margin of appreciation to decide on the form of the remedy[8] and that the remedy may differ

---

2 G. Malinverni, 'Variations sur un thème encore méconnu: l'Article 13 de la Convention européenne des droits de l'homme', *Rev.Trim.D.H.* 1998, p647 at 649.

3 *Gebremedhin v. France*, 26 April 2007, appl. no. 25389/05, §64ff; and G. Malinverni, 'Variations sur un thème encore méconnu', p647 at 650.

4 *Boyle and Rice v. the United Kingdom*, 27 April 1988, appl. nos. 9659/82 and 9658/82, §55; and D. Shelton, *Remedies in International Human Rights Law*, Oxford, Oxford University Press, 1999, at 24.

5 H. Petzold, 'The Convention and the Principle of Subsidiarity' in R. Macdonald, F. Matscher en H. Petzold (eds.), *The European System for the Protection of Human Rights*, Dordrecht, Martinus Nijhoff Publishers,1993, p41 at 47.

6 *Kudla v. Poland*, 26 October 2000 (Grand Chamber), appl. no. 30210/96, §159. See also: T. Barkhuysen and M. Van Emmerik, 'Constitutionalization of Private Law: The European Convention on Human Rights Perspective' in T. Barkhuysen and S.D. Lindenbergh, *Constitutionalization of Private Law*, Leiden, Martinus Nijhoff Publishers, 2006, at 43–57. Apart from this judgment, one must also refer to the jurisprudence of the Strasbourg Court which finds that internal legal means are not exhausted because the applicants still had the possibility to file a case in tort law against the government in order to obtain compensation for the damages caused by the violation of the reasonable time requirement: *Gonzalez Marin v. Spain*, 5 October 1999, appl. no. 39521/98; and *Brusco v. Italy*, 6 September 2001 (decision), appl. no. 69789/01.

7 *Swedish engine drivers' union v. Sweden*, 6 February 1976, appl. no. 5614/72, §50; *Silver et al. v. the United Kingdom*, 25 March 1983, appl. nos. 5947/72, 6205/73, 7052/75, 7061/75, 7107/75, 7113/75 and 7136/75, §113; *James et al. v. the United Kingdom*, 21 February 1986 (Grand Chamber), appl. no. 8793/79, §86; *Lithgow et al. v. the United Kingdom*, 8 July 1986 (Grand Chamber), appl. no. 9006/80 et al, §205; *Vilvarajah et al. v. the United Kingdom*, 30 October 1991, appl. no. 13163/87 et al., §122; and *Iovchev v. Bulgaria*, 2 February 2006, appl. no. 41211/98, §§142–143.

8 *Aksoy v. Turkey*, 18 December 1996, appl. no. 21987/93, §95; *Chahal v. the United Kingdom*, 15 November 1996 (Grand Chamber), appl. no. 22414/93, §145; *Jabari v. Turkey*,

according to the type of human rights violation.[9] The Court nevertheless requires the state to provide legal remedies that are effective in a preventive or a compensatory way.[10] It thereby does not require states to satisfy the claimants in every claim that they file under these procedures,[11] but it does require states to judge these claims within a reasonable time.[12]

Take for example the right to have a judgment within a reasonable time. In *Sürmeli*, the Court ruled that the mere declaration by the German Constitutional Court that the reasonable timeframe was exceeded without fixing a deadline for the procedure and without granting any financial compensation could not be regarded as an effective remedy.[13] The Court requires states to provide financial redress if they cannot prevent an exceeding of the reasonable timeframe.[14] As a consequence it can be concluded that in cases where it is impossible to provide a remedy to prevent a violation of the requirement of a judgment within a reasonable

---

11 July 2000, appl. no. 40035/98, §48; and D. Harris, M. O'Boyle, E. Bates and C. Buckley, *Law of the European Convention*, Oxford, Oxford University Press, 2009, at 559.

9 *Vilvarajah et al. v. the United Kingdom*, 30 October 1991, appl. no. 13163/87 et al., §62; *Kudla v. Poland*, 26 October 2000 (Grand Chamber), appl. no. 30210/96, §157; *Grzinčič v. Slovenia*, 3 May 2007, appl. no. 26867/02, §98; *M.S.S. v. Belgium and Greece*, 21 January 2011 (Grand Chamber), appl. no. 30696/09, §288; *Hirsi Jamaa et al. v. Italy*, 23 February 2012 (Grand Chamber), appl. no. 27765/09, §197; and *Sedminek v. Slovenia*, 23 October 2013, appl. no. 9842/07, §58.

10 *Aksoy v. Turkey*, 18 December 1996, appl. no. 21987/93, §95; *McGlinchey et al. v. the United Kingdom*, 29 April 2003, appl. no. 50390/99, §62; *Sürmeli v. Germany*, 8 June 2006 (Grand Chamber), appl. no. 75529/01, §§99–101; *Stanev v. Bulgaria*, 17 January 2012 (Grand Chamber), appl. no. 36760/06, §217; *Kirins v. Latvia*, 12 January 2017, appl. no. 34140/07, §87; F. Jacobs, R. White and C. Ovey, *The European Convention*, Oxford, Oxford University Press, 2010, at 141. It must be noted that compensatory instruments should only be used in case prevention is impossible: J. Velaers, 'De proliferatie van de zgn. klassieke "liberale" grondrechten in de XXIe eeuw' in X. (ed.), *De Grondwet in groothoekperspectief. Liber amicorum discipuloremque Karel Rimanque*, Antwerp, Intersentia, 2007, p99 at 133.

11 *Costello-Roberts v. the United Kingdom*, 25 March 1993, appl. no. 13134/87, §40; *Conka v. Belgium*, 5 February 2002, appl. no. 51564/99, §75; and *Lorsé et al. v. the Netherlands*, 4 February 2003, appl. no. 52750/99, §96.

12 *Doran v. Ireland*, 31 July 2003, appl. no. 50389/99, §66; and *Sürmeli v. Germany*, 8 June 2006 (Grand Chamber), appl. no. 75529/01, §108.

13 *Sürmeli v. Germany*, 8 June 2006 (Grand Chamber), appl. no. 75529/01, §106–108; *Herbst v. Germany*, 11 January 2007, appl. no. 20027/02, §65; *Skugor v. Germany*, 10 May 2007, appl. no. 76680/01, §63 and *Ommer v. Germany (no. 2)*, 13 November 2008, appl. no. 26073/03, §59.

14 *Doran v. Ireland*, 31 July 2003, appl. no. 50389/99, §66; and *Sürmeli v. Germany*, 8 June 2006 (Grand Chamber), appl. no. 75529/01, §108.

timeframe from occurring, one has to provide a legal remedy with the possibility of granting financial compensation.[15]

States have a margin of appreciation to decide on what an effective remedy must look like. The Court cannot oblige them to provide, for example, tort law remedies. The Court does not oblige states to provide a form of state liability for human rights violations either. However, Jean François Flauss argued in 2002 that, taking *Kudla* into account, it seems necessary to provide state liability for the violation of Art. 6. He noticed that neither a tort procedure for the personal liability of judges, a fast procedure to prevent the occurrence of violations, the possibility of diminished punishments in criminal law, nor the combination of these three procedures could fulfil the requirements of Art. 13 read in conjunction with the reasonable time requirement.[16] This conclusion became even stronger after *Kudla*. After this judgment, many states introduced a remedy in national law to sue the government for damages for violating the requirement of a judgment within a reasonable time.[17] Since then the Court has developed more requirements. First of all, the Court ruled that Art. 13 is violated if a member state cannot approve the legal basis of the obligation of the government to pay damages for violating the reasonable time requirement.[18] Secondly, the Court found that Art. 13 is violated if a state cannot indicate on what ground the size of the compensation is based, regardless of the fact that the violation of the reasonable time requirement as such can be challenged in Court (e.g. via constitutional procedures).[19] If, on the other hand, a state provides

---

15 *McFarlane v. Ireland*, 10 September 2010 (Grand Chamber), appl. no. 31333/06, §108. Exceptionally, the Court found that a financial compensation could also be a sufficient effective remedy when a case was still pending before a national court: *Krasuski v. Poland*, 14 June 2005, appl. no. 61444/00, §66. In *Žunič*, the Court even found that the state had to provide financial redress in a situation where it also required that the procedure was sped up to provide a judgment within a reasonable time: *Žunič v. Slovenia*, 18 October 2007 (decision), appl. no. 24342/04, §54.

16 J.-F. Flauss, 'Le droit à un recours effectif au secours de la règle du délai raisonnable: un revirement de la jurisprudence historique', *Rev.Trim.D.H.* 2002, p179 at 189–195.

17 M.-A. Beernaert, 'De l'épuisement des voies de recours internes en cas de dépassement du délai raisonnable', *Rev.Trim.D.H.* 2004, p905 at 906ff.

18 EComHR *O' Reilly v. Ireland*, 22 January 1996 (Decision), appl. no. 24196/94; and ECtHR, *Vilho Eskelinen et al. v. Finland*, 19 April 2007 (Grand Chamber), appl. no. 63235/00, §82*in fine*.

19 *Kudla v. Poland*, 26 October 2000 (Grand Chamber), appl. no. 30210/96, §159; *Matthies-Lenzen v. Luxemburg*, 5 February 2002 (Decision), appl. no. 45165/99; *Doran v. Ireland*, 31 July 2003, appl. no. 50389/99, §66; and *Sürmeli v. Germany*, 8 June 2006 (Grand Chamber), appl. no. 75529/01, §108.

a compensatory scheme for when the reasonable time is exceeded, if this scheme is effective in the sense that financial compensation is offered on a regular basis,[20] and if this compensation is in line with the compensation that the Court itself grants under Art. 41, it finds the regulation to be in compliance with Art. 13.[21]

In *Wasserman*, the Court summarized this as follows:

> An action for compensation must be heard within a reasonable time; the compensation must be paid promptly and generally no later than six months from the date on which the decision awarding compensation becomes enforceable; the procedural rules governing an action for compensation must conform to the principle of fairness guaranteed by Article 6 of the Convention; the rules regarding legal costs must not place an excessive burden on litigants where their action is justified; the level of compensation must not be unreasonable in comparison with the awards made by the Court in similar cases.[22]

Although the Court indicates that the size of the compensation in a national procedure must be in line with the awards that the Court grants itself in similar cases, it also rules that national judges are in principle better placed to estimate damages.[23] This, however, is only the case for material damages. For immaterial damages the Court argues that:

> there exists a strong but rebuttable presumption that excessively long proceedings will occasion non-pecuniary damage. The Court accepts that, in some cases, the length of proceedings may result in only minimal non-pecuniary damage or no non-pecuniary damage at all. In such cases the domestic courts will have to justify their decision by giving sufficient reasons.[24]

---

20 The Court is not satisfied when there is no settled case law at hand: *A.K. v. Liechtenstein*, 18 February 2016, appl. no. 10722/13, §101.

21 *Eskilsson v. Sweden*, 24 January 2012 (Decision), appl. no. 14628/08. It must be noted that the inadmissible request of the applicants was framed in the context of Art. 6. This book nevertheless refers to this case in the context of Art. 13 because the Court in this decision applied the same criteria as it applies in the context of Art. 13.

22 *Wasserman v. Russia (no.2)*, 10 April 2008, appl. no. 21071/05, §49. See also: *Burdov v. Russia (no.2)*, 15 January 2009, appl. no. 33509/04, §99.

23 *Carvalho Pinto De Sousa Morais v. Portugal*, 25 July 2017, appl. no. 17484/15, §51.

24 *Wasserman v. Russia (no.2)*, 10 April 2008, appl. no. 21071/05, §50. See also: *Scordino v. Italy (no.1)*, 29 March 2006 (Grand Chamber), appl. no. 36813/97, §204; *Sürmeli v. Germany*, 8 June 2006 (Grand Chamber), appl. no. 75529/01, §113; *Herbst v. Germany*, 11 January 2007, appl. no. 20027/02, §66; *Ommer v. Germany (no. 2)*, 13 November 2008, appl. no. 26073/03, §63; *Burdov v. Russia (no.2)*, 15 January 2009, appl. no. 33509/04, §100; and *Rutkowski et al. v. Poland*, 7 July 2015, appl. nos. 72287/10, 13927/11 and 46187/11, §182.

As a result, it may not come as a surprise that the Court does not hesitate to judge that Art. 13 is violated if a member state provides only a very limited amount of financial compensation for immaterial damages.[25] Moreover, if a national judge decides not to grant any compensation for the violation of the reasonable time requirement, he must motivate this.[26]

2. ARTICLE 13 READ IN CONJUNCTION WITH OTHER TREATY PROVISIONS

Apart from the reasonable time requirement, Art. 13 can be read in conjunction with every substantial Convention right. However, the jurisprudence is not evenly elaborated regarding every provision in the Convention. As a consequence, this section only discusses Arts 2, 3 and 8 of the Convention.

2.1. ARTICLES 2 AND 3 OF THE CONVENTION

With regard to the requirement to compensate human rights victims in order to provide an effective remedy under Art. 13, the most interesting jurisprudence of the Court is that concerning the right to life (Art. 2) and the prohibition of torture (Art. 3). Interestingly, the Court in these cases does not always refer to Art. 13 but sometimes absorbs Art. 13 in Arts 2 and 3. For instance in *Kaya*, the Court found a violation of Arts 2 and 3 because a state did not provide financial redress for the violation of these rights.[27] In *Poghosyan and Baghdasaryan* the Court explained that a national remedy for a violation of Art. 3 must be able to provide financial compensation for the moral damages suffered by the victims of these human rights violations.[28] Concerning the right to life, the Court judged in *Gül*:

> Given the fundamental importance of the right to protection of life, Article 13 requires, in addition to the payment of compensation where appropriate,

[25] *Wasserman v. Russia (no.2)*, 10 April 2008, appl. no. 21071/05, §56.

[26] *Scordino v. Italy (no.1)*, 29 March 2006 (Grand Chamber), appl. no. 36813/97, §204; and *Herbst v. Germany*, 11 January 2007, appl. no. 20027/02, §66.

[27] *Kaya v. Turkey*, 19 February 1998, appl. no. 22729/93, §108.

[28] *Poghosyan and Baghdasaryan v. Armenia*, 12 June 2012, appl. no. 22999/06, §§45–48. However, the compensatory function is only one aspect of an effective remedy. The remedy must also prevent the violation from occurring: *Butrin v. Russia*, 22 March 2016, appl. no. 16179/14, §41; and *Baştovoi v. the Republic of Moldova*, 5 July 2016, appl. no. 36125/14, §17.

a thorough and effective investigation capable of leading to the identification and punishment of those responsible for the deprivation of life and including effective access for the complainant to the investigation procedure.[29]

Consequently, it seems that a national remedy for the violation of the right to life or the prohibition of torture must at least provide financial compensation for moral damages in order to be effective.[30] Thus, just as for the reasonable time requirement, an action in tort law against the state seems to be a necessary remedy to protect these rights. This was also illustrated in *Z. et al. v. the United Kingdom*. The applicants in this case were four children who were neglected by their parents. The local authorities were aware of this fact but did not intervene. The children filed a tort claim against the local authorities, but their claim was dismissed. They brought a case before the ECtHR. The Court found a violation of Arts 3 and 8, arguing that governments have the duty to make sure that 'individuals within their jurisdiction are not subjected to torture, inhuman or degrading treatment, including such ill-treatment administered by private individuals.'[31]

Regarding Art. 13, the Court argued that in cases where a violation of Arts 2 or 3 was caused by the omission of the state to protect private persons against the acts of other private persons, it is not necessary to provide an action in criminal law to investigate the cause of death, but it has to be possible to sue the government or one of its staff in a civil liability case.[32] Furthermore, the Court considered it necessary to provide the possibility for victims of violations of the right to life or the prohibition of torture to get financial compensation for moral damages.

---

29 *Gül v. Turkey*, 14 December 2000, appl. no. 22676/93. See also: *Aktaş v. Turkey*, 24 April 2003, appl. no. 24351/94, §329; *Ananyev et al. v. Russia*, 10 January 2001, appl. nos. 42525/07 and 60800/08, §98; *El-Masri v. The former Yugoslav Republic of Macedonia*, 13 December 2012, appl. no. 39630/09, §255; and *Pereira Henriques v. Luxemburg*, 9 May 2006, appl. no. 60255/00, §90.

30 *Bilgin v. Turkey*, 17 July 2001, appl. no. 25659/94, §156; *Tanis et al. v. Turkey*, 2 August 2005, appl. no. 65899/01, §225; *Mikhno v. Ukraine*, 1 September 2016, appl. no. 32514/12, §118; and *Kirins v. Latvia*, 12 January 2017, appl. no. 34140/07.

31 *Z. et al. v. the United Kingdom*, 10 May 2005 (Grand Chamber), appl. no. 29392/95, §73.

32 *Ibid.*, §109. See in the same sense: *Paul and Audrey Edwards v. the United Kingdom*, 14 March 2002, appl. no. 46477/99, §97; *Iurcu v. Moldavia*, 9 April 2013, appl. no. 33759/10, §46; *D.P. and J.C. v. the United Kingdom*, 10 January 2013, appl. no. 38719/97, §§135 and 138; *Lopes De Sousa Fernandes v. Portugal*, 19 December 2017 (Grand Chamber), appl. no. 56080/13, §223.

Since English law at that time did not provide this possibility, the Court ruled that Art. 13 was violated.[33] The Court argues, as with the reasonable time requirement, that the amount of damages must be in line with the awards that the Court itself grants under Art. 41 in cases where Arts 2 or 3 are violated.[34]

2.2. ARTICLE 8 OF THE CONVENTION

The most interesting judgment concerning the requirement of an effective remedy to protect Art. 8 ECHR is probably *T.P. and K.M.*[35] The case concerns an incident of sexual abuse within a family. In a conversation with the police that was filmed on tape, a child gave some indications concerning the identity of its sexual abuser which suggested that the child's mother's partner was the sexual abuser. Consequently, it was decided that the child should be removed from its family. The allegations were false however, but they could not easily be refuted because the police denied access to the video recording of the conversation with the child. Nevertheless, the family obtained access to the minutes of the conversation. With this document, they filed a claim for damages against the state in a national court arguing that the police easily jumped to conclusions about the identity of the sexual abuser. This, they argued, led to the government's negligence in tracking down the real assailant in a timely manner. These arguments were ignored by the national judges who argued that police officers have immunity in this type of case. As a result, they brought an action before the Court. The Court ruled that the national judges should have accepted the claim because:

> the tort of negligence was the only remedy in national law capable of determining the substance of their complaint and which (but for the alleged immunity) would closely match the requirements of the Convention.[36]

---

33 See also: *Bubbins v. the United Kingdom*, 17 March 2005, appl. no. 50196/99, §171; and A. Janczuk and M. Veloso Gomes, 'Claims for non-pecuniary losses by "third persons" upon death or injury' in G. Brüggemeier, A. Colombi Ciacchi and G. Commandé (eds.), *Fundamental Rights and Private Law in the European Union*, Cambridge, Cambridge University Press, 2010, p200 at 219–220.

34 *Kontrová v. Slovakia*, 31 May 2007, appl. no. 7510/04, §64.

35 *V.P. and K.M. v. the United Kingdom*, 10 May 2001 (Grand Chamber), appl. no. 28945/95.

36 *Ibid.*, §105.

With these words, the Court explicitly recognized that in this case a claim in tort law would have been the only effective remedy in national law. The Court also found that the immunity of the police officers might not prevent a judicial procedure from being opened. The defending government argued that the national judges had dealt with the case but that they had ruled that they could not grant financial compensation because the separation of a mother and its child did not qualify for moral damages. The Court, however, did not take these objections into account. It argued that it must be possible to hold public agencies or its staff liable for human rights violations and that in some cases compensation for both material and moral damages must be provided. Consequently it argued that the possibility to receive moral damages in national law was necessary in this case because if, 'as is alleged, psychiatric damage occurred, there may have been elements of medical costs as well as significant pain and suffering to be addressed.'[37] The Court thus found that Art. 13 was violated. Moreover, the ECtHR found that the claimants had suffered moral damages because of the unwillingness of the police to give access to the minutes and the recording of the interview with the child. As a result of this unwillingness, the mother and her child lost the chance to reunite earlier. Consequently, the Court granted them financial compensation of £10,000 for moral damages.

Another interesting case concerning this topic is *Georgel and Georgeta Stoicescu*.[38] An elderly woman that lived in Bucharest was attacked by a pack of wild dogs. The woman sued the government for damages in a national court on the basis of a legal obligation for communities to take action against groups of stray dogs. In the first instance, the community was sentenced to pay compensation to the woman, but she never received this money because the appellate court ruled that she had sued the wrong public agency. The woman then brought a case before the ECtHR and argued that her right to private life and her right of access to a court had been violated. The Court found that there was indeed a serious interference with the applicant's rights under Art. 8. The question, however, was whether the government could be blamed for this. The Romanian government argued that the problem of wild dogs could not be imputed to the government alone but should be imputed to society as a whole. The Court expressed some support for this viewpoint. It stated that it does not fall within the authority of the Court to decide which measures are necessary to tackle

37 *Ibid.*, §109.

38 *Georgel and Georgeta Stoicescu v. Romania*, 26 July 2011, appl. no. 9718/03.

the problem of wild dogs, that the state could only be held responsible if it could have been aware of the problem and that one cannot require the state to reach unachievable goals. The Court nevertheless found a violation of the positive obligation to protect the right to private life. It argued that the government was aware of the dangerous situation as the problem had existed since the 1980s. The Court also noted that the state had enacted legislation to tackle this problem and thus must have been aware of it. But since the government did not take any measures to implement this legislation in practice, the Court ruled that Art. 8 was violated and granted the applicant a compensation of €9,000 for moral damages.

In both these cases, it seems that the Court would not have found a violation of Art. 8 in conjunction with Art. 13 if a national tort law remedy was effective. In contrast, it must be noted that the Court sometimes does not find a violation of these provisions if an applicant had an effective remedy in tort law at hand but did not use it.[39]

2.3. CONCLUSION

One of the things that the jurisprudence mentioned above illustrates, is that in cases where a state cannot prevent a human rights violation from occurring, it must provide the possibility for human right victims to receive financial redress for moral damages in a national procedure.[40] These cases however only relate to some substantive rights. So, one cannot easily draw conclusions about the necessity to enact mechanisms of state liability for human rights violations in general. Nevertheless, it is clear that the Court has the authority to require national legal systems to provide financial compensation for the moral damages that are caused by human rights violations. In fact, the Court has expressed this possibility in a more general way:

> Where an arguable breach of one or more of the rights under the Convention is in issue, there should be available to the victim a mechanism for establishing any liability of State officials or bodies for that breach. Furthermore, in appropriate

39 E.g.: *Cacuci and S.C. Virra & Cont Pad S.R.L. v. Romania*, 17 January 2017, appl. no. 27153/07.

40 A similar argument has been developed in: A. Collignol-Smit Sibinga and S. Mewa, 'Fundamentele rechten in de personenschadepraktijk', *Letsel & Schade* 2011, p9 at 15.

cases, compensation for the pecuniary and non-pecuniary damage flowing from the breach should in principle be available as part of the range of redress.[41]

Moreover, since the jurisprudence of the Court always evolves, it seems that in practice, Art. 13 does require states to enact a general clause for governmental liability for human rights violations.[42] Such a clause would make it possible for the national judiciaries to apply the principles on state liability in the jurisprudence of the ECtHR without having to adopt statutory law every time the jurisprudence of the Court evolves. It seems clear that a legal statute such as the Human Rights Act, which has been adopted in the United Kingdom and provides a separate tort for violations of the Convention by the government, could be a useful instrument to catch up with the development of the jurisprudence of the ECtHR. However, in countries where tort law is regulated by very general and broad statutory provisions, as is the case in Belgium and France, it is possible for courts to adapt the interpretation of these provisions to the requirements of the Convention. That this is possible can be illustrated by the fact that the possibility to hold the state liable for torts committed by the judiciary and the legislature, has been accepted in Belgium in cases where a violation of the Convention was at stake and where the Belgian Court of Cassation implicitly took into account the requirements of Art. 13.[43] Also in Sweden, the possibility of state liability for torts committed by the judiciary has been accepted by the Swedish Supreme Court in a case where Art. 6 had been violated.[44] The Swedish Supreme Court explicitly stated that it had

---

41 E.g.: *Tanrikulu v. Turkey*, 8 July 1999 (Grand Chamber), appl. no. 23763/94, §117; *Ilhan v. Turkey*, 27 June 2000 (Grand Chamber), appl. no. 22277/93, §97; *Salman v. Turkey*, 27 June 2000 (Grand Chamber), appl. no. 21986/93, §121; *Hugh Jordan v. the United Kingdom*, 4 May 2001, appl. no. 24746/94, §160; *Anguelova v. Bulgaria*, 13 June 2002, appl. no. 38361/97, §161; *Gongadze v. Ukraine*, 8 November 2005, appl. no. 34056/02, §191; *Luluyev et al. v. Russia*, 9 November 2006, appl. no. 69480/01, §137; and *E.S. et al. v. Slovakia*, 15 September 2009, appl. no. 8227/04, §34.

42 This argument has also been formulated by Cees Van Dam: C. Van Dam, *European Tort Law*, Oxford, Oxford University Press, 2013, at 25. One author even argues that the Convention in itself provides a legal ground for state liability for the violation of the substantial rights of the Convention: W. Berka, 'Human Rights and Tort Law' in A. Fenyves, E. Karner, H. Koziol and E. Steiner (eds.), *Tort Law in the Jurisprudence of the European Court of Human Rights*, Göttingen, De Gruyter, 2011, p237 at 265.

43 S. Somers, *Aansprakelijkheidsrecht en mensenrechten: Kruisbestuiving in een meergelaagde rechtsorde*, Antwerp, Intersentia, 2016, at 185–210.

44 B. Dufwa, 'Horizontal effect of the European Convention: Swedish Case Law' in A. Colombi Ciacchi, C. Godt, P. Rott and L. Smith (eds.), *Liber Amicorum Gert Brüggemeier. Liability in the Third Millenium*, Baden-Baden, Nomos, 2009, p85 at 99.

to provide an effective remedy for the violation of this Convention right. Because the Court found that the violation had already occurred and could not be prevented anymore, it found that it had to provide financial compensation for immaterial damages, although Swedish law did not provide a legal basis for such a compensation in this concrete case.[45] Thus, the Swedish Supreme Court appealed directly to Art. 13 to provide financial redress for human right victims.

45 M. Schultz, 'Rights Through Torts: The Rise of a Rights Discourse in Swedish Tort Law', *European Review of Private Law* 2009, p305 at 323. Similar solutions have also been applied in the Czech Charter of Fundamental Rights: J. Hradek, 'Czech Republic' in H. Koziol and B. Steininger (eds.), *European Tort Law 2002*, Vienna, Springer, 2003, p119 at 121–123; and in Lithuania: S. Selelionyte-Drukteiniene and L. Saltinyte, 'Lithuania' in K. Oliphant and B. Steininger (eds.), *European Tort Law 2011*, Berlin, De Gruyter, 2012, p386 at 405.

CHAPTER 3

THE INTERACTION BETWEEN ARTICLES 13 AND 41 ECHR AND LIABILITY IN HORIZONTAL RELATIONS

1. TORT LAW AS AN EFFECTIVE REMEDY FOR UNINTENTIONAL INFRINGEMENTS OF HUMAN RIGHTS BY PRIVATE PERSONS

The requirements that the ECtHR poses to governments under Art. 13 are also applicable to positive obligations. This includes the possible requirement to provide financial redress.[1] This is interesting when looking at the positive obligations to protect human rights in horizontal relations. Since the ECtHR on the one hand requires states to provide a remedy and financial redress when the government violates the Convention, and on the other hand requires states to protect human rights in horizontal relations, a compensatory remedy must be provided in case human rights are violated in horizontal relations.[2]

This poses the question of whether the state can fulfill this requirement by providing actions in tort law against private individuals. In 1979 Andrew Drzemczewski argued that an action in tort law against a private

---

1. See for instance with regard to Art. 6: *Osman v. the United Kingdom*, 28 October 1998, appl. no. 23452/94; Art. 3: *Z. et al. v. the United Kingdom*, 10 May 2005 (Grand Chamber), appl. no. 29392/95; Art. 2 in conjunction with Art. 13: *Öneryildiz v. Turkey*, 30 November 2004 (Grand Chamber), appl. no. 48939/99; *L.C.B. v. the United Kingdom*, 9 June 1998, appl. no. 23413/94; and *Guerra et al. v. Italy*, 19 February 1998 (Grand Chamber), appl. no. 14967/89.
2. D. Harris, M. O'Boyle, E. Bates and C. Buckley, *Law of the European Convention*, Oxford, Oxford University Press, 2009, at 342. An example of this can be found in the case discussed above of *Z. et al. v. the United Kingdom*, *Z. et al. v. the United Kingdom*, 10 May 2001, appl. no. 29392/95.

person would constitute an effective remedy in the meaning of Art. 13.[3] This approach was followed for the first time by the Court in the case of *X and Y v. the Netherlands*.[4] As was discussed before, the applicants in this case were a girl with mental disability and her father. The girl had been raped, but the Dutch police did not investigate the crime because rape could only be investigated after someone filed a complaint. The problem was that the victim was judicially unable to file such a complaint because she had a mental disability and yet her father could not do it in her place because she was already of age. Because of this, the Court found a violation of Arts 8 and 13. What is interesting about this case is that the government argued that it had a margin of appreciation and thus could decide on the appropriate remedies it had to take under Art. 13 and that it had chosen to provide an action in tort law.[5] The claimants, on the other hand, objected that an action in civil law could not be qualified as effective in this case because it puts the burden of proof on the victims. Moreover, they argued that actions in tort law take a long time and are thus very demanding for the victims. In civil lawsuits, victims have to play a much more active role than in criminal lawsuits. The European Commission for Human Rights agreed with the plea of the claimants and added to this plea that actions in tort law could only be filed against a limited number of persons, that actions in tort law lack the deterrent effect of a criminal procedure and that it doubted whether the claimants could receive any compensation for moral damages via Dutch tort law. The Court responded to these considerations as follows:

> The Court finds that the protection afforded by the civil law in the case of wrongdoing of the kind inflicted on Miss Y is insufficient. This is a case where fundamental values and essential aspects of private life are at stake. Effective deterrence is indispensable in this area and it can be achieved only by criminal-law provisions; indeed, it is by such provisions that the matter is normally regulated. Moreover, as was pointed out by the Commission, this is in fact an area in which the Netherlands has generally opted for a system of protection based on the criminal law. The only gap, so far as the Commission and the Court have been made aware, is as regards persons in the situation of Miss Y; in such cases, this system meets a procedural obstacle which the Netherlands legislature had apparently not foreseen.[6]

---

3 A. Drzemczewski, 'The European Human Rights Convention and Relations between private parties', *Netherlands International Law Review*, 1979, p163 at 168.

4 *X and Y v. the Netherlands*, 26 March 1985 (Grand Chamber), appl. no. 8978/80.

5 *Ibid.*, §§24–25.

6 *Ibid.*, §27.

Because the ECtHR argued that an action in tort law against a private person in this specific case could not constitute an effective remedy in the meaning of Art. 13 since it is not sufficiently dissuasive,[7] one wonders whether the Court would come to the same conclusion in other cases.[8] Indeed, it is possible to argue that criminal law, with its dissuasive effect, is only the *ultimum remedium*[9] in conflicts between private persons and that tort law might constitute an effective remedy if dissuasion is not as necessary to protect human rights.

The ECtHR made these kinds of observations in later judgments.[10] Take for example the case of *Vo*. The claimant in this case was Miss Thi-Nho Vo, a French woman of Vietnamese origin, who was pregnant and had an appointment with her gynecologist. On the same day, Miss Thi Thanh Van Vo had an appointment with the same gynecologist. The gynecologist made a mistake as to the identity of both patients and applied the medical treatment that was meant for Miss Thi Thanh Van Vo on Miss Thi-Nho Vo. As a result, the unborn child of Miss Thi-Nho Vo had to be aborted. Miss Thi-Nho Vo sued the gynecologist in tort law before a national court and obtained financial compensation. She could not, however, file a criminal complaint for the accidental manslaughter. Because of this, she believed that France did not provide an effective remedy to protect the right to life of her unborn child. The ECtHR, however, responded to this claim as follows:

> the Court has stated on a number of occasions that an effective judicial system, as required by Article 2, may, and under certain circumstances must, include

---

7 See also: *Akdivar et al. v. Turkey*, 16 September 1996 (Grand Chamber), appl. no. 21893/93, §§71–72; *Khachiev and Akaieva v. Russia*, 24 February 2005, appl. nos. 57942/00 and 57945/00, §§121 and 185; and *Gambulatova v. Russia*, 26 March 2015, appl. no. 11237/10, §52.

8 For an in-depth analysis of the question about the requirement to deter rape, see: P. Londono, 'Positive Obligations, Criminal Procedure and Rape Cases', *EHRLR* 2007, p158 at 159ff.

9 J. Velaers, 'De proliferatie van de zgn. klassieke "liberale" grondrechten in de XXIe eeuw' in X. (ed.), *De Grondwet in groothoekperspectief. Liber amicorum discipuloremque Karel Rimanque*, Antwerp, Intersentia, 2007, p99 at 140.

10 *Calvelli and Ciglio v. Italy*, 17 January 2002 (Grand Chamber), appl. no. 32967/96; *Lazzarini and Ghiacci v. Italy*, 7 November 2002 (Decision), appl. no. 53749/00, §1; *Sindicato dos Pilotos de Aviação Civil v. Portugal*, 29 January 2004 (Decision), appl. no. 38176/02; *Vo v. France*, 8 July 2004 (Grand Chamber), appl. no. 53924/00; *Tarariyeva v. Russia*, 14 March 2007, appl. no. 4353/03, §75; *Spyra and Kranczkowski v. Poland*, 25 September 2012, appl. no. 19764/07, §87; *Sıdıka İmren v. Turkey*, 13 September 2013, appl. no. 47384/11, §58; and *Cevrioğlu v. Turkey*, 4 October 2016, appl. no. 69546/12, §54.

> recourse to the criminal law. However, if the infringement of the right to life or to physical integrity is not caused intentionally, the positive obligation imposed by Article 2 to set up an effective judicial system does not necessarily require the provision of a criminal-law remedy in every case. In the specific sphere of medical negligence, "the obligation may for instance also be satisfied if the legal system affords victims a remedy in the civil courts, either alone or in conjunction with a remedy in the criminal courts, enabling any liability of the doctors concerned to be established and any appropriate civil redress, such as an order for damages and for the publication of the decision, to be obtained. Disciplinary measures may also be envisaged.[11]

This judgment demonstrates the possibility that suing someone in tort law might be an effective remedy in the meaning of Art. 13 if the infringement of a human right is caused unintentionally.[12] Of course this has to be done

---

11 *Vo v. France*, 8 July 2004 (Grand Chamber), appl. no. 53924/00, §90. See in the same sense: *Calvelli and Ciglio v. Italy*, 17 January 2002 (Grand Chamber), appl. no. 32967/96, §51; *Byrzykowski v. Poland*, 27 June 2006, appl. no. 11562/05, §105; *Benderskiy v. Ukraine*, 15 November 2007, appl. no. 22750/02, §§61–62; *Dodov v. Bulgaria*, 17 January 2008, appl. no. 59548/00, §80; *Karchen et al. v. France*, 4 March 2008 (Decision), appl. no. 5722/04; *Colak and Tsakiridis v. Germany*, 5 March 2009, appl. nos. 77144/01 and 35493/05, §30; *Šilih v. Slovenia*, 9 April 2009 (Grand Chamber), appl. no. 71463/01, §156; *Codarcea v. Romania*, 2 June 2009, appl. no. 1675/04, §102; *G.N. et al. v. Italy*, 1 December 2009, appl. no. 43134/05, §82; *Maiorano et al. v. Italy*, 15 December 2009, appl. no. 28634/06, §128; *Fedina v. Ukraine*, 2 September 2010, appl. no. 17185/02, §62; *Stoyanovi v. Bulgaria*, 9 November 2010, appl. no. 42980/04, §60; *Romokhov v. Russia*, 16 December 2010, appl. no. 4532/04, §100; *Anna Todorova v. Bulgaria*, 24 May 2011, appl. no. 23302/03, §73; *Ciechońska v. Poland*, 4 June 2011, appl. no. 19776/04, §66; *V.C. v. Slovakia*, 8 November 2011, appl. no. 18968/07, §125; *Igor Shevchenko v. Ukraine*, 12 January 2012, appl. no. 22737/04, §51; *Ilbeyi Kemaloğlu en Meriye Kemaloğlu v. Turkey*, 10 April 2012, appl. no. 19986/06, §38; *Mitkus v. Latvia*, 2 October 2012, appl. no. 7259/03, §76; *Z. v. Poland*, 13 November 2012, appl. no. 46132/08, §94; *Bajić v. Croatia*, 13 November 2012, appl. no. 41108/10, §78; *Kudra v. Croatia*, 18 December 2012, appl. no. 13904/07, §91; *Arskaya v. Turkey*, 5 December 2013, appl. no. 45076/05, §65; *Valeriy Fuklev v. Ukraine*, 16 January 2014, appl. no. 6318/03; *Binişan v. Romania*, 20 May 2014, appl. no. 39438/05, §75; *Gray v. Germany*, 22 May 2014, appl. no. 49278/09, §81; *Starčević v. Croatia*, 13 November 2014, appl. no. 80909/12, §54; *Barańska v. Poland*, 16 December 2014 (Decision), appl. no. 46863/09, §56; *Ciobanu v. Moldavia*, 24 February 2015, appl. no. 62578/09, §32; *Ateş v. Turkey*, 24 March 2015 (Decision), appl. no. 38332/11, §18; *Ioniță v. Romania*, 10 January 2017, appl. no. 81270/12, §73; and *Lopes De Sousa Fernandes v. Portugal*, 19 December 2017 (Grand Chamber), appl. no. 56080/13, §§214–238.

12 However, in one judgment the Court required instruments in criminal law to remedy unintentional violations of human rights by governmental officials. For this, the Court took into account criteria such as the grade of responsibility of the government in a specific policy field, the gravity of the infringement on human rights and the number of (potential) victims of the human rights violation: *Öneryildiz v. Turkey*, 30 November 2004 (Grand Chamber), appl. no. 48939/99, §§93, 117 and 118. See also: A. Gerry,

in a fast and effective way.[13] The Court requires that access to a civil court not be impeded. For instance, in *Ilbeyi Kemaloğlu and Meriye Kemaloğlu*, the Court argued that the right to life was violated in the situation where a child died of undercooling after it was sent back home from school and the parents could not file a claim in court because they were unable to pay the court fees.[14]

More interesting with regard to tort law is the case of *Colak and Tsakiridis*.[15] A doctor diagnosed a married man with HIV. The doctor urged the patient to inform his wife about the diagnosis. The doctor did not inform the woman of her husband's HIV infection himself because he thought that he would violate his duty of confidentiality if he did so. Only when the man died a few years later did the doctor inform the woman about the HIV-infection of her husband. A short while later, the woman was also diagnosed with HIV. She believed that if the doctor had informed her earlier, this infection might have been prevented. For this reason, she filed an action in tort law against the doctor. The German court dismissed this claim because the woman could not prove the causal connection between her infection and the fact that the doctor had withheld information about the infection of her husband. However, the causal link was difficult to demonstrate in this case because the woman had to prove that she was infected with HIV after the doctor diagnosed her husband with HIV and not before. German law provides a reversal of the burden of proof if a suspected tortfeasor makes a gross error. Thus, the woman argued that the doctor made a gross error by not informing her about her husband's infection. The German courts did not agree with this line of reasoning however. They argued that no medical legislation existed in this field, and that in the field of medical deontology disagreement existed as to how a doctor should balance his duty of confidentiality towards one patient with

---

'Öneryildiz v Turkey', *EHRLR* 2005, p203 at 209–212. But apart from governmental officials, the Court can also require a state to provide remedies in criminal law in cases of medical negligence if a doctor did not give any medical treatment to a person who is obviously in need of urgent treatment: *Mehmet Şentürk en Bekir Şentürk v. Turkey*, 9 April 2013, appl. no. 13423/09, §§104–106.

13 *Dodov v. Bulgaria*, 17 January 2008, appl. no. 59548/00, §98; *Šilih v. Slovenia*, 9 April 2009 (Grand Chamber), appl. no. 71463/01, §195; *Anna Todorova v. Bulgaria*, 24 May 2011, appl. no. 23302/03, §83; *Ciechońska v. Poland*, 14 June 2011, appl. no. 19776/04, §79; *Igor Shevchenko v. Ukraine*, 12 January 2012, appl. no. 22737/04, §54ff; *Z. v. Poland*, 13 November 2012, appl. no. 46132/08, §95; *Kudra v. Croatia*, 18 December 2012, appl. no. 13904/07, §100ff; and *Ciobanu v. Moldavia*, 24 February 2015, appl. no. 62578/09, §34.

14 *Ilbeyi Kemaloğlu en Meriye Kemaloğlu v. Turkey*, 10 April 2012, appl. no. 19986/06, §44.

15 *Colak and Tsakiridis v. Germany*, 5 March 2009, appl. nos. 77144/01 and 35493/05.

the right to life of another. Accordingly, the judges found that the doctor did not commit a grave error by prioritizing the right to privacy of man above the rights of his wife. The woman then brought a claim before the ECtHR and argued that German law did not provide an effective remedy to protect her right to life.

The Court started its judgment by stating that the state's positive obligations under Art. 2 require an effective independent judicial system so that the cause of death of patients in the care of the medical profession can be determined and those responsible made accountable. In cases of medical malpractices, the Court has found that an effective remedy might consist of a remedy in a tort action before a civil court. It noticed that Germany did not have specific legislation concerning the conflict between a doctor's duty of confidentiality and the right to life and physical integrity of another patient. Moreover, because no domestic case-law existed on this issue, the Court found that the German lawyers had applied the claims of the applicant in the spirit of the treaty. Because the Court used the words 'in the spirit of the treaty' it seems that the Court was not entirely sure about its judgment. Interestingly, the Court also noted that in the future German courts might have to apply higher standards of diligence for doctors since they had made an indication as to how a doctor should act when confronted with a conflict between his duty of confidentiality and the right to life of one of his patients. Consequently, it is possible that the Court will decide differently in future cases. At this point, however, this case illustrates that at the least a form of action for damages should be provided, whether or not the action will be successful.

2. TORT LAW AS AN ACCESSORY REMEDY FOR INTENDED INFRINGEMENTS OF HUMAN RIGHTS

When infringements of human rights are caused intentionally, it seems that tort law lacks enough dissuasive effect to be effective. Indeed, when human right violations are caused intentionally, the Court argues that states must provide criminal[16] or (in exceptional cases) administrative

16 *Jeronovičs v. Latvia*, 5 July 2016 (Grand Chamber), appl. no. 44898/10, §76; and Y. Arai, 'Right to an effective remedy before a National Authority (Article 13)' in P. Van Dijk, F. Van Hoof, A. Van Rijn and L. Zwaak (eds.), *Theory and Practice of the European Convention on Human Rights*, Antwerp, Intersentia, p997 at 1007.

actions,[17] and must pursue a criminal investigation.[18] For example in *Şentürk*, the Court ruled that an action in criminal law must be at hand if doctors in full consciousness and in conflict with their deontological code do not take the necessary precautionary measures.[19] This is an interesting observation for two reasons. The first reason is that it illustrates that states have a duty to enact mechanisms that deter people from infringing each others' rights. As a consequence, there need to be remedies that are dissuasive enough to prevent human rights violations from occurring. This shows that human rights cannot be protected in an effective manner if protective measures are only directed towards the state. Human rights must also be protected in horizontal relationships, both by criminal and civil law remedies. The differentiation between the necessity to provide these two types of remedies then seems to come from their dissuasive effect, which is the second interesting observation of this jurisprudence.[20]

This distinction does not mean that civil law is irrelevant for situations where criminal law remedies are required. Indeed, in cases where a criminal action is necessary to provide an effective remedy in national law, tort law has its role to play. In national legal systems, victims of crimes normally have the possibility to sue the criminal for damages via an action in tort law. This stems from the fact that tort law has a compensatory function that criminal law lacks. And this compensatory function is important because if the ECtHR requires a national remedy to provide financial compensation in order to be effective, it obviously does so for compensatory reasons. Thus, it comes as no surprise that the ECtHR in the case of *Akalli* made clear that criminal sanctions cannot suffice as a mean to compensate human rights violations. In its judgment the Court stated that the fact that some police officers who had infringed upon human rights of others were condemned in criminal law, which gave some satisfaction to the applicants, did not keep the Court from granting these victims financial compensation for moral damages under Art. 41 of the Convention. The Court ruled that

---

17 *Tre Traktörer Aktiebolag v. Sweden*, 7 July 1989, appl. no. 10873/84, §49.

18 When, for example, a person is missing, a claim in tort law against the suspected criminal cannot provide an effective remedy since the victims do not know his identity. It is up to the state to investigate who committed the crime: *Ranđelović and Others v. Montenegro*, 19 September 2017, appl. no. 66641/10, §105.

19 *Mehmet Şentürk en Bekir Şentürk v. Turkey*, 9 April 2013, appl. no. 13423/09, §104ff.

20 In an exceptional judgment, the Court required a criminal investigation in a case where the applicant complained that he had been infected with HIV during his imprisonment and where the applicant himself had no means to collect proof: *Mitkus v. Latvia*, 2 October 2012, appl. no. 7259/03, §77.

the imposed penalties could not be considered sufficient to repair the non-pecuniary damage suffered by the applicant.[21]

3. LIMITATIONS IN REQUIRING HORIZONTAL TORT LAW

Now that it has been illustrated how tort law can provide the effective remedy required by Art. 13 and how the Court requires states to enact legal rules to prevent private persons from infringing each others' human rights, the question arises of whether the Court can explicitly require states to enact horizontal liability regulations.

At first glance this seems unlikely since the Convention is directed towards states. One cannot sue a private individual before the Court. The only mechanism to enforce human rights in horizontal relationships in the Convention is through the so-called positive obligations of states to protect human rights in horizontal relationships. The result is that the Court under Art. 41 can only command the government to pay compensation to a human rights victim. The Court cannot command private entities to provide compensatory damages. On the other hand, it argues that states do have to compensate for the damages in cases where it did not protect human rights in private relationships. This possibility has been limited by some cases where the Court judged that the government cannot be told under Art. 41 to compensate for the damages caused by private persons,[22] and that the government cannot be held responsible for the fact that a private person who violated human rights is insolvent.[23]

This jurisprudence will be examined further from the perspective of causality. For now, this jurisprudence is interesting because if the ECtHR itself cannot obligate private persons to compensate human right victims under Art. 41, one wonders whether the Court can require states to do so under Art. 13. Indeed, the Court requires a national remedy to provide a similar compensation as it grants itself under Art. 41 in order to be effective. It is, however, a different thing for the Court to command private persons to compensate human rights victims under Art. 41 as it is to

---

21 *Okkali v. Turkey*, 17 October 2006, appl. no. 52067/99, §82.

22 *Venema v. the Netherlands*, 17 December 2002 (just satisfaction), appl. no. 35731/97, §112. See also: *M.C. v. Bulgaria*, 4 December 2003, appl. no. 39272/98, §149; *Mascolo v. Italy*, 16 December 2004, appl. no. 68792/01, §55; and *Lo Tufo v. Italy*, 21 April 2005, appl. no. 64663/01, §68.

23 *Magherini v. Italy*, 1 June 2006, appl. no. 69143/01, §43.

require states under Art. 13 to enact liability regimes that have to uphold the compensatory principles of Art. 41 in horizontal relationships. For this reason, it is interesting to look into the – very scarce – jurisprudence of the Court concerning this topic.

A first case is *Zavoloka*.[24] The facts were tragic, but simple. A 12-year-old girl died in a car accident. All the parties involved were private persons. After the parents of the girl filed a claim at a Latvian court that held another private party liable, it seemed that the parents could not receive compensation for the immaterial damages that were caused by the loss of their young daughter. Accordingly, the victims filed a complaint at the ECtHR and argued that Latvian law, by not providing this possibility in the concrete case, violated the Convention. The Court did not agree with this point of view. It noted that the Latvian law stipulates that immaterial damages in case of death are covered by the material damages. Moreover, the Court also stressed that the applicants had not claimed compensation for the hospital and funeral expenses.[25]

It is clear in this case that the Court did not push for a further protection of human rights in horizontal tort law. Nevertheless, it did not reject the possibility as such. On the contrary, by referring to the principle in Latvian law that immaterial damages are covered by the compensation that is awarded for material damages and by referring to the fact that the applicants had failed to claim all relevant costs, it seems that the Court has kept open the possibility that in some cases, it would find a violation of the Convention.[26]

Such a violation was found in *Codarcea*.[27] The applicant was a woman that had undergone plastic surgery. In one of the operations, a doctor made an error causing a permanent injury. The woman sued the doctor and the hospital in civil courts, but these procedures brought her nothing. In one of the judgments, the doctor was held liable for the injury, but since he was insolvent, she could not receive any compensation. The law prevented every liability claim against the hospital. The ECtHR argued that states have a positive obligation to provide a regulatory framework so that

---

24 *Zavoloka v. Latvia*, 7 July 2009, appl. no. 58447/00.

25 *Ibid.*, §§40–41.

26 In the case of *Howald Moor* (*Howald Moor et al. v. Switzerland*, 11 March 2014, appl.nos. 52067/10 and 41072/11), the Court applied this argument in the opposite way. It seems that the Court took into account the fact that a compensation fund for injuries caused by asbestos did not provide restitution for non-pecuniary damages.

27 *Codarcea v. Romania*, 2 June 2009, appl. no. 1675/04.

hospitals (whether or not they are public agencies or private owned) will respect the rights that patients have under Arts 2 and 8 ECHR.[28] Since neither a claim against the hospital nor against the doctor brought the woman any real compensation, Art. 8 was violated.[29] Although the Court did not refer to Art. 13 in an explicit way, it seems that because it required an effective remedy to be provided under Art. 8, a victim of a violation of Art. 8 in the context of medical malpractice must be able to obtain a real compensation from the human rights infringer. The Court did not require the doctor or the hospital to pay damages since this falls outside of its authority, but it forced the government to provide a remedy in national law by commanding the government to compensate the victim.

The practical implications of this case are limited however. The Romanian government had already enacted a law to obligate doctors to insure themselves against medical errors. This law only entered into force after the case of *Codarcea* occurred. The only reason that the new rules were not applied in this case stems from the fact that the new law had no retroactive application. However, one can wonder whether the Court would also have found a violation of the Convention if the Romanian parliament had not yet enacted a law that obliged doctors to have insurance for medical errors. In such a situation, the Court might have been less strict.

From these cases it is not clear whether the Court can require states to provide horizontal tort law. To the extent that the Court seems to do this, it seems to be very cautious. Nevertheless, it cannot be ignored that the Court accepts that tort law can be an effective remedy in cases where it deems it unnecessary to enact criminal law. Indeed, a number of cases have been discussed in this book in which the Court judged that it was not necessary to enact criminal law in order to provide an effective remedy for an infringement by other private persons. It is clear that the Court in these cases would have found a violation if national law did not provide a remedy in tort law. By doing so, the Court does not only require tort law as an instrument to grant compensation to human rights victims (that must not necessarily come from tort law but might for example also come from social security law), but also requires that the private person who infringes a human right of another person is somehow deterred by tort law. Thus, the Court does not only perceive tort law as an instrument to compensate human rights victims, but also as an instrument to deter private persons from violating human rights.

---

28 *Ibid.*, §§102–103.

29 *Ibid.*, §§107–109.

The necessity to provide remedies that can both compensate the victim as well as deter the tortfeasor is indicated in *Ciechońska*:

> … the Court reiterates that an issue of State responsibility under Article 2 of the Convention may arise in the event of the inability of the domestic legal system to secure accountability for any negligent acts endangering or resulting in the loss of human life. In such a case the Court must examine whether the available legal remedies, taken together, as provided in law and applied in practice, could be said to have amounted to legal means capable of establishing the facts, holding accountable those at fault and providing appropriate redress to the victim.[30]

Another important judgment is *Söderman*.[31] In September 2014, a 14-year-old Swedish girl discovered that her stepfather had hidden a video-camera in the laundry basket in the bathroom, which was in recording mode and directed towards the spot where she had undressed before taking a shower. Immediately after the incident, the film was burned without anyone seeing it. Two years later, after the girl's mother separated from her stepfather, the mother reported the incident to the police. This led to a criminal investigation. Although it was proved that the applicant's stepfather had intended to film his minor stepdaughter in the bathroom and that this was obviously of a sensitive nature as regards the applicant's personal integrity, and although the violation was particularly serious on account of the applicant's age and relationship to her stepfather, the Swedish court of appeal found that the stepfather could not be held criminally responsible for sexual molestation for the isolated act of filming the applicant without her consent. The court of appeal noted that the act of the stepfather might, at least theoretically, have constituted the crime of attempted child pornography. However, since no charge of that kind had been brought against the applicant's stepfather, the court could not examine whether he could be held responsible for that crime.

This judgment in criminal law influenced the civil law procedure for damages. Before the Swedish courts, the applicant had claimed compensation based on the provision that provides compensation to crime victims. She had not invoked the more general liability provision of negligence in Swedish tort law. Consequently, the victim appealed to the ECtHR and argued that the Convention was violated because there were no

30 *Ciechońska v. Poland*, 14 June 2004, appl. no. 19776/04, §71. See also: *Furdik v. Slovakia*, 2 December 2008, appl. no. 42994/05.

31 *Söderman v. Sweden*, 12 November 2013, appl. no. 5786/08.

criminal-law remedies at hand and because the lack of an effective private-law remedy made it impossible for her to receive compensation. After the Court found that Sweden indeed did not provide a criminal remedy for the human rights infringement, but noted that it fell within the margin of appreciation of the member states as to decide in this type of case whether it would provide criminal instruments or whether civil-law remedies sufficed, the Swedish government contended that Swedish law provided an effective remedy because the applicant could have relied on the grounds that her stepfather had caused her personal injury by acting negligently under Chapter 2, s. 1, of the Swedish Tort Liability Act, which could have covered any physical and psychological injury. The ECtHR observed that the applicant's stepfather had at no time during the investigation nor the criminal proceedings alleged that he had left the camera in recording mode in the laundry basket in the bathroom by accident. On the contrary, he acknowledged that it had been a willful but impulsive act. Therefore, the Court found that the applicant and her counsel could not be expected to have invoked negligence just for the sake of ensuring that her claim be dealt with in the event that the act was not deemed to be covered by the offence of sexual molestation. As a result, the Court ruled that Swedish law did not provide an effective remedy as required under Art. 13 of the Convention.

This judgment illustrates that the Court does not always require states to provide remedies in criminal law to deteriorate intended infringements of human rights. The Court explicitly noted that the case concerned 'less serious acts' than, for instance child abuse, and thus civil-law remedies afforded sufficient protection.[32] The line of reasoning indicates that the Court requires civil-law remedies to be somehow dissuasive. Indeed, an instrument to protect human rights against willful infringements can only be effective if it can be used to hold the infringer accountable in order to deter him from infringing the same rights again.

This deterrence is important. If the Court would only require civil-law remedies as instruments to compensate the damages of victims, an effective remedy in this case could have been found in state liability. The Swedish government indeed argued that Swedish law in this case provided an effective remedy because the applicants could have filed a claim in Swedish law against the state for violating the Convention. The Court however noted that this remedy could only be used against the state, and that it could not believe that it could have made up for the absence of a

---

32 *Ibid.*, §85.

civil remedy in the specific situation at hand.[33] Thus, in some cases it is not enough that the state provides compensation when it failed to protect human rights in horizontal relations. Sometimes states are also obliged to make sure that private persons are deterred from infringing the human rights of others. In order to do so, they have a margin of appreciation as to decide which instruments they will use. But if they do not provide criminal law remedies, they have to assure that a deterrent civil-law instrument is at hand, such as a claim in tort law.

Concluding, it seems that although the Court can require national legal orders to provide sufficient compensation for violations of the Convention, the Court is reluctant to request that states provide tort law in horizontal relations. States have a margin of appreciation to decide how they will compensate human right victims. However, since tort law in most legal systems is the main compensatory scheme, it seems quite reasonable to adapt this field of law to the requirements of the Court. This is especially true since a lot of human rights violations can be qualified as torts. This idea is endorsed by the fact that the primary aim of a national remedy must be to deter human rights violations. Of course, this will often be done by criminal law, but in cases where states do not want to provide criminal sanctions or where the legislator did not yet have the chance to enact criminal law, tort law seems to be the only possible instrument that can both deter and compensate. If an effective remedy only requires compensation, a state could rely on social security law or on state liability for not providing a compensation scheme in horizontal tort law. But these options would have budgetary consequences for the government and lack a deterrent effect. As a result, it is advisable for national judges to interpret tort law provisions in such a way that they do provide an effective remedy (both from a deterrent and a compensatory point of view) to protect human rights in vertical as well as in horizontal relations.

[33] *Ibid.*, §116.

CHAPTER 4

TORT LIABILITY AS A VIOLATION OF HUMAN RIGHTS

The previous chapters illustrated that the Convention can influence tort law via the theory of positive obligations and the requirement of an effective remedy. But the Convention can also influence tort law in a whole different way. While the previous chapters also illustrated how tort law can serve as an effective remedy in case of a violation of human rights, tort liability can also violate the treaty rights of the liable person.

The most distinct example of a tort liability that was in violation of human rights can be found in *Tolstoy Miloslavsky*.[1] The applicant in this case was a British historian who had issued a pamphlet entitled 'War Crimes and the Wardenship of Winchester College'. In this pamphlet, he argued that Lord Aldington, the administrator of the prestigious Winchester College, was responsible for the extradition of almost 70,000 persons of Yugoslavian nationality to the Communist regime of Tito and to Russia. Mr Tolstoy distributed this pamphlet among the personnel of Winchester College, the students of the college, their parents, members of parliament and the press. Lord Aldington pressed charges before a civil court for libel. The procedures in this case were very complex. In short, Lord Aldington won the case and received damages of £15 million. For an appeal to this judgement to be admissible, Mr Tolstoy had to pay Lord Aldington a guarantee of £124,000 for damages and £22,000 as a guarantee for the litigation costs in higher appeal. Mr Tolstoy challenged this decision before the Court. He argued that the guarantees he had to deliver in order to lodge an appeal violated his right to be heard by a judge and that his freedom of expression was violated because he had to pay £1.5 million in damages. The ECtHR did not establish a violation of the right to be heard by a judge but found a violation of Art. 10.[2]

1 *Tolstoy Miloslavsky v. the United Kingdom*, 13 July 1995, appl. no. 18139/91.
2 *Ibid.*, §55.

With regard to the violation of the freedom of expression, Mr Tolstoy brought two arguments. He first argued that the damages were not prescribed by law (as Art. 10, §2 requires). The applicant accepted that the condition that an exception to the freedom of expression had to be prescribed by law could also relate to case-law rules, but argued that 'the law in question did not enable him to foresee to a reasonable degree that the amount would be as high as 1.5 million pound.'[3] He argued that even if the damages did not entail 'punitive damages', they were three times higher than any sum that had been granted in previous libel cases and was even higher than the sums that are granted in cases of serious personal injury.

The ECtHR decided that 'prescribed by law' did not imply that the applicant must be able to assess the damages that he would have to pay.[4] With regard to the question whether the attributed damages were necessary in a democratic society, the Court considered:

> it should be noted that, at the material time, the national law allowed a great latitude to the jury. The Court of Appeal could not set aside an award simply on the grounds that it was excessive but only if the award was so unreasonable that it could not have been made by sensible people and must have been arrived at capriciously, unconscionably or irrationally (see paragraph 26 above). In a more recent case, Rantzen v. Mirror Group Newspapers Ltd, the Court of Appeal itself observed that to grant an almost limitless discretion to a jury failed to provide a satisfactory measurement for deciding what was "necessary in a democratic society" for the purposes of Article 10 (Art. 10) of the Convention. It noted that the common law – if properly understood – required the courts to subject large awards of damages to a more searching scrutiny than had been customary. As to what guidance the judge could give to the jury, the Court of Appeal stated that it was to be hoped that in the course of time a series of decisions of the Court of Appeal, taken under section 8 of the Courts and Legal Services Act 1990, would establish some standards as to what would be "proper" awards. In the meantime the jury should be invited to consider the purchasing power of any award which they might make and to ensure that any award they made was proportionate to the damage which the plaintiff had suffered and was a sum which it was necessary to award him to provide adequate compensation and to re-establish his reputation.[5]

The Court decided that in the underlying case there were not enough stimuli for the jury to grant proportional damages and that the damages

---

3 *Ibid.*, §38.

4 *Ibid.*, §41*in fine*.

5 *Ibid.*, §50.

granted of £1.5 million was disproportionately high taking into account the intended aim, namely the protection of the good name and reputation of Lord Aldington. A fundamental consideration seemed to be the unfettered discretionary power of the jury to determine the amount of the compensation.[6]

The same conclusion was also reached in *Independent news and media and Independent newspapers v. Ireland*.[7] In this case the highest court of Ireland had granted damages that were three times higher than the highest damages that had ever been granted before. The liable persons argued that their freedom of speech was violated in light of the *Miloslavsky* case. The Court decided that in this case the freedom of speech was not violated. On the one hand, the Court pointed out that even if the highest court of Ireland had never granted such a high amount of compensation in a similar case, lower courts had done so before. The Court found that the amount of compensation was not entirely unpredictable. Moreover, it pointed out that the judges in this case had paid a lot of attention to the amount of the compensation to award, e.g. in similar cases.

In his dissenting opinion Judge Cabral Barreto criticized this judgment. He was of the opinion that the Court does not have to examine whether the national judges follow a procedure that takes into account the proportionality of the seriousness of the violation of the freedom of speech and the amount of the compensation, but that the Court does have to assess whether the results obtained under national law are in line with the jurisprudence of the Court.[8] Despite this critique the Court recently considered in *Krone Verlag* that it is its duty to verify that the member states take the necessary procedural measures to prevent unreasonably high amounts of compensation.[9] In the case of *Krone Verlag* the Court found that the state did so because the law prescribed an upper limit for compensation of moral damages caused in the context of press liability.

---

6 W. Berka, 'Human Rights and Tort Law' in A. Fenyves, E. Karner, H. Koziol and E. Steiner (eds.), *Tort Law in the Jurisprudence of the European Court of Human Rights*, Göttingen, De Gruyter, 2011, p237 at 282. It is not surprising that English law has developed different guidelines to instruct the jury about the amount of compensation: A. Mullis, 'The law of defamation – part II' in K. Oliphant (ed.), *The Law of Tort*, Suffolk, LexisNexis Butterworths, 2007, p1361 at 1483–1484.

7 *Independent news and media and Independent newspapers Ireland v. Ireland*, 16 June 2005, appl. no. 55120/00, §§119–125.

8 Dissenting opinion of Judge Cabral Barreto in *Independent news and media and Independent newspapers Ireland v. Ireland*, 16 June 2005, appl. no. 55120/00, §2.

9 *Krone Verlag GMBH v. Austria*, 19 June 2012, appl. no. 27306/07, §61.

Later the Court more or less followed the reasoning of Judge Cabral Barreto in the case of *Steel and Morris*.[10] The applicants in this case were London members of the environmental organization Greanpeace, which had distributed a pamphlet in which they challenged the policies of the burger chain McDonald's. McDonald's started a case of libel against the applicants. The Court of appeal held Ms Steel liable for £36,000 and Mr Morris for £40,000. Consequently, Steel and Morris challenged the decision before the ECtHR on the basis of Art. 6, §1 and Art. 10. Within the framework of Art. 6, §1, the Court found a violation of the rights of defense because of the ineligibility for legal aid. According to the Court this led to an 'unacceptable inequality of arms' between the applicant and McDonald's.[11] For the same reason the freedom of expression (Art. 10) was also violated.

10 *Steel and Morris v. the United Kingdom*, 15 February 2005, appl. no. 68416/01.
11 *Ibid.*, §§59–72.

CHAPTER 5
ARTICLE 41 AS AN ALTERNATIVE TORT LAW SYSTEM

The previous chapters discussed how states can be forced to provide tort law remedies in order to provide an effective remedy under Art. 13 ECHR. A consequence of this is that states must provide compensation that are in line with those of the ECtHR based on Art. 41. This raises the question of whether the Court can act as an alternative forum when national courts grant only a limited financial compensation for human rights violations. If this would be the case, the Court could be used as an instrument to get full compensation when national courts refuse to grant full compensation. The Court could then be used as leverage in national compensatory schemes.

1. REQUIREMENTS OF ADMISSABILITY

Before the ECtHR can award compensation to a human rights victim, the victim needs to file an admissible claim. This raises the question whether a claim will be admissible if an applicant has already been awarded compensation under national law. Indeed, if someone files a claim before the ECtHR, he must exhaust all national remedies and must prove that he has an interest.[1] Since the 14th protocol entered into force, an applicant must not only prove that he has an interest in the claim, but also that the alleged violation of the Convention caused him some significant disadvantage.[2] What is of utmost importance in the context of this book,

[1] The fact that the Court sometimes investigates the applicability together with the merits of the case and not separately must be highlighted: *Zborovský v. Slovenia*, 23 October 2012, appl. no. 14325/08; and *Migalska v. Poland*, 4 December 2012, appl. no. 10368/05.

[2] For an in-depth analysis of this criteria see: F. Vanneste, 'A new inadmissibility ground' in P. Lemmens and W. Vandenhole (eds.), *Protocol No. 14 and the Reform of the European Court of Human Rights*, Antwerp, Intersentia, 2004, 69–88; X.-B. Ruedin,

is the fact that the Court often takes its own jurisprudence on Art. 41 into account when ruling on the admissibility of a claim.[3]

In a study that was carried out by the registry of the ECtHR, it was pointed out that almost all of the applicants that filed a claim for an alleged violation of Arts 2 or 3, or for an alleged violation of the reasonable time requirement, were deemed to have suffered a significant disadvantage due to the alleged violation.[4] This is interesting for two reasons. The first reason is that an effective national remedy for the protection of these rights requires moral damages. Secondly, it must be noted that, in principle, under Art. 41 the Court always grants financial redress if the substantial aspects of these Convention rights are violated. It is also striking that these cases where the Court decides that an alleged violation of one of these rights does not cause a significant disadvantage to the applicant do not relate to substantial aspects of these rights but to the procedural aspects of these rights (except for one case).[5] Moreover, in the cases concerning procedural aspects of these rights, the applicants of cases concerning criminal law are more often deemed to have experienced a significant disadvantage than the applicants of alleged violations of procedural aspects of Arts 2 and 3 that do not relate to criminal law. This is something that might be ascribed to the severity of criminal punishments.[6]

'De minimis non curat the European Court of Human Rights: The Introduction of a New Admissibility Criterion (Article 12 of Protocol No. 14)', *EHRLR* 2008, 80–105. There is one exception to this requirement. Even if an alleged violation of the Convention does not put the applicant at a significant disadvantage, the Court can declare a claim to be admissible if it is required for the observance of the treaty or in case the complaint of the applicant was not handled with due care in the national courts. For instance, in the case of *Živić*, it seemed that the Court declared the request admissible, not because the applicant had suffered a significant disadvantage, but because the alleged violation affected a lot of people and seemed to create a situation that could not be reconciled with the Convention: *Živić v. Serbia*, 13 September 2011, appl. no. 37204/08, §§38–42.

3 *Holzinger v. Austria (no. 1)*, 30 January 2001, appl. no. 23459/94, §21; *Romokhov v. Russia*, 16 December 2010, appl. no. 4532/04, §102; and *Šablij v. Slovakia*, 28 April 2015, appl. no. 78129/11, §42. There is however no clear consistency in the way the Court refers to its own practice in awarding damages, as there isn't in its use of judicial precedents in general. See on this last topic: H. Ruiz Fabri, 'The Use of International Judicial Precedents by the European Court of Human Rights: On the Trail of Judicial Policy', *European Journal of Human Rights* 2017, 231–248.

4 Impact assessment of some of the reform proposals under consideration. Document prepared by a study group of the Registry, CDDH-GDR (2003) 017.

5 *Ştefănescu v. Romania*, 12 April 2011 (Decision), appl. no. 11774/04.

6 The Court for instance found that applicants suffered a serious disadvantage in case their imprisonment was not shortened because of the illegal character of the

The severity of criminal punishments cannot explain everything however. For example, the Court judges that someone who has been held in detention for unlawful reasons and who has received compensation under national procedure, has still been placed at a significant disadvantage if the state has not officially admitted that it had violated the Convention.[7] This approach can be compared to cases where the Court judges that an applicant who had not been punished but who was accused of criminal offences and who was not allowed to prove his innocence in a criminal procedure still suffers a significant disadvantage.[8] This was clear in *Aydin* where the state raised the fact that the applicants were not at a significant disadvantage because they had already received financial assistance.[9] The Court however found that the state had not acknowledged the treaty violation and so the fact that the applicant received financial assistance could not undo the applicants' significant disadvantage. In *Wolfmeyer*, the Austrian government argued in the same sense that an applicant who complained of discrimination because of the criminalization of some homosexual acts was not at a significant disadvantage because the courts did not implement the punishment since it was retained by a judgment of the Constitutional Court. The ECtHR however judged:

> The applicant had to stand trial and was convicted by the first instance court. In such circumstances, it is inconceivable how an acquittal without any compensation for damages and accompanied by the reimbursement of a minor part of the necessary defence costs could have provided adequate redress. This is all the more so as the Court itself has awarded substantial amounts of compensation for non-pecuniary damage in comparable cases, having particular regard to the fact that the trial during which details of the applicants' most intimate private life were laid open to the public, had to be considered as a profoundly destabilising event in the applicants' lives.[10]

imprisonment (*Van Velden v. the Netherlands*, 19 July 2011, appl. no. 30666/08) or in case an imprisonment could be prolonged (*Van Der Velden v. the Netherlands*, 31 July 2012, appl. no. 21203/10, §23). However, when an applicant only had to pay a limited amount of money as a fine, the Court found that the applicants did not suffer a significant disadvantage: *Boelens et al. v. Belgium*, 11 September 2012 (Decision), appl. nos. 20007/09 et al.

7 *Sýkora v. the Czech Republic*, 22 November 2012, appl. no. 23419/07, §§50 and 75.

8 *Sereny v. Romania*, 18 June 2013, appl. no. 13071/06, §104.

9 *Aydin v. Turkey*, 1 February 2000 (Decision), appl. nos. 28293/95, 29494/95 and 30219/96. Also: *Akman v. Turkey*, 26 June 2001, appl. no. 37453/97, §30.

10 *Wolfmeyer v. Austria*, 26 May 2005, appl. no. 5263/03, §33. Also: *Dalban v. Romania*, 28 September 1999 (Grand Chamber), appl. no. 28114/95, §44.

Thus, it seems that states not only have to provide financial compensation (or at least a procedure on the basis of which a human rights victim might be able to receive a compensation),[11] but also have to recognize the violation of the Convention.[12] This raises the question of whether the Court is of the opinion that this recognition in itself has a compensatory function, a problem that will be discussed later. For now, it suffices to point to the fact that if a national judge orders a government to pay compensation to redress the damages caused by a human rights violation, the ECtHR normally rules that the applicant has no interest in filing a case with the Court anymore. In *Doubtfire*, for example, the applicant argued that his right to a fair trial was violated in a criminal law procedure because he was refused access to some documents that were used by the public prosecutor.[13] The Court stated that the conviction of the applicant had already been annulled because he had been refused access to these documents and that the applicant could file a claim in national tort law to receive compensation. The state had recognized the violation of Art. 6 of the Convention, and the applicant had not exhausted all national remedies because he could still file an action in tort law.

In cases where an applicant had already received compensation from a national judge, the Court should in principle find that the applicant simply has no interest anymore.[14] The ECtHR also ruled that applicants lack an interest if a national judge recognized the violation of the reasonable time requirement and awarded an adequate compensation.[15] If the domestic courts award a compensation that is inadequate, the Court will find the claim to be admissible. To judge whether an award is adequate, the Court looks at whether the amount is in line with what it grants itself under

---

11 *Mozer v. the Republic of Moldova and Russia*, 23 February 2016 (Grand Chamber), appl. no. 11138/10, §§115–121.

12 This rerequires a motive: *Bourdov v. Russia (no.1)*, 7 May 2002, appl. no. 59498/00.

13 *Doubtfire v. the United Kingdom*, 23 April 2002 (Decision), appl. no. 31825/96.

14 E.g.: *Caraher v. the United Kingdom*, 11 January 2000 (Decision), appl. no. 24520/94. In the case of *Tupa*, the Court observed that in principle compensation in tort law could have made up for the disadvantage that an applicant has suffered because of an involuntary confinement. However, since the national courts had not awarded compensation to the applicant, the Court accepted the application to be admissible: *Tupa v. The Czech Republic*, 26 May 2011, appl. no. 39822/07, §§40–42.

15 EComHR, *Van Laak v. the Netherlands*, 31 March 1993 (Decision), appl. no. 17669/91; EComHR, *Byrn v. Denmark*, 1 July 1992 (Decision), appl. no. 13156/87. See also: P. Leach, *Taking a Case to the European Court of Human Rights*, Oxford, Oxford University Press, 2011, at 134ff.

Art. 41[16] and allows states a certain margin of appreciation if they act within reasonable time.[17] In the case of *Havelka* the Court stated:

> While the award cannot, strictly speaking, be considered as providing adequate and sufficient redress under the Court's relevant case-law, the sum does not differ from the appropriate just satisfaction to such an extent as to cause the applicant a significant disadvantage.[18]

It must be concluded that a human rights victim must file a claim in national tort law if he is able to do so (otherwise he has in principle not exhausted the national remedies)[19] and that he lacks an interest to file a complaint before the ECtHR if he has already received (or reasonably could have received)[20] a compensation that is both appropriate and in line with what the Court itself would grant in a similar case under Art. 41 ECHR. This rule does not apply in cases where a crime was committed.[21] Indeed, as was discussed before in the context of Art. 13, a national remedy cannot be perceived as effective if it only awards compensation in cases where the right to life has been violated intentionally and no deterrent criminal remedy is provided.

2. ADDITIONAL COMPENSATION UNDER ARTICLE 41

2.1. ADDITIONAL COMPENSATION IN CASES WHERE APPLICANTS RECEIVED PARTIAL REDRESS VIA NATIONAL LAW

Since the ECtHR can judge that an applicant still has an interest in filing a complaint even though he has already received redress for an alleged

---

16 Or whether the compensation is 'reasonable in comparison with what the Court awards in similar situations': *Jurica v. Croatia*, 2 May 2017, appl. no. 30376/13, §65.

17 *Vanchev v. Bulgaria*, 19 October 2017, appl. no. 60873/09, §§36–39.

18 *Havelka v. The Czech Republic*, 20 September 2011, appl. no. 7332/10.

19 As an exception to this principle, an applicant sometimes must not exhaust a state liability procedure in case his rights for a fair trial were violated and the liability procedure cannot have as a result that the procedure is re-opened: *Scheszták v. Hungary*, 21 November 2017, appl. no. 5769/11.

20 This is not the case if, for example, a tortfeasor is immune to tort claims: *Nasr and Ghali v. Italy*, 23 February 2016, appl. no. 44883/09, §§204ff.

21 *Mikhno v. Ukraine*, 1 September 2016, appl. no. 32514/12, §118.

human rights violation, it is likely that the Court sometimes grants additional compensation under Art. 41 of the Convention. The consequence of this is that the Court must take national remedies into account when granting awards under Art. 41.[22] The Court will take the national compensation into account[23] in order to reduce the award that it would normally grant with the compensation that the applicant has already received under national law.[24] An example can be found in *Oyal*.[25] Shortly after his birth, baby Oyal underwent surgery that was accompanied by blood transfusions. Four months after the surgery his parents were informed that Oyal was infected with HIV. In the tort law procedure, it became known that the *Kizilay*, the Turkish division of the Red Cross, had neither tested the blood for HIV nor screened the blood donors in the way required by the law. The parents of Oyal won the lawsuit. Nevertheless, Oyal's parents only obtained financial redress for one year of medical aid, and Oyal himself received only a limited amount of compensation for his moral damages. Accordingly, the parents sued the government before an administrative court. They also won this procedure, but again they received only a very limited amount of compensation. At that point, the financial situation of the family worsened because the government withdrew all financial aid that the family received via social programs after they had received their compensation in tort law. Since from that moment on Oyal's family had to pay for all the healthcare themselves, they became impoverished and fell below the poverty line. This situation led the family to bring a case before the ECtHR. They argued that their right to life had been violated because the state had failed to organize supervision for the safety of blood transfusions and had been negligent in organizing appropriate training for the medical staff. The Court ruled that, as a principle, the positive obligations to protect the right to life against infringements from private persons in a medical context can be guaranteed by tort law. However, it found that the compensation the applicants had received from the tort law procedure was inadequate. The Court argued that an effective remedy in

---

22 The same line of argument can be found in: F. Sundberg, 'Le principe de l'octroi subsidiaire des dommages-intérêts – coté comité des ministres' in J.-F. Flauss and E. Lambert Abdelgawad (eds.), *La pratique d'indemnisation par la Cour européenne des droits de l'homme*, Brussels, Bruylant, 2011, 27–51; and The Law Commission and the Scottish Law Commission, Damages under the Human Rights Act 1998. Report on a Reference under Section 3(1) (e) of the Law Commissions Act 1965, SE/2000/182, 2000, <http://www.lawcom.gov.uk>, at 60.

23 *Vanchev v. Bulgaria*, 19 October 2017, appl. no. 60873/09, §61.

24 *Saliba et al. v. Malta*, 22 January 2013 (just satisfaction), appl. no. 20287/10, §21.

25 *Oyal v. Turkey*, 23 March 2010, appl. no. 4864/05.

this case consisted of compensation for the moral damages that the family had suffered and of compensation for all the medical costs that Oyal would need throughout his life because of the HIV infection.[26] By doing so, under Art. 41 of the Convention the Court granted the applicants additional compensation for moral damages and ordered the state to cover all Oyal's medical costs caused by the HIV infection throughout his life.

Another interesting case is *Armonienė*.[27] Armonienė was the widow of L.A., who had HIV and died in 2002. Before his death, one of the biggest Lithuanian newspapers had indicated that L.A. was infected with HIV and had two illegitimate children with a woman who was also infected with HIV. Consequently, L.A. sued the newspaper in tort law and won the lawsuit. The civil court could only grant compensation of €2,896 because of a Lithuanian law that stated that this was the maximum amount of compensation that could be awarded for cases of unintentional defamation by the press. L.A. and his wife found this compensation insufficient and brought a case before the ECtHR. They argued that their right to privacy could not be protected in an effective way if compensation under tort law was so limited. The Court agreed with this line of reasoning. It argued that there had been a very serious infringement of Art. 8, especially considering that the publication did not contribute to a debate of general societal interest. The Court mentioned that although member states have a margin of appreciation, they are obliged to provide effective legal remedies in national law to protect human rights. With regard to the liability of the press, the Court also recalled that sanctions against the press should not be too severe in order to prevent a chilling effect on the freedom of the press. It nevertheless judged that the compensation that the applicants had received in this case was too low. The Court found that the severe legislative limitations on judicial discretion in addressing the damage failed to provide the applicant with the protection that could have legitimately been expected under Art. 8. The Court did so because it considered the fact that there had been an outrageous abuse of press freedom and the fact that compensation should sufficiently deter the recurrence of such abuses. Consequently, the Court found a violation of Art. 8 and granted an additional compensation of €6,500 for moral damages.

This principle can be illustrated by many more judgments. *Schuler Zgraggen and Wasserman* illustrates that the Court can award additional compensation for damages if a national court erroneously calculated the

---

26 *Ibid.*, §72.

27 *Armonienė v. Lithuania*, 25 November 2008, appl. no. 36919/02.

interest of the damages[28] or forgot to take into account the interest at all.[29] *Khachiev and Akaieva* illustrates that the Court sometimes awards additional compensation for moral damages if it deems the compensation received in national procedures to be too limited for victims of a violation of Arts 2, 3 and 13 of the Convention.[30] In the same way *Ernestina Zullo* can be pointed to,[31] one of the many cases in which the Court found that the compensation awarded in Italy for the violation of the reasonable time requirement was insufficient;[32] to *Kormos* where the Court made the same argument in the framework of the immaterial damages that result from an unlawful detention;[33] to some judgments concerning the inhuman treatment of prisoners;[34] to cases concerning the freedom of speech;[35] and to judgments where the Court made the same argument in the context of the right to property.[36]

Although all these judgments illustrate that the Court can grant additional compensation when it deems a compensation of national judges to be insufficient, the Court does find that national courts are better placed in principle to estimate the amount of damages. It is only when the Court finds that the compensation that human rights victims receive under national law are substantially lower than the compensation that the Court itself awards under Art. 41 that it judges that a human rights victim can still bring its case before the Court and can receive additional compensation.[37]

---

28 *Schuler-Zgraggen v. Switzerland*, 31 January 1995 (just satisfaction), appl. no. 14518/89, §15.

29 *Wasserman v. Russia (no.1)*, 18 November 2004, appl. no. 15021/02, §49.

30 *Khachiev and Akaieva v. Russia*, 24 February 2005, appl. nos. 57942/00 and 57945/00, §§189 and 193.

31 *Ernestina Zullo v. Italy*, 29 March 2006 (Grand Chamber), appl. no. 64897/01.

32 *Ibid.*, §142. See also: *Zarb v. Malta*, 4 July 2006, appl. no. 17209/02, §§59–61; *Central Mediterranean Development Corporation Limited v. Malta*, 24 October 2006, appl. no. 35829/03, §§59–61; *Solarova et al. v. Slovakia*, 5 December 2006, appl. no. 77690/01, §62; *Hajdukovich v. Croatia*, 12 April 2007, appl. no. 38303/02, §§35–36; ECtHR, *Pasanec v. Croatia*, 3 May 2007, appl. no. 41567/02, §§38–39; *Milasinovic v. Croatia*, 24 May 2007, appl. no. 41751/02, §§37–38; *Jakupovic v. Croatia*, 31 July 2007, appl. no. 12419/04, §33; and *Husic v. Croatia*, 25 October 2007, appl. no. 14878/04, §31. See also with regard to an insufficient judicial motivation: *Ceachir v. Moldavia*, 15 January 2008, appl. no. 50115/06, §52.

33 *Kormos v. Slovakia*, 8 November 2011, appl. no. 46092/06, §109.

34 *Kopylov v. Russia*, 29 July 2010, appl. no. 3933/04, §§180–181; *Romokhov v. Russia*, 16 December 2010, appl. no. 4532/04, §§144–145; and *Shishkov v. Bulgaria*, 9 January 2003, appl. no. 26746/05, §§159–160.

35 *Centro Europa 7 S.R.L. and Di Stefano v. Italy*, 7 June 2012, appl. no. 38433/09, §§216 and 222.

36 *Prodan v. Moldavia*, 18 May 2004, appl. no. 49806/99, §48.

37 *Romokhov v. Russia*, 16 December 2010, appl. no. 4532/04, §104.

In *Scordino*, for instance, the Court argued that the applicants had already received compensation in national procedures for the violation of the reasonable time requirement but that the amount of the compensation: 'is approximately 10% of what the Court would have awarded them. In the Court's view, this factor in itself leads to a result which is manifestly unreasonable having regard to the criteria established in its case-law.'[38]

2.2. ADDITIONAL COMPENSATION IN CASES WHERE STATES PROVIDED MEASURES TO REDRESS THE DAMAGES

Sometimes member states do not redress damages by granting financial compensation but by taking measures to redress the harm. In such situations the ECtHR can judge that these measures are inappropriate to redress all of the damages.[39] At first sight this is remarkable because the Court appreciates that the awards it grants under Art. 41 and the measures to redress the damages must be viewed separately:

> The State Party in question will be under an obligation not just to pay those concerned the sums awarded by way of just satisfaction, but also to take individual and/or, if appropriate, general measures in its domestic legal order to put an end to the violation found by the Court and to redress the effects, the aim being to put the applicant, as far as possible, in the position he would have been in had the requirements of the Convention not been disregarded.[40]

These observations suggest that financial compensation might be combined with measures taken to restore the victim of a human rights violation to the state he would have been in had the human rights violation not occurred. This seems to contradict the notion of compensation as such, but it is possible to combine measures taken to redress damages with a monetary compensation if the measures can prevent the damages from occurring again. Financial compensation is meant to compensate for the damages that

---

38 *Scordino v. Italy (no.1)*, 29 March 2006 (Grand Chamber), appl. no. 36813/97, §272.

39 The Court sometimes makes this kind of observation regarding the requirement of the lawmaker to enact legislation: *Norris v. Ireland*, 26 October 1988 (Plenary), appl. no. 10581/83, §50; and *Christine Goodwin v. the United Kingdom*, 11 July 2002, appl. no. 28957/98, §120.

40 *Verein gegen Tierfabriken Schweiz (VgT) v. Switzerland (no.2)*, 30 June 2009 (Grand Chamber), appl. no. 32772/02, §85.

had previously occurred. In the past, the Court had found that violations of the right to a fair procedure (Art. 6) in criminal law cases could best be redressed by redoing the procedure.[41] It found in these cases that it was only necessary to take measures for the future. In recent cases the Court increasingly requires states both to take measures to prevent a violation from reoccurring in the future and to grant financial compensation to compensate for the damages that have already occurred.[42] In some cases the Court explicitly argues that these measures only have effect for future damages and that the financial compensation is meant to compensate for the damages that had already occurred.[43] Because of this practice, here it is concluded by considering Michel de Salvia's indication that the amount of compensation that the Court grants will partly depend on whether a state has taken or will take measures to prevent future damages.[44]

---

41 *Hirst v. the United Kingdom (no.2)*, 30 March 2004, appl. no. 74025/01, §60. This has been confirmed by the Grand Chamber: *Hirst v. the United Kingdom (no.2)*, 6 October 2005 (Grand Chamber), appl. no. 74025/01, §93. See also: *Aziz v. Cyprus*, 22 June 2004, appl. no. 69949/01, §43; *Öcalan v. Turkey*, 12 May 2005 (Grand Chamber), appl. no. 46221/99, §210; *Bülent Zengin v. Turkey*, 29 November 2007, appl. no. 60848/00, §27; *Hadzhiev v. Bulgaria*, 23 October 2012, appl. no. 22373/04, §65; and *I.G. et al. v. Slovakia*, 13 November 2012, appl. no. 15966/04, §63.

42 *Brumarescu v. Romania*, 23 January 2001 (just satisfaction) (Grand Chamber), appl. no. 28342/95; *Assanidze v. Georgia*, 8 April 2004 (Grand Chamber), appl. no. 71503/01; *Ilascu et al. v. Moldavia and Russia*, 8 July 2004 (Grand Chamber), appl. no. 48787/99; *Strain et al. v. Romania*, 21 July 2005, appl. no. 57001/00; *Rusu et al. v. Romania*, 19 July 2007, appl. no. 4198/04; *Driza v. Albania*, 1 November 2007, appl. no. 33771/02; *Suciu Werle v. Romania*, 13 December 2007, appl. no. 26521/05; *Grigoras v. Romania*, 7 October 2008, appl. no. 19188/03; *Chiorean v. Romania*, 21 October 2008, appl. no. 20535/03; *Teodorescu Olimpia-Maria v. Romania*, 4 November 2008, appl. no. 43774/02; *Reichardt v. Romania*, 13 November 2008, appl. no. 6111/04; *Veniamin v. Romania*, 26 January 2010, appl. no. 19438/05; *Maria Violeta Lazarescu v. Romania*, 23 February 2010, appl. no. 10636/06; *Fatullayev v. Azerbaijan*, 22 April 2010 (Grand Chamber), appl. no. 40984/07; *M.S.S. v. Belgium and Greece*, 21 January 2011 (Grand Chamber), appl. no. 30696/09; *Denisova and Moiseyeva v. Russia*, 14 June 2011, appl. no. 16903/03; *Hirsi Jamaa et al. v. Italy*, 23 February 2012 (Grand Chamber), appl. no. 27765/09; and *Oleksandr Volkov v. Ukraine*, 9 January 2013, appl. no. 21722/11. *Papamichalopoulos v. Greece*, 31 October 1995 (just satisfaction), appl. no. 14556/89, §34.

43 In this context, one must also refer to the case of *Ilic* where the Court on the one hand awarded a just satisfaction for material damages and on the other hand referred to measures that the state can take to end the human rights violation: *Ilic v. Serbia*, 9 October 2007, appl. no. 30132/04, §112.

44 M. de Salvia, 'Can the Reparation Awarded to Victims of Violations under the ECHR be Considered a Real "Just" Satisfaction' in A. Fenyves, E. Karner, H. Koziol and E. Steiner (eds.), *Tort Law in the Jurisprudence of the European Court of Human Rights*, Göttingen, De Gruyter, 2011, p387 at 392.

CHAPTER 6

GENERAL OUTLINE OF ARTICLE 41 OF THE CONVENTION

The previous chapters indicated how the Convention can influence private law in general and tort law in particular. For tort law, it has been shown that Art. 41 of the Convention is very important, both as an interpretative tool in the context of Art. 13 of the Convention and as a possibility for the Court to act as a tort law institution in its own way. This raises the question of how this provision is applied. This chapter will deal with the basic outline of this provision.

1. THE TEXT OF ARTICLE 41 OF THE CONVENTION

Although the text of Art. 41 (previously Art. 50) has changed since the 11th protocol entered into force, the provision did not change substantially. The text is now a bit shorter than before and explicitly refers to the protocols, but this did not mark a substantial change because the Court implicitly judged that the previous Art. 50 could not only be applied when the Convention is violated but also in cases where the protocols are violated.[1] Today Art. 41 reads as follows:

> If the Court finds that there has been a violation of the Convention or the Protocols thereto, and if the internal law of the High Contracting Party concerned allows only partial reparation to be made, the Court shall, if necessary, afford just satisfaction to the injured party.

There are four points of concern to be found in the wording of the text. The first is the fact that Art. 41 can only be applied if the Court finds a

1 K. Wolfram, 'Just Satisfaction in Art 41 ECHR and Public International Law – Issues of Interpretation and Review of International Materials' in A. Fenyves, E. Karner, H. Koziol and E. Steiner (eds.), *Tort Law in the Jurisprudence of the European Court of Human Rights*, Göttingen, De Gruyter, 2011, p345 at 351.

violation of the Convention. The second point is related to the principle of subsidiarity. The text indicates that the provision can only be applied 'if the internal law of the High Contracting Party concerned allows only partial reparation to be made'. It thus seems that Art. 41 is only applicable if a national legal system does not provide full compensation. Thirdly, the provision states that the Court does not have to apply the Convention when the first two conditions are fulfilled, but that the Court only has to afford just satisfaction 'if necessary'. This raises the question of whether the Court has a discretionary competence to decide when a satisfaction is necessary. While these three points all relate to the conditions of the legal rule, the fourth and last point has to do with the consequences or the remedy of the rule. The text of Art. 41 mentions 'just satisfaction'. It does not use the words compensation or restitution. This of course raises the question as to what the difference between a just satisfaction and a restitution is.

The following sections examine these four points of interest. For now, it is necessary to briefly explore some of the procedural aspects of Art. 41. It is important to know that the Court can postpone its decision on Art. 41 on the basis of Art. 75 of the rules of the Court. Thus, the Court can choose whether it will deal with Art. 41 in the same judgment as the judgment on the merits or whether it will decide to reserve this question in whole or in part. If the Court opts for the latter, which it only does in a minority of cases, it does so on the grounds that the case is not ready for a decision yet at the time that it makes a judgment on the merits.[2] The Court will then make a different judgment on Art. 41. This is important to know because it raises the question of whether a procedure in national law can take place between the judgment on the merits and the judgment on Art. 41. This in turn raises the question of whether such a national procedure can influence the ECtHR's decision on Art. 41. It is interesting in this context to know that governments sometimes argue that an applicant can receive reparation under national law.[3] A consequence of this possibility is the fact that the Court can strike out a case if it is informed of an agreement between the applicant and the liable state on the reparation and if the Court finds this agreement to be reasonable.[4]

---

2 M.E. Mas, 'Right to Compensation under Article 50' in R. Macdonald, F. Matscher and H. Petzold (eds.), *The European System for the Protection of Human Rights*, Dordrecht, Martinus Nijhoff Publishers, 1993, p775 at 779.

3 M.L. Van Emmerik, *Schadevergoeding bij schending van mensenrechten. De rechtspraktijk onder het EVRM vergeleken met die in Nederland*, Stichting NJCM-Boekerij, Leiden, 1997, at 110ff.

4 The fact that the Court strikes out a case if the applicant and the defendant state can reach an agreement on the reparation of the caused damages, indicates that restitution

2. THE VIOLATION OF THE CONVENTION

For Art. 41 ECHR to be applicable, it is necessary for the Court to find a violation of the Convention. This criterion does not only stem from a textual reading of the provision but also derives from its positioning in the Convention. The provision is included in a part concerning the procedural aspects before the Court. Thus, as with all procedural provisions, Art. 41 cannot be seen as an autonomous provision that grants a subjective right to file a case before the Convention. Article 41 is a procedural provision that can only be invoked if another treaty provision is violated.

3. THE PRINCIPLE OF SUBSIDIARITY

Article 41 ECHR stipulates that the ECtHR can only grant a just satisfaction 'if the internal law of the High Contracting Party concerned allows only partial reparation to be made.' These words refer to the principle of subsidiarity. This principle is a general principle in the Convention according to which the Convention is only a subsidiary protection-mechanism. The first and most important mechanism to protect human rights must be found in national law.[5] This has two consequences: one substantial and one procedural. From a substantial point of view, the principle of subsidiarity requires the Court to take into account a margin of appreciation for the member states as they are, in principle, in a better position than the Court itself to protect human rights.[6] From a procedural

is an important factor for an applicant to file a claim with the ECtHR. For the applicant, such an agreement can have as an advancement that he can receive restitution at an earlier time: L. Zwaak, 'The Procedure before the European Court of Human rights' in P. Van Dijk, F. Van Hoof, A. Van Rijn and L. Zwaak (eds.), *Theory and Practice of the European Convention on Human Rights*, Antwerp, Intersentia, 2006, p95 at 223. In the context of this book the practice of the Court to accept friendly settlements is not elaborated. However, for further lecture, see: F. Ang and E. Berghmans, 'Friendly settlements and striking out of applications' in P. Lemmens and W. Vandenhole (eds.), *Protocol No. 14 and the Reform of the European Court of Human Rights*, Antwerp, Intersentia, 2005, 89–104; I. Sevinc 'La pratique par la Turquie des règlements amiables et de leur composante indemnitaire' in J.-F. Flauss and E. Lambert Abdelgawad (eds.), *La pratique d'indemnisation par la Cour européenne des droits de l'homme*, Brussels, Bruylant, 2011, 85–110.

5 23 July 1968, appl. nos. 1474/62, 1677/62, 1691/62, 1769/63, 1994/63 and 2126/64, §10 *in fine*; and K. Wolfram, 'Just Satisfaction in Art 41 ECHR', 2011, above n. 1, p345 at 359.

6 *Handyside v. the United Kingdom*, 7 December 1976 (Grand Chamber), appl. no. 5493/72, §48.

point of view, the principle of subsidiarity (as enshrined in Art. 35, §1) requires applicants to exhaust the national remedies and has as a result that the Court will not question the facts that were already subject of a national procedure.[7]

By enshrining this principle in Art. 41, it seems that the ECtHR must take into account the remedies that are offered by national law when it grants damages.[8] Indeed, one cannot imagine that the Court would not take into account the remedies provided by national law if it may only grant an award in cases where the national legal system of the applicant allows only partial reparation to be made.[9]

3.1. THE NEGLIGENCE OF THE PRINCIPLE OF SUBSIDIARITY BY THE COURT

Although the test of Art. 41 does not raise many doubts about the necessity of taking the principle of subsidiarity into account, there are not many traces of this principle in the jurisprudence of the Court.[10] This originated back to the first judgments in which the Court had to deal with Art. 41. In these cases, the defendant states invoked this criterion and argued that their national legal system provided mechanisms for the applicants to receive full restitution of their damages. A famous case in this context was

---

7 *Garcia Ruiz v. Spain*, 21 January 1999, appl. no. 30544/96, §28; *Sisojeva et al. v. Latvia*, 15 January 2007, appl. no. 60654/00, §89; *Kononov v. Latvia*, 24 July 2008, appl. no. 36376/04, §108; and M. Smith, 'The Adjudicatory Fact-finding Tools of the European Court of Human Rights', *EHRLR* 2009, p206 at 207–208.

8 W. Berka, 'Human Rights and Tort Law', in A. Fenyves, E. Karner, H. Koziol and E. Steiner (eds.), *Tort Law in the Jurisprudence of the European Court of Human Rights*, Göttingen, De Gruyter 2011, p237 at 249; H. Koziol, 'Concluding Remarks regarding the Methods of Interpreting Art. 41 ECHR' in A. Fenyves, E. Karner, H. Koziol and E. Steiner (eds.), *Tort Law in the Jurisprudence of the European Court of Human Rights*, Göttingen, De Gruyter, 2011, p825 at 828.

9 H. Golsong, 'Quelques réflexions a propos du pouvoir de la Cour Européenne des Droits de l'homme d'accorder une satisfaction équitable' in René Cassin, *Amicorum Discipulorumque*, I, *Problèmes de protection internationale des droits de l'homme*, Editions A. Pedone, Paris, 1969, p89 at 91.

10 The English and Scottish Law Commissions argue that the principle of subsidiarity in the context of Art. 41 'is of no more than historical significance for the Strasbourg Court': The Law Commission and the Scottish Law Commission, *Damages under the Human Rights Act 1998. Report on a Reference under Section 3(1) (e) of the Law Commissions Act 1965*, SE/2000/182, 2000, at 23 <https://www.scotlawcom.gov.uk/files/3012/7989/6877/rep180.pdf>.

De Wilde, Ooms and Versyp v. Belgium.[11] In the judgment on Art. 41, the Belgian government developed two lines of reasoning based on both the procedural aspect of the principal of subsidiarity and on the substantial principle of subsidiarity. The government first argued that the applicants had not exhausted the national remedies as required by Art. 35, §1, between the judgment of the ECtHR on the merits and the judgment on Art. 41. The government argued that although the Court had already found a violation of the Convention in its judgment on the merits on 18 June 1971,[12] the applicants had not filed a case since then in the Belgian legal system in order to receive reparation. Secondly, the government argued that the Court could not know whether or not the Belgian legal system could provide full reparation of the damages that were caused by the Convention violation because the applicant had not filed a claim in Belgian law. The Belgian government argued that if the applicants had filed an action in Belgian tort law, they would have been able to receive full reparation.[13]

The Court nevertheless rejected these arguments. It found that it did not have to judge based on Art. 41 because the applicants filed a new request. Moreover, the Court judged that its separate judgment based on Art. 41 was only a continuation of the judgment on the merits.[14] It further judged that the requirement to exhaust the national remedies as is enshrined in Art. 35, §1, cannot be read in conjunction with Art. 41.[15]

As a result, the Court ruled that the fact that the applicants had the option to file a claim in national tort law after its judgment on the merits, could not withhold the Court from applying Art. 41, since the Court only pursues a procedure that is already pending before it.[16] This ruling received a lot of criticism. In a separate opinion, Judges Holmbäck, Ross and Wold argued that the Court went beyond its jurisdiction. They argued that Art. 41 is only applicable if a national legal system makes it impossible

---

11 *De Wilde, Ooms and Versyp v. Belgium*, 10 March 1972 (just satisfaction) (Plenary), appl. nos. 2832/66, 2835/66 and 2899/66.

12 *De Wilde, Ooms and Versyp v. Belgium*, 18 June 1971 (Plenary), appl. nos. 2832/66, 2835/66 and 2899/66.

13 *De Wilde, Ooms and Versyp v. Belgium*, 10 March 1972 (just satisfaction) (Plenary), appl. nos. 2832/66, 2835/66 and 2899/66, §20.

14 As enshrined in Arts 35 and 36 of the Convention.

15 *De Wilde, Ooms and Versyp v. Belgium*, 10 March 1972 (just satisfaction) (Plenary), appl. nos. 2832/66, 2835/66 and 2899/66, §16.

16 *Ibid.*, §21ff. For other examples see: *König v. Germany*, 10 March 1980 (just satisfaction) (Plenary), appl. no. 6232/73, §15; *Eckle v. Germany*, 21 June 1983 (just satisfaction), appl. no. 8130/78, §13; and *Barberà, Messegué and Jabardo v. Spain*, 13 June 1994 (just satisfaction) (Plenary), appl. nos. 10588/83, 10589/83 and 10590/83, §§12–16.

to receive full reparation, something the Court had not examined in this case.[17] Judge Verdross criticized the judgment in the same way in his separate opinion,[18] and Judge Mosler in his separate opinion added the argument that the Court may not prevent states from developing their own mechanisms to redress the damages caused by human rights violations.[19]

The Court, however, did not take this criticism into account as can be illustrated by *Bönisch.*[20] The applicant in this case owned a company that produced smoked meat. He had been prosecuted by the Federal Food Control Institute of Austria and was sentenced to imprisonment, a punishment that was reduced to a fine. Bönisch believed that the procedure that led to his conviction was not in accordance with the requirements of a fair trial under Art. 6 of the Convention. He argued that the expert that was appointed by himself had not been treated in the same way as the expert of the Federal Food Control Institute. This argument was followed by both the European Commission on Human Rights and the Court. Because the Austrian government had not yet been able to give all the necessary information, the Court postponed its decision on Art. 41. Thus, when the procedure based on Art. 41 started, the Austrian government argued that it in the meantime had taken all measures to grant the applicant a *resitutio in integrum*. The government pointed to the fact that it had officially apologized and that Bönisch's criminal record was cleared. The Court found that Bönisch had also suffered moral damages. It pointed out that Bönisch had lost the chance to prove his innocence in a lawsuit. As a result, the Court judged that the measures taken by the Austrian government did not redress all of the damages that Bönisch had suffered.[21]

What is striking about this case is the fact that the Court did not investigate whether or not the applicant could have filed a claim in national tort law to receive moral damages. This is, however, not surprising. Michel de Salvia illustrated that from the 1960s to the 1990s (the period of time that De Salvia was secretary of the Court) the Court never investigated

---

17 Joint separate opinion of Judges Holmbäck, Ross and Wold in *De Wilde, Ooms and Versyp v. Belgium*, 10 March 1972 (just satisfaction), appl. nos. 2832/66, 2835/66 and 2899/66.

18 Separate opinion of Judge Verdross in *De Wilde, Ooms and Versyp v. Belgium*, 10 March 1972 (just satisfaction) (Plenary), appl. nos. 2832/66, 2835/66 and 2899/66.

19 Separate opinion of Judge Mosler in *De Wilde, Ooms and Versyp v. Belgium*, 10 March 1972 (just satisfaction) (Plenary), appl. nos. 2832/66, 2835/66 and 2899/66.

20 *Bönisch v. Austria*, 2 July 1986 (just satisfaction), appl. no. 8658/79.

21 *Ibid.*, §§11–13.

whether the damages of a human rights victim could be repaired by a national legal system.[22] Consequently, it can be concluded that the Court in most cases neglects the principle of subsidiarity.

3.2. THE NATIONAL STATE'S ABILITY TO RESTORE THE DAMAGES WHEN THE COURT CANNOT

Although the Court does not in principle investigate whether or not an applicant can receive full reparation under his national legal system, it does argue that states are better placed to restore damages. In *Piersack* the Court argued that after it had found a violation of the Convention in the judgment on the merits of the ground, the state made a new procedure in national law possible that brought about a result as close to *restitutio in integrum* as was possible.[23] This case concerned a violation of the right to a fair trial (Art. 6). The Court found that these damages could best be redressed by a retrial, as was offered by the national state. The same principle is also seen in *Windisch.* In this case the Court found a violation of Art. 6 because Austrian criminal judges had condemned someone based on anonymous witnesses that the defendant could not challenge. Since the representative of the government argued before the ECtHR that the case could be retrialled in Austria, the Court found that it could not address the questions under Art. 41 until the retrial had taken place.[24] When this had been done, the Court found that the retrial had conformed to Art. 6 and thus found that the applicant (although he was convicted again) had been put in a position that reached the *restitutio in integrum* as was possible in the nature of things.[25]

---

22 M. de Salvia, 'Can the Reparation Awarded to Victims of Violations under the ECHR be Considered a Real "Just" Satisfaction' in A. Fenyves, E. Karner, H. Koziol and E. Steiner (eds.), *Tort Law in the Jurisprudence of the European Court of Human Rights*, Göttingen, De Gruyter, 2011, p387 at 389.

23 *Piersack v. Belgium*, 26 October 1984 (just satisfaction), appl. no. 8692/79, §11. In *De Cubber*, the Court ruled in the opposite way, while referring to the case of *Piersack*, that the further procedures in Belgium had not led to a situation that brought about a result as close to *restitutio in integrum* as possible: *De Cubber v. Belgium*, 14 September 1987 (just satisfaction), appl. no. 9186/80, §21. It must be noted that an applicant's request to reopen the case in national law after a conviction by the ECtHR was accepted in *Piersack* but was rejected in *De Cubber.*

24 *Windisch v. Austria*, 27 September 1990, appl. no. 12489/86, §35.

25 *Windisch v. Austria* (just satisfaction), 28 June 1993, appl. no. 12489/86, §14; and *Zadumov v. Russia*, 12 December 2017, appl. no. 2257/12, §81. The Court made

These cases concerning Art. 6 differ fundamentally from the case of *De Wilde, Ooms and Versyp*. What is notable in cases such as *Piersack* and *Windisch* is that the member states could grant something that came as close to a *restitutio in integrum* as possible. The ECtHR in these cases could not offer a similar form of restitution for the simple reason that it is not a criminal court. What this illustrates is that the Court takes into account the principle of subsidiarity in cases where it does not have the authority to grant full reparation. In some cases, the Court has explained this criterion very explicitly:

> If the nature of the breach allows of restitutio in integrum, it is for the respondent State to effect it, the Court having neither the power nor the practical possibility of doing so itself. If, on the other hand, national law does not allow – or allows only partial – reparation to be made, Article 41 empowers the Court to afford the injured party such satisfaction as appears to it to be appropriate.'[26]

With this reasoning, the Court indicated that first it is up to the state to redress the damages *in natura*. If states can provide such redress, the Court requires them to do so and will not grant a monetary compensation[27]

---

similar observations with regard to the deduction of the temporary custody from an imprisonment: *NeuMayster v. Austria*, 7 May 1974 (just satisfaction), appl. no. 1936/63, §40; *contra*: *Ringeisen v. Austria*, 22 June 1972 (just satisfaction), appl. no. 2614/65, §21. See also with regard to Art. 5 of the Convention: *Engel et al. v. the Netherlands*, 23 November 1976 (just satisfaction) (Plenary), appl. nos. 5100/71, 5101/71, 5102/71, 5354/72 and 5370/72, §69.

26 *Papamichalopoulos v. Greece*, 31 October 1995 (just satisfaction), appl. no. 14556/89, §34. See also: *Latridis v. Greece*, 19 October 2000 (just satisfaction) (Grand Chamber), appl. no. 31107/96, §33; *Brumarescu v. Romania*, 23 January 2001 (just satisfaction) (Grand Chamber), appl. no. 28342/95, §20; *Former King of Greece et al. v. Greece*, 23 November 2002 (Grand Chamber), appl. no. 25701/94, §73; *Bocos-cuesta v. the Netherlands*, 10 November 2005, appl. no. 54789/00, §80; 24 November 2005 (just satisfaction), §15; *Scordino v. Italy (no.1)*, 29 March 2006 (Grand Chamber), appl. no. 36813/97, §247; *Devecioglu v. Turkey*, 24 November 2009 (just satisfaction), appl. no. 17203/03, §13; *Mutishev et al. v. Bulgaria*, 28 February 2012 (just satisfaction), appl. no. 18967/03, §23; *Varfis v. Greece*, 13 November 2014, appl. no. 40409/08, §19; *Saghinadze v. Georgia* 13 January 2015 (just satisfaction), appl. no. 18768/05, §14; *Stolyarova v. Russia*, 29 January 2015, appl. no. 15711/13, §75; *Chinnici v. Italy (no.2)*, 14 April 2015, appl. no. 22432/03, §58; *Magyar Keresztény Mennonita Egyház et al. v. Hungary*, 28 June 2016 (just satisfaction), appl. no. 70945/11 et al., §45; *B.K.M. Lojistik Tasimacilik Ticaret Ltd Sirketi v. Slovenia*, 17 January 2017, appl. no. 42079/12; and *Joannou v. Turkey*, 12 December 2017, appl. no. 53240/14, §114.

27 *Guiso-Gallisay v. Italy*, 22 December 2009 (just satisfaction) (Grand Chamber), appl. no. 58858/00, §90; *Sargsyan v. Azerbaijan*, 12 December 2017 (Grand Chamber), appl. no. 40167/06, §35; and *Chiragov et al. v. Armenia*, 12 December 2017 (Grand Chamber), appl. no. 13216/05, §§49–52.

or will only award a partial compensation, for example a compensation for moral damages only.[28] What is also interesting is that this indicates that the Court perceives redress *in natura* and financial compensation as two alternatives,[29] and grants precedence to redress *in natura*.[30]

3.3. THE EFFECTIVENESS OF THE NATIONAL PROCEDURE

The fact that the Court is sometimes unable to grant *restitutio in integrum* when a member state is able to do so cannot itself explain all the cases where the Court has applied the principle of subsidiarity. This principle cannot, for instance, explain *Pressos Compania Naviera*.[31] In this case the ECtHR found that a law retroactively providing immunity for actions in tort law to ship pilots, violated the right to property of those people whose action in tort law now became aimless. In its judgment on the merits, the Court did not grant a just satisfaction as the applicants requested for the following reason:

> In the circumstances of the case, the Court finds that the question is not ready for decision. It is indeed for the national courts to determine the beneficiaries and amounts of the damages claims generated by the accidents that lay at the origin of the case. It is accordingly necessary to reserve the matter of pecuniary damage,

[28] E.g.: *Joannou v. Turkey*, 12 December 2017, appl. no. 53240/14, §§116–117.

[29] A similar observation has been made by De Salvia and Pettiti: M. De Salvia, 'Le principe de l'octroi subsidiaire des dommages-intérêts: d'une morale des droits de l'homme à une morale simplement indemnitaire?' in J.-F. Flauss and E. Lambert Abdelgawad (eds.), *La pratique d'indemnisation par la Cour européenne des droits de l'homme*, Brussels, Bruylant, 2011, p9 at 18ff; and C. Pettiti, 'Stratégie de la partie requérante face à la perspective d'octroi de dommages et intérêts par la cour Européenne des droits de l'homme' in J.-F. Flauss and E. Lambert Abdelgawad (eds.), *La pratique d'indemnisation par la Cour européenne des droits de l'homme*, Brussels, Bruylant, 2011, p56 at 64ff.

[30] E. Lambert Abdelgawad, 'Comment chifrer la réparation des traitements inhumains/dégradants et de la torture' in J.-F. Flauss and E. Lambert Abdelgawad (eds.), *La pratique d'indemnisation par la Cour européenne des droits de l'homme*, Brussels, Bruylant, 2011, p189 at 201; L. Loucaides, 'Reparation for Violations of Human Rights under the European Convention and Restitutio in Integrum', *EHRLR* 2008, p182 at 184–185; and D. Shelton, *Remedies in International Human Rights Law*, Oxford, Oxford University Press, 1999, at 111.

[31] *Pressos Compania Naviera S.A. et al. v. Belgium*, 20 November 1995, appl. no. 17849/91; and *Pressos Compania Naviera S.A. et al. v. Belgium*, 3 July 1997 (just satisfaction), appl. no. 17849/91.

> account being taken of the possibility of an agreement being reached between the respondent State and the applicants.[32]

In these observations the Court refers explicitly to the principle of subsidiarity and the possibility that the state and the applicants may reach an agreement. Such an agreement was not reached however. The applicants (26 shipping companies) wanted 1,547,508,885 Belgian Franc to compensate for their material damages. On top of that, they claimed compensation for immaterial damages. Although they had filed a claim in national tort law, they argued that the Belgian judicial system had exceeded the reasonable timeframe required by Art. 6 and thus that the ECtHR, to prevent a further violation of Art. 6, had to appoint experts to estimate the damages (as the Court had previously done in the case of *Papamichalopoulos*).[33] The Court however found that the experts in *Papamichalopoulos* had a rather limited appointment. In *Papamichalopoulos* the experts only had to estimate the value of a piece of expropriated land, but in the case of *Pressos Compania Naviera* 'before damages are assessed, liability for each of the accidents has to be determined and the beneficiaries and the compensation due identified.'[34] The ECtHR accordingly found that it is not up to experts but up to national judges to determine the liability of the accidents. The Court moreover pointed out that national judges had, since its judgment on the merits, decided on the tort claims of the applicants in accordance with the requirements that it had posed in its judgment on the merits. These two judgments, according to the Court, granted the required *restitutio in integrum*.[35] As a result, the Court found that it could not judge the applications on a just satisfaction as long as the national judges had not yet made their final decision.[36] It did however grant a just satisfaction to one of the applicants. The reason for this was the fact that this applicant had filed a claim in national tort law long before the ECtHR had granted

32 *Ibid.*, §51.

33 *Papamichalopoulos v. Greece*, 31 October 1995 (just satisfaction), appl. no. 14556/89. For an in-depth analysis of the competence of the Court to appoint experts, see: S. Turgis, 'La recours aux expertises' in J.-F. Flauss and E. Lambert Abdelgawad (eds.), *La pratique d'indemnisation par la Cour européenne des droits de l'homme*, Brussels, Bruylant, 2011, pp113–125.

34 *Pressos Compania Naviera S.A. et al. v. Belgium*, 3 July 1997 (just satisfaction), appl. no. 17849/91, §10.

35 *Ibid.*, §11.

36 The Court made similar observations in: *Clooth v. Belgium*, 12 December 1991, appl. no. 12718/87, §52.

its judgment on the merits. In that national procedure, the national court had applied the rules of immunity retroactively and so had not granted any compensation. Since it was no longer possible to file an appeal against this judgment,[37] the ECtHR granted just satisfaction.

Interestingly, in this judgment the Court applied the principle of subsidiarity in a case where an action in tort law was already filed in national law and that stood a good chance of success. Two of the applicants had already received compensation in national law. Thus, the Court could count on the fact that the other applicants would also receive compensation in the pending procedures. It is not only important that applicants have a good chance to receive compensation under national law, but it is also important that they presumably receive this compensation within a reasonable time. In the case of *Pressos Compania Naviera* this criterion can implicitly be derived from the fact that all the applicants had cases pending under national law. In *Barberà, Messegué and Jabardo* the Court stated this more explicitly:

> If, after having exhausted domestic remedies without success before complaining in Strasbourg of a violation of their rights, then doing so a second time, successfully, to secure the setting aside of the convictions, and finally going through a new trial, the applicants were required to exhaust domestic remedies a third time in order to be able to obtain just satisfaction from the Court, the total duration of the proceedings would be hardly consistent with the effective protection of human rights and would lead to a situation incompatible with the aim and object of the Convention.[38]

This reasoning illustrates that the ECtHR sometimes grants just satisfaction (mainly in its judgment on the merits) so that applicants do not have to file a new claim under national law.[39]

---

37 *Pressos Compania Naviera S.A. et al. v. Belgium*, 3 July 1997 (just satisfaction), appl. no. 17849/91, §§15–21.

38 *Barberà, Messegué and Jabardo v. Spain*, 13 June 1994 (just satisfaction) (Plenary), appl. nos. 10588/83, 10589/83 and 10590/83, §17.

39 Kissling and Kelliher make a more extensive interpretation of this jurisprudence by arguing that the Court only takes into account compensations that an applicant can receive under national law if these compensations were already awarded before the Court judged on the merits: C. Kissling and D. Kelliher, 'Compensation for Pecuniary and Non-Pecuniary Loss' in A. Fenyves, E. Karner, H. Koziol and E. Steiner (eds.), *Tort Law in the Jurisprudence of the European Court of Human Rights*, Göttingen, De Gruyter, 2011, p579 at 581.

From the above, it can be concluded that the ECtHR will only require the applicants to follow a national procedure to get redress if they have a good chance of receiving compensation within a reasonable time from the national courts.[40] In most of its judgments the Court only applies this criterion implicitly. Consequently, it is not easy to know when the Court deems an applicant to have a good chance of receiving compensation in a national procedure within a reasonable time. If a case is already pending before the national court, such as in *Pressos Compania Naviera*,[41] the Court seems to judge that the applicants will receive compensation in a reasonable time. However, in most cases it will find that a judgment in national law will probably not be granted within a reasonable time. The reason for this is that a claim can only be applicable if the applicants have already exhausted the national remedies.[42] Thus, in most cases that come to the Court, an applicant can only receive compensation in national law if he starts a new lawsuit all over again to claim damages. This of course is an incredibly time-consuming procedure. As a consequence, the ECtHR has set new requirements. In more recent cases the court has judged, with reference to *De Wilde, Ooms and Versyp*, that if an applicant had exhausted national remedies before he went to the ECtHR, one cannot expect this applicant to file a new claim under national law to receive compensation and exhaust all national remedies again before he can sue the government

---

40 The criteria that the Court discusses in the context of Art. 41 are very similar to the admissibility criteria. Indeed, in order to have an admissible claim, an applicant must exhaust all the effective national procedures. However, if an applicant proves that some national procedures are not effective because judgments are not given in a reasonable time or because a vast jurisprudence does not award damages in the particular situation of the applicant, he must not exhaust that procedure: D. Harris, M. O'Boyle, E. Bates and C. Buckley, *Law of the European Convention on Human Rights*, Oxford, Oxford University Press, 2009, at 764ff; H. Krüger and C. Norgaard, 'The Right of Application' in R. Macdonald, F. Matscher and H. Petzold (eds.), *The European System for the Protection of Human Rights*, Dordrecht, Martinus Nijhoff Publishers, 1993, p657 at 670–671; and D. Shelton, *Remedies*, 1999, above n. 30, at 23.

41 *Zanghi v. Italy*, 19 February 1991, appl. no. 11491/85, §25. See also *Salah v. the Netherlands*, 6 July 2006, appl. no. 8196/02, §81. In the subsequent judgments on Art. 41 the Court only observed that the parties had agreed on a settlement: *Salah v. the Netherlands*, 8 March 2007 (just satisfaction), appl. no. 8196/02, §7; and *Zanghi v. Italy*, 10 February 1993 (just satisfaction), appl. no. 11491/85, §12.

42 As was, for example, the situation of one applicant in *Pressos Compania Naviera SA* whose claim on Art. 41, in opposition to the claims of the other applicants, had been awarded by the Court. The Court did not award the claims of the other applicants because it found that they still had a good chance to receive compensation in a national procedure.

under Art. 41.[43] The Court, in other words, judged that the requirement to exhaust all national remedies does not apply to Art. 41 as such.[44]

It is important to note that these criteria are very similar to the one that the Court uses in the context of the admissibility test. Indeed, for a case to be admissible with the ECtHR, the Court requires that applicants not exhaust *all* remedies just all *effective* remedies. The applicants thus do not have to exhaust all remedies but only those remedies that might offer a chance of success within a reasonable time and before an independent judge.[45] The only difference between the general admissibility criteria and the subsidiarity requirements under Art. 41 is the fact that the Court does not want the applicants to exhaust the national remedies for a second time in order to receive compensation. In one exceptional case, the Court argued that it is suitable for the compensation of a human rights violation to be awarded by a tribunal that has also judged on the merits of the case.[46]

4. A DISCRETIONARY COMPETENCE OF THE COURT

The third point of interest in the wording of Art. 41 of the Convention is that the Court only has to afford just satisfaction 'if necessary.' This raises the question of whether the Court has a discretionary competence as to decide whether or not it will grant a just satisfaction. The problem with answering this question lies in the fact that these words do not have specific meaning and that the preparatory works do not offer any guidelines for the application of Art. 41 in general.[47] As a result, it seems that the Court

43 *Anguelova v. Bulgaria*, 13 June 2002, appl. no. 38361/97, §172; *Shishkov v. Bulgaria*, 9 January 2003, appl. no. 26746/05, §97; *Levin v. Russia*, 2 February 2006, appl. no. 33264/02, §31; *Jalloh v. Germany*, 11 July 2006 (Grand Chamber), appl. no. 54810/00, §129; *Lenev v. Bulgaria*, 4 December 2012, appl. no. 41452/07, §178; and *Korobov et al. v. Estland*, 28 March 2013, appl. no. 10195/08, §153.

44 *Becciev v. Moldavia*, 4 October 2005, appl. no. 9190/03, §80; *Paladi v. Moldavia*, 10 July 2007, appl. no. 39806/05, §104; *Dolneanu v. Moldavia*, 13 November 2007, appl. no. 17211/03, §54; and Joint concurring opinion of Judges Zupančič, Gyulumyan, David Thor Bjorgvinsson, Nicolaou, Sajo, Lazarova Trakjkovska, Power-Forde, Vucinic and Pinto de Albuerque in *Cyprus v. Turkey*, 12 May 2014 (just satisfaction) (Grand Chamber), appl. no. 25781/94, §11.

45 On this topic, see: L. Zwaak, 'The Procedure', 2006, above n. 4, p95 at 147–151.

46 *Ringeisen v. Austria*, 22 June 1972 (just satisfaction), appl. no. 2614/65, §15.

47 F. Bydlinski, 'Methodological Approaches to the Tort Law of the ECHR' in A. Fenyves, E. Karner, H. Koziol and E. Steiner (eds.), *Tort Law in the Jurisprudence of the European Court of Human Rights*, Göttingen, De Gruyter, 2011, p29 at 38.

has a wide margin of appreciation in applying Art. 41[48] in that it can decide on a case-by-case basis whether or not it grants just satisfaction.[49] Accordingly, in one early case in 1980 the Court argued that applicants do not have a subjective right to compensation if their Convention rights are violated.[50] It is nevertheless obvious that the Court does take into account its own jurisprudence when applying Art. 41 ECHR.[51]

5. THE MEANING OF JUST SATISFACTION

The last point of interest is that Art. 41 uses the phrase 'just satisfaction' and not 'compensation' or 'restitution'. This raises the question as to what the difference is between a just satisfaction and a restitution or compensation. This question encompasses two sub-questions. The first question concerns the amount of the just satisfaction: can the Court compensate less than the totality of the caused damages? The second question concerns the form of the just satisfaction: does the Court always have to grant financial redress (as already mentioned) or are there alternatives? The next two sections will deal with both of these questions separately.

5.1. CAN THE COURT COMPENSATE LESS THAN THE TOTALITY OF THE CAUSED DAMAGES?

According to Art. 41, the ECtHR does not have to award a total compensation for the damages that are caused by a violation of the Convention, but it usually does. Article 41 only requires the Court to award a just satisfaction. According to Elisabeth Steiner, this term means that the Court can compensate less than the total amount of damages for reasons of equity.[52] Indeed, if the words 'just satisfaction' are read literally,

---

48 *Guzzardi v. Italy*, 6 November 1980 (Plenary), appl. no. 7367/76, §114; *Shesti Mai Engineering OOD et al. v. Bulgaria*, 20 September 2011, appl. no. 17854/04, §101; D. Shelton, *Remedies*, 1999, above n. 30, at 218; and J. Vande Lanotte and Y. Haeck, *Handboek EVRM. Part 1, Algemene beginselen*, Antwerp, Intersentia, 1995, at 625.

49 M.E. Mas, 'Right to Compensation', 1993, above n. 2, p775 at 783.

50 *Sunday Times v. the United Kingdom*, 6 November 1980 (just satisfaction) (Plenary), appl. no. 6538/74, §15.

51 C. Kissling and D. Kelliher, 'Compensation for Pecuniary and Non-Pecuniary Loss' in A. Fenyves, E. Karner, H. Koziol and E. Steiner (eds.), *Tort Law in the Jurisprudence of the European Court of Human Rights*, Göttingen, De Gruyter, 2011, p579 at 623.

52 E. Steiner, 'Just Satisfaction under Art. 41 ECHR: A compromise in 1950 – Problematic Now' in A. Fenyves, E. Karner, H. Koziol and E. Steiner (eds.), *Tort Law in the*

it seems that equity has a role to play in deciding how the satisfaction must look. Nevertheless, it must also be pointed out that Art. 41 stipulates that the ECtHR can only grant such a just satisfaction 'if the internal law of the High Contracting Party concerned allows only partial reparation to be made'. From the perspective of these words, it seems plausible that the Court must try to grant an award that compensates the totality of the damages.[53]

Thus, it seems that the text of Art. 41 provides contradictory directions. This paradox can be untangled by giving another meaning to equity. Indeed, in Belgian tort law for example, the use of equity reasonings in the compensation of damages in tort law does not necessarily mean that the judge does not have the obligation to provide full compensation.[54] A reasoning in this context mainly refers to the fact that it is often impossible to estimate the size of the damages precisely. This is of course often the case with immaterial damages, which from their nature can never be estimated precisely.[55] Thus, if a judge has to grant full compensation in a situation where it is impossible to estimate the size of the damages, he will have to rely on equity to determine the size of a compensation that – taking into account all the conditions of the case – compensates the damages as much as possible.

This last interpretation of a just satisfaction is supported by the jurisprudence of the ECtHR. Although the Court has never stated that the reference to equity in just satisfaction must be seen as meaning that damages often cannot be estimated precisely, the Court has often declared that a just satisfaction in principle must compensate all the damages:

> the Court will proceed from the principle that the applicant should as far as possible be put in the position he would have been in had the requirements of Article 6 not been disregarded.[56]

Jurisprudence of the European Court of Human Rights, Göttingen, De Gruyter, 2011, p3 at 14.

53 J. Sharpe, 'Article 50' in L.E. Pettiti, E. Decaux and P.-H. Imbert (eds.), *La Convention Européenne des droits de l'homme. Commentaire Article par Article*, Paris, Economica, 1999, p809 at 811.

54 L. Cornelis, 'Werkelijkheids- en zekerheidsgehalte van schade en schadeherstel' in M. Van den Bossche (ed.), *de nieuwe 'Indicatieve Tabel': een praktisch werkinstrument voor de evaluatie van menselijke schade*, Gent, Larcier, 2001, p21 at 38.

55 H. Koziol, *Basic questions of tort law from a Germanic perspective*, Vienna, Jan Sramek Verlag, 2012, at 113.

56 *Piersack v. Belgium*, 26 October 1984 (just satisfaction), appl. no. 8692/79, §12. See in the same way also: *Scozzari and Giunta v. Italy*, 13 July 2000 (Grand Chamber), appl. nos. 39221/98 and 41963/98, §250; *Former King of Greece et al. v. Greece*, 23 November 2002

This phrase illustrates that a just satisfaction, according to the Court, must pursue the *restitutio in integrum*.[57] This principle can also be found in Art. 2 of the Practice Direction concerning Just Satisfaction Claims that the registry of the Court drew up in 2007.[58] In this provision it is stipulated that the Court in principle grants *restitutio in integrum* but that it can award less in exceptional cases. These exceptional cases concern situations where there is a contributory fault of the human rights victim and the situations where the Court makes a declaratory judgment.

Although the Court's practice of making a declaratory judgment and the contributory fault of the victim of a human rights violation, amongst other issues, will be dealt with later in this book, it must already be said that the situations where the Court makes declaratory judgments can be explained on the basis of some jurisprudential rules. Thus, as a general rule, a just satisfaction requires full compensation. A more limited compensation is an exception to this rule. As Judge Costa once remarked, these exceptions are the consequence of material or juridical reasons that make the *restitutio in integrum* impossible.[59] If the words of Costa

---

(Grand Chamber), appl. no. 25701/94, §72; *Haase v. Germany*, 8 April 2004, appl. no. 11057/02, §115; *Saliba et al. v. Malta*, 22 January 2013 (just satisfaction), appl. no. 20287/10, §22; *Gera de Petri Testaferrata Bonici Ghaxaq v. Malta*, 3 September 2013 (just satisfaction), appl. no. 26771/07, §25; *S.B. v. Romania*, 23 September 2014, appl. no. 24453/04, §94; *Zaieţ v. Romania*, 24 March 2015, appl. no. 44958/05, §67; *Chinnici v. Italy (no.2)*, 14 April 2015, appl. no. 22432/03, §57; and *Magyar Keresztény Mennonita Egyház et al. v. Hungary*, 28 June 2016 (just satisfaction), appl. nos. 70945/11, 23611/12, 26998/12, 41150/12, 41155/12, 41553/12, 54977/12 and 56581/12, §45. It is interesting to note that in *Papamichelopoulos* the Court refers to the jurisprudence of the International Court of Justice: *Papamichalopoulos v. Greece*, 31 October 1995 (just satisfaction), appl. no. 14556/89, §36.

57 T. Barkhuysen and M. Van Emmerik, 'Rechtsherstel bij schending van het EVRM in Nederland en Straatsburg', *NJCM-Bulletin* 2006, p39 at 43; C. Birsan, 'Les aspects nouveaux de l'application des Articles 41 et 46 de la convention dans la jurisprudence de la cour européenne des droits de l'homme' in H. Hartig (ed.), *Trente ans de droit européen des droits de l'homme. Etudes à la mémoire de Wolfgan Strasser*, Brussels, Bruylant, 2007, p19 at 21; J.-P. Costa, 'The provision of compensation under Article 41 of the European Convention on Human Rights' in D. Fairgrieve, M. Adenas and J. Bell (eds.), *Tort Liability of Public Authorities in Comparative Perspective*, London, The British Institute of International and Comparative Law, 2002, p3 at 6; D. Scorey and T. Eicke, *Human Rights Damages. Principles and Practice*, London, Sweet & Maxwell, 2001, at A2–14; and K. Wolfram, 'Just Satisfaction in Art 41 ECHR', 2011, above n. 1, p345 at 350.

58 Practice Direction on Just Satisfaction Claims, 28 March 2007.

59 J.-P. Costa, 'The provision of compensation under Article 41 of the European Convention on Human Rights' in D. Fairgrieve, M. Adenas and J. Bell (eds.), *Tort Liability of Public Authorities in Comparative Perspective*, London, The British Institute of International and Comparative Law, 2002, p3 at 11.

seem correct, victims of human rights violations have a subjective right, not only to a kind of satisfaction but also to a full compensation of their damages.[60]

5.2. HAS THE COURT OTHER MEANS TO GRANT *RESTITUTIO IN INTEGRUM?*

Knowing that the Court in principle pursues full compensation, the question arises as to what instruments the Court possesses to achieve this goal. It is interesting to approach this question from a historical perspective. Historically, it is important to know that the ECtHR was the first international tribunal that obtained the authority to award just satisfaction to private applicants.[61] It did not use this authority in the first ten years of its existence.[62] Although this might be a bit strange from a contemporary perspective, it is a reminder of the fact that the authority of the Court to grant just satisfaction was contested at the time of the Court's foundation. The founding members of the Council of Europe were aware of the fact that the ECtHR might threaten their sovereignty by granting just satisfaction, so they chose to limit the authority by only allowing it to grant just satisfaction in the form of a sum of money and that it could not impose measures on the states.[63] As a result, Art. 41 only permits the Court

60 See on this topic: S. Somers, 'Declaratory judgments and the right to compensation in the jurisprudence of the European Court of Human Rights: Does art. 41 ECHR grants human right victims a right to financial compensation?', *JEDH* 2016, pp57–82.

61 E. Steiner, 'Just Satisfaction under Art. 41 ECHR', 2011, above n. 52, p3 at 4. In this context, it must be noted that Art. 5 has its own remedy. This remedy is not discussed separately from Art. 41 because the Strasbourg Court applies both provisions in the same manner: The Law Commission and the Scottish Law Commission, *Damages under the Human Rights Act 1998*, 2000, at 114 <https://www.scotlawcom.gov.uk/files/3012/7989/6877/rep180.pdf>.

62 D. Shelton, *Remedies*, 1999, above n. 30, at 154.

63 E. Steiner, 'Just Satisfaction under Art. 41 ECHR', 2011, above n. 52, p3 at 9. One can conceive that this is a consequence of the fact that the Court can only judge in the context of the subjective contentieux and not in the context of the objective contentieux. The Court can judge on an individual case but not on the existence of rules as such: M. de Salvia, 'Can the Reparation Awarded to Victims of Violations under the ECHR be Considered a Real "Just" Satisfaction', 2011, above n. 22, p387 at 388. Consequently, in the past the Court rejected claims to take measures: *Le Compte, Van Leuven and De Meyere v. Belgium*, 18 October 1982 (just satisfaction), appl. nos. 6878/75 and 7238/75, §13; *Dudgeon v. the United Kingdom*, 24 February 1983 (just satisfaction), appl. no. 7525/76, §15; *Campbell and Cosans v. the United Kingdom*, 22 March 1983 (just satisfaction), appl. nos. 7511/76 and 7743/76, §16;

to grant financial compensation or moral satisfaction to victims of human rights violations.[64]

This was, however, not an inevitable fact. Some of the drafters of the Convention pleaded in favor of a broader competence for the Court. Pierre-Henri Teitgen for instance argued that the Court also had to be in the position to annul, suspend or amend decisions that were made by national governments.[65] He argued that the mere authority to award human right victims a sum of money or a moral satisfaction would not be sufficient to protect the Convention rights. He argued for this as follows:

> Si demain, la France sombrait dans un régime de dictature et si son dictateur supprimait la liberté de la presse, La Cour Européenne donnerait-elle un franc de dommages-intérêts à tous les Français pour réparer le tort que leur aurait causé la suppression de cette liberté fondamentale? Cela n'a pas de sens. [If tomorrow, France would become a dictatorship and if its dictator suppresses the freedom of the press, would the European Court then grant one franc in compensation to all French citizens in order to repair the harm they suffered because of the removal of this fundamental freedom? That does not make any sense.] (author's translation)[66]

It is hard to disagree with Teitgen. Can one really believe that the mere giving of financial compensation to human right victims would stop a state from violating these rights? In recent times, it can be doubted that the obligations of Russia to pay compensation for human rights infringements had led to a radical shift in its human rights policies.[67] But these issues are

---

Gillow v. the United Kingdom, 14 September 1987 (just satisfaction), appl. no. 9063/80, §9; *W. v. the United Kingdom*, 9 June 1988 (just satisfaction) (Plenary), appl. no. 9749/82, §14; *Demicoli v. Malta*, 27 August 1991, appl. no. 13057/87, §45; *Saïdi v. France*, 20 September 1993, appl. no. 14647/89, §47; *Pelladoah v. the Netherlands*, 22 September 1994, appl. no. 16737/90, §44; *Allenet de Ribemont v. France*, 10 February 1995, appl. no. 15175/89, §65; *Yagci and Sargin v. Turkey*, 8 June 1995, appl. nos. 16419/90 and 16426/90; *Tolstoy Miloslavsky v. the United Kingdom*, 13 July 1995, appl. no. 18139/91, §72; *Duclos v. France*, 17 December 1996, appl. nos. 20940/92, 20941/92 and 20942/92, §92; and *Selmouni v. France*, 28 July 1999, appl. no. 25803/94, §126.

64 M.L. Van Emmerik, *Schadevergoeding*, above n. 3, 1997, at 89; and M.E. Mas, 'Right to Compensation', 1993, above n. 2, p775 at 778.

65 *Collected Edition of the "Travaux Préparatoires" of the European Convention on Human Rights*, Vol. I, Den Haag, Martinus Nijhof Publishers, 1975, at 212. For an elaborate analysis of the preparatory work of Art. 41 of the Convention see: E. Steiner, 'Just Satisfaction under Art. 41 ECHR', 2011, above n. 52, p3 at 4–10.

66 *Collected Edition of the "Travaux Préparatoires" of the European Convention on Human Rights*, Vol.V. Den Haag, Martinus Nijhof Publishers, 1979, at 301.

67 On this topic, see: K. Malfliet and S. Parmentier (eds.), *Russia and the Council of Europe: 10 years after*, London, Palgrave Macmillan, 2010.

beyond the scope of this book. What is important here is the fact that the limited authority of the Court has also been criticized from a compensatory perspective. Jeremy McBride pointed out that it is probably more important for victims of human rights violations to end the violation than to receive compensation.[68] Other scholars have also argued that the Convention does not sufficiently deter member states since they only have to fear being sentenced to pay a sum of money.[69] But no matter how reasonable these critiques may be, one cannot change the fact that the contracting states did not provide this possibility in the Convention.

The restricted authority of the Court under Art. 41 does not prevent the Court from requiring states to take some measures. Indeed, Art. 46 obliges member states to take measures to stop the consequences of human rights violations.[70] This is not however a strict obligation. Because of the principle of subsidiarity, the convicted member states are free to decide as to which measures they deem to be appropriate to meet the requirements of Art. 46.[71] If a convicted state fails to meet these requirements, the court can convict the state and can encourage the judges of the member states to confirm their jurisprudence with the conviction in cases where the lawmaker fails to take initiative.[72] By using these instruments creatively,

---

68 J. McBride, 'Redress for human rights violations' in G. Hand and J. McBride (eds.), *Essays in honour of L. Neville Brown*, Oxford Monographs in International Law, Oxford, Oxford University Press, 1991, p161 at 166–167. One author also regrets that the Court never ordered the installation of a truth commission: I. Boerefijn, 'Billijker genoegdoening', *NJCM-Bulletin* 2004, pp920–923.

69 L. Loucaides, 'Reparation for Violations', 2008, above n. 30, p182 at 186; and P. Van Dijk, 'Een efficient en effectief stelsel van toezicht op de naleving van het EVRM. De rolverdeling bij de rechtsvorming en rechtshandhaving', *NJCM-Bulletin* 2003, p394 at 400–401.

70 This reading of Arts 41 and 46 is in line with the general rules of state responsibility in international law. According to these rules, the primary obligation of a state is to end its illegal acts: D. Shelton, *Remedies*, 1999, above n. 30, at 31; K. Wolfram, 'Just Satisfaction in Art 41 ECHR', 2011, above n. 1, p345 at 365. One author even argues that the Convention in itself, and aside from Art. 41, obliges states to restore human rights victims to the situation they would have been in if the violation had not occurred: R. Bernhardt, 'The Convention and Domestic Law' in R. Macdonald, F. Matscher and H. Petzold (eds.), *The European System for the Protection of Human Rights*, Dordrecht, Martinus Nijhoff Publishers, 1993, p25 at 37.

71 *Papamichalopoulos v. Greece*, 31 October 1995 (just satisfaction), appl. no. 14556/89, §34; *Scozzari and Giunta v. Italy*, 13 July 2000 (Grand Chamber), appl. nos. 39221/98 and 41963/98, §249; and *Haase v. Germany*, 8 April 2004, appl. no. 11057/02, §115.

72 This stems from *Vermeire* where the Court found a violation of Art. 8 read in conjunction with Art. 14 because love children were discriminated in the field of inheritance law. Since the Court had already convicted Belgium for the same reason in the famous *Marckx* judgment (*Marckx v. Belgium*, 13 June 1979 (Plenary),

the Court has appropriated the authority to order member states to take measures to restore the caused damages. This is illustrated by the following case-law.

The first case in which the Court provided measures to a state for the restitution of damages was *Stran Greek Refineries*.[73] The applicant in this case was the owner of a refinery that had contracted with the Greek government at the time of the Greek military junta. When this regime was overthrown, and Greece had become a democracy once again, the Greek government found that this contract violated the national interest and decided not to give it any further effect. There was an arbitration clause included in the contract, and on the basis of this clause every dispute concerning the execution of the contract had to be settled by an arbitration tribunal. Accordingly, the owner of the refinery filed a complaint before the tribunal, and the tribunal convicted the state on 27 February 1984, ordering them to pay a sizable amount of damages. The Greek government filed an appeal against this decision, but they were convicted again. To undo this conviction, the Greek parliament adopted a law on the 22 May 1987 that annulled the arbitration clauses that were included in the contracts that were agreed upon under the military junta. After this law entered into force, the Greek government filed a cessation appeal and obtained an annulment of the arbitration tribunal's decision. As a result, the owner of the refinery argued that his rights to property (Art. 1 FP) and his right to a fair trial (Art. 6) were violated. He sued the Greek government before the ECtHR who found a violation of both of these Convention rights. With relation to Art. 41, the Court did not grant just satisfaction itself, but ordered the Greek government to execute the decision of the arbitration tribunal. It also ordered the Greek government to pay 6 percent in interest for the delay.

Although the Court in *Stran Greek Refineries* did not order the national state to do anything other than pay an amount of money, it did not award this compensation itself. From that point, it was a small step to order the state to take more specific measures. This happened for the first time in *Papamichalopoulos*.[74] The facts that gave rise to this case were quite similar

appl. no. 6833/74), it found that the Belgian judges had been able to confirm their jurisprudence to the Court's findings in the *Marckx* case by appealing directly to the Convention: *Vermeire v. Belgium*, 29 November 1991, appl. no. 12849/87, §§26–28.

73 *Stran Greek Refineries and Stratis Andreadis v. Greece*, 9 December 1994, appl. no. 13427/87.

74 *Papamichalopoulos v. Greece*, 31 October 1995 (just satisfaction), appl. no. 14556/89. See in the same way also: *Brumarescu v. Romania*, 23 January 2001 (just satisfaction)

to those in *Stran Greek Refineries*. The applicants in *Papamichalopoulos* pleaded that their right to property as enshrined by Art. 1 FP was violated because the Greek army had expropriated their properties without paying any compensation. After the ECtHR found a violation of Art. 1 FP, it indicated that the state had to take measures to ensure that the judgment would be complied with and to provide *restitutio in integrum* for the victims. The Court further remarked that in principle the states are free to choose the means of compliance with a judgment in which the Court has found a violation. It nevertheless also argued that it is for the national state to affect a *restitutio in integrum* if the nature of the violation allows such a *restitutio in integrum*. If national law does not allow – or allows only partial – reparation to be made for the consequences of the violation, the Court has the power to grant just satisfaction to the injured parties on the basis of Art. 41 ECHR.[75]

In this case, the Greek government had neglected to grant damages or to take measures so that the applicants could take possession of their properties again. The Court found that this was an unlawful expropriation and argued that this could not be compensated by a lawful expropriation. It further referred to international law and more specifically to the *Chorzow* judgment of the Permanent Court of International Justice from which the ECtHR used the following quote:

> … reparation must, as far as possible, wipe out all the consequences of the illegal act and reestablish the situation which would, in all probability, have existed if that act had not been committed. Restitution in kind, or, if this is not possible, payment of a sum corresponding to the value which a restitution in kind would bear; the award, if need be, of damages for loss sustained which would not be

(Grand Chamber), appl. no. 28342/95, §§22–23; *Strain et al. v. Romania*, 21 July 2005, appl. no. 57001/00, §§80–81; *Scordino v. Italy (no.1)*, 29 March 2006 (Grand Chamber), appl. no. 36813/97, §247; *Sylla v. the Netherlands*, 6 July 2006, appl. no. 14683/03, §75; *Paudicio v. Italy*, 24 May 2007, appl. no. 77606/01, §59; *Rusu et al. v. Romania*, 19 July 2007, appl. no. 4198/04, §§34–35; *Driza v. Albania*, 1 November 2007, appl. no. 33771/02, §138; *Suciu Werle v. Romania*, 13 December 2007, appl. no. 26521/05, §§29–30; *Grigoras v. Romania*, 7 October 2008, appl. no. 19188/03, §§29–30; *Chiorean v. Romania*, 21 October 2008, appl. no. 20535/03, §§28–29; *Teodorescu Olimpia-Maria v. Romania*, 4 November 2008, appl. no. 43774/02, §§34–35; *Reichardt v. Romania*, 13 November 2008, appl. no. 6111/04, §§35–36; *Guiso-Gallisay v. Italy*, 22 December 2009 (just satisfaction) (Grand Chamber), appl. no. 58858/00, §90; *Veniamin v. Romania*, 26 January 2010, appl. no. 19438/05, §§29–30; and 23 February 201023 February 2010, appl. no. 10636/06, §34.

75 *Papamichalopoulos v. Greece*, 31 October 1995 (just satisfaction), appl. no. 14556/89, §34.

> covered by restitution in kind or payment in place of it – such are the principles which should serve to determine the amount of compensation due for an act contrary to international law.[76]

The ECtHR consequently argued that the applicants had not only been harmed because they had lost their property as such, but also because the expropriation had taken place more than 20 years earlier. They had lost the enjoyment of their property for more than 20 years. The Court then found that the restitution could best be reached if the state returned the property to the applicants. Although the value of the properties had increased because the government had erected buildings on the lands, the Court found that the government could not demand any compensation for this. The Court instead found that these buildings could compensate the applicants for the loss of enjoyment of the properties. In the end the Court ruled that if the Greek government did not implement this judgment within six months, it would order them to pay a large sum of money with added interest.[77] In addition, the Court also awarded the applicants a limited amount of money for moral damages.

By ordering the state to return the land to the applicants, in *Papamichelapolous* for the first time the Court ordered a state to take measures to provide *restitutio in integrum*. Since then, it has ordered states more and more to take measures to restore the damages and thus to protect the Convention in an effective way.[78] Although the Court often does so in its reasonings on the merits (and afterwards only makes a declaratory judgment), it sometimes does this under Art. 41.[79] As a result, it seems that the Court takes into account the measures that it orders the state to take

76 ICJ, *Chorzow Factory Case*, 13 September 1928.

77 *Papamichalopoulos v. Greece*, 31 October 1995 (just satisfaction), appl. no. 14556/89, §39. In the case of *Hentrich*, the Court effectively convicted a state to pay damages after it failed to take the required measures: *Hentrich v. France*, 3 July 1995 (just satisfaction), appl. no. 13616/88, §§10–11.

78 One can note that the Court, in a similar way, also uses its competence more and more to take interim measures. With this regard, see: C. Harby, 'The Changing Nature of Interim Measures before the European Court of Human Rights', *EHRLR* 2010, 73–84.

79 *Hirst v. the United Kingdom (no.2)*, 30 March 2004, appl. no. 74025/01; *Aleksanyan v. Russia*, 22 December 2008, appl. no. 46468/06; *Layijov v. Azerbaijan*, 10 April 2014, appl. no. 22062/07; *Aleksandr Valeryevich Kazakov v. Russia*, 4 December 2014, appl. no. 16412/06; and *Volkov and Adamskiy v. Russia*, 26 March 2015, appl. nos. 7614/09 and 30863/10. However, it must be pointed out that some judges find that the Court should always refer to the measures in its reasoning on the merits, which seems to be motivated by the rule that the Court in principle only reasons on the just satisfaction if applicants claim a just satisfaction. See: Joint concurring opinion of Judges Spielmann and Jebens in *Panovits v. Cyprus*, 11 March 2009, appl. no. 4268/04.

when it has to apply Art. 41.[80] Indeed, the Court will indicate measures in its opinions if it thinks that a state can provide restitution in kind by taking measures.[81] As already stated, the Court argues that if someone is condemned in a criminal lawsuit where the requirements of a right to a fair trial were not respected, the best way to grant restitution to the human rights victim is by the reopening of the lawsuit.[82] The same also holds true when Art. 6 was violated for the lack of access to a court.[83] If on the other hand someone had been imprisoned from a violation of the Convention, the Court finds that the best way to redress the damages is to release him.[84] If someone would be extradited to a country that falls outside the jurisprudence of the ECtHR and this might be a violation of the extradited person's Convention rights, the best way to redress this violation is to require guarantees from the receiving state.[85] Other examples of measures

---

80 The Law Commission and the Scottish Law Commission, 'Damages under the Human Rights Act 1998', 2000, at 30 <https://www.scotlawcom.gov.uk/files/3012/7989/6877/rep180.pdf>.

81 E. Lambert, 'La pratique récente de reparation des violations de la convention européenne de sauvegarde des droits de l'homme et des libertés fondamentales: plaidoyer pour la preservation d'un acquis remarquable', *Rev.Trim.D.H.* 2000, p199 at 201.

82 *Öcalan v. Turkey*, 12 May 2005 (Grand Chamber), appl. no. 46221/99, §210; *Bocos-cuesta v. the Netherlands*, 10 November 2005, appl. no. 54789/00, §82; *Sejdovic v. Turkey*, 1 March 2006 (Grand Chamber), appl. no. 56581/00, §126; *Salduz v. Turkey*, 27 November 2008 (Grand Chamber), appl. no. 36391/02, §72; *Panovits v. Cyprus*, 11 March 2009, appl. no. 4268/04, §103; *Maksimov v. Azerbaijan*, 8 October 2009, appl. no. 38228/05, §46; *Cudak v. Lithuania*, 23 March 2010 (Grand Chamber), appl. no. 15869/02, §79; *Nechiporuk and Yonkalo v. Ukraine*, 21 April 2011, appl. no. 42310/04, §297; *Schüth v. Germany*, 28 June 2012 (just satisfaction), appl. no. 1620/03, §17; *Harabin v. Slovakia*, 20 November 2012, appl. no. 58688/11, §177; *Aleksandr Valeryevich Kazakov v. Russia*, 4 December 2014, appl. no. 16412/06; *Volkov and Adamskiy v. Russia*, 26 March 2015, appl. nos. 7614/09 and 30863/10, §68; *Shumikhin v. Russia*, 16 July 2015, appl. no. 7848/06, §28; *Lorefice v. Italy*, 29 June 2017, appl. no. 63446/13, §52; *M. v. The Netherlands*, 25 July 2017, appl. no. 2156/10; *Zadumov v. Russia*, 12 December 2017, appl. no. 2257/12, §81; and Joint concurring opinion of Judges Rozakis, Spielmann, Ziemele and Lazarova Trajkovska in *Salduz v. Turkey*, 27 November 2008 (Grand Chamber), appl. no. 36391/02, §8ff. If the violation of Art. 6 only had as a consequence that a criminal was unable to provide a national court with documents that might influence the severity of his punishment, the Court will award a compensation for non-pecuniary damages: *Matanović v. Croatia*, 4 April 2017, appl. no. 2742/12, §203.

83 *Naku v. Lithuania and Sweden*, 8 November 2016, appl. no. 26126/07, §110.

84 *Assanidze v. Georgia*, 8 April 2004 (Grand Chamber), appl. no. 71503/01, §202; *Ilascu et al. v. Moldavia and Russia*, 8 July 2004 (Grand Chamber), appl. no. 48787/99, §§487 and 490; *Aleksanyan v. Russia*, 22 December 2008, appl. no. 46468/06, §240; *Fatullayev v. Azerbaijan*, 22 April 2010 (Grand Chamber), appl. no. 40984/07, §174; and *Del Rio Prada v. Spain*, 10 July 2012 (Grand Chamber), appl. no. 42750/09, §83.

85 *Hirsi Jamaa et al. v. Italy*, 23 February 2012 (Grand Chamber), appl. no. 27765/09, §211.

that the Court has ordered are the handling of an asylum request within a reasonable time[86] or the order to put a pension right in a fund.[87] In a recent case the Court ordered a state to restore a judge back to the position he possessed before he was deposed in a way that violated the Convention.[88]

What is interesting in all of these cases is the fact that the Court remarks that its judgments are only declaratory and that states have a margin of appreciation as to the manner in which they grant restitution.[89] Then the Court always argues that 'Sometimes the nature of the violation found may be such as to leave no real choice as to the measures required.' Thus, as was carefully suggested before, the Court only orders states to take measures if there is only one way to grant the victims restitution in kind.[90] By doing so, the Court takes into account the principle of subsidiarity[91] in a prudent way.[92] Consequently, Art. 41 is a secondary provision that can only be applied in cases where states neglect to take appropriate measures to offer restitution in kind.[93] It is regrettable that the Court does not always invoke the measures that it orders in its reasoning on the merits or in its application of Art. 46 in its reasonings on Art. 41. We can however applaud some recent judgments of the ECtHR where it deals with Arts 41 and 46 under the same heading.[94]

---

86 *M.S.S. v. Belgium and Greece*, 21 January 2011 (Grand Chamber), appl. no. 30696/09, §402.

87 *Karanovic v. Bosnia and Herzegovina*, 20 November 2007, appl. no. 39462/03, §28ff.

88 *Oleksandr Volkov v. Ukraine*, 9 January 2013, appl. no. 21722/11, §208.

89 If the Committee of ministers finds the measures to be inadequate (e.g. to offer the applicants *restitutio in integrum*), it files the case with the ECtHR: F. Sundberg, 'Le principe de l'octroi subsidiaire des dommages-intérêts – coté comité des ministres' in J.-F. Flauss and E. Lambert Abdelgawad (eds.), *La pratique d'indemnisation par la Cour européenne des droits de l'homme*, Brussels, Bruylant, 2011, p27 at 43ff.

90 *Grande Stevens et al. v. Austria*, 4 March 2014, appl. nos. 18640/10, 18647/10, 18663/10, 18668/10 and 18698/10, §234. In contrast, the Court rejects claims to take measures itself if there are still effective remedies at hand in the national legal order: *Muminov v. Russia*, 11 December 2008, appl. no. 42502/06, §145; *Khodorkovskiy v. Russia*, 31 May 2011, appl. no. 5829/04, §271; and *O.H. v. Germany*, 24 November 2011, appl. no. 4646/08, §119.

91 Consequently, the Court sometimes explicitly deals with Arts 41 and 46 together: *Varnava et al. v. Turkey*, 18 September 2009 (Grand Chamber), appl. nos. 16064/90, 16065/90, 16066/90, 16068/90, 16069/90, 16070/90, 16071/90, 16072/90 and 16073/90, §212ff.

92 P. Leach, 'Beyond the Bug River – A New Dawn for Redress Before the European Court of Human Rights', *EHRLR* 2005, p148 at 149.

93 G. Nicolau, 'The New Perspective of the European Court of Human Rights on the Effectiveness of its judgments', *HRLJ* 2011, p269 at 271.

94 E.g.: *Sürmeli v. Germany*, 8 June 2006 (Grand Chamber), appl. no. 75529/01, §135ff; and *Orlandi et al. v. Italy*, 14 December 2017, appl. nos. 26431/12 et al. §§214–216.

Although Art. 41 theoretically has a secondary character in the sense that the state's measures to offer restitution in kind to the victims have precedence over the application of Art. 41,[95] there are in practice more cases where the Court grants financial compensation under the heading of Art. 41 than there are cases where the Court orders states to take measures to offer restitution in kind. The reason for this is the fact that damages in many cases cannot be restored in kind, regardless of the types of measures that can be taken.[96] If, for instance, the reasonable time requirement has already been violated, one can no longer restore this violation.[97] The same is true in cases where someone had not been able to make use of his right to free speech[98] or where someone had been imprisoned unlawfully.[99] It is possible to imagine hundreds of situations where human rights violations cause damages, such as moral damages, that by their nature cannot be restored in kind. Indeed, how can one restore the death of a relative in violation of Art. 2 in kind? In all these cases (probably the majority of its case-law) the Court awards a sum of money as just satisfaction.[100]

---

95 Because of this, one could say that Art. 41 is subsidiary to Art. 46: C. Birsan, 'Les aspects nouveaux de l'application des Articles 41 et 46 de la convention dans la jurisprudence de la cour européenne des droits de l'homme' in H. Hartig (ed.), *Trente ans de droit européen des droits de l'homme. Etudes à la mémoire de Wolfgan Strasser*, Brussels, Bruylant, 2007, p19 at 23ff; M. De Salvia, 'La satisfaction equitable au titre des mesures individuelles et la pratique des organs de la convention européenne des droits de l'homme: qu'en est-il du principe de sécurité juridique?' in H. Hartig (ed.), *Trente ans de droit européen des droits de l'homme. Etudes à la mémoire de Wolfgan Strasser*, Brussels, Bruylant, 2007, p45 at 46ff; J. Hartshorne, 'The Human Rights Act 1998 and Damages for Non-Pecuniary Loss', *EHRLR* 2004, p660 at 661; and L. Loucaides, 'Reparation for Violations', 2008, above n. 30, p182 at 188.

96 In this sense, see: Concurring opinion of Judge Yudkivska in 9 January 2013; J. Hartshorne 'The Human Rights Act', 2004, above n. 95, p660 at 661 and L. Loucaides, 'Reparation for Violations', 2008, above n. 30, p182 at 188.

97 *König v. Germany*, 10 March 1980 (just satisfaction) (Plenary), appl. no. 6232/73, §15.

98 *Sunday Times v. the United Kingdom*, 6 November 1980 (just satisfaction) (Plenary), appl. no. 6538/74, §13.

99 *Guzzardi v. Italy*, 6 November 1980 (Plenary), appl. no. 7367/76, §113. There is an impossibility to repair damages in this type of case when the damages already occurred before the human rights violation was found. One cannot undo an imprisonment from the past. However, for the future, an unlawful imprisonment can be restored by an immediate release. See in this sense: *Assanidze v. Georgia*, 8 April 2004 (Grand Chamber), appl. no. 71503/01, §202.

100 In *Claeys*, the Court only awarded a financial compensation for non-pecuniary damages arising out of the violation of the right to a fair trial in criminal matters after it observed that (at that time) it was impossible to reopen a criminal case in the legal order of the defendant state: *Claes et al. v. Belgium*, 2 June 2005, appl. no. 46825/99 et al., §§53, 57 and 62.

CHAPTER 7
DAMAGES

Since the Court aims to award human rights victims full compensation of their damages on the basis of Art. 41, the question arises whether it should develop a notion of damages that is similar to the notion of damages in national tort law. An inquiry into this question will have to develop insight on the functions of damages, starting from the idea that the primary aim of damages in national tort law is to compensate the suffered loss of an injured person.[1] Examining this question will also shed light on the question whether the Convention influences the concept of damages in national tort law.

1. DEFINITION AND FINDING OF DAMAGES

1.1. DEFINITION OF DAMAGES

The text of Art. 41 of the Convention does not mention the notion of damages. The provision only stipulates that the ECtHR has the authority to award a just satisfaction if the Convention is violated and if the internal law of the state concerned only allows partial reparation to be made. The ECtHR does not provide a definition of damages in its jurisprudence either. It only gives a sort of definition of restitution, from which one might deduce a definition of damages. The Court in some cases states that the full compensation of the damages exists in putting an applicant as far as possible in the situation equivalent to the one in which he would find himself had there not been a breach of the Convention.[2]

---

1 U. Magnus, 'Comparative Report on the Law of Damages' in U. Magnus et al. (eds.), *Unification of Tort Law: Damages*, The Hague, Kluwer, 2001, (185) at 185.

2 *Latridis v. Greece*, 19 October 2000 (just satisfaction) (Grand Chamber), appl. no. 31107/96, §35; *Brumarescu v. Romania*, 23 January 2001 (just satisfaction) (Grand Chamber), appl. no. 28342/95, §19; *Kingsley v. the United Kingdom*, 28 May 2002

Assuming that a full compensation redresses all the suffered damages, a definition of damages can be deduced from this wording that reads as follows: damages are the difference between the actual situation of the victim of a human rights violation and the situation in which he would find himself had there not been a breach of the violation. In essence, this definition reduces the notion of damages to a comparison between two situations: if there is a difference between the two situations, damages exist. Apart from that, the Court does not provide a substantial definition of damages. One might argue that damages can be defined as an interest for the reason that there seems to be a link between the application of Art. 41 and the admissibility criteria according to which an applicant must have an interest in bringing a case before the Court. Nevertheless, there might be a difference between an interest as required under the admissibility criteria and the notion of damages under Art. 41 since the last one can contain an additional threshold.

The question arises then, when does an infringement of what interest qualify as damages. It will take more time to answer this question. For now, it is sufficient to know that the ECtHR is not bound by the definition that national legal systems apply. The Court can give an autonomous meaning to the notion of damages.[3] According to Peter Bydlinski, the definition of

(Grand Chamber), appl. no. 35605/97, §40; *Wilson, National Union of Journalists et al. v. the United Kingdom*, 2 July 2002, appl. nos. 30668/96, 30671/96 and 30678/96, §54; *Lungoci v. Romania*, 26 January 2006, appl. no. 62710/00, §55; *Yanakiev v. Bulgaria*, 10 August 2006, appl. no. 40476/98, §89; *Andrejeva v. Latvia*, 18 February 2009 (Grand Chamber), appl. no. 55707/00, §111; *Danilenkov et al. v. Russia*, 30 July 2009, appl. no. 67336/01, §142; *Javaugue v. France*, 11 February 2010, appl. no. 39730/06, §53; *Harabin v. Slovakia*, 20 November 2012, appl. no. 58688/11, §177; *Oleksandr Volkov v. Ukraine*, 9 January 2013, appl. no. 21722/11, §193; *Dimitar Krastev v. Bulgaria*, 12 February 2013, appl. no. 26524/04, §92; *Petko Petkov v. Bulgaria*, 19 February 2013, appl. no. 2834/06, §43; *Vilnes et al. v. Norway*, 5 December 2013, appl. nos. 52806/09 and 22703/10, §269; *Layijov v. Azerbaijan*, 10 April 2014, appl. no. 22062/07, §84; *Aleksandr Valeryevich Kazakov v. Russia*, 4 December 2014, appl. no. 16412/06, §44; *Ceni v. Italy*, 16 December 2014 (just satisfaction), appl. no. 25376/06, §20; *Volkov and Adamskiy v. Russia*, 26 March 2015, appl. nos. 7614/09 and 30863/10, §68; and *Shumikhin v. Russia*, 16 July 2015, appl. no. 7848/06, §28.

3 K. Oliphant and K. Ludwichowska, 'Damage' in A. Fenyves, E. Karner, H. Koziol and E. Steiner (eds.), *Tort Law in the Jurisprudence of the European Court of Human Rights*, Göttingen, De Gruyter, 2011, p397 at 397. This stems from the fact that the Court is not bound by national tort law: *Sunday Times v. the United Kingdom*, 6 November 1980 (just satisfaction) (Plenary), appl. no. 6538/74, §15. Nevertheless, this does not mean that the Court cannot take rules and principles of national tort law into account: *Gault v. the United Kingdom*, 20 November 2007, appl. no. 1271/05, §30.

damages that the Court uses does at least encompass the types of damages that are also recognized in national law.[4] Whether this is the case, and more importantly whether the opposite is the case, will be discussed in the following chapters.

1.2. FINDING OF DAMAGES

From the wording of the Convention, one cannot see whether or not an applicant has to prove that he experienced damages. What is clear is the fact that the Court can only award a just satisfaction if it finds a violation of the Convention. As a result, one cannot discuss the rules of evidence with regard to the application of Art. 41 without looking at those that are applied for finding a violation of the Convention.

1.2.1. The Finding of a Violation of the Convention

The proof of the facts is often not an important issue in the jurisprudence of the Court because they have often already been found in a national procedure.[5] It is nevertheless important to note that it is up to the applicants to demonstrate a starting point for proof, but that the Court can order the government to participate in finding proof. It is important to know that the Court, before finding a violation of the Convention, requires that there cannot be a reasonable doubt on the existence of a violation.[6] The Court however finds that the rules of evidence vary according to the nature and

4 F. Bydlinski, 'Methodological Approaches to the Tort Law of the ECHR' in A. Fenyves, E. Karner, H. Koziol and E. Steiner (eds.), *Tort Law in the Jurisprudence of the European Court of Human Rights*, Göttingen, De Gruyter, 2011, p29 at 43.

5 P. Leach, C. Paraskeva and G. Uzelac, 'Human rights fact-finding. The European Court of Human Rights at a crossroads', *NQHR* 2010, p41 at 41–42.

6 *Ireland v. the United Kingdom*, 18 January 1978 (Plenary), appl. no. 5310/71, §161; *Aydin v. Turkey*, 25 September 1997 (Grand Chamber), appl. no. 23178/94, §72; *Kaya v. Turkey*, 19 February 1998, appl. no. 22729/93, §76; *Aktaş v. Turkey*, 24 April 2003, appl. no. 24351/94, §270; *Fadeyeva v. Russia*, 9 June 2005, appl. no. 55723/00, §79; *Bouyid v. Belgium*, 21 November 2013, appl. no. 23380/09, §43; and *Bataliny v. Russia*, 23 July 2015, appl. no. 10060/07, §86. See also: K. Oliphant and K. Ludwichowska, 'Damage', 2011, above n. 3, p397 at 398.

the character of the case and the severity of the human rights infringement. The Court judged in this way in *Nachova*:

> ... in assessing evidence, the Court has adopted the standard of proof "beyond reasonable doubt". However, it has never been its purpose to borrow the approach of the national legal systems that use that standard. Its role is not to rule on criminal guilt or civil liability but on Contracting States' responsibility under the Convention. The specificity of its task under Article 19 of the Convention – to ensure the observance by the Contracting States of their engagement to secure the fundamental rights enshrined in the Convention – conditions its approach to the issues of evidence and proof. In the proceedings before the Court, there are no procedural barriers to the admissibility of evidence or pre-determined formulae for its assessment. It adopts the conclusions that are, in its view, supported by the free evaluation of all evidence, including such inferences as may flow from the facts and the parties' submissions. According to its established case-law, proof may follow from the coexistence of sufficiently strong, clear and concordant inferences or of similar unrebutted presumptions of fact. Moreover, the level of persuasion necessary for reaching a particular conclusion and, in this connection, the distribution of the burden of proof are intrinsically linked to the specificity of the facts, the nature of the allegation made and the Convention right at stake. The Court is also attentive to the seriousness that attaches to a ruling that a Contracting State has violated fundamental rights.[7]

This shows that the ECtHR is very flexible with regard to proving violations of the Convention and that it has not developed a general theory on this issue.[8] The Court used this freedom to apply presumptions of fact. This happened in cases where an applicant complained that his rights or his relatives' rights under Arts 2 or 3 were violated because of death or injury in prison. In these cases strong presumptions of fact will arise in respect of the injuries and death so that the burden of proof should be regarded as resting on the authorities.[9] The reason for this

---

7 *Nachova et al. v. Bulgaria*, 6 July 2005 (Grand Chamber), appl. nos. 43577/98 and 43579/98, §147. See also: *Cobzaru v. Romania*, 26 July 2007, appl. no. 48254/99, §93; *Rupa v. Romania*, 16 December 2008, appl. no. 58478/00, §96; *El-Masri v. The former Yugoslav Republic of Macedonia*, 13 December 2012 (Grand Chamber), appl. no. 39630/09, §151; *Hassan v. the United Kingdom*, 16 September 2014 (Grand Chamber), appl. no. 29750/09, §48; and *Bataliny v. Russia*, 23 July 2015, appl. no. 10060/07, §86.

8 P. Leach, C. Paraskeva and G. Uzelac, 'Human rights fact-finding', 2010, above n. 5, p41 at 44; and M. Smith, 'The Adjudicatory Fact-finding Tools of the European Court of Human Rights', *European Human Rights Law Review* 2009, p206 at 209–212.

9 *Demiray v. Turkey*, 21 November 2000, appl. no. 27308/95, §44; *Anguelova v. Bulgaria*, 13 June 2002, appl. no. 38361/97, §109; *Ipek v. Turkey*, 17 February 2004,

is that the victims of the violations are unable to provide evidence in a context that is so strongly controlled by the state.[10] In one case, the Court even applied this criterion explicitly when it had to decide whether tort law provided an effective remedy in the context of Art. 5 when the victim did not receive adequate medical treatment in detention. In this case, the Court found a violation of Art. 13 because the applicant had to prove that the state committed a fault which was highly unlikely because of the control of the state and the fact that the state officials had followed clear protocols.[11] Apart from that, the Court also takes into account the way in which the parties appearing before the Court cooperate in providing evidence.[12]

1.2.2. The Finding of Damages

If the ECtHR finds a violation of the Convention, it does not automatically award a just satisfaction.[13] The Court will only award just satisfaction

appl. no. 25760/94, §165; *Rupa v. Romania*, 16 December 2008, appl. no. 58478/00, §97; *El-Masri v. The former Yugoslav Republic of Macedonia*, 13 December 2012 (Grand Chamber), appl. no. 39630/09, §152; *Reshetnyak v. Russia*, 8 January 2013, appl. no. 56027/10, §92; *Lonić v. Croatia*, 4 December 2014, appl. no. 8067/12, §72; and *Varga et al. v. Hungary*, 10 March 2015, appl. nos. 14097/12, 45135/12, 73712/12, 34001/13, 44055/13 and 64586/13, §68.

10 Nevertheless, the Court is sometimes criticized for being too strict in its approach to change the burden of proof to the state: Partly Dissenting Opinion of Judge Bonello in *Anguelova v. Bulgaria*, 13 June 2002, appl. no. 38361/97, §§10–13.

11 *Khayletdinov v. Russia*, 12 January 2016, appl. no. 2763/13, §108.

12 *Salman v. Turkey*, 27 June 2000 (Grand Chamber), appl. no. 21986/93, §100; *Berktay v. Turkey*, 1 March 2001, appl. no. 22493/93, §127; and *Aktaş v. Turkey*, 24 April 2003, appl. no. 24351/94, §270.

13 *Ryabykh v. Russia*, 24 July 2003, appl. no. 52854/99, §§67–68; *Timofeyev v. Russia*, 23 October 2003, appl. no. 58263/00, §§51–52; *Vasyagin v. Russia*, 22 September 2005, appl. no. 75475/01, §40; *Yayan v. Turkey*, 2 February 2006, appl. no. 66848/01, §25; *Sidorenko v. Russia*, 26 July 2007, appl. no. 4459/03, §§35–36; *Larionov v. Russia*, 14 November 2008, appl. no. 42431/02, §33; *Rysev v. Russia*, 18 June 2009, appl. no. 924/03, §41; P. Leach, *Taking a Case to the European Court of Human Rights*, Oxford, Oxford University Press, 2011, at 468; J. Sharpe, 'Article 50' in L.E. Pettiti, E. Decaux and P.-H. Imbert (eds.), *La Convention Européenne des droits de l'homme. Commentaire Article par Article*, Paris, Economica, 1999, p809 at 812–813; D. Shelton, *Remedies in International Human Rights Law*, Oxford, Oxford University Press, 1999, at 189; E. Steiner, 'Just Satisfaction under Art. 41 ECHR: A compromise in 1950 – Problematic Now' in A. Fenyves, E. Karner, H. Koziol and E. Steiner (eds.), *Tort Law in the Jurisprudence of the European Court of Human Rights*, Göttingen, De Gruyter, 2011, p3 at 13; K. Reid, *A practitioner's guide to the European Convention on Human Rights*, London, Thomson, 2008, 603.

if it is effectively claimed[14] in due time.[15] The Court also does not award a just satisfaction if the applicants indicate that they only want to get a proclamation of the violation from the Court.[16] If on the other hand a defendant does not make any objections against the satisfaction that the applicant claims, the Court will award the claimed satisfaction.[17] One can

---

14 Article 60 of the Rules of Court, 1 September 2012; 6 November 1980 (just satisfaction) (Plenary), appl. no. 6538/74, §14; *Benthem v. the Netherlands*, 23 October 1985 (Plenary), appl. no. 8848/80, §45; *Deumeland v. Germany*, 29 May 1986 (Plenary), appl. no. 9384/81, §98; *Inze v. Austria*, 28 October 1987, appl. no. 8695/79, §46; *Bouamar v. Belgium*, 29 February 1988, appl. no. 9106/80, §68; *Ekbatani v. Sweden*, 26 May 1988 (Plenary), appl. no. 10563/83, §34; *Brogan v. the United Kingdom*, 30 May 1989 (just satisfaction) (Plenary), appl. nos. 11209/84, 11234/84, 11266/84 and 11386/85, §7; *Kostovski v. the Netherlands*, 20 November 1989 (Plenary), appl. no. 11454/85, §46; *Huvig v. France*, 24 April 1990, appl. no. 11105/84, §38; *Nasri v. France*, 13 July 1995, appl. no. 19465/92, §49; *Moore and Gordon v. the United Kingdom*, 29 September 1999, appl. nos. 36529/97 and 37393/97, §27; *Coëme et al. v. Belgium*, 22 June 2000, appl. nos. 32492/96, 32547/96, 32548/96, 33209/96 and 33210/96, §155; *Porubova v. Russia*, 8 October 2009, appl. no. 8237/03, §53; *Tkachevy v. Russia*, 4 April 2013 (just satisfaction), appl. no. 35430/05, §16; *Delvina v. Albania*, 21 May 2013 (just satisfaction), appl. no. 49106/06, §18; *Frendo Randon et al. v. Malta*, 9 July 2013 (just satisfaction), appl. no. 2226/10, §28; and *Albergas and Arlauskas v. Lithuania*, 27 May 2014, appl. no. 17978/05, §37. See also: T. Barkhuysen and M.L. Van Emmerik, 'Rechtsherstel bij schending van het EVRM in Nederland en Straatsburg', *NJCM-Bulletin* 2006, p39 at 47; F. Edel, 'L'indemnisation par la Cour européenne des droits de l'homme des victimes de violations de la liberté d'expression' in J.-F. Flauss and E. Lambert Abdelgawad (eds.), *La pratique d'indemnisation par la Cour européenne des droits de l'homme*, Brussels, Bruylant, 2011, p229 at 234; and D. Scorey and T. Eicke, *Human Rights Damages. Principles and Practices*, London, Sweet & Maxwell, at A2–12.

15 If the claim for compensation reaches the Court too late, it will in principle not award just satisfaction: *Vučković et al. v. Serbia*, 28 August 2012 (Grand Chamber), appl. nos. 17153/11, et al., §93; *Anđelković v. Serbia*, 9 April 2013, appl. no. 1401/08, §33; *Malofeyeva v. Russia*, 30 May 2013, appl. no. 36673/04, §147; *Neshkov et al. v. Bulgaria*, 27 January 2015, appl. nos. 36925/10, 21487/12, 72893/12, 73196/12, 77718/12 and 9717/13, §303; and *Traustason et al. v. Iceland*, 4 May 2017, appl. no. 44081/13, §60.

16 *Deweer v. Belgium*, 27 February 1980, appl. no. 6903/75, §59; *Pham Hoang v. France*, 25 September 1992, appl. no. 13191/87, §45; and *Tolstoy Miloslavsky v. the United Kingdom*, 13 July 1995, appl. no. 18139/91, §§69–72. In one case the Court required that a waiver for a compensation is made explicitly: *NeuMayster v. Austria*, 7 May 1974 (just satisfaction), appl. no. 1936/63, §36.

17 *De Jong, Baljet and Van den Brink v. the Netherlands*, 22 May 1984, appl. nos. 8805/79, 8806/79 and 9242/81, §65; and *Akdeniz et al. v. Turkey*, 31 May 2001, appl. no. 23954/94, §129. It is also possible that a party does not object to a part of the claimed damages and that the Court afterwards compensates the full damages on an equitable basis: *Berrehab v. the Netherlands*, 21 June 1988, appl. no. 10730/84, §§33–34. The same principles also apply to procedural costs: *Airey v. Ireland*, 6 February 1981 (just satisfaction), appl. no. 6289/73, §13; and *Johnston et al. v. Ireland*, 18 December 1986 (Plenary), appl. no. 9697/82, §86. If an applicant claims procedural costs and the defendant state does not object to this claim, the Court will award the claimed costs: *Belilos v. Switzerland*, 29 April 1988 (Plenary), appl. no. 10328/83, §81;

thus conclude that the Court starts considering the award of just satisfaction by examining the will of the parties and not the size of the damages.

The burden of proof lies with the applicant who must document his claims.[18] As a consequence, the Court refuses to award a satisfaction if the applicant cannot prove the existence of the claimed damages.[19] In principle, it seems as if the applicant also has to prove the size of the damages. In the case of *Ausiello* the Court for example found that the violation of the reasonable time requirement 'certainly suffered prejudice', but it did not award a sum of money because it had no precise quantification at hand.[20] In the same way, in *Mehmet Şentürk and Bekir Şentürk* the Court rejected a claim for pecuniary damages for the violation of the right to life, but it awarded a very high sum of money for non-pecuniary damages.[21] Another example can be found in *Storck*. The Court in this case refused to grant compensation for the loss of income to an applicant who had been locked up in a psychiatric clinic for a year in a way that violated the Convention because it could not speculate what the income of the applicant would have been if she had not had been locked up in the clinic.[22]

In *Buzescu*, a case concerning a lawyer who had been excluded from the Bar,[23] and where the applicant had claimed compensation for his loss of income, the Court could not calculate the precise size of the damages but nevertheless found that there had been a loss:

> An award may still be made notwithstanding the large number of imponderables involved in the assessment of future losses, though the greater the lapse of time involved the more uncertain the link becomes between the breach and the damage.[24]

Wassink v. the Netherlands, 27 September 1990, appl. no. 12535/86, §42; and *Koendjbiharie v. the Netherlands*, 25 October 1990, appl. no. 11487/85, §35. On the other hand, the Court can also accept an offer of the defendant state that is smaller than the claimed damages: *Van Leer v. the Netherlands*, 21 February 1990, appl. no. 11509/85, §§41–42.

18 Article 60 of the *Rules of Court*, 1 September 2012; and C. Kissling and D. Kelliher, 'Compensation for Pecuniary and Non-Pecuniary Loss' in A. Fenyves, E. Karner, H. Koziol and E. Steiner (eds.), *Tort Law in the Jurisprudence of the European Court of Human Rights*, Göttingen, De Gruyter, 2011, p579 at 587.

19 *Savda v. Turkey (no.2)*, 15 November 2016, appl. no. 2458/12, §32; and *Dinu v. Romania*, 7 February 2017, appl. no. 64356/14, §90.

20 21 May 1996, appl. no. 20331/92.

21 9 April 2013, appl. no. 13423/09, §115. See also: 9 April 2013, appl. no. 62590/09, §40.

22 16 June 2005, appl. no. 61603/00, §172ff.

23 24 May 2005, appl. no. 61302/00, §107.

24 *Ibid.*, §105. See also: 28 June 2016 (just satisfaction), appl. no. 70945/11 et al., §47.

Although in principle the ECtHR requires applicants to prove the existence and the size of the damages, the case of *Buzescu* illustrates that the Court does not always apply the second requirement in a strict manner. Sometimes it seems as if an applicant only has to document the existence of his damages. Nevertheless, if the Court requires applicants to provide further evidence on the size of their damages, and the applicants refuse to offer such evidence, the Court sometimes refuses to grant compensation.[25]

Even more remarkable is the fact that the Court sometimes awards a just satisfaction for non-pecuniary damages in cases where the applicants have not claimed them. It does so in cases where it found violations of Arts 2, 3 and/or 5, arguing that it normally does not award satisfaction if the applicants did not claim it, but that these cases concern very serious violations of fundamental,[26] or even absolute,[27] rights of the Convention. As far as is known, the Court awarded a just satisfaction to an applicant for a violation of another Convention right in only one case. This was *X v. Croatia*, where the Court found a violation of Arts 6 and 8 for the reason that a daughter had been given up for adoption without her mother's knowledge, consent or participation in the adoption proceedings and without the mother having ever been formally divested of her parental rights.[28] Since one cannot doubt the seriousness of this violation of the Convention, it seems that in this case the seriousness of the violation can also explain the award of compensation for non-pecuniary damages. As a result, it seems that the Court sometimes awards satisfactions for non-pecuniary damages to elaborate the efficiency of the Convention by strengthening the dissuasive effect.[29]

---

25 5 December 2017, appl. no. 16554/06, §§19–21.

26 With regard to Art. 2 see: *Kats et al. v. Ukraine*, 18 December 2008, appl. no. 29971/04, §149. With regard to Art. 5 see: *Rusu v. Austria*, 2 October 2008, appl. no. 34082/02, §62; *Khudyakova v. Russia*, 8 January 2009, appl. no. 13476/04, §107; and *Crabtree v. The Czech Republic*, 25 February 2010, appl. no. 41116/04, §60.

27 With regard to Art. 3 see: *Mayzit v. Russia*, 20 January 2005, appl. no. 63378/00, §88; *Igor Ivanov v. Russia*, 7 June 2007, appl. no. 34000/02, §50; *Babushkin v. Russia*, 18 October 2007, appl. no. 67253/01, §62; *Chember v. Russia*, 3 July 2008, appl. no. 7188/03, §77; *Nadrosov v. Russia*, 31 July 2008, appl. no. 9297/02, §54; *Denisenko and Bogdanchikov v. Russia*, 12 February 2009, appl. no. 3811/02, §142; *Alibekov v. Russia*, 14 May 2009, appl. no. 8413/02, §73; *Vladimir Fedorov v. Russia*, 30 July 2009, appl. no. 19223/04, §87; *Maksimov v. Azerbaijan*, 8 October 2009, appl. no. 38228/05, §98; *Dorogaykin v. Russia*, 10 February 2011, appl. no. 1066/05, §49; *Chudun v. Russia*, 21 June 2011, appl. no. 20641/04, §129; *Grigoryev v. Russia*, 23 October 2012, appl. no. 22663/06, §103; *Borodin v. Russia*, 6 November 2012, appl. no. 41867/04, §166; and *Neshkov et al. v. Bulgaria*, 27 January 2015, appl. nos. 36925/10, 21487/12, 72893/12, 73196/12, 77718/12 and 9717/13, §303; and *Traustason et al. v. Iceland*, 4 May 2017, appl. no. 44081/13, §302.

28 *X. v. Croatia*, 17 July 2008, appl. no. 11223/04.

29 In one case, Judge Sajo found that the majority made an unproportionate decision by rejecting a claim that reached the Court four days too late: Partly concurring and

2. THE BENEFICIARIES

2.1. THE INJURED PARTY

Regarding the people who can claim a just satisfaction before the ECtHR, Art. 41 only refers to the *injured party.* According to the doctrine, the injured party is the person who is directly affected or the individual applicant.[30] The individual applicant is the person who is the victim of a human rights violation in the meaning of Art. 34. Because of this, everyone who can file a claim before the Court, can claim compensation under Art. 41.[31] This also applies to states, when they file a claim against another state.[32] This raises the question as to the conditions under which one can file a claim before the Court. To file a claim before the ECtHR, an applicant has to demonstrate that he is personally and directly affected by the alleged human rights violation.[33] In *Brudnicka*, the Court moreover found that:

> to be a victim of a violation of the Convention, there must be a sufficiently direct link between the applicant and the harm which they consider they have sustained on account of the alleged violation.[34]

---

partly dissenting opinion of Judge Sajo in *Vučković et al. v. Serbia*, 28 August 2012 (Grand Chamber), appl. no. 17153/11, et al.

30 F. Bydlinski, 'Methodological Approaches', 2011, above n. 4, p29 at 69; D. Shelton, *Remedies*, 1999, above n. 13, at 183; D. Scorey and T. Eicke, *Human Rights Damages*, above n. 14, at A1-09; E. Steiner, 'Just Satisfaction under Art. 41 ECHR', 2011, above n. 13, p3 at 13; L. Zwaak, 'The Procedure before the European Court of Human rights' in P. Van Dijk, F. Van Hoof, A. Van Rijn and L. Zwaak (eds.), *Theory and Practice of the European Convention on Human Rights*, Antwerp, Intersentia, 2006, p95 at 258; M.L. Van Emmerik, *Schadevergoeding bij schending van mensenrechten. De rechtspraktijk onder het EVRM vergeleken met die in Nederland*, Stichting NJCM-Boekerij, Leiden, 1997, at 88; K. Wolfram, 'Just Satisfaction in Art 41 ECHR and Public International Law – Issues of Interpretation and Review of International Materials' in A. Fenyves, E. Karner, H. Koziol and E. Steiner (eds.), *Tort Law in the Jurisprudence of the European Court of Human Rights*, Göttingen, De Gruyter, 2011, p345 at 353. A third party that gives an opinion in a case cannot, however, claim just satisfaction: *Koua Poirrez v. France*, 30 September 2003, appl. no. 40892/98, §69.

31 O. Ichim, *Just Satisfaction under the European Convention on Human Rights*, Cambridge, Cambridge University Press, 2015, at 79.

32 B. Rainey, E. Wicks and C. Ovey, *Jacobs, White and Ovey: The European Convention on Human Rights*, Oxford, Oxford University Press, 2017, at 52.

33 P. Leach, *Taking a Case to the European Court*, 2011, above n. 13, at 115.

34 *Brudnicka et al. v. Poland*, 3 March 2003, appl. no. 54723/00, §26. See also the references in this case.

What is interesting about this phrase, is that the ECtHR quite clearly indicates that to be a victim of a human rights violation, one has to sustain harm. The Court seems to indicate that damages are somehow linked to the infringements of interests. The Court only requires a sufficient direct link, which seems to indicate that it is willing to accept a broader notion of beneficiaries than merely the direct victim of the human rights violation. What is also worth mentioning is that it is not required that the human rights violation should have already occurred. An applicant can also bring a case before the Court if there exists a real risk that he will become victim of a human rights violation in the future.[35]

Although the Court finds that the notion of applicants is broader than merely the direct victim of the human rights violation, it does not accept an *actio popularis.* One cannot bring a case before the Court in order to contest national measures or laws that might violate the Convention if the applicants themselves are not affected by the measures.[36] The Court does accept that someone can contest a measure or a law that will potentially harm the interests of the applicant for the reason that he is a member of a group that will be affected by the measure or law.[37] By appealing to this reasoning, in the past applicants have been allowed to contest legislation that made it possible for the police to tap telephones and check the post, although these applicants could not prove that their mail or telephone had been intercepted by the police.[38]

---

35 P. Leach, *Taking a Case to the European Court*, above n. 13, 2011, at 115.

36 *Klass et al. V. Germany*, 6 September 1978 (Plenary), appl. no. 5029/71, §33; *Norris v. Ireland*, 26 October 1988 (Plenary), appl. no. 10581/83, §30; *Russian Conservative Party of Entrepreneurs et al. v. Russia*, 11 January 2007, appl. nos. 55066/00 and 55638/00, §77; *Burden v. the United Kingdom*, 29 April 2008 (Grand Chamber), appl. no. 13378/05, §§33–34; *ReligionsgeMaynschaft der zeugen Jehovas et al. v. Austria*, 31 July 2008, appl. no. 40825/98, §90; *Tănase v. Moldavia*, 27 April 2010 (Grand Chamber), appl. no. 7/08, §104; and *Michaud v. France*, 6 December 2012, appl. no. 12323/11, §51. See also: H. McGregor, *McGregor on Damages*, London, Sweet & Maxwell, 2009, at 1733; H. Krüger and C. Norgaard, 'The Right of Application' in R. Macdonald, F. Matscher en H. Petzold (eds.), *The European System for the Protection of Human Rights*, Dordrecht, Martinus Nijhoff Publishers, 1993, p657 at 663 and L. Zwaak, 'General Survey of the European Convention' in P. Van Dijk, F. Van Hoof, A. Van Rijn and L. Zwaak (eds.), *Theory and Practice of the European Convention on Human Rights*, Antwerp, Intersentia, 2006, p1 at 55.

37 *Marckx v. Belgium*, 13 June 1979 (Plenary), appl. no. 6833/74, §27; *Johnston et al. v. Ireland*, 18 December 1986 (Plenary), appl. no. 9697/82, §42; *Open Door and Dublin Well Woman v. Ireland*, 29 October 1992 (Plenary), appl. nos. 14234/88 and 14235/88, §§41ff; and *Burden v. the United Kingdom*, 29 April 2008 (Grand Chamber), appl. no. 13378/05, §34.

38 *Klass et al. V. Germany*, 6 September 1978, appl. no. 5029/71, §34.

2.2. JURISTIC PERSONS

Article 34 ECHR allows 'non-governmental organisations' to bring a case before the ECtHR for an alleged violation of the Convention. Accordingly, there is no doubt as to whether juristic persons can contest human rights violations.[39] This does not mean that corporations have the same rights under the Convention as natural persons. First and foremost, some Convention rights by their nature cannot be attributed to juristic persons.[40] The Court for example found that juristic persons cannot appeal to the right to life (Art. 2) since this is a right that is 'an inalienable attribute of human beings.'[41] The same is true for the prohibition of torture (Art. 3),[42] the protection of personal liberty (Art. 5) and the right to marry (Art. 12).[43]

A juristic person has to illustrate that it has an interest in bringing a case before the Court.[44] Since juristic persons are always found to pursue a specific aim, it is necessary to control whether the alleged violation conforms to the character and aims of a juristic person. The Court for instance accepts that a church may bring a case before the Court for the alleged violation of the right to freedom of religion,[45] but it will not accept a complaint on an alleged violation of the right to privacy of an organization

---

39 J.-P. Costa, 'The provision of compensation under Article 41 of the European Convention on Human Rights' in D. Fairgrieve, M. Adenas and J. Bell (eds.), *Tort Liability of Public Authorities in Comparative Perspective*, London, The British Institute of International and Comparative Law, 2002, p3 at 5; F. Jacobs, R. White and C. Ovey, *The European Convention on Human Rights*, Oxford, Oxford University Press, 2010, at 30–31; V. Wilcox, *A Company's Right to Damage for Non-Pecuniary Loss*, Cambridge, Cambridge University Press, 2016, at 34ff; A. Schild, 'De betekenis van artikel 1, eerste protocol voor het ondernemingsrecht', *NJCM-Bulletin* 2007, p603 at 604. Thus, the Court sometimes finds violations of the Convention rights of legal person, e.g.: *Özgür Gündem v. Turkey*, 16 March 2000, appl. no. 23144/93, §71; *Comingersoll S.A. v. Portugal*, 6 April 2000 (Grand Chamber), appl. no. 35382/97, §36; *SC Editura Orizonturi SRL v. Romania*, 13 May 2008, appl. no. 15872/03, §89; and *Dacia S.R.L. v. Moldavia*, 24 February 2009 (just satisfaction), appl. no. 3052/04, §60.

40 For an in-depth study on this topic see: V. Wilcox, *A Company's Right to Damage for Non-Pecuniary Loss*, 2016, above n. 39, at 40ff.

41 *K-HW v. Germany*, 22 March 2001 (Grand Chamber), appl. no. 37201/97, §96.

42 EComHR, *Verein Kontakt-Information-Therapie (KIT) and Hagen v. Austria*, 12 October 1998 (Decision), appl. no. 11921/86.

43 V. Wilcox, *A Company's Right to Damage*, 2016, above n. 39, at 49–50.

44 EComHR, *X. v. Germany*, 14 July 1981 (Decision), appl. no. 9234/81.

45 *Metropolitan Church of Bessarabia et al. v. Moldavia*, 13 December 2001, appl. no. 45701/99, §101.

that champions rights for homosexuals.[46] For an alleged violation of the right to privacy, the members of the organization have to sue the government personally. In some cases, the ECtHR has also accepted the fact that public legal persons can bring a case before the Court for alleged human rights violations. Indeed, the Court has allowed autonomous radio stations that were state-owned to bring a case before the Court in case they operate as a player in a wider market and in case they have a certain degree of autonomy.[47]

The approach of the Court in allowing corporations to bring a case before it is rather flexible. A remarkable illustration of this flexibility was shown in the recent case *Center for Legal Resources on behalf of Valentin Câmpeanu.*[48] In this case, the non-governmental organization *Center for Legal Resources* brought a case before the ECtHR for the alleged violation of the right to life of Valentin Câmpeanu. The Center did so because Valentin Câmpeanu had died and had no relatives who could have filed a claim. Since the Court found that the right to life must be protected in any case, whether or not there are relatives, it found the request admissible. This case clearly illustrates that the Court always tries to protect the Convention rights[49] in an effective manner.

The fact that juristic persons can bring a case before the Court does not automatically have as a consequence that they can also receive a just satisfaction on the basis of Art. 41. At first glance it seems clear that this must be possible. Since juristic persons can bring a case before the Court, they can appeal to Art. 41 and thus receive a just satisfaction.[50] Nevertheless, the Court might interpret the provision in a way so that it does not apply to juristic persons. It might be that the Court judges that a juristic person, because of its statutory function, cannot receive compensation for some pecuniary or non-pecuniary damages.

With regard to the possibility of corporations receiving a just satisfaction for pecuniary damages, the jurisprudence of the ECtHR does not seem

---

46 EComHR, *Norris and National Gay Federation v. Ireland, Norris and National Gay Federation v. Ireland*, 16 May 1985 (Decision), appl. no. 10581/83.

47 *Radio France et al. v. France*, 23 September 2003 (Decision), appl. no. 53984/00 and *Österreichischer Rundfunk v. Austria*, 7 December 2006, appl. no. 35841/02, §§46–54.

48 *Centre for Legal Resources on behalf of Valentin Câmpeanu v. Romania*, 17 July 2014 (Grand Chamber), appl. no. 47848/08. The applicants in this case did not claim damages.

49 For an in-depth analysis of this case and its consequences, see: H. Keller and A. Garin, 'Câmpeanu: quo vadis? – Le recours individuel en péril' *Revue Trimestrielle des Droits de l'Homme* 2017, 485–509.

50 M.L. Van Emmerik, *Schadevergoeding*, 1997, above n. 30, at 134.

to pose many problems. Corporations can receive compensation for pecuniary damages.[51] For non-profit organizations this question is more complicated. An interesting case on this topic, is *Open Door and Dublin Well Woman*.[52] The applicants here were two non-profit organizations in Ireland that informed women on health topics and advised women that although abortion was prohibited in Ireland, they could go to England to have an abortion. The government found that the help these organizations offered in finding a way to get an abortion violated the right to life of an unborn child as enshrined in the Irish constitution. Consequently, they ordered the non-profit organizations to cease their activities. When these organizations filed a complaint before the ECtHR, the Court found that the prohibition on giving information on abortion violated the right to free speech. The Court remarked that the right to free speech also protects contested opinions. As a result, the organization Dublin Well Woman claimed a compensation of 62,172 Irish pounds under Art. 41 for the reason that it had suffered a loss of income because it had to stop its activities during a certain period. Although the Irish state argued that a non-profit organization cannot claim to have suffered a loss of income since it does not pursue profit, the Court awarded a just satisfaction of 25,000 Irish pounds for this category of damages.[53]

Regarding the possibility of juristic persons receiving compensation for non-pecuniary damages, more problems come to the surface. At present there is no doubt that this is possible, as was cogently demonstrated by Vanessa Wilcox.[54] The first plea for this possibility was given in *Open Door and Dublin Well Woman* where in his dissenting opinion Judge Matscher argued that it should be recognized that idealistic or non-profit corporations can suffer non-pecuniary damages.[55] This, however, was only the opinion of one judge in a dissenting opinion. The jurisprudence suggests that the ECtHR did not accept this possibility for a long time. For example, in *Manifattura FL*, the Court judged that a corporation

---

51 *Union Alimentaria Sanders SA v. Spain*, 7 July 1989, appl. no. 11681/85, §45; and 9 February 1993 (just satisfaction), appl. no. 12742/87, §15.

52 *Open Door and Dublin Well Woman v. Ireland*, 29 October 1992 (Plenary), appl. nos. 14234/88 and 14235/88.

53 29 October 1992, §§85–87.

54 V. Wilcox, *A Company's Right to Damage*, 2016, above n. 39, at 62ff.

55 This judge found that an idealistic organization that does not pursue profit can suffer non-pecuniary damages: Partly dissenting opinion of Judge Matscher in *Open Door and Dublin Well Woman v. Ireland*, 29 October 1992 (Plenary), appl. nos. 14234/88 and 14235/88, §5.

could not be awarded compensation for the violation of the reasonable time requirement.[56] In its conclusions, the Court noted that this was a commercial corporation, but that specification does not seem to matter. Indeed, why should a corporation because of its commercial character not be frightened and distressed because of the excessive length of legal procedures? In the case of *Matos and Silva Lda. et al.*, the Court seemed to change its jurisprudence. Here, the Court awarded a just satisfaction for the distress that was caused by the excessive length of a legal procedure. There were however two applicants in this case, a corporation and a person, and since the Court did not specify to whom it awarded the satisfaction,[57] one cannot be sure about the impact of this judgment.

By the mid-1990s, it seemed that the Court had definitively changed its jurisprudence in the sense that corporations could be awarded a just satisfaction for non-pecuniary damages. The first case that paved the way for this was *Vereinigung Demokratischer Soldaten Österreichs and Gubi.* Although the Court here did not award a sum of money to the applicants, it declared that the mere finding of a human rights violation in this case offered sufficient satisfaction for the non-pecuniary damages that the applicants had suffered.[58] From 2000 onwards, this jurisprudence was confirmed in different cases. The Court in this period awarded a sum of money to profit- and non-profit corporations for the non-pecuniary damages that were caused by the violation of the freedom of assembly,[59] by the violation of the reasonable time requirement,[60] and by the violation of the right to have access to a court.[61] Just as was the case with the admissibility criteria, the Court did so on the basis of the principle of effectivity:

> The Court reiterates that, if the rights guaranteed by the Convention are to be effective, it must necessarily be empowered to award pecuniary compensation for non-pecuniary damage also to commercial companies. In such cases, account should be taken of the company's reputation, uncertainty in decision-planning, disruption in the management of the company (for which there is no precise

56 *Manifattura FL v. Italy*, 27 February 1992, appl. no. 12407/86, §22.

57 *Matos e Silva Lda. et al. v. Portugal*, 16 September 1996, appl. no. 15777/89, §40.

58 *Vereinigung Demokratischer Soldaten Österreichs and Gubi v. Austria*, 19 December 1994, appl. no. 15153/89, §62.

59 *Freedom and Democracy Party (Özdep) v. Turkey*, 8 December 1999 (Grand Chamber), appl. no. 23885/94, §57.

60 *Comingersoll S.A. v. Portugal*, 6 April 2000 (Grand Chamber), appl. no. 35382/97, §36; *Bielectric S.R.L. v. Italy*, 16 November 2000, appl. no. 36811/97, §28; *Société Comabat v. France*, 26 March 2002, appl. no. 51818/99, §19; and *Begus v. Slovenia*, 15 December 2011, appl. no. 25634/05.

61 *S.A. Sotiris and Nikos Koutras Attee v. Greece*, 16 November 2000, appl. no. 39442/98, §29.

method of calculating the consequences) and lastly the anxiety and inconvenience caused to the members of the management team.[62]

With this jurisprudence, it became clear that the Court accepts the possibility that juristic persons can suffer non-pecuniary damages, but it only does so under specific circumstances.[63] Moreover, even if it does award compensation for non-pecuniary damages, it seems that they are often more limited than the compensation that the Court would award to natural persons, as was demonstrated with regard to compensation for violations of the right to privacy.[64] A corporation can only suffer non-pecuniary damages in cases where the reputation of the corporation is harmed, when the violation caused disruption in the management or when the violation caused anxiety because of inconvenience to the members of the management of the team.[65] Since it is hard to imagine that a violation of a Convention right does not cause any anxiety or inconvenience to the members of the management of a corporation, the limitations of the possibility of corporations to receive a just satisfaction for non-pecuniary damages seems to be rather theoretical. Indeed, since some countries only accept the existence of non-pecuniary damages for the head of a corporation if the honor and reputation of a corporation is violated,[66] it seems that the ECtHR might force some national states to broaden their approach.

2.3. YOUNG CHILDREN AND MENTALLY ILL PERSONS

Another question to pose is whether young and disabled persons are able to receive compensation for non-pecuniary damages. An answer to this

62 *Comingersoll S.A. v. Portugal*, 6 April 2000 (Grand Chamber), appl. no. 35382/97, §35 and *Meltex Ltd and Movsesyan v. Armenia*, 17 June 2008, appl. no. 32283/04, §105.

63 For instance, the German *Bundesverfassungsgericht* judged that legal persons cannot have personal rights such as the right to free speech: *Bundesverfassungsgericht* 18 November 2004. See on this theme: J. Fëdtke, 'Germany' in H. Koziol and B. Steininger (eds.), *European Tort Law 2005*, Vienna, Springer, 2006, p281 at 290–291.

64 B. van der Sloot, 'Where is the Harm in a Privacy Violation? Calculating the Damages Afforded in Privacy Cases by the European Court of Human Rights' *J.Intell.Prop.Info. Tech.&Elec.Com.L.* 2017, at 333–336.

65 *Rodinná záložna, spořitelní a úvěrní družstvo et al. v. the Czech Republic*, 19 January 2012 (just satisfaction), appl. no. 74152/01, §16.

66 This is for instance the case in Belgium: M. Coipel, 'Introduction au droit des societies et autres groupenements' in X. (ed.), *Guide juridique de l'entreprise*, Book 11.1., Brussels, Kluwer, 2002, p1 at 14.

question cannot be formulated easily. Since non-pecuniary damages can only be redressed in a symbolic way by awarding a sum of money, it seems possible to argue that young children and mentally ill persons are not able to understand the compensatory function of a sum of money.[67] This approach might conflict with Art. 13 since this provision not only requires that a remedy exists for mentally ill persons who become victims of human rights abuses,[68] but also requires that for a remedy to be effective, financial compensation is required.[69] Moreover, Art. 13 can be read together with the principle of equality as enshrined in Art. 14. And although the Court has never applied Art. 14 in conjunction with Art. 13 in this way, it must be stressed that it does find that Art. 14 contains a positive obligation to provide facilities for disabled persons.[70]

Although it seems likely from the perspective of Arts 13 and 14 of the Convention that young children should be granted a sum of money as compensation for non-pecuniary damages, the ECtHR itself has not always done so. In the case of *Sylvester* for example, the Court found a violation of Arts 6 and 8 for the reason that a state did not enforce a judgment where the right of custody of a child was granted to the father.[71] With regard to Art. 41, the Court in this case awarded a sum of €20,000 for the father's non-pecuniary damages because it saw no reason 'to doubt that the first applicant suffered distress as a result of the non-enforcement of the return order and that sufficient just satisfaction would not be provided solely by the finding of a violation.'[72] With regard to the non-pecuniary damages of the two-year-old daughter, the Court found that the mere

---

67 For Belgian law see: J. Ronse, L. De Wilde, A. Claeys and I. Mallems, *Schade en schadeloosstelling*, Ghent, Story-Scientia, 1984, at 379. However, in most countries young children and mentally ill persons can receive financial compensation for non-pecuniary damages: House of Lords, *H. West & Son*, 1963, 2 All ER 625; W. Van Gerven et al. (eds.), *Casebook on Torts*, Oxford, Hart Publishing, 2000, 99 (for England); Hoge Raad 20 September 2002, *RvdW* 2002, 142 (for the Netherlands); Cass.fr. 3 April 1978, *J.C.P.* 1979, II, 19168, noot S. Brousseau; Cass.fr. 22 February 1995, *Rev.trim.dr.civ.* 1995, 639 (for France). In French law, there are however authors who criticize this possibility, see: P. Brun, *Responsabilité civile extracontractuelle*, Paris, Lexisnexis, 2014, at 136–138.

68 *X and Y v. the Netherlands*, 26 March 1985 (Grand Chamber), appl. no. 8978/80.

69 As seen in the first part of this book.

70 O. De Schutter, 'Reasonable Accommodation and Positive Obligations in the European Convention on Human Rights' in A. Lawson and C. Gooding (eds.), *Disability Rights in Europe: From Theory to Practice*, Oxford, Hart Publishing, 2005, 35–64; and B. Rainey, E. Wicks and C. Ovey, *Jacobs, White and Ovey: The European Convention on Human Rights*, 2017, above n. 32, at 652–654.

71 *Sylvester v. Austria*, 24 April 2003, appl. nos. 36812/97 and 40104/98, §§72 and 77.

72 *Ibid.*, §84.

declaration of a violation constituted a just satisfaction.[73] It did not give any reason as to why it found that it did not have to award a sum of money to the daughter. However, Judges Bonello, Tulkens and Vajic did not agree with this approach and formulated the following critiques in their partly dissenting opinion:

> Personally, we do not share the view that, owing to its tender age, the child has not suffered or may not in the future suffer any non-pecuniary damage (such as stress or anxiety) of its own, warranting an award of compensation for the violation of Article 8 of the Convention which the Court has found as a result of the Austrian authorities' failure to take, without delay, the measures they could reasonably have been expected to take in order to enforce the return order, in breach of the second applicant's right to respect for her family life (see paragraph 72 of the judgment). We consider that, as in the Scozzari and Giunta v. Italy judgment of 13 July 2000, in which the Court held that it had to take into account the non-pecuniary damage sustained by the children in view of their position as applicants (§253), the Court should have granted the second applicant, whose conduct cannot be criticised in any way, compensation reflecting the level of damage she sustained.[74]

It is from this partly dissenting opinion that we learn that the Court found that the daughter could not be awarded a sum of money 'owing to its tender age'. The Court does not always have to exclude the possibility of receiving a sum of money as a means to compensate non-pecuniary damages: it can also take the young age into account when estimating the size of compensation for the reason that it only grants financial redress for future damages, or in other words for the time that the young child will be aware of her loss. This seems to have happened in the case of *Z. et al. v. the United Kingdom*:

> The report on C indicated that she was not psychiatrically ill and was coping well, rendering the conclusion that she had emotional and practical difficulties beyond the average girl of her age difficult to understand. The statements concerning likely future need and alleged impact of the failure of the compensation claim were unsupported by the evidence.[75]

---

73 Similarly: *Iosub Caras v. Romania*, 27 July 2006, appl. no. 7198/04, §62.

74 Joint partly dissenting opinion of Judges Bonelle, Tulkens and Vajic in *Sylvester v. Austria*, 24 April 2003, appl. nos. 36812/97 and 40104/98.

75 *Z. et al. v. the United Kingdom*, 10 May 2005 (Grand Chamber), appl. no. 29392/95, §117.

Indeed, the fact that the Court in *Z. et al. v. the United Kingdom* only granted financial redress for future damages seems to be in accordance with *Sylvester*. In *Sylvester*, there were no future damages, so it seems obvious that the Court did not award a just satisfaction to the two-year-old child. Another possible explanation that might be given in these cases is the fact that the Court, as discussed later in this book, takes into account the total amount of damages for non-pecuniary damages that it awards to all the human rights victims. Indeed, in both *Sylvester* and *Z. et al. v. the United Kingdom*, the Court also awarded a sum of money to the relatives of the young child.

With regard to mentally disabled persons, it seems that the Court accepts that mentally disabled persons can receive financial compensation for immaterial damages. Indeed, in *X and Y v. the Netherlands*, which concerned the impossibility for a disabled woman to file a complaint under criminal law for rape, the Court found a violation of Art. 13 and awarded a just satisfaction of €3,000 to the applicant making the following argument:

> No one contests that Miss Y suffered damage. In addition, it is hardly deniable that the Netherlands authorities have a degree of responsibility resulting from the deficiency in the legislation which gave rise to the violation of Article 8.[76]

In *Perks et al.*, the Court awarded a sum of £5,500 to compensate for the non-pecuniary damages because the mentally disabled applicant would not have been imprisoned for medical reasons if the requirements enshrined in Art. 6 had been respected.[77] Although there were also other applicants who had claimed compensation for the violation of Art. 6, the Court did not grant them monetary compensation because it found that since they were not mentally disabled, it could not speculate as to the outcome of their procedures had Art. 6 been respected.[78] Another example where the Court awarded a monetary compensation for the non-pecuniary damages of a mentally disabled person is *Pla en Puncernau*.[79]

In none of these cases did the Court examine whether mentally disabled persons understand the purpose of a financial compensation

---

76 *X and Y v. the Netherlands*, 26 March 1985 (Grand Chamber), appl. no. 8978/80, §40.

77 In this case, one witness made the following statement: 'I believe that anyone who has had contact with [the applicant] would quickly realise that he is severely mentally handicapped … There is no way that [he] has deliberately avoided paying his community charge, as I have explained, he is simply unable to understand.': *Perks et al. v. the United Kingdom*, 12 October 1999, appl. no. 25277/94 et al., §10.

78 *Ibid.*, §81.

79 *Pla and Puncernau v. Andorra*, 13 July 2004, appl. no. 69498/01, §67.

for non-pecuniary damages. It would have been possible for the Court in these cases to find that the applicants were able to understand the compensatory function of the money, but this cannot be deduced from the wordings of the judgment. The Court did not even discuss this problem in the case of *D.D. v. Lithuania*, where psychiatric institutions had raised the fact that the applicant, who claimed a monetary compensation for the violation of Arts 5 and 6 for the reason that she had been locked up without her consent, had no clue of the value of money.[80] It seems then that the ECtHR does not pay any attention to the question of whether or not a person is conscious enough to understand the relationship between receiving a sum of money and the non-pecuniary damages that he suffered, but this does not prevent the Court from awarding sums of money to very young children. Because this practice is not explained by the Court and is contradictory to its jurisprudence with regard to mentally disturbed persons, it seems advisable for the Court to abandon this approach and argue that both young children and disabled persons can receive a financial compensation for their non-pecuniary damages.

An additional argument for this approach can be found in the fact that it is often hard to distinguish non-pecuniary and pecuniary damages and that one can also ask whether mentally disabled persons or young children are able to understand the compensatory function of money that is awarded for pecuniary damages. Indeed, if persons have no clue about the value of money, it seems strange that they would understand the connection between damages caused on material issues and the receiving of a sum of money. Can one imagine that a young child or a mentally disturbed person always understands that a sum of money or even a reparation in kind is meant to compensate the loss of a pet, a stuffed animal or a family heirloom on which it attached great value?

2.4. THE SUCCESSORS OF THE DIRECTLY INJURED PARTY

Although Art. 34 of the Convention only refers to the injured party, it is clear that the successors of a directly injured party can also bring a case

---

80 *D.D. v. Lithuania*, 14 February 2012, appl. no. 13469/06. Although the Court in the similar case of *Kędzior* did not accept that an applicant was unable to accept or refuse to be locked up in a psychiatric institution (*Kędzior v. Poland*, 16 October 2012, appl. no. 45026/07, §58), it would be too far-reaching to conclude that the Court also found that the applicant was unable to understand the function of compensation for non-pecuniary damages.

before the Court.[81] With regard to Art. 41, the ECtHR does not differentiate between the personal damages of the directly injured party and the damages that the successors suffered by reflection. Indeed, in national tort law, it is possible for the successor of a directly injured party to receive compensation for the damages that the directly injured party suffered before he died and the damages that the successor suffered by reflection.[82] Since the Court does not distinguish these two categories of damages, other criteria of differentiation will be used. A distinction must be made between two sets of cases. The first set of cases concerns those where a successor brings a case before the Court because one of his relatives had died as a result of a violation of the Convention (mainly for the violation of the right to life). In these cases, the successors often suffer reflected damages because of the death of their relative. The second set of cases concerns situations where the directly injured party died for a reason that has nothing to do with the violation of the Convention. Within this last set of cases, two situations can occur. On the one hand it can happen that the directly injured party died after he brought a case before the ECtHR and his successors continued his case. On the other hand, it is possible that the directly injured party did not bring a case before the Court himself, but that his successors did so after he died. In these cases, the successors of the directly injured party often claim a compensation for the damages that the directly injured party suffered due to the violation of the Convention. They then argue that they, as heirs of the deceased person, are entitled to the compensation.

2.4.1. The Damages are Caused by the Death of a Relative

If an injured party dies because of a violation of Art. 2 or, in an exceptional case, Art. 3, his successors will be able to claim compensation under the heading of Art. 41 of the Convention.[83] This concerns the damages that

---

81 D. Harris, M. O'Boyle, E. Bates and C. Buckley, *Law of the European Convention on Human Rights*, Oxford, Oxford University Press, 2009, at 797; M.L. Van Emmerik, *Schadevergoeding*, 1997, above n. 30, at 121. It is important to note that the Court has never made a list of relatives that are able to claim a just satisfaction under Art. 41. The ability to claim compensation is judged on a case-by-case level: F. Bydlinski, 'Methodological Approaches', 2011, above n. 4, p29 at 70.

82 C. Van Dam, *European Tort Law*, Oxford, Oxford University Press, 2013, at 170.

83 *Velikova v. Bulgaria*, 18 May 2000, appl. no. 41488/98, §22; *Solomou et al. v. Turkey*, 24 June 2008, appl. no. 36832/97, §41; and *Pitsayeva et al. v. Russia*, 9 January 2014, appl. no. 53036/08 et al., §537. See also: B. Girard, *Responsabilité civile extracontractuelle et droits fondamentaux*, Paris, LGDJ, 2015, at 121–122.

the successors themselves suffered by reflection (e.g. the mental harm that is caused by the death of their relative or the loss of income or help in the household). What is interesting here is that the Court does not require the relatives to be the legal heirs of the deceased person.[84] An extramarital partner can also receive compensation for these damages.[85] If, however, the violation of another provision such as Arts 2 or 3 caused the death of the relative, the Court finds that this does not automatically create reflected damages for the successors of the directly injured party.[86]

The successors of the directly injured party can only receive compensation for the violation of a human rights provision if there is a causal link between the reflected damages of the successors and the death of the directly injured party. For reflected pecuniary damages, the applicants will have to prove that they depended on the income of the deceased person for their living.[87] With regard to this type of damages, the applicants and the defended state often make a settlement.[88] With regard to reflected non-pecuniary damages, the Court is very flexible in finding a causal link between the violation that caused the death of the relative and the reflected damages of the successors. The Court in this context accepts that the death of a relative in principle causes non-pecuniary damages.[89] This approach is very similar to the requirement in the context of Art. 13 to provide financial redress for the moral damages that are caused by a

---

84 H. McGregor, *McGregor on Damages*, London, Sweet & Maxwell, 2009, at 1734.

85 This was stated explicitly in: *Velikova v. Bulgaria*, 18 May 1999 (Decision), appl. no. 41488/98. Moreover, it must be noted that the Court awarded the full claimed damages in the judgment on the merits: *Velikova v. Bulgaria*, 18 May 2000, appl. no. 41488/98, §98.

86 'The Court has consistently rejected as inadmissible ratione personae applications lodged by the relatives of deceased persons in respect of alleged violations of rights other than those protected by Articles 2 and 3 of the Convention': *Gradinar v. Moldavia*, 8 April 2008, appl. no. 7170/02, §91. See also: *Makri et al. v. Greece*, 24 March 2005 (Decision), appl. no. 5977/03; *Bic et al. v. Turkey*, 2 February 2006, appl. no. 55955/00, §22; *Gül et al. v. Turkey*, 5 December 2006 (Decision), appl. no. 956/02; *Gakiyev and Gakiyev v. Russia*, 23 April 2009, appl. no. 3179/05, §166; and *Micallef v. Malta*, 15 October 2009 (Grand Chamber), appl. no. 17056/06, §26.

87 *Ogur v. Turkey*, 20 May 1999 (Grand Chamber), appl. no. 21594/93, §98; *Çakici v. Turkey*, 8 July 1999 (Grand Chamber), appl. no. 23657/94, §127; *Salman v. Turkey*, 27 June 2000 (Grand Chamber), appl. no. 21986/93, §137; *Öneryildiz v. Turkey*, 30 November 2004 (Grand Chamber), appl. no. 48939/99, §168; *Utsayeva et al. v. Russia*, 29 May 2008, appl. no. 29133/03, §208; and *Solomou et al. v. Turkey*, 24 June 2008, appl. no. 36832/97, §100.

88 *Diaz Ruano v. Spain*, 26 April 1994, appl. no. 16988/90, §§17–19.

89 *Velikova v. Bulgaria*, 18 May 2000, appl. no. 41488/98, §22; *Solomou et al. v. Turkey*, 24 June 2008, appl. no. 36832/97, §41; *Pitsayeva et al. v. Russia*, 9 January 2014, appl. no. 53036/08 et al., §537; and B. Girard, *Responsabilité*, 2015, above n. 83, at 121–122.

violation of Arts 2 and 3[90] and also seems to be related to the jurisprudence where the Court awards satisfaction for the violation of these provisions out of its own motion.[91]

The Court accepts that the successors of a person that died because of a violation of Arts 2 or 3 can receive compensation for pecuniary reflected damages if they can prove that they depended on the income of the deceased person for their living. It also easily finds that the successors have suffered non-pecuniary damages if a relative died due to a violation of the Convention. This last notion has interesting implications for national tort law. Indeed, although some legal systems accept the possibility of relatives receiving compensation for the moral damages that successors suffer by reflection, other legal systems do not offer this possibility, or only in a limited way.[92] Consequently, it does not come as a surprise that in England, where this possibility does not exist, it is argued in the doctrine that judges will have to use the Human Rights Act to provide the possibility of awarding successors of deceased persons financial compensation.[93]

2.4.2. The Damages are Not Caused by the Death of a Relative

Some authors indicate that the Court rejects claims for reflected damages in cases where the damages are not caused by the deceased or the directly injured party.[94] In *Kucheruk*, the Court found that the mother of a victim of inhuman treatment in the meaning of Art. 3 had not suffered harm

---

90 *Gül v. Turkey*, 14 December 2000, appl. no. 22676/93; *Aktaş v. Turkey*, 24 April 2003, appl. no. 24351/94, §329; *Ananyev et al. v. Russia*, 10 January 2001, appl. nos. 42525/07 and 60800/08, §98; *El-Masri v. The former Yugoslav Republic of Macedonia*, 13 December 2012, appl. no. 39630/09, §255; and *Pereira Henriques v. Luxemburg*, 9 May 2006, appl. no. 60255/00, §90.

91 *Mayzit v. Russia*, 20 January 2005, appl. no. 63378/00, §88; *Igor Ivanov v. Russia*, 7 June 2007, appl. no. 34000/02, §50; *Babushkin v. Russia*, 18 October 2007, appl. no. 67253/01, §62; *Chember v. Russia*, 3 July 2008, appl. no. 7188/03, §77; *Nadrosov v. Russia*, 31 July 2008, appl. no. 9297/02, §54; *Denisenko and Bogdanchikov v. Russia*, 12 February 2009, appl. no. 3811/02, §142; *Alibekov v. Russia*, 14 May 2009, appl. no. 8413/02, §73; *Vladimir Fedorov v. Russia*, 30 July 2009, appl. no. 19223/04, §87; *Maksimov v. Russia*, 18 March 2010, appl. no. 43233/02, §98; *Dorogaykin v. Russia*, 10 February 2011, appl. no. 1066/05, §49; *Chudun v. Russia*, 21 June 2011, appl. no. 20641/04, §129; *Grigoryev v. Russia*, 23 October 2012, appl. no. 22663/06, §103; and *Borodin v. Russia*, 6 November 2012, appl. no. 41867/04, §166.

92 C. Van Dam, *European Tort Law*, 2013, above n. 82, at 370–372.

93 K. Oliphant, 'England and Wales' in H. Koziol and B. Steiniger (eds.), *European Tort Law 2001*, Vienna, Springer, 2002, p131 at 146.

94 C. Kissling and D. Kelliher, 'Compensation', 2011, above n. 18, p579 at 619.

due to the violation of the Convention since her son had not died as a result of this violation.[95] It would be rash to conclude from this case that the ECtHR never accepts that relatives can suffer reflected damages. The Court did not explain this decision at all. In the case of *Mubilanzila Mayeka and Kaniki Mitunga* it did award a compensation for reflected damages for the following reasons:

> the issue whether a parent qualifies as a "victim" of the ill-treatment of his or her child will depend on the existence of special factors which give the applicant's suffering a dimension and character distinct from the emotional distress which may be regarded as inevitably caused to relatives of a victim of a serious human rights violation. Relevant elements will include the proximity of the family tie – in that context, a certain weight will attach to the parent-child bond – the particular circumstances of the relationship and the way in which the authorities responded to the parent's enquiries. The essence of such a violation lies in the authorities reactions and attitudes to the situation when it is brought to their attention. It is especially in respect of this latter factor that a parent may claim directly to be a victim of the authorities' conduct.[96]

The Court continued this approach in later cases where a relative of the directly injured party claimed damages. This, however, only happened in cases where it had found a violation of Art. 3 ECHR.[97]

With regard to violations of other treaty provisions, the Court traditionally found that the violation of these provisions did not constitute damages for the relatives of the directly injured party. The Court gave two important reasons for this. It first noted that relatives of an applicant who had died for another reason such as a violation of the Convention could be

---

95 *Kucheruk v. Ukraine*, 6 September 2007, appl. no. 2570/04, §§203–205.

96 *Mubilanzila, Mayeka and Kaniki Mitunga v. Belgium*, 12 October 2006, appl. no. 13178/03.

97 *Çakici v. Turkey*, 8 July 1999 (Grand Chamber), appl. no. 23657/94, §98; *Tas v. Cyprus*, 14 November 2000, appl. no. 24396/94, §79; *Cyprus v. Turkey*, 10 May 2001 (Grand Chamber), appl. no. 25781/94, §156; *Tekdag v. Turkey*, 15 January 2004, appl. no. 27699/95, §85; *Gongadze v. Ukraine*, 8 November 2005, appl. no. 34056/02, §184; *Bazorkina v. Russia*, 27 July 2006, appl. no. 69481/01, §139; *Magomadov and Magomadov v. Russia*, 12 July 2007, appl. no. 68004/01, §118; *Aziyevy v. Russia*, 20 March 2008, appl. no. 77626/01, §102; *Khantiyeva et al. v. Russia*, 29 October 2009, appl. no. 43398/06, §127; *Vakayeva et al. v. Russia*, 10 June 2010, appl. no. 2220/05, §171; *Vitayeva et al. v. Russia*, 7 June 2011, appl. no. 27459/07, §143; *Salakhov and Islyamova v. Ukraine*, 14 March 2013, appl. no. 28005/08, §200; *Akhmatov et al. v. Russia*, 16 January 2014, appl. no. 38828/10 et al., §240; *Makayeva v. Russia*, 18 September 2014, appl. no. 37287/09, §117; *Elberte v. Latvia*, 13 January 2015, appl. no. 61243/08, §137; and *Islamova v. Russia*, 30 April 2015, appl. no. 5713/11, §69.

awarded compensation 'at least in respect of material damage and costs.'[98] On the other hand, the Court pointed out that the European Commission for Human Rights had never before awarded a satisfaction to the relatives of a directly injured party in its jurisprudence concerning the violation of the reasonable time requirement.[99] In *Deumeland*, the Court argued that this was related to the fact that the relatives of a directly injured party cannot receive compensation in cases where the directly injured party could not receive compensation:

> As far as the alleged non-material damage is concerned, it cannot be excluded that Mr. Deumeland's mother suffered some psychological distress during the period when the reasonable time had been exceeded. However, even supposing that she might have obtained financial compensation on this score, the Court sees no reason to grant any to the applicant himself since the present judgment affords him adequate just satisfaction.[100]

The Court makes a connection between the possibility of relatives receiving compensation for reflected damages with their possibility (as heirs) to receive compensation for the moral damages that the deceased person had suffered. Regarding this last type of case, the Court made an interesting judgment in *X. v. the United Kingdom*.[101] The Court here found that the heirs of a directly injured party could not receive compensation for the non-pecuniary damages that the directly injured party suffered.[102] Judge Vilhjalmsson opposed this decision. Whether or not the damages were pecuniary or non-pecuniary in nature, he found that:

> in so far as X, if still alive, would have been entitled to financial compensation by way of just satisfaction under Article 50 [old Art. 41] of the Convention, such compensation should now be paid to his estate, in accordance with the claim put forward on its behalf.[103]

Ten years later, the Court explicitly awarded compensation for non-pecuniary damages to the relatives of a deceased person for the violation

98 18 October 1982 (just satisfaction), appl. no. 7215/75, §12.

99 EComHR, *Kofler v. Italy*, 9 October 1982 (Decision), appl. no. 8261/78, §§16–17; and EComHR, *Mathes v. Austria*, 13 January 1992 (Decision), appl. no. 12973/87, §§18–20.

100 *Deumeland v. Germany*, 29 May 1986 (Plenary), appl. no. 9384/81, §97.

101 *X. v. the United Kingdom*, 18 October 1982 (just satisfaction), appl. no. 7215/75.

102 18 October 1982 (Art. 50), §§12 and 19.

103 Dissenting opinion of Judge Vilhjalmsson in *X. v. the United Kingdom*, 18 October 1982 (just satisfaction), appl. no. 7215/75.

of the requirement to provide a judgment within a reasonable time in the case of *X. v. France.*[104] This approach was continued in other judgments.[105] The Court argues that this is only possible in situations where the relatives continue a case that had been brought before the Court by the deceased person.[106] In such a situation, they can receive compensation for the continuing violation after the death of the direct victim.[107] The relatives also have to prove that they have an interest in continuing the procedure, but this additional criteria does not seem to be a big hurdle since the Court accepts that an interest can be found in the financial interest of receiving compensation under the heading of Art. 41.[108]

3. THE ACTUAL CONTENT OF DAMAGES

3.1. DEFINITION

Article 41 of the Convention does not mention the word 'damages' but 'just satisfaction'. The fact that the Convention does not uses the term damages, does not mean that the Convention system lacks a notion of damages. This book has already shown that the ECtHR uses *restitutio in integrum* as a starting point to determine a just satisfaction and that one can describe the damages as the difference between the actual state of the human rights victim and the situation he would have been in if the violation had not occurred. It also has to be shown that the notion of damages can be related to the notion of an interest in the meaning of Art. 34. Moreover, according

---

104 *X. v. France*, 31 March 1992, appl. no. 18020/91, §§26 and 52. See also: *Deweer v. Belgium*, 27 February 1980, appl. no. 6903/75, §37.

105 *Colozza v. Italy*, 12 February 1985, appl. no. 9024/80, §38; *Deumeland v. Germany*, 29 May 1986 (Plenary), appl. no. 9384/81, §95; *Gillow v. the United Kingdom*, 14 September 1987 (just satisfaction), appl. no. 9063/80, §23; *Vocaturo v. Italy*, 24 May 1991, appl. no. 11891/85, §§2 and 19; *Pandolfelli and Palumbo v. Italy*, 27 February 1992, appl. no. 13218/87, §2; *X. v. France*, 31 March 1992, appl. no. 18020/91, §54; *A. et al. v. Denmark*, 8 February 1996, appl. no. 20826/92, §86; *Meulendijks v. the Netherlands*, 14 May 2002, appl. no. 34549/97, §59; and *Lemo et al. v. Croatia*, 10 July 2014, appl. no. 3925/10 et al., §60.

106 *Ahmet Sadik v. Greece*, 15 November 1996, appl. no. 18877/91, §26; *Dalban v. Romania*, 28 September 1999 (Grand Chamber), appl. no. 28114/95, §39; *Craxi v. Italy*, 7 December 2000 (Decision), appl. no. 25337/94; *Taskin et al. v. Turkey*, 10 November 2004, appl. no. 46117/99, §102; *Goktas v. Turkey*, 29 November 2007, appl. no. 66446/01, §19; *Gradinar v. Moldavia*, 8 April 2008, appl. no. 7170/02, §91; and *Stoyan Mitev v. Bulgaria*, 7 January 2010, appl. no. 60922/00, §47.

107 *Sargsyan v. Azerbaijan*, 12 December 2017 (Grand Chamber), appl. no. 40167/06, §54.

108 *Ahmet Sadik v. Greece*, 15 November 1996, appl. no. 18877/91, §26.

to Helmut Koziol the Court applies a broad concept of damages.[109] He argues that the scope of the concept of damages must be as broad as the rights that are protected by the Convention because Art. 41 can be applied after any Convention right has been violated. This stems from the idea that, as already pointed out, the Court is not bound to the content that national tort law uses when awarding compensation for damages.[110] Indeed, the fact that a national legal system does not qualify an interest that is protected by the Convention as damages will not hinder the Court from qualifying this as damages.

These ideas are very preliminary. To understand the actual content of damages under Art. 41 or, in other words, the concept of damages in the jurisprudence of the ECtHR, more research is required. The most important question in this context is whether a violation of the Convention automatically causes damages. In contrast, one must inquire whether the presence of damages is a required condition in order to find a violation of the Convention. Both of these questions are quite similar. If the presence of damages would constitute a necessary requirement for finding a violation of the Convention, then a violation of the Convention would always constitute damages. If the presence of damages is not a necessary condition for the finding of a violation of the Convention, the Court has to inquire whether the violation has caused damages.

At first glance it seems as if both questions must be answered negatively for two reasons. The first reason relates to the practice of the ECtHR to make declaratory judgments under Art. 41. As will be discussed further on, the Court in some judgments, after it has found a violation of the Convention, does not grant any sum of money as compensation but where the Court argues that the finding of the violation by the Court in itself awards sufficient satisfaction to the victims of the human rights violation. The second reason concerns the jurisprudence of the Court where it found that it is possible to find a violation of the Convention if no damages occurred for the reason that the harm of the applicants is only a condition for the application of Art. 41.[111] According to this jurisprudence, it seems

---

109 H. Koziol, 'Concluding Remarks on Compensatory and Non-Compensatory Remedies' in A. Fenyves, E. Karner, H. Koziol and E. Steiner (eds.), *Tort Law in the Jurisprudence of the European Court of Human Rights*, Göttingen, De Gruyter, 2011, p863 at 868.

110 F. Bydlinski, 'Methodological Approaches', 2011, above n. 4, p29 at 119.

111 *Artico v. Italy*, 13 May 1980, appl. no. 6694/74, §35; *Adolf v. Austria*, 26 March 1982, appl. no. 8269/78, §37; *Eckle v. Germany*, 15 July 1982, appl. no. 8130/78, §66; *Corigliano v. Italy*, 10 December 1982, appl. no. 8304/78, §31; *van der Sluijs, Zuiderveld and Klappe v. the Netherlands*, 22 May 1984, appl. nos. 9362/81, 9363/81 and

quite clear that the violation of the Convention as such cannot be qualified as the notion of damages that the Court applies in the context of Art. 41. The result would be that it is not required that applicants suffer damages in order to find a violation of the Convention and that the finding of a violation of damages does not automatically result in the finding of damages.

Ken Oliphant and Katarzyna Ludwichowska, however, argue that this jurisprudence has to be relativized. They give two reasons for this. The first reason is that for a violation of the right to property as is enshrined in Art. 1 of the first protocol, it is required that the applicants have suffered pecuniary damages.[112] Secondly, the Court often accepts that non-pecuniary damages are at hand for the reason that the applicant had suffered stress or anxiety because of the violation of the Convention.[113]

9387/81, §37; *Inze v. Austria*, 28 October 1987, appl. no. 8695/79, §32; *Wassink v. the Netherlands*, 27 September 1990, appl. no. 12535/86, §38; *Lüdi v. Switzerland*, 15 June 1992, appl. no. 12433/86, §34; *Amuur v. France*, 25 June 1996, appl. no. 19776/92, §36; *Nsona v. the Netherlands*, 28 November 1996, appl. no. 23366/94, §106; *Brumarescu v. Romania*, 23 January 2001 (just satisfaction) (Grand Chamber), appl. no. 28342/95, §50; *Guisset v. France*, 26 September 2000, appl. no. 33933/96, §67; *Walston v. Norway (no.1)*, 3 June 2003, appl. no. 37372/97, §58; *Politikin v. Poland*, 27 April 2004, appl. no. 68930/01, §23; *Voytenko v. Ukraine*, 29 June 2004, appl. no. 18966/02, §34; *Shmalko v. Ukraine*, 20 July 2004, appl. no. 60750/00, §33; *Romashov v. Ukraine*, 27 July 2004, appl. no. 67534/01, §26; *Milatova et al. v. the Czech Republic*, 21 June 2005, appl. no. 61811/00, §65; *Siliadin v. France*, 26 July 2005, appl. no. 73316/01, §62; *Monnat v. Switzerland*, 21 September 2006, appl. no. 73604/01, §31; *Moskow Branch of the Salvation Army v. Russia*, 5 October 2006, appl. no. 72881/01, §65; *Church of Scientology Moscow v. Russia*, 5 April 2007, appl. no. 18147/02, §77; *Voskuil v. the Netherlands*, 22 November 2007, appl. no. 64752/01, §79; *Pankiewicz v. Poland*, 12 February 2008, appl. no. 34151/04, §29; *ReligionsgeMaynschaft der zeugen Jehovas et al. v. Austria*, 31 July 2008, appl. no. 40825/98, §68; *Godlevskiy v. Russia*, 23 October 2008, appl. no. 14888/03, §36; *Duca v. Moldavia*, 3 March 2009, appl. no. 75/07, §23; *Polonskiy v. Russia*, 19 March 2009, appl. no. 30033/05, §151; *Stephens v. Malta (no.1)*, 21 April 2009, appl. no. 11956/07, §87; *Gaspari v. Slovenia*, 21 July 2009, appl. no. 21055/03, §52; *Ananyin v. Russia*, 30 July 2009, appl. no. 13659/06, §92; *Sorokin v. Russia*, 30 July 2009, appl. no. 7739/06, §65; *Frasik v. Poland*, 5 January 2010, appl. no. 22933/02, §71; *Puto et al. v. Albania*, 20 July 2010, appl. no. 609/07, §22; *J.M. v. the United Kingdom*, 28 September 2010, appl. no. 37060/06, §27; *Finger v. Bulgaria*, 10 May 2011, appl. no. 37346/05, §65; *Communist Party of Russia et al. v. Russia*, 19 June 2012, appl. no. 29400/05, §71; *Nada v. Switzerland*, 12 September 2012 (Grand Chamber), appl. no. 10593/08, §128; *Khayrov v. Ukraine*, 15 November 2012, appl. no. 19157/06, §84; *Yefimenko v. Russia*, 12 February 2013, appl. no. 152/04, §93; *Zahirović v. Croatia*, 25 April 2013, appl. no. 58590/11, §48; *Wallishauser v. Austria (no.2)*, 20 June 2013, appl. no. 14497/06, §50; *Lonić v. Croatia*, 4 December 2014, appl. no. 8067/12, §84; *D'Asta v. Italy*, 16 December 2014, appl. no. 26010/04, §22; and *Russo v. Italy*, 5 May 2015, appl. no. 14231/05, §26.

112 It must be noted that the protection of pecuniary rights in the Convention is linked to the right to property: O. Ichim, *Just Satisfaction*, 2015, above n. 31, at 27–28 and 98.

113 K. Oliphant and K. Ludwichowska, 'Damage', 2011, above n. 3, p397 at 398; M.L. Van Emmerik, *Schadevergoeding*, 1997, above n. 30, at 178–179. Examples can be found

It seems that in cases where the Convention protects pecuniary interests, pecuniary damages are required to find a violation of the Convention and that the wrestling of the Court with the notion of non-pecuniary damages can be attributed to the nature of these types of damages. Indeed, apart from the right to property, the Convention rights above all protect non-pecuniary interests: interests from which the infringement cannot be estimated in a pecuniary value.[114] From this perspective, the question of whether a violation of the Convention automatically causes damages, first and foremost concerns non-pecuniary damages. With regard to pecuniary damages, one can point to the right to property and the notion that an infringement of this right can constitute a violation of this treaty right. Because a claim for compensation can be qualified as property within the meaning of Art. 1 of the first protocol and since the Court has to apply the Convention in a harmonized way, one can expect that the Court will require the presence of damages to find a violation of the Convention if the only interest at stake in a specific case are pecuniary interests.

Finally, it is also worth mentioning that the Court recognizes future damages. Indeed, the Court in one case has even found that national tort law was not effective in a case where the remedies in tort law were not effective to end a continuing human rights violation.[115]

3.2. THE CONTENT OF IMMATERIAL DAMAGES

According to Bydlinski, it is obvious that the Court can grant a just satisfaction immaterial or non-pecuniary damages. He noted that the German translation of the satisfaction is called 'Genuugtung', a term that in all three legal systems using the German language is associated with non-pecuniary damages.[116] Bydlinski also argues that the recognition of non-pecuniary damages is the logical consequence of the obligation to interpret the Convention in a teleological way and that the rights enshrined in the Convention, according to Art. 1 of the Convention, have to be protected in

in: *Deweer v. Belgium*, 27 February 1980, appl. no. 6903/75, §60; *Goddi v. Italy*, 9 April 1984, appl. no. 8966/80, §35; and *Tomasi v. France*, 27 August 1992, appl. no. 12850/87, §130.

114 This does not mean that the compensation for pecuniary damages are unimportant in the jurisprudence of the Court. The highest amounts that the Court awarded aimed to compensate pecuniary damages: O. Ichim, *Just Satisfaction*, 2015, above n. 31, at 99.

115 *Khayletdinov v. Russia*, 12 January 2016, appl. no. 2763/13, §118.

116 F. Bydlinski, 'Methodological Approaches', 2011, above n. 4, p29 at 50–51.

an effective and not in a theoretical and illusionary way.[117] Thus, since most of the provisions in the Convention relate to non-pecuniary interests, it seems very unlikely that the Court cannot qualify non-pecuniary damages as damages in the context of Art. 41. According to Bydlinski, one would fail to appreciate the Convention if the notion of damages under Art. 41 were interpreted in another way.[118]

The argument of Bydlinski must be accepted because the Convention first and foremost aims to protect non-pecuniary interests, something that is illustrated by the fact that the Court more often awards a just satisfaction for non-pecuniary damages as for pecuniary damages.[119] It must be stressed that this book has already found that a consequence of the principle of effectivity is that legal persons should be able to receive compensation for moral damages, and that the Court in some cases awards compensation for non-pecuniary damages out of its own motion for reasons of effectivity. Nonetheless, it must be recognized that the very nature of non-pecuniary damages is such as not to lend itself to precise calculation. The Court in one case even judged that an applicant 'cannot be required to furnish any proof of non-pecuniary damages'.[120]

If the ECtHR describes non-pecuniary damages, it often indicates that a victim of human rights violations, because of the violations, suffers anxiety and distress of considerable inconvenience,[121] because of the infringement of someone's good name and reputation,[122] or because the violation of the Convention caused a certain feeling of isolation and helplessness.[123] From this wording, it seems clear that the Court protects a wide range of non-pecuniary interests. An overview of these interests has been provided in

117 *Ibid.*, at 51 See also: C. Kissling and D. Kelliher, 'Compensation', 2011, above n. 18, p579 at 615–616.

118 F. Bydlinski, 'Methodological Approaches', 2011, above n. 4, p29 at 109.

119 D. Harris, M. O'Boyle, E. Bates and C. Buckley, *Law of the European Convention*, 2009, above n. 81, at 860; K. Oliphant and K. Ludwichowska, 'Damage', 2011, above n. 3, p397 at 413; C. Pettiti, 'Stratégie de la partie requérante face à la perspective d'octroi de dommages et intérêts par la cour Européenne des droits de l'homme' in J.-F. Flauss and E. Lambert Abdelgawad (eds.), *La pratique d'indemnisation par la Cour européenne des droits de l'homme*, Brussels, Bruylant,, 2011, p56 at 72; D. Shelton, *Remedies*, 1999, above n. 13, at 219.

120 *Belousov v. Russia*, 2 October 2008, appl. no. 1748/02, §78.

121 *Olsson v. Sweden (no.1)*, 24 March 1988 (Plenary), appl. no. 10465/83, §102; *Eriksson v. Sweden*, 22 June 1989 (Plenary), appl. no. 11373/85, §§97–98; 25 February 1992, §107; and *McMichael v. the United Kingdom*, 24 February 1995, appl. no. 16424/90, §103.

122 *Brincat v. Italy*, 26 November 1992, appl. no. 13867/88, §26; and *Helmers v. Sweden*, 29 October 1991 (Plenary), appl. no. 11826/85, §42.

123 *Megyeri v. Germany*, 12 May 1992, appl. no. 13770/88, §32; and *Pham Hoang v. France*, 25 September 1992, appl. no. 13191/87, §45.

an outstanding publication of Oliphant and Ludwichowka.[124] Accordingly, this question will not be dealt with in detail in the context of this book. It is however important to know that the Convention protects a broad range of non-pecuniary interests. Thus, the Court, for example, has awarded just satisfaction for the infringement of someone's physical integrity that resulted from a body search that had not caused physical injuries.[125] The Court has also awarded just satisfaction for both pecuniary and non-pecuniary damages that soldiers suffered because they had to undergo an investigation of their sexual orientation;[126] it has offered just satisfaction for broadcasting images of a mentally handicapped person on television without asking permission to do so;[127] for the stress, the nuisance and the fear of medical problems that could be caused by the presence of a nearby waste-disposal factory;[128] for the stress that people experience when their rights to property are violated;[129] for the loss of a family relation in cases where a child is taken away from its parents because this is an infringement of Art. 8;[130] and for a violation of the right to a fair trial because national judges applied the procedural rules in a far too formalistic manner.[131] As was discussed earlier on in this book and taking into account a margin of appreciation, states can be pushed to grant compensation for the infringements of Convention rights in order to offer an effective remedy in national law.[132] In other words, one can say that national tort law has to recognize these notions of damage.[133]

---

124 K. Oliphant and K. Ludwichowska, 'Damage', 2011, above n. 3, p397 at 416–447.

125 *Wainwright v. the United Kingdom*, 26 September 2006, appl. no. 12350/04, §60.

126 *Lustig-Prean and Beckett v. the United Kingdom*, 25 July 2000 (just satisfaction), appl. nos. 31417/96 and 32377/96, §12.

127 *Peck v. the United Kingdom*, 28 January 2003, appl. no. 44647/98, §120.

128 *Lopez Ostra v. Spain*, 9 December 1994, appl. no. 16798/90, §65.

129 *Jokela v. Finland*, 21 May 2002, appl. no. 28856/95, §88; *Kakamoukas et al. v. Greece*, 15 February 2008 (Grand Chamber), appl. no. 38311/02, §44; and *Shesti Mai Engineering OOD et al. v. Bulgaria*, 20 September 2011, appl. no. 17854/04, §115.

130 *H. v. the United Kingdom*, 9 June 1988 (just satisfaction) (Plenary), appl. no. 9580/81, §10.

131 *Walchli v. France*, 26 July 2007, appl. no. 35787/03, §41.

132 In the Netherlands, this has led to the recognition of non-pecuniary damages in cases where the right to have a judgment within a reasonable time was violated: S. Jansen and D. Wenders, 'Een kroniek van de redelijke termijn', *NJCM-Bulletin* 2006, p1091 at 1111 and 1119ff; T. Barkhuysen, M. Van Emmerik and J.-P. Loof, 'Mensenrechten-Actualiteiten.NL', *NJCM-Bulletin* 2006, p258 at 263–264; and T. Barkhuysen, M. Van Emmerik and J.-P. Loof, 'Mensenrechten-Actualiteiten.NL', *NJCM-Bulletin* 2008, p423 at 435.

133 Interestingly, the notion of environmental damages widened in some countries because of the jurisprudence of the Court: F. McManus, 'Noise Pollution and Human Rights', *EHRLR* 2005, pp575–587.

In this context, it is interesting to note that the Convention has caused a debate in the Netherlands on the question of whether Dutch tort law had to broaden its notion of non-pecuniary damages.[134] Moreover, some judges in Eastern European legal orders proved to be far more willing to grant compensation for non-pecuniary damages after these countries joined the Convention than they were before.[135] This might in some countries be relevant for environmental damages. The ECtHR has indeed decided that infringements of the home, the health and the private and family life by environmental pollution can constitute a violation of Art. 8. This does not mean that every pollution can be qualified as a violation of Art. 8. The Court grants the member states a broad margin of appreciation with regard to this problem[136] and consequently argues that the pollution has to reach a minimum seriousness.[137]

3.3. DECLARATORY JUDGMENTS AS JUST SATISFACTION

The previous section demonstrated that the concept of damages under Art. 41 seems to include non-pecuniary damages. The Court nevertheless often made 'declaratory judgments'. It did so for the first time in the famous *Golder* case.[138] Afterwards, the Court continued to do so more and more.[139]

---

134 See: M. Faure and T. Hartlief, 'The Netherlands' in H. Koziol and B. Steininger (eds.), *European Tort Law 2006*, Vienna, Springer, 2007, p338 at 360; A. Keirse, 'EVRMering' 2011, Vol.1, p5 at 7; A. Van, 'Recente ontwikkelingen op het gebied van de vergoeding van immateriële schade in de praktijk' in P. Kottenhagen-Edzes (ed.), *Immateriële schade: tendensen en wensen*, Groningen, Intersentia, 2000, p19 at 23; and M.L. Van Emmerik, *Schadevergoeding*, 1997, above n. 30, at 352.

135 E.g.: I. Raduletu, 'Romania' in H. Koziol en B. Steininger (eds.), *European Tort Law 2006*, Vienna, Springer, 2007, (516) at 531.

136 J. Vanpraet and C. Van de Heyning, 'Hoe fundamentele rechten het leefmilieu beschermen. Overzicht van het instrumentarium', *Nieuw Juridisch Weekblad*, 2010, p562 at 572.

137 *Lopez Ostra v. Spain*, 9 December 1994, appl. no. 16798/90, §51; *Hatton et al. v. the United Kingdom*, 8 July 2003 (Grand Chamber), appl. no. 36022/97, §118; *Fadeyeva v. Russia*, 9 June 2005, appl. no. 55723/00, §69; and *Borysiewicz v. Poland*, 1 July 2008, appl. no. 71146/01, §51.

138 *Golder v. the United Kingdom*, 21 February 1975, appl. no. 4451/70, §46. This principle does not apply to the costs of the legal procedures: 'In fact, it is, difficult to imagine that the finding of a violation could of itself constitute just satisfaction as regards costs': *Sunday Times v. the United Kingdom*, 6 November 1980 (just satisfaction), appl. no. 6538/74, §16.

139 Later on, the Court confirmed this approach: *Marckx v. Belgium*, 13 June 1979, appl. no. 6833/74, §68; *Le Compte, Van Leuven and De Meyere v. Belgium*, 18 October 1982 (just satisfaction), appl. nos. 6878/75 and 7238/75, §16; *Abdulaziz, Cabales and Balkandali v. the United Kingdom*, 28 May 1985, appl. no. 9214/80 et al., §96; *Barthold v. Germany*,

The Court only does so in cases where an applicant claims compensation for immaterial damages. The declaratory judgment does not seem to be an appropriate remedy to redress the judicial costs and the pecuniary damages of human rights victims.[140] The number of declaratory judgments the Court makes has been decreasing in the last decades,[141] but the Court does continue to issue them. When the Court makes a declaratory judgment, it argues that the finding of a violation of the Convention provides sufficient satisfaction and that it is unnecessary to award a financial compensation.[142]

Thus, declaratory judgments seem to be an exception to the principle of *restitutio in integrum*, which is the starting point of restitution in the context of Art. 41. It is regrettable that the ECtHR poorly explains the reasons for its declaratory judgments. The Court leaves one in ignorance as to the reasons why it only makes a declaratory judgment in some cases. In the rare cases where the Court gives an explanation, it mainly refers to equity but does not show how equity explains why the mere declaratory judgment suffices as a means of granting just satisfaction.[143] At first glance, the only reason that matters is the freedom of the Court to decide whether or not to grant financial compensation. This stems from *Varnava*. In this exceptional case, the Grand Chamber granted financial compensation to the victims of human rights violations after the Chamber had only made a declaratory judgment. In its judgment, the Court made the following observations:

> In many cases where a law, procedure or practice has been found to fall short of Convention standards this is enough to put matters right. In some situations,

31 January 1986, appl. no. 8734/79, §8ff; *Brogan v. the United Kingdom*, 30 May 1989 (just satisfaction), appl. no. 11209/84 et al., §§8–9; *Bricmont v. Belgium*, 7 July 1989, appl. no. 10857/84, §99; and *Kamasinski v. Austria*, 19 December 1989, appl. no. 9783/82, §113.

140 Although the Court had in the past made declaratory judgments for material and immaterial damages together, it has abandoned this approach: M. Jozon, 'Satisfaction by Finding a violation' in A. Fenyves, E. Karner, H. Koziol and E. Steiner (eds.), *Tort Law in the Jurisprudence of the European Court of Human Rights*, Göttingen, De Gruyter, 2011, p741 at 759–761.

141 M. Sirinelli 'La stratégie des parties face à la perspective d'octroi de dommages-intérêts par la Cour – côté etat défendeur' in J.-F. Flauss and E. Lambert Abdelgawad (eds.), *La pratique d'indemnisation par la Cour européenne des droits de l'homme*, Brussels, Bruylant, 2011, p75 at 78.

142 Although the use of declaratory judgments by the Court seems self-evident now, one must remember that Art. 41 was initially based on older arbitration agreements that did not recognize declaratory judgments: C. Gray, *Judicial Remedies in International Law*, Oxford, Clarendon Press, 1987, at 17.

143 D. Shelton, *Remedies*, 1999, above n. 13, at 201.

> however, the impact of the violation may be regarded as being of a nature and degree as to have impinged so significantly on the moral well-being of the applicant as to require something further. Such elements do not lend themselves to a process of calculation or precise quantification. Nor is it the Court's role to function akin to a domestic tort mechanism court in apportioning fault and compensatory damages between civil parties. Its guiding principle is equity, which above all involves flexibility and an objective consideration of what is just, fair and reasonable in all the circumstances of the case, including not only the position of the applicant but the overall context in which the breach occurred.[144]

This statement indicates that the ECtHR has a discretionary power for granting financial compensation to victims of human rights violations. It seems as if human rights victims have no right to compensation, let alone a right to full compensation or *restitutio in integrum* as is required by domestic tort law. From this perspective, studying the application of Art. 41 seems to be a desperate undertaking. It takes the heart out of every jurist who tries to understand the Court's practice for granting just satisfactions. Indeed, there are many reasons that lead one to think the Court's statement cannot be taken too seriously. The first reason is the admissibility criteria that the Court takes into account in its jurisprudence under Art. 41 in order to judge whether an applicant has an interest in the meaning of Art. 34. Accordingly, the discretionary power of the Court to award just satisfaction would have an impact on the admissibility criteria. The second reason is that the Court also takes into account its practice of awarding just satisfaction when it has to judge whether or not a national remedy is effective in the meaning of Art. 13. The Court finds violations in the context of Art. 13 if member states cannot indicate the legal basis on which victims of human rights violations claim compensation and in cases where the member states do not provide a mechanism that controls the size of these compensations. If the Court requires all these guarantees from the states, it would be very strange for the Court not to respect these guarantees. This is especially true since the Court attaches great importance to legal certainty.[145] Moreover, one wonders how a national

---

144 *Varnava et al. v. Turkey*, 18 September 2009 (Grand Chamber), appl. nos. 16064/90, 16065/90, 16066/90, 16068/90, 16069/90, 16070/90, 16071/90, 16072/90 and 16073/90, §224.

145 The Court often observes that it cannot easily deviate from previous jurisprudence: *Cossey v. the United Kingdom*, 27 September 1990, appl. no. 10843/84, §35; *Chapman v. the United Kingdom*, 18 January 2001, appl. no. 27238/95, §70; *Coster v. the United Kingdom*, 18 January 2001, appl. no. 24876/94, §84, 2nd section; *Stafford v. the United Kingdom*, 28 May 2002, appl. no. 46295/99, §68; *Christine Goodwin v. the*

state can award a satisfaction in line with the Court's judgment under Art. 41 if the Court does not develop jurisprudential rules but acts as if it has a discretionary power. For these reasons, it is necessary for the Court to follow its jurisprudence on Art. 41 on clear principles. In order to do so, it is necessary to find the principles on the basis of which the Court makes declaratory judgments.

3.3.1. *Situations Where the Court Never Makes Declaratory Judgments*

To know whether the Court has a discretionary power to make declaratory judgments, one first has to look to the situations where the Court never makes declaratory judgments and always grants compensation. Indeed, in some cases where the substantial aspects of the right to life, the prohibition of torture[146] or the right to liberty and security of a person[147] are violated, the Court assumes that moral damages resulting from these kinds of violations cannot be redressed by the mere declaration by the Court that Convention rights have been violated.[148]

That the Court often assumes this when the substantial aspects of Arts 2, 3 or 5 are violated does not necessarily mean that it never makes the

United Kingdom, 11 July 2002, appl. no. 28957/98, §74; *Mamatkulov and Abdurasulovic v. Turkey*, 6 February 2003, appl. nos. 46827/99 and 46951/99, §105; *Aoulmi v. France*, 17 January 2006, appl. no. 50278/99, §109; *Scoppola v. Italy (no.2)*, 17 September 2009 (Grand Chamber), appl. no. 10249/03, §104; and *Sabri Güneş v. Turkey*, 29 June 2012 (Grand Chamber), appl. no. 27396/06, §50.

146 The Court, on the other hand, does make declaratory judgments if only the procedural aspects of Art. 3 are violated: *Melinte v. Romania*, 9 November 2006, appl. no. 43247/02, §§41 and 43; *Gebremedhin v. France*, 26 April 2007, appl. no. 25389/05, §79; *Dumitru Popescu v. Romania (no.2)*, 26 April 2007, appl. no. 71525/01, Merits, §84.

147 The Court does not only act in this way when it applies Art. 5 but also when it applies Art. 41: *Witold Litwa v. Poland*, 4 April 2000, appl. no. 26629/95, §88; *Magalhães Pereira v. Portugal*, 26 February 2002, appl. no. 44872/98, §66; *Enhorn v. Sweden*, 25 January 2005, appl. no. 56529/00, §60; *Gavula v. Ukraine*, 16 May 2013, appl. no. 52652/07, §115; *K. v. Russia*, 23 May 2013, appl. no. 69235/11, §106; and *Baran v. Poland*, 28 May 2013, appl. no. 53315/09, §42.

148 *Tanis et al. v. Turkey*, 2 August 2005, appl. no. 65899/01, §235; *Imakayeva v. Russia*, 9 November 2006, appl. no. 7615/02, §216; *Akhmadova and Sadulayeva v. Russia*, 10 May 2007, appl. no. 40464/02, §146; *Gekhayeva et al. v. Russia*, 29 May 2008, appl. no. 1755/04, §151; *Meshayeva et al. v. Russia*, 12 February 2009, appl. no. 27248/03, §143; *Khatuyeva v. Russia*, 22 April 2010, appl. no. 12463/05, §114; *Iskandarov v. Russia*, 23 September 2010, appl. no. 17185/05, §156; *Nechiporuk and Yonkalo v. Ukraine*, 21 April 2011, appl. no. 42310/04, Merits, §296; *Shokkarov et al. v. Russia*, 3 May 2011, appl. no. 41009/04, §143; *Vitayeva et al. v. Russia*, 7 June 2011, appl. no. 27459/07, §173; *Ilayeva et al. v. Russia*, 10 July 2012, appl. no. 27504/07, §116; and *Yefimenko v. Russia*, 12 February 2013, appl. no. 152/04, §171.

same assumption when other Convention rights are violated. Indeed, in the case of *Aslakhanova* the Court stated that wherever it finds a violation of the Convention, 'it may accept that the applicants have suffered non-pecuniary damage which cannot be compensated for solely by the findings of violations and make a financial award.'[149] And although this consideration has been used in the context of other treaty provisions,[150] it is remarkable that the ECtHR has never made a declaratory judgment when a substantial aspect of Arts 2 or 3 were violated but has often done so in cases where other treaty provisions were violated.[151]

An explanation can be found in international law. Article 14 of the UN Convention against Torture and Other Cruel, Inhuman or Degrading Treatment or Punishment stipulates that every state has to provide a judicial remedy that can put the victim of torture as much as possible in the position he would have been in had he not been tortured, and that if the victim is already deceased his successors would receive financial compensation.[152] Elisabeth Lambert Abdelgawad also noted that the victims of torture in international law first and foremost have the right to psychological assistance.[153] The financial compensation is a secondary consideration. In line with this reasoning, in the case of *Z. et al. v. the*

---

149 *Aslakhanova v. Russia*, 18 December 2012, appl. no. 2944/06 et al., §258.

150 See with regard to Art. 5: *James, Wells and Lee v. the United Kingdom*, 18 September 2012, appl. nos. 25119/09, 57715/09 and 57877/09, §244; *Sýkora v. the Czech Republic*, 22 November 2012, appl. no. 23419/07, §117. With regard to Art. 6: *Gana v. Italy*, 27 February 1992, appl. no. 13024/87, §19; *Billi v. Italy*, 26 February 1993, appl. no. 15118/89, §24; *Beaumartin v. France*, 24 November 1994, appl. no. 15287/89, §44; *Chevrol v. France*, 13 February 2003, appl. no. 49636/99, §89; *Putter v. Bulgaria*, 2 December 2010, appl. no. 38780/02, §60; *Neziraj v. Germany*, 8 November 2012, appl. no. 30804/07, §72; *Petko Petkov v. Bulgaria*, 19 February 2013, appl. no. 2834/06 2834/06, §43. With regard to Art. 8 (in conjunction with Art. 14): *Elsholz v. Germany*, 13 July 2000, appl. no. 25735/94, §71; *Zavřel v. The Czech Republic*, 18 January 2007, appl. no. 14044/05, §76; *Lashin v. Russia*, 22 January 2013, appl. no. 33117/02, §128; *X. et al. v. Austria*, 19 February 2013, appl. no. 19010/07, §157. With regard to Art. 10: *Nikula v. Finland*, 21 March 2002, appl. no. 31611/96, §65; and *Otegi Mondragon v. Spain*, 15 March 2011, appl. nos. 2034/07 and 2034/07, §72.

151 In a case where it found a violation of both Arts 3 and 11, the Court judged that the moral harm resulting from the violation of Art. 11 can be compensated by a declaratory judgment whereas the moral harm resulting from Art. 3 cannot: 7 October 2008, appl. no. 4327/02, §54.

152 Article 14, Convention against torture and other cruel, inhuman or degrading treatment or punishment, 1465 UNTS, 85.

153 E. Lambert Abdelgawad, 'Comment chifrer la réparation des traitements inhumains/ dégradants et de la torture' in J.-F. Flauss and E. Lambert Abdelgawad (eds.), *La pratique d'indemnisation par la Cour européenne des droits de l'homme*, Brussels, Bruylant, 2011, p189 at 197–198.

United Kingdom the ECtHR seems to award financial compensation for the violation of Arts 2 and 3 in order to cover the costs of psychological assistance:

> Notwithstanding their current positive prognosis, it may be considered as reasonably possible that in the future they will have some need of professional help in coping with problems which may arise as they grow older and in coming to terms with their childhood experience. An award to cover future psychotherapeutic care will assist in providing them with the support necessary to that process.[154]

The argument that financial compensation for violations of Arts 2 or 3 of the Convention, in accordance with international law, aims to cover the psychological costs is not satisfying. Article 14 of the Convention against Torture and Other Cruel, Inhuman or Degrading Treatment or Punishment could only explain the jurisprudence of the Court regarding Art. 3. It cannot explain why the Court never makes a declaratory judgment if Arts 2, 3 or another provision of the Convention are violated. Because of this, it seems that another criterion is more relevant: the gravity of the human rights violation.[155] Indeed, in the case of *Lashin*, the Court awarded financial compensation for the non-pecuniary damages caused by a violation of Art. 8, for the following reason: 'the cumulative effect of the violations of the applicant's rights, their duration, and the particular vulnerable situation of the applicant who suffered from a mental disorder.'[156] In *Z. et al. v. the United Kingdom*, another case where the Court found a violation of Art. 8, the Court once more found:

> The children in this case suffered very serious abuse and neglect over a period of more than four years. Z, A and B suffered, and in the case of the two boys, still suffer psychiatric illness as a result. A and B also suffered physical injury and C suffered neglect in respect of an eye condition. The description of the

---

154 *Z. et al. v. the United Kingdom*, 10 May 2005 (Grand Chamber), appl. no. 29392/95, §124.

155 It must be noted that infringements of Arts 2, 3 and 5 are almost always serious because these rights are 'notstandsfeste', which means that they cannot be suspended in cases of emergency.

156 *Lashin v. Russia*, 22 January 2013, appl. no. 33117/02, §128. For a more elaborate discussion of this jurisprudence, see: S. Touzé, 'Les limites de l'indemnisation devant la Cour européenne des droits de l'homme: le constat de violation comme satisfaction équitable suffisante' in J.-F. Flauss and E. Lambert Abdelgawad (eds.), *La pratique d'indemnisation par la Cour européenne des droits de l'homme*, Brussels, Bruylant, 2011, p127 at 151–152.

> conditions which they endured and the traumatic effects which this had on the children leave the Court with no doubt that a substantial award to reflect their pain and suffering is appropriate.[157]

It is remarkable that the ECtHR applies similar criteria as it uses in the context of the requirement of an effective national remedy as enshrined in Art. 13. Indeed, it has been shown in this book that the Court in principle requires a national remedy to provide financial compensation for non-pecuniary damages caused by a violation of Arts 2 or 3 in order to be considered as an effective remedy within the meaning of Art. 13. In view of these requirements, it is advisable for the Court to apply these criteria itself. Otherwise its jurisprudence in the future might contradict the standards that it requires the states to provide.

3.3.2. Situations Where the Court Makes Declaratory Judgments

The situations where the Court never makes a declaratory judgment indicate that there are certain boundaries to this practice of the Court. This does not however prevent the Court from making declaratory judgments in a number of other cases. Indeed, the exclusion of situations where a substantial aspect of Arts 2, 3 or 5 was violated, leaves numerous possibilities open. Thus the situations where the Court does make declaratory judgments must be explored.

In legal doctrine, it has been noted that the Court often makes declaratory judgments if it has found a violation of the right to a fair trial as enshrined in Art. 6 or in cases where it has found a violation of the procedural aspects of Arts 5 or 8.[158] It thus seems that the Court more often makes declaratory judgments in cases where procedural aspects of the Convention are violated than in cases where substantial aspects of the Convention are violated.[159] Monika Jozon and Dinah Shelton have found

---

157 *Z. et al. v. the United Kingdom*, 10 May 2005 (Grand Chamber), appl. no. 29392/95, §130.

158 M. De Salvia, 'Le principe de l'octroi subsidiaire des dommages-intérêts: d'une morale des droits de l'homme à une morale simplement indemnitaire?' in J.-F. Flauss and E. Lambert Abdelgawad (eds.), *La pratique d'indemnisation par la Cour européenne des droits de l'homme*, Brussels, Bruylant, 2011, p9 at 14. See also: The Law Commission and the Scottish Law Commission, Damages under the Human Rights Act 1998. Report on a Reference under Section 3(1) (e) of the Law Commissions Act 1965, SE/2000/182, 2000, <https://www.scotlawcom.gov.uk/files/3012/7989/6877/rep180.pdf>, at 97ff and 119ff.

159 The Law Commission and the Scottish Law Commission, Damages under the Human Rights Act 1998. Report on a Reference under Section 3(1) (e) of the Law Commissions

for instance that the Court made 51 declaratory judgments in the period between 1982 and 1991. In 40 cases, the applicants had been convicted by a criminal court, the other cases were mainly related to the procedural guarantees that are enshrined in Arts 5 and 6.[160] In the period after 1992, it seems that the Court made use of declaratory judgments more often, but this was still mainly the case in situations where procedural aspects of the Convention were violated.[161] Moreover, Jozon and Shelton argue that the Court more often makes declaratory judgments in cases where the Court was divided as to the final judgment, as is illustrated by the number of dissenting opinions.[162]

In *Abdi*, the Court seems to give a reason for its just satisfactions. The Court in this case acknowledged that it does in principle only make declaratory judgments and does not award financial compensation in cases where a detention of the applicant had only been unlawful for mere technical reasons, and where the applicant would also have been detained if the Convention had not been violated.[163] The finding of a violation in this case seems to indicate that there was a violation of the Convention without the appearance of damages. Indeed, the Court indicates that the applicant would have suffered the same damages if the Convention had not been violated. This, however, is related more to the topic of causality as to damages. What is at stake here is the absence of a causal link between the claimed damages (the damages caused by the detention), and the violation of the Convention. This is also a reminder that it has been demonstrated that the Court sometimes argues that it cannot speculate on the outcome that a national procedure would have had if the Convention had not been violated, a situation where the Court under Art. 46 sometimes requires states to award reparation in kind. In these last cases, the Court makes a declaratory judgment but that does not mean that it does not require states to repair the damages.

What this illustrates is that declaratory judgments can be explained if one takes into account criteria such as causality, criteria that are very common in tort law. Thus, in what follows, this book will try to explain the situations where the Court makes declaratory judgments. This topic has

---

Act 1965, SE/2000/182, 2000, <https://www.scotlawcom.gov.uk/files/3012/7989/6877/rep180.pdf>, at 34.

160 M. Jozon, 'Satisfaction by Finding a violation', 2011, above n. 140, p741 at 205.

161 *Ibid.*, at 743.

162 *Ibid.*, at 741–742; and D. Shelton, *Remedies*, 1999, above n. 13, at 205.

163 *Abdi v. the United Kingdom*, 9 April 2013, appl. no. 27770/08, §92.

been studied in the past by Michiel Van Emmerik.[164] He noted that the Court makes declaratory judgments if the applicant only claimed a declaratory judgment, if the damages are only limited, if the damages were already (partly) repaired by other measures, if the causal link was not established, if the damages were not proved, if there were only future damages, in case the damages could be ascribed to the own fault of the applicant, if the damages were not suffered by the applicant himself but by someone else and if only a part of the alleged violations is accepted.

3.3.2.1. The Damages are Very Limited

The first group of cases where the Court makes a declaratory judgment, can be seen as the opposite category of the cases where it never makes a declaratory judgment. This group consists of the cases where the Court finds that the applicants suffered some harm because of the violation of the Convention, but where the Court found that these damages were so 'insignificant' so that they do not justify financial compensation.[165] An illustration of this can for instance be found in the case of *Kamasinski*, a case where the Court found a breach of the right to a fair trial because the applicants had not been heard in a part of the criminal investigation.[166] Though the Court found a violation of the Convention in this case, it did not award financial compensation because it found that the part of the investigation where the applicants had not been heard had only a limited impact on the entire criminal procedure.[167] By stating so, the Court seems to refer to the limited size of the damages[168] and not to the limited reprehensibility of the fault, as some commentators have argued.[169] A similar approach can also be found in *Eckle*, where the Court refused to award a financial compensation for the reason that:

> [t]he applicants themselves, it has to be pointed out, did not allege that the unreasonable length of the proceedings in question provoked in them feelings of

---

164 M.L. Van Emmerik, *Schadevergoeding*, 1997, above n. 30, at 139ff.

165 *Kanayev v. Russia*, 27 July 2006, appl. no. 43726/02, §36.

166 *Kamasinski v. Austria*, 19 December 1989, appl. no. 9783/82, §102.

167 *Kamasinski v. Austria*, 19 December 1989, appl. no. 9783/82, §113. See also: *Brogan v. the United Kingdom*, 30 May 1989 (just satisfaction) (Plenary), appl. no. 11209/84 et al., §9; and *Wassink v. the Netherlands*, 27 September 1990, appl. no. 12535/86, §41.

168 It is also possible that the Court based this decision on the absence of a causal link.

169 In this context, Shelton refers to the low level of culpability of the defending state: D. Shelton, *Remedies*, 1999, above n. 13, at 201.

> anxiety and distress. Moreover, at the time they evinced no particular concern to have the proceedings conducted as speedily as possible.[170]

Although the Court later found that the applicants must have suffered some harm, it did take into account the limited impact of the non-pecuniary damages.[171] The Court confirmed this approach explicitly in the case of *Burdov*.[172] The defendant state in this case argued that the Court often does not award financial compensation for the violation of the reasonable time requirement and thus found that the Court in *Burdov* had to follow this approach. The Court however argued that the judgments that the state referred to were quite exceptional for the reason that they concerned national cases where only a limited financial compensation or a non-essential interest of the applicants was at stake. The interest that was at stake seemed to be too limited to justify financial compensation. It thus seems that the Court applied the *de minimis* rule: *De minimis non curat praetor*, the court does not concern itself with trifles, or trivial matters. As a consequence, it seems that if the reasonable time requirement is violated in national procedures where important interests are at stake, the Court will find that the applicants suffered harm that justifies a financial compensation.

Since this book has shown that a link exists between the ECtHR's application of Art. 41 of the Convention and the criteria of admissibility, it is important to note that with the coming into force of the twelfth protocol, the *de minimis* rule also became inscribed in the admissibility criteria.[173] Since this protocol entered into force, an applicant has to prove that he suffered a significant disadvantage because of the human rights violation. The Court applied this criterion for the first time in the cases of *Ionescu*[174] and *Korolev*.[175] In this last case, the applicant argued that his rights under Art. 6 were violated because the Russian government had not paid a sum of 22.5 roubles (approximately €1) to the applicant as it

---

170 *Eckle v. Germany*, 21 June 1983 (just satisfaction), appl. no. 8130/78, §24.

171 See also: *Oberschlick v. Austria*, 23 May 1991 (Plenary), appl. no. 11662/85, §69.

172 *Burdov v. Russia (no.2)*, 15 January 2009, appl. no. 33509/04, §153.

173 F. Vanneste, 'A new inadmissibility ground' in P. Lemmens and W. Vandenhole (eds.), *Protocol No. 14 and the Reform of the European Court of Human Rights*, Antwerp, Intersentia, 2004, p69 at 69; and X.-B. Ruedin, 'De minimis non curat the European Court of Human Rights: The Introduction of a New Admissibility Criterion (Article 12 of Protocol No. 14)', *European Human Rights Law Review*, 2008, p80 at 80.

174 *Ionescu v. Romania*, 1 June 2010 (Decision), appl. no. 36659/04.

175 *Korolev v. Russia*, 1 July 2010 (Decision), appl. no. 25551/05.

was ordered to do by a national judge. The Court in this case made the following reasoning:

> It is common ground that these terms are open to interpretation and that they give the Court some degree of flexibility, in addition to that already provided by the existing admissibility criteria. In the Court's view, these terms are not susceptible to exhaustive definition, like many other terms used in the Convention. The High Contracting Parties thus expected the Court to establish objective criteria for the application of the new rule through the gradual development of the case-law. Inspired by the abovementioned general principle de minimis non curat praetor, the new criterion hinges on the idea that a violation of a right, however real from a purely legal point of view, should attain a minimum level of severity to warrant consideration by an international court. The assessment of this minimum level is, in the nature of things, relative and depends on all the circumstances of the case. The severity of a violation should be assessed, taking account of both the applicant's subjective perceptions and what is objectively at stake in a particular case.[176]

With regard to the starting point of the Court not to concern itself with trifles, or trivial matters (*De minimis non curat praetor*), it is not surprising that the Court in the end found that the applicants did not suffer a significant disadvantage:

> In the circumstances of the present case, the Court is struck at the outset by the tiny and indeed almost negligible size of the pecuniary loss which prompted the applicant to bring his case to the Court. The applicant's grievances were explicitly limited to the defendant authority's failure to pay a sum equivalent to less than one euro awarded to him by the domestic court.[177]

---

176 See also: *Gagliano Giorgi v. Italy*, 6 March 2012, appl. no. 23563/07, §55.

177 See also: *Ionescu v. Romania*, 1 June 2010 (Decision), appl. no. 36659/04, §35; *Vasilchenko v. Russia*, 23 September 2010, appl. no. 34784/02; *Rinck v. France*, 19 October 2010 (Decision), appl. no. 18774/09; *Gaftoniuc v. Romania*, 22 February 2011 (Decision), appl. no. 30934/05, §33; *Ştefănescu v. Romania*, 12 April 2011 (Decision), appl. no. 11774/04; *Fedotov v. Moldavia*, 24 May 2011 (Decision), appl. no. 51838/07; *Burov v. Moldavia*, 14 June 2011 (Decision), appl. no. 38875/03, §§26–31; *Kiousi v. Greece*, 20 September 2011 (Decision), appl. no. 52036/09; *Havelka v. The Czech Republic*, 20 September 2011, appl. no. 7332/10; *Jancev v. The former Yugoslav Republic of Macedonia*, 4 October 2011 (Decision), appl. no. 18716/09; *Pantelimon and Vasilica SAVU v. Romania*, 11 October 2011 (Decision), appl. no. 29218/05; *Gururyan v. Armenia*, 24 January 2012 (Decision), appl. no. 11456/05; *Shefer v. Russia*, 13 March 2012 (Decision), appl. no. 45175/04, §27; *Bazelyuk v. Ukraine*, 27 March 2012 (Decision), appl. no. 49275/08; *Boelens et al. v. Belgium*, 11 September 2012 (Decision), appl. no. 20007/09 et al.; *Uhl v. The Czech Republic*, 25 September 2012 (Decision), appl. no. 1848/12, §23; *Eon v. France*, 14 March 2013, appl. no. 26118/10,

In spite of this use of the *de minimis* rule, the Court did note that it has to take into account the financial situation of the applicant to judge whether he suffered a significant disadvantage. Thus, if there is only a low amount of money at stake in a case, one cannot *mutatis mutandis* conclude that the applicants do not suffer a significant disadvantage.[178] In addition, the Court found that non-pecuniary damages can also constitute a significant disadvantage. In *Korolev*, the Court however found that there was nothing other than pecuniary interests at stake. Indeed, the applicant in this case had been awarded the sum of 22.5 roubles for his inability to look into some documents concerning his person, but because he had since had the opportunity to look into the documents, there were no non-pecuniary interests at stake anymore.

In *Giuran*, the Court found that the impossibility to receive a sum of a few hundred euros could cause a serious disadvantage for a man who was retired and has to survive with a limited income.[179] In *Piętka*, the Court more concretely found that a sum that constituted 120 percent of someone's monthly income is significant.[180] In the case of *Hudecova*, the Court argued *a contrario* that a financial sum that was less than a monthly income did not constitute a significant disadvantage.[181] In the case of *Rudyk* the Court found in the same sense that the applicant had not suffered a significant disadvantage in a case where the government did not enforce a national judgment that awarded the applicant a sum of less than €500.[182] With regard to a company, the Court found in the case of *Kirovogradoblenergo* that the impossibility to enforce the payment of the debts of half of its clients, caused a significant disadvantage for the company.[183]

---

§34; *Cecchetti v. San Marino*, 9 April 2013 (Decision), appl. no. 40174/08; *Bartl v. Slovakia*, 4 June 2013 (Decision), appl. no. 48638/09, §20; *Kiselyov v. Ukraine*, 13 June 2013, appl. no. 42953/04, §18; *Komanicky v. Slovakia*, 18 June 2013 (Decision), appl. no. 53364/07, §28; *Khvorostyanoy et al. v. Ukraine*, 25 July 2013, appl. no. 54552/09 et al., §16; *Makara et al. v. Ukraine*, 12 December 2013, appl. no. 40934/06 et al., §§18–19; *Khaynatskyy et al. v. Ukraine*, 9 January 2014, appl. no. 12895/08 et al., §18; *Shchukin et al. v. Ukraine*, 13 February 2014, appl. no. 59834/09 et al., §25; *Shtefan et al. v. Ukraine*, 31 July 2014, appl. no. 36762/06 et al., §30; and *Škubonja v. Croatia*, 19 May 2015 (Decision), appl. no. 27767/13, §32.

178 In *Diacenco* the Court, for instance, refers to the relationship between the amount of money that is at stake and the modest income of the applicant: *Diacenco v. Romania*, 7 February 2012, appl. no. 124/04, §45.

179 *Giuran v. Romania*, 21 June 2011, appl. no. 24360/04, §§15–25. See also: *Asmayev v. Russia*, 14 March 2013, appl. no. 44142/05, §50.

180 *Piętka v. Poland*, 16 October 2012, appl. no. 34216/07, §39.

181 *Hudecova et al. v. Slovakia*, 18 December 2012 (Decision), appl. no. 53807/09, §27.

182 *Rudyk et al. v. Ukraine*, 9 April 2013 (Decision), appl. no. 52932/07 et al.

183 *Kirovogradoblenergo, Pat v. Ukraine*, 27 June 2013, appl. no. 35088/07, §28.

In *Giusti*, the Court developed further criteria as to determine the content of a significant disadvantage.[184] The Court in this case identified the nature of the violated Convention right, the gravity of the impact of the violation and the potential impact of the violation on the personal situation of the applicant. The Court had to decide whether the applicant had suffered a significant disadvantage because the Italian government had neglected to enforce a contract to sell an apartment for six and a half years. The Italian government objected that this did not cause a significant disadvantage, but the Court did not agree with this. It found that the contract related to a substantial value: real property.[185] In the same way, the Court found that when someone did not receive compensation after an expropriation, he suffered a significant disadvantage.[186] If the exceeding of the reasonable time requirement is not excessive however, the Court often finds that the applicant did not suffer a significant disadvantage.[187] The Court on the other hand finds that a mere sense of injustice cannot be qualified as a sufficient significant disadvantage to bring a case before the Court. In *Ladygin*, the Court argued in this context:

> Although the applicant's subjective perception is relevant, this element does not suffice for the Court to conclude that the applicant suffered a significant disadvantage. The applicant's subjective perception has to be justifiable on objective grounds.[188]

From this point of view, a complaint about the violation of the right to privacy as enshrined in Art. 8 will be dismissed if the applicant cannot prove that the infringement of his privacy caused him some discomfort or inconvenience.[189]

It one takes this reason back to Art. 41, it will be applied mainly when a human rights violation only caused non-pecuniary damages. When a

---

184 *Giusti v. Italy*, 18 October 2011, appl. no. 13175/03, §34.

185 See also: *Finger v. Bulgaria*, 10 May 2011, appl. no. 37346/05, §63.

186 *Sancho Cruz and 14 other "Agrarian Reform" cases v. Portugal*, 18 January 2011, appl. nos. 8851/07, 8854/07, 8856/07, 8865/07, 10142/07, 10144/07, 24622/07, 32733/07, 32744/07, 41645/07, 19150/08, 22885/08, 22887/08, 26612/08 and 202/09, §§32–35. See also: *Čadek et al. v. the Czech Republic*, 22 November 2012, appl. no. 31933/08 et al., §56.

187 *Pantelimon and Vasilica SAVU v. Romania*, 11 October 2011 (Decision), appl. no. 29218/05.

188 *Ladygin v. Russia*, 30 August 2011 (Decision), appl. no. 35365/05. The Court explicitly confirmed this in: *Sylka v. Poland*, 3 June 2014 (Decision), appl. no. 19219/07, §30.

189 *Zwinkels v. the Netherlands*, 9 October 2012 (Decision), appl. no. 16593/10, §26.

victim only suffers moral loss, it will be more easily accepted that his loss can be redressed by a mere declaratory judgment. From this perspective, the Court made an interesting observation with regard to the application of Art. 41 in cases of non-pecuniary damages:

> Situations where the applicant has suffered evident trauma, whether physical or psychological, pain and suffering, distress, anxiety, frustration, feelings of injustice or humiliation, prolonged uncertainty, disruption to life, or real loss of opportunity can be distinguished from those situations where the public vindication of the wrong suffered by the applicant, in a judgment binding on the Contracting State, is an appropriate form of redress in itself. In some situations, where a law, procedure or practice has been found to fall short of Convention standards this is enough to put matters right. In other situations, however, the impact of the violation may be regarded as being of a nature and degree as to have impinged so significantly on the moral well-being of the applicant as to require something further.[190]

As a result, it must be concluded that the ECtHR applies a *de minimis* rule both in its application of Art. 41 and in its jurisprudence concerning the admissibility criteria. What is interesting about this is that this practice is not unknown in national tort law. Indeed, the *principles of European tort law* do provide the *de minimis* rule.[191] The rule does, moreover, also exist in national legal systems in one way or another. The German *Bundesgerichtshof* has for example judged that courts must dismiss claims for non-pecuniary damages if the damages are only trivial, except in cases where the damage was caused intentionally.[192] In Austria, the *Oberste Gerichtshof* has found that the adage *minima non curat praetor* can be applied in the context of *troubles des voisinages*,[193] and in Portuguese law it is said that the one can deduct the *de minimis* rule, at least with regard to non-pecuniary damages, from Art. 398 of the civil code that stipulates

---

190 *Sargsyan v. Azerbaijan*, 12 December 2017 (Grand Chamber), appl. no. 40167/06, §39; and *Chiragov et al. v. Armenia*, 12 December 2017 (Grand Chamber), appl. no. 13216/05, §57.

191 H. Koziol, *Basic questions of tort law from a Germanic perspective*, Vienna, Jan Sramek Verlag, 2012, at 179; and C. Von Bar, *Principles of European Law. Non-Contractual Liability Arising out of Damage Caused to Another*, München, European Law Publishers, 2009, at 927.

192 Bundesgerichtshof 14 January 1992, *Neue Juristische Wochenschrift* 1992, 1043 and Bundesgerichtshof 27 May 1993, *Neue Juristische Wochenschrift* 1993, 2173.

193 Oberste Gerichtshof 3 February 2005, Ob 11/05i.

that a judge must only award compensation if an interest is infringed that is worth receiving legal protection.[194]

One might wonder whether this criterion is not implicitly present in every tort law system, at least regarding non-pecuniary damages. Unlike Austrian and Portuguese tort law, Belgian tort law for example does not accept the *de minimis* rule, but it implicitly applies the same criteria. The reason for this is that Belgian tort law uses a legal connotation of damages.[195] The meaning of damages under the civil code is more limited as in real life. Only what a judge conceives as damages under the civil code will be taken into account. One can have '*damages sine injuria*'. This is particularly interesting with regard to moral damages. Since moral damages cannot be estimated concretely, there cannot be a real difference between judging whether damages are grave enough as to be qualified as legal damages or judging whether a *de minimis* rule is guaranteed. Consequently it can be argued that the *de minimis* rule as applied in Portuguese law can be applied to non-pecuniary damages in Belgian tort law and probably in every other legal system as well.

3.3.2.2. The Damages are Already Repaired by Other Measures

In some cases, the consequences of a violation of the Convention have already been redressed by measures. This happened for instance in *Dudgeon* and *Norris*.[196] These cases concerned the penalization of homosexual acts between adult men in Northern Ireland and Ireland. In both these cases the Court found a violation of Art. 8. The Court nevertheless refused to grant financial compensation and argued instead that the mere declaration of the violation offered sufficient satisfaction. In *Dudgeon*, the Court moreover pointed out that the legislator in Northern Ireland had already unpenalized homosexual acts between adult men.[197] In *Norris*, the Court underlined that there were debates in the Irish parliament going on to do the same.[198] The Court in this case also stressed that the Irish parliament

194 C. Von Bar, *Principles of European Law*, 2009, above n. 191, at 930.

195 Belgian tort law is far from unique in this approach since it is common to every tort law system to limit the rights and interests that are protected by tort law. For an overview in this sense, see: C. Van Dam, *European Tort Law*, 2013, above n. 82, at 167ff.

196 *Dudgeon v. the United Kingdom*, 24 February 1983 (just satisfaction), appl. no. 7525/76 and *Norris v. Ireland*, 26 October 1988 (Plenary), appl. no. 10581/83.

197 *Dudgeon v. the United Kingdom*, 24 February 1983 (just satisfaction), appl. no. 7525/76, §18.

198 *Norris v. Ireland*, 26 October 1988 (Plenary), appl. no. 10581/83, §50. See also: *Christine Goodwin v. the United Kingdom*, 11 July 2002, appl. no. 28957/98, §120.

had to succeed in this quest so as to meet the requirement to comply with the judgment under Art. 46 of the Convention.

The cases of *Dudgeon* and *Norris* illustrate that the Court makes a declaratory judgment in cases where states have already taken measures so as to comply with the judgment and where the state will take measures in the near future. Implicitly, these cases also illustrate the application of the *de minimis* rule. Indeed, it seems as if the Court found that the damages that the applicants had suffered for the mere fact that some of their handlings were criminalized, did not cause enough stress and anxiety as to legitimize a just satisfaction as is required by the *de minimis* rule. From this perspective, it seems as if the Court would have granted financial compensation if the applicants had already been punished. This is what happened in *Wolfmeyer*. In this case, the Court, as in *Dudgeon* and *Norris*, had to deal with the criminalization of homosexual acts. In this case the applicant had been convicted for homosexual acts, but his punishment was not affected. The Austrian government argued that the applicant had no interest in the application because the punishment he had received had not been implemented after a judgment of the Austrian Constitutional Court. The Court however argued:

> The applicant had to stand trial and was convicted by the first instance court. In such circumstances, it is inconceivable how an acquittal without any compensation for damages and accompanied by the reimbursement of a minor part of the necessary defence costs could have provided adequate redress. This is all the more so as the Court itself has awarded substantial amounts of compensation for non-pecuniary damage in comparable cases, having particular regard to the fact that the trial during which details of the applicants' most intimate private life were laid open to the public, had to be considered as a profoundly destabilising event in the applicants' lives.[199]

After finding a violation of the principle of equality, the Court granted the applicant in this case financial compensation for moral damages. If this case is compared with *Dudgeon* and *Norris*, at first sight this seems remarkable because the applicant in *Wolfmeyer* had – just as the applicants in *Dudgeon* and *Norris* – not been punished for homosexual acts. The applicants in all these three cases would also not be punished in the future because the

199 *Wolfmeyer v. Austria*, 26 May 2005, appl. no. 5263/03, §33. See also, although less explicit: *Dalban v. Romania*, 28 September 1999 (Grand Chamber), appl. no. 28114/95, §44.

Convention requires the states to comply with the judgment of the ECtHR under Art. 46 of the Convention. Consequently, the only reason why the Court granted a financial compensation in this case and not in *Dudgeon* and *Norris*, seems to be the fact that the moral damages that the applicant had suffered in the past were graver in *Wolfmeyer*. Indeed, in the cases of *Dudgeon* and *Norris*, the applicant could only have suffered moral damages because of the fact that homosexual actions were criminalized without them being sentenced for these actions. In *Wolfmeyer* on the other hand, the applicant had been the subject of a criminal procedure and had been sentenced. That some of his most private intimacies had been made public during the criminal procedure was an element that the ECtHR stressed when granting financial compensation for moral damages.

The use of the *de minimis* rule in *Dudgeon* and *Norris* also illustrates that the ECtHR applies the principle of subsidiarity. Regarding the application of the principle of subsidiarity in the context of Art. 41, this book has shown that the Court does not grant financial compensation under Art. 41 if the state is able to take measures to restitute the damages as far as possible in kind. Accordingly, the cases where the Court makes declaratory judgments in this context can be explained by a principle that is comparable to national tort law. Indeed, in Belgian tort law it is accepted that when compensation in kind is possible, it has priority over financial compensation.[200]

3.3.2.3. There is Only a Potential Violation of the Convention

Another type of case that Van Emmerik indicates as a case where the Court makes a declaratory judgment, are those where the Court only found a potential violation of the Convention. Typical examples are those where the Convention would be violated if a state executed a deportation order.[201] That the Court does not grant financial compensation in this type

200 Belgian Court of Cassation, 21 April 1994, appl. no. AR C.93.0225.F; Belgian Court of Cassation, 13 May 1997, appl. no. AR P.96.0539.N; Belgian Court of Cassation, 22 January 2007, appl. nos. AR S.04.0088.N and S.04.0169.N; Belgian Court of Cassation. 25 September 2008, appl. no. AR C.07.0207.F; Belgian Court of Cassation, 5 May 2011, appl. no. AR C.10.0496.F; and Belgian Court of Cassation, 17 December 2012, appl. no. AR S.11.0099.F.

201 *Soering v. the United Kingdom*, 7 July 1989 (Plenary Session), appl. no. 14038/88, §127; *Beldjoudi v. France*, 26 March 1992, appl. no. 12083/86, §86; *Chahal v. the United Kingdom*, 15 November 1996, appl. no. 22414/93, §157; *Ahmed v. Austria*, 17 December 1996, appl. no. 25964/94, §51.

of case is evident. Since the damage is only potential, the damages will be redressed if the state meets its obligations under Art. 46. If the applicants on the other hand had been locked up in a detention center before the deportation order were to be executed, the Court would grant compensation for the damages that were caused by the detention.[202]

3.3.2.4. The Fault of the Applicant and the Principle of *Fraus Omnia Corrumpit*

Other types of cases where the ECtHR makes a declaratory judgment are those where the applicant himself has made a fault. The most renowned example is *McCann*.[203] The facts of this case are well known. The secret services of the United Kingdom were aware of the plan of three members of the IRA to commit a terrorist attack in Gibraltar. When these men were prospecting in Gibraltar and left their car alone on a marketplace, members of the police followed them. When one of the men made a suspicious movement that was interpreted by the police as an attempt to activate a car bomb, the police officers killed them. Although the Court in this case found that Art. 2 was violated because the operation of the security services was not planned in an adequate way, it did not grant financial compensation. It found that, 'having regard to the fact that the three terrorist suspects who were killed had been intending to plant a bomb in Gibraltar, the Court does not consider it appropriate to make an award under this head.'[204] Thus one can conclude that the Court found that, as Judges Bonello and Marusto also noted in their dissenting opinion,[205] at least a part of the damage was due to the acts of the human rights victims.[206]

That this approach was not an ephemera is illustrated by a case where the Court referred to the *McCann* case to distinguish it from a situation where it was not proved that the applicants had been involved in the preparation of a terrorist attack. In such a case, the Court did grant financial compensation for the violation of the right to life.[207] In addition, this principle also seems to be applied in different cases where the Court, without making reference to the fault of the applicant,

202 *Saadi v. Italy*, 28 February 2008, appl. no. 37201/06, §§182–188.
203 *McCann et al. v. the United Kingdom*, 27 September 1995, appl. no. 18984/91.
204 *Ibid.*, §219.
205 See in the same sense: Partly dissenting opinion of Judge Bonello joined by Judge Maruste in 25 March 1999, appl. no. 31195/96.
206 D. Shelton, *Remedies*, 1999, above n. 13, at 209ff.
207 *A. et al. v. the United Kingdom*, 19 February 2009, appl. no. 3455/05, §251.

refused to grant compensation to human rights victims who had committed criminal acts.[208]

The same conclusion can also be drawn from the jurisprudence concerning the unreasonable length of judicial procedures.[209] In *Corrigliano* the Court for instance found that because of the tactical manoeuvers of the applicant in the national procedures, it seemed that it was not of a primary concern for him that the judgment should be delivered within a reasonable time.[210] In *Storck* the Court also found that the declaratory judgment in itself provided just satisfaction because the applicants had asked the judges in the national procedures over and over again whether they could give additional evidence.[211] In their dissenting opinion, some of the judges argued that a declaratory judgment was not appropriate in this case because they considered that only a part of the delay in the national procedure could be attributed to the applicants. If the entire delay of the procedure could have been attributed to the applicants, they argued, the Court could not have found a violation of the requirement to give a judgment within a reasonable time. The dissenters found that in this case the Court should have granted a limited financial compensation.[212] But although these dissenters argued that a declaratory judgment was inappropriate in this case, their considerations illustrate that the *restitutio in integrum* must be the target for just satisfaction under Art. 41 but that the fault of the applicant must be seen as an exception to this rule.

According to Monika Jozon, the use of the principle of the own fault of the victim is problematic in the framework of the Convention because the Convention cannot be implemented in a discriminatory manner.[213] It is the opinion of the author of this book that one cannot agree with this criticism. Indeed, the principle that a wrongdoer must be responsible for the consequences of his own wrongful conduct must also be applicable to victims. This is an established principle in several tort law systems and is

---

208 *Migon v. Poland*, 25 June 2002, appl. no. 24244/94; *Chalkley v. the United Kingdom*, 12 June 2003, appl. no. 63831/00; *Kafkaris v. Cyprus*, 12 February 2008, appl. no. 21906/04. See also the jurisprudence cited by Edel in: F. Edel, 'L'indemnisation par la Cour européenne', 2011, p229 at 252, nn. 61 et seq.

209 *Buscemi v. Italy*, 16 September 1999, appl. no. 29569/95, §77; *Peryt v. Poland*, 2 December 2003, appl. no. 42042/98, §33; and *Gisela Müller v. Germany*, 6 October 2005, appl. no. 69584/01, §93.

210 *Corigliano v. Italy*, 10 December 1982, appl. no. 8304/78, §53.

211 *Stork v. Germany*, 13 July 2006, appl. no. 38033/02, §51.

212 Joint dissenting opinion of Judges Butkevych, Tsatsa-Nikolovska and Botoucharova in 13 July 2006, appl. no. 38033/02.

213 M. Jozon, 'Satisfaction by Finding a violation', 2011, above n. 140, p741 at 749.

known as contributory negligence. On top of this, this jurisprudence of the ECtHR must be welcomed because it expresses the principle of *fraus omnia corrumpit*, according to which a wrongdoer cannot make profit out of his own intentional wrongful acts.

3.3.2.5. Only a Part of the Alleged Violations is Accepted by the Court

In the literature it has been noted that the ECtHR makes declaratory judgments in cases where only a part of the alleged human rights violations was accepted by the Court.[214] An example is *Johnston*.[215] The case concerned the lovechild born of a father who was married to a woman other than the mother of the child. Since Irish law at that time did not recognize the possibility to divorce and since under the same law children that were born outside marriage had lesser legal protection in the context of *inter alia* inheritance law, the parents argued that their rights under Art. 8 were violated because the father could not divorce and because children that were born outside marriage did not have the same rights as children born within a marriage. The Court found that the impossibility to divorce did not constitute a violation of Art. 8 but that the unequal treatment of love children did.[216]

Concerning the award of just satisfaction, the ECtHR found that a large part of the moral damages of the applicants was caused by the impossibility to divorce. Since this did not however constitute a violation of the convention, the Court did not grant any compensation for it. Concerning the remaining immaterial damages, the Court stated:

> If and in so far as the remaining matters are connected with the legal situation of the third applicant – a point which does not emerge clearly from the material before the Court -, they could in principle form the object of such an award. Nevertheless, the Court considers that, in the particular circumstances of the case, its findings of violation on that issue of themselves constitute sufficient just satisfaction.[217]

Consequently, it seems that the Court in this case did not grant compensation on the one hand because, as in *Dudgeon* and *Norris*, most

214 M.L. Van Emmerik, *Schadevergoeding*, 1997, above n. 30, at 145.
215 *Johnston et al. v. Ireland*, 18 December 1986, appl. no. 9697/82. See also: *Olsson v. Sweden (no.1)*, 24 March 1988, appl. no. 10465/83, §111.
216 *Johnston et al. v. Ireland*, 18 December 1986, appl. no. 9697/82, §75.
217 *Ibid.*, §84.

of the damages would occur in the future and, on the other hand, because the remaining immaterial damages were too small to be remedied. Indeed, in other cases where the Court only found a part of the alleged violations to be violated, it did grant limited moral damages.[218] As a result, it must be concluded that the fact that only a part of the alleged human rights violations was actually violated in itself has no influence on the practice under Art. 41 to grant compensation apart from the influence of the *de minimis* rule.

3.3.3. Criticism on the Use of Declaratory Judgments

Up until now this book has shown that declaratory judgments can be explained and thus that the freedom of the Court to choose whether or not to grant compensation seems to be based on principles. It is however also important to know that this freedom has been criticized. Indeed, the use of declaratory judgments is not self-evident. It has never been used by international arbitration councils[219] and the Inter-American Court of Human Rights has always rejected the requests of states to make a declaratory judgment.[220] Thus it comes as no surprise that the practice of making declaratory judgments by the ECtHR has been criticized.

The first important criticism was formulated by Judges Ganshof Van Der Meersch and Evrigenis in their dissenting opinion in *Engel*:

> According to Article 50 [Art. 41] of the Convention, the Court shall afford, on the conditions laid down in that provision, 'just satisfaction' to the injured party if it finds a breach of the Convention. It seems difficult to accept the proposition that the finding by the Court of a breach of the substantive provisions of the Convention, whilst constituting a condition for the application of Article 50, can at the same time be the consequence in law following from that same provision.[221]

---

218 *Helmers v. Sweden*, 29 October 1991, appl. no. 11826/85, §42. The fact that these damages were more limited could be subtracted from the legal costs that the Court had granted under Art. 41. These costs are granted proportionate to the violation: *Nikolova v. Bulgaria*, 25 March 1999, appl. no. 31195/96, §79; *Beyeler v. Italy*, 28 May 2002, appl. no. 33202/96, §27; *Sahin v. Germany*, 8 July 2003, appl. nos. 30943/96 and 30943/96, §105; *Sakkopoulos v. Greece*, 15 January 2004, appl. no. 61828/00, §59; *Cianetti v. Italy*, 22 April 2004, appl. no. 55634/00, §56; and *Debono v. Malta*, 7 February 2006, appl. no. 34539/02, §54.

219 C. Gray, *Judicial Remedies in International Law*, 1987, above n. 142, at 17.

220 D. Shelton, *Remedies*, 1999, above n. 13, at 211.

221 Joint Separate opinion of Judges Ganshof Van Der Meersch and Evrigenis in 23 November 1976 (just satisfaction), appl. no. 5100/71 et al.

The critique of these judges seems to be reasonable. If the condition to apply Art. 41 of the Convention is the same as the result, the provision threatens to become meaningless. In the case of *Marckx*, Judges Ganshof Van Der Meersch and Evrigenis, together with Ballador Pallieri, Pederson and Pinheiro, gave further interpretation to their criticism.[222] In this case the Court found a violation of a free family life (Art. 8) and the principle of equality because Belgian law treated children who were born outside a legal marriage different from children who were born inside a legal marriage. The applicants, both the mother and her child, claimed one Belgian franc (about 2.5 eurocent) nominal damages for their immaterial injury. The Court however refused to grant them this little amount of money. The dissenters were of the opinion that this refusal was unacceptable. They found that the moral satisfaction that the applicants required could indeed be granted by a declaratory judgment. But they also found that this moral satisfaction could be personalized by commanding the state to grant them a symbolic sum of money. The purpose of the satisfaction according to the dissenters is that the applicants are 'recognised individually as victims of the legal situation brought about by the State.'[223] If the victims of human rights violations only receive declaratory judgments, it seems as though they did not really receive just satisfaction.[224]

In *Nikolova*, Judge Bonello – joined by Judge Maruste – made a similar criticism.[225] He also added the argument that declaratory judgments are not very common in domestic legal systems where judges at least grant symbolic damages for the violation of immaterial values. Thus, if the Court would not accept the possibility to grant symbolic or nominal damages, it would lead to the contradictory situation where people whose normal domestic rights are violated would receive a larger amount of damages

---

222 Joint dissenting opinion of Judges Balladore Pallieri, Pederson, Ganshof Van Der Meersch, Evrigenis, Pinheiro Farinha and Garcia de Enterria in *Marckx v. Belgium*, 13 June 1979, appl. no. 6833/74.

223 *Ibid.*

224 In this sense: Partly dissenting opinion of Judge Loucaïdes in *Kingsley v. the United Kingdom*, 7 November 2000 (Grand Chamber), appl. no. 35605/97; Partly dissenting opinion of Judge Casadevall in *Swiersko v. Poland*, 10 January 2006, appl. no. 9013/02; and M. De Salvia, 'Le principe de l'octroi subsidiaire des dommages-intérêts', 2011, above n. 158, p9 at 14.

225 Partly dissenting opinion of Judge Bonello joined by Judge Maruste in *Nikolova v. Bulgaria*, 25 March 1999, appl. nos. 31195/96 and 31195/96. A similar line of criticism was also formulated by Judge Casadevall: Partly dissenting opinion of Judge Casadevall joined by Judges Bonello and Kovler in *Kingsley v. the United Kingdom*, 28 May 2002, appl. no. 35605/97.

then people whose rights under the Court are violated. On top of that, Judge Bonello criticized the lack of motivation of the Court when it makes declaratory judgments. He thereby criticized the argument of the Court that it only has to grant satisfaction 'if necessary'. According to Bonello:

> 'If necessary' is applicable only where there is a concurrence of both the conditions posited by Article 41, i.e. the finding of a violation of the Convention and the ability of the domestic system to provide for some partial reparation. When these two conditions combine (and only then) the Court can find it unnecessary to award additional just satisfaction. This is what Article 41 clearly states.[226]

Bonello thus argues that when the domestic legal order does not grant compensation, the ECtHR has no choice but to grant the compensation itself. According to Bonello this also derives from Art. 46, §2, according to which the Committee of ministers must supervise the execution of judgments. This however requires that a judgment must be executed, which is not the case if the judgment in itself is the execution. The practice of declaratory judgments in itself is thus not reconcilable with Art. 46 of the Convention.

Although the criticism of Bonello at first sight seems to be plausible, it cannot be entirely agreed with here. The problem is that Bonello does not differentiate between the different situations where declaratory judgments are made. Where Bonello finds the declaratory judgment incompatible with Art. 46, it has been seen that the Court sometimes makes a declaratory judgment just because it takes into account the fact that the government still has to take measures under Art. 46. Thus the arguments of Bonello seem to be a bit confusing. But if it is thought through, what bothers Bonello is not the practice of declaratory judgments as such, what bothers him is the *de minimis* rule. The problem with the declaratory judgment for Bonello is the fact that the Court does not always grant financial compensation when it finds a violation of a human right. For Bonello, the violation of the Convention in itself causes damages that should be redressed automatically by financial compensation.

That the rejection of the *de minimis* rule is the true ground for Bonello's criticism also stems from the fact that Bonello argues that the Court, with making declaratory judgments, fails in its judicial and its pedagogical

---

226 Partly dissenting opinion of Judge Bonello joined by Judge Maruste in *Nikolova v. Bulgaria*, 25 March 1999, appl. no. 31195/96.

functions. The award of damages, according to Bonello, is not only meant to redress the damages of the victim but also has a dissuasive function towards the government. Bonello is of the opinion that the Court must at least grant nominal or symbolic damages to victims of human rights violations. A similar critique towards declaratory judgments are sometimes also formulated against specific refusals of the Court to award compensation for non-pecuniary damages, and where it does award compensation for pecuniary damages.[227]

Similar arguments have also been formulated in legal doctrine. Evert Alkema for instance found that the Court, by not granting financial compensation for some types of human rights violations, creates categories of less important human rights.[228] Van Emmerik on the other hand complained about the practice of declaratory judgments in cases where a law would annul the human rights violation in the future. He rightly points out that the victims in such cases have already suffered some damages in the past and thus should be granted some compensation.[229] Van Emmerik, just as Judge Rozakis does in his partial dissenting opinion in *Claes*, rightly argues that it would be better if the Court in the future would make a clear distinction between the measures that should be taken to redress the human rights violation in the future and the satisfaction that serves as a means to compensate the suffered damages. But on the other hand, one must admit that also in national tort law, judges sometimes do not clearly separate the damages for past and future losses.[230]

In *Salduz* the Court seems to take this criticism into account. In this case, where the Court found a violation of the right to a fair trial in a criminal procedure, it argued under Art. 41 that redress could best be reached by reopening the criminal case but it also granted financial compensation for the remaining non-pecuniary damages.[231] The same was also clear in

---

227 E.g. Partly dissenting opinion of Judge Pastor Vilanova in *Paunović and Milivojević v. Serbia*, 24 May 2016, appl. no. 41683/06.

228 E. Alkema, 'Case report on ECtHR, Bunkate v the Netherlands, *Bunkate v. the Netherlands*, 26 May 1993, appl. no. 13645/88', *Nederlandse Jurisprudentie* 1993, at 1664.

229 M.L. Van Emmerik, *Schadevergoeding*, 1997, above n. 30, at 147.

230 See, for instance on Belgian law: P. Wéry, 'La réparation en nature du dommage en matière de responsabilité civile extracontractuelle', *Tijdschrift voor Belgisch Burgerlijk Recht* 2012, p249 at 253.

231 *Salduz v. Turkey*, 27 November 2008, appl. no. 36391/02, §73. See also: *Brumarescu v. Romania*, 23 January 2001 (just satisfaction), appl. no. 28342/95; *Assanidze v. Georgia*, 8 April 2004, appl. no. 71503/01; *Ilascu et al. v. Moldavia and Russia*, 8 July 2004, appl. no. 48787/99; *Strain et al. v. Romania*, 21 July 2005, appl. no. 57001/00; *Rusu et al. v. Romania*, 19 July 2007, appl. no. 4198/04; *Driza v. Albania*, 1 November 2007,

K.U. v. Finland.[232] The applicant in this case complained that under Finish law he was unable to sue a person in Court who had made a profile under his name on a dating site. The Court indeed found that the inability to file such a claim violated the right to privacy under Art. 8. While the procedure for the ECtHR was pending, Finland had adopted a law that foresaw criminal charges against people who present themselves as someone else on the internet. Nevertheless, the Court found that the applicant had suffered moral distress and granted him damages under Art. 41.[233] In *Ilic* the Court explicitly suggested some measures that the state could take to prevent future damages and granted compensation for the damages that had already occurred.[234] Thus, as De Salvia already pointed out, it seems reasonable that the Court should reward lesser damages when a state takes measures to prevent future damages.[235]

But the Court does not only differentiate past and future damages, it also changed its view on nominal or symbolic damages. In recent cases the Court sometimes grants these types of damages if the applicants claim them.[236] Indeed, the Court does not grant compensation on its own initiative.[237]

---

appl. no. 33771/02; *Suciu Werle v. Romania*, 13 December 2007, appl. no. 26521/05; *Grigoras v. Romania*, 7 October 2008, appl. no. 19188/03; *Chiorean v. Romania*, 21 October 2008, appl. no. 20535/03; *Teodorescu Olimpia-Maria v. Romania*, 4 November 2008, appl. no. 43774/02; *Reichardt v. Romania*, 13 November 2008, appl. no. 6111/04; *Veniamin v. Romania*, 26 January 2010, appl. no. 19438/05; *Maria Violeta Lazarescu v. Romania*, 23 February 2010, appl. no. 10636/06; *M.S.S. v. Belgium and Greece*, 21 January 2011, appl. no. 30696/09; *Denisova and Moiseyeva v. Russia*, 14 June 2011, appl. no. 16903/03; *Hirsi Jamaa et al. v. Italy*, 23 February 2012, appl. no. 27765/09; and *Oleksandr Volkov*, 9 January 2013, appl. no. 21722/11.

232 *K.U. v. Finland*, 2 December 2008, appl. no. 2872/02.

233 *Ibid.*, §55.

234 In *Ilic* the Court granted partial compensation for material damages and suggested some measures to stop the human rights violation: *Ilic v. Serbia*, 9 October 2007, appl. no. 30132/04, §112.

235 M. De Salvia, 'Can the Reparation Awarded to Victims of Violations under the ECHR be Considered a Real "Just Satisfaction"' in A. Fenyves, E. Karner, H. Koziol and E. Steiner (eds.), *Tort Law in the Jurisprudence of the European Court of Human Rights*, Göttingen, De Gruyter,, 2011, p387 at 392.

236 *Lorsé et al. v. the Netherlands*, 4 February 2003, appl. no. 52750/99, §98 and 100; *Vaney v. France*, 30 November 2004, appl. no. 53946/00, §§55 and 57; *Cruz de Carvalho v. Portugal*, 10 July 2007, appl. no. 18223/04, §§31 and 33; *Clinique psychiatrique 'Athina' Vrilission SARL and Clinique Lyrakou SA v. Greece*, 2 July 2009, appl. no. 32838/07, §49 and 52. *contra*: *Karacay v. Turkey*, 27 March 2007, appl. no. 6615/03; *Grande Oriente D'Italia de Palazzo Giustiniani v. Italy (no.2)*, 31 May 2007, appl. no. 35972/97, §§68 and 70.

237 *Ryabykh v. Russia*, 24 July 2003, appl. no. 52854/99, §§67–68; *Timofeyev v. Russia*, 23 October 2003, appl. nos. 58263/00 and 58263/00, §§51–52; *Vasyagin v. Russia*, 22 September 2005, appl. no. 75475/01, §40; *Yayan v. Turkey*, 2 February 2006,

As a rule, damages must be claimed and proven.[238] Thus, the last group of cases where the Court makes declaratory judgments are those where the applicants did not claim any damages.[239] There is however an exception to this rule. In cases where the Court found a violation of a substantial aspect of Arts 2, 3 or 5 (the provisions for which the Court never makes a declaratory judgment) the Court had already granted damages out of its own motion and argued that although the applicants had not claimed redress, the fundamental character of the violated rights made compensation necessary.[240]

---

appl. no. 66848/01, §25; *Sidorenko v. Russia*, 26 July 2007, appl. no. 4459/03, §§35–36; *Larionov v. Russia*, 14 November 2008, appl. no. 42431/02, §33; *Rysev v. Russia*, 18 June 2009, appl. no. 924/03, §41; P. Leach, *Taking a Case to the European Court*, 2011, above n. 13, at 468; J. Sharpe, 'Article 50', 1999, above n. 13, p809 at 812–813; D. Shelton, *Remedies*, 1999, above n. 13, at 189; E. Steiner, 'Just Satisfaction under Art. 41 ECHR', 2011, above n. 13, p3 at 13; and K. Reid, *A practitioner's guide*, 2008, above n. 13, at 603.

238 Article 60 of the Rules of Court, 1 September 2012; M. De Salvia, 'Le principe de l'octroi subsidiaire des dommages-intérêts', 2011, above n. 158, p9 at 15; and C. Kissling and D. Kelliher, 'Compensation', 2011, above n. 18, p579 at 587.

239 *Sunday Times v. the United Kingdom*, 6 November 1980 (art. 41), appl. no. 6538/74, §14; *Benthem v. the Netherlands*, 23 October 1985, appl. no. 8848/80, §45; *Deumeland v. Germany*, 29 May 1986, appl. no. 9384/81, §98; *Inze v. Austria*, 28 October 1987, appl. no. 8695/79, §46; *Bouamar v. Belgium*, 29 February 1988, appl. no. 9106/80, §68; *Ekbatani v. Sweden*, 26 May 1988, appl. no. 10563/83, §34; *Brogan v. the United Kingdom*, 30 May 1989 (art. 41), appl. no. 11209/84 et al., §7; *Kostovski v. the Netherlands*, 20 November 1989, appl. no. 11454/85, §46; *Huvig v. France*, 24 April 1990, appl. no. 11105/84, §38; *Nasri v. France*, 13 July 1995, appl. no. 19465/92, §49; *Moore and Gordon v. the United Kingdom*, 29 September 1999, appl. no. 36529/97 and 37393/97, §27; *Coëme et al. v. Belgium*, 22 June 2000, appl. no. 32492/96 et al., §155; *Porubova v. Russia*, 8 October 2009, appl. no. 8237/03, §53; *Tkachevy v. Russia*, 4 April 2013 (just satisfaction), appl. no. 35430/05, §16; *Delvina v. Albania*, 21 May 2013 (just satisfaction), appl. no. 49106/06, §18; *Frendo Randon et al. v. Malta*, 9 July 2013 (just satisfaction), appl. no. 2226/10, §28; and *Albergas and Arlauskas v. Lithuania*, 27 May 2014, appl. no. 17978/05, §37. T. Barkhuysen and M. Van Emmerik, 'Rechtsherstel bij schending', 2006, above n. 14, p39 at 47; F. Edel, 'L'indemnisation par la Cour européenne', 2011, above n. 14, p229 at 234; and D. Scorey and T. Eicke, *Human Rights Damages*, above n. 14, A2 at 12.

240 *Mayzit v. Russia*, 20 January 2005, appl. no. 63378/00, §88; *Igor Ivanov v. Russia*, 7 June 2007, appl. no. 34000/02, §50; *Babushkin v. Russia*, 18 October 2007, appl. no. 67253/01, §62; *Chember v. Russia*, 3 July 2008, appl. no. 7188/03, §77; *Nadrosov v. Russia*, 31 July 2008, appl. no. 9297/02, §54; *Denisenko and Bogdanchikov v. Russia*, 12 February 2009, appl. no. 3811/02, §142; *Alibekov v. Russia*, 14 May 2009, appl. no. 8413/02, §73; *Vladimir Fedorov v. Russia*, 30 July 2009, appl. no. 19223/04, §87; *Maksimov v. Azerbaijan*, 8 October 2009, appl. no. 38228/05, §98; *Dorogaykin v. Russia*, 10 February 2011, appl. no. 1066/05, §49; *Chudun v. Russia*, 21 June 2011, appl. no. 20641/04, §129; *Grigoryev v. Russia*, 23 October 2012, appl. no. 22663/06, §103; and *Borodin v. Russia*, 6 November 2012, appl. no. 41867/04, §166.

3.4. DEFINING DAMAGES BY HUMAN RIGHTS

From the preceding sections, different conclusions can be drawn. The first is that the Court uses declaratory judgments if restitution in kind can only be delivered at the national state. As was discussed before, this is one of the situations where the Court applies the principle of subsidiarity. Secondly, the Court applies the principle that the damaged person has to bear the damages that were caused by his own fault and that in some cases the Court finds that the damages, because of the seriousness of its fault, has to bear all the damages. Thirdly, the Court makes a declaratory judgment if there are only future damages or if the causal connection between human rights violation and the claimed damages is missing. On top of that, the ECtHR applies a *de minimis* rule. If the (non-pecuniary) damages are almost irrelevant, the Court finds it appropriate to make a declaratory judgment.

Although the practice of making declaratory judgments has been criticized in the past, the Court has always continued to do so. Nevertheless, the use of the declaratory judgments should not be exaggerated. In the majority of cases where the Court finds a violation of the Convention, it awards a sum of money under Art. 41.[241] Moreover, the use of declaratory judgments in some cases does not contradict the idea of restitution of damages. This is especially so in cases where the Court argues that restitution in kind can be offered at the national level. That the Court in a lot of cases makes declaratory judgments in situations where national tort law would not grant financial redress either, gives the impression that the Court, when it makes declaratory judgments, does not want to deviate from the principle of *restitutio in integrum*. This might also stem from the fact that the Court, when making declaratory judgments, does speak of satisfaction, just as it does when it grants financial compensation. Accordingly, it seems as if the Court assumes that a violation of the Convention in itself constitutes damages.[242] Indeed, does a satisfaction not

---

241 For instance, in 1988, the Court awarded a financial compensation in 82 percent of the cases where it found a violation: B. Fontana, 'Damage awards for human rights violations in the European and the Inter-American courts of human rights', *Santa Clara L. Rev.* 1991, p1127 at 1138.

242 From this perspective, see: F. Bydlinski, 'Methodological Approaches', 2011, above n. 4, p29 at 120; K. Oliphant and K. Ludwichowska, 'Damage', 2011, above n. 3, p397 at 399; M. Kellner and I. Durant, 'Causation' in A. Fenyves, E. Karner, H. Koziol and E. Steiner (eds.), *Tort Law in the Jurisprudence of the European Court of Human Rights*, Göttingen, De Gruyter, 2011, p449 at 462; The Law Commission and the Scottish Law Commission, *Damages under the Human Rights Act 1998*, 2000, <https://www.scotlawcom.gov.uk/files/3012/7989/6877/rep180.pdf>, at 32; K. Wolfram, 'Just Satisfaction in Art 41 ECHR', 2011, above n. 30, p345 at 354.

require (non-pecuniary) damages that need to be compensated? If so, one can argue that the declaratory judgments are a form of restitution in kind to satisfy human rights victims that suffer non-pecuniary damages because of the violation of their human rights.[243] If an international court finds a violation of a human right, one cannot act as if this is just an unimportant event. The finding of a violation of the Convention by the ECtHR must be perceived – also for the victims of the violation – as a highly symbolic act.[244]

If declaratory judgments do compensate damages, an infringement of the Convention that constitutes moral damages does not always have to be compensated by a sum of money. The primacy of restitution in kind and the *de minimis* rule preclude the Court from granting sums of money for all non-pecuniary damages. Indeed, in cases where the Court makes a declaratory judgment because of the own fault of the victim or the absence of a causal link, it seems that the violation of the Convention in itself causes some moral damages that do not however have to be compensated by a sum of money because of the primacy of the restitution in kind and the *de minimis* rule. The ECtHR, by making declaratory judgments in these cases, gives another perspective on restitution of non-pecuniary damages. By making declaratory judgments, it does not put the financial redress in the center of restitution for non-pecuniary damages, but the moral recognition of the suffered harm.

From the perspective of national law, this approach is not strange. This stems from the main function of tort law. Tort law is not in the first place meant to award financial redress to victims but is meant to settle conflicts in a peaceful manner. Indeed, if a system of tort law awards a sum of money for non-pecuniary damages, than this sum of money is not primarily meant to compensate the damages, but to award a satisfaction to limit the moral sufferings and to recognize, as a society, that the victim has been treated in an unjust manner.[245] It has also been said that compensation

---

243 M. Kellner and I. Durant, 'Causation', 2011, above n. 242, p449 at 463.

244 D. Shelton, *Remedies*, 1999, above n. 13, at 201. Leach is of the opinion that the Court often only makes a declaratory judgment or awards a small amount of compensation because the primary function of the Court is, as described in Art. 19, to enforce the compliance with the Convention: P. Leach, *Taking a Case to the European Court*, 2011, above n. 13, at 467.

245 H. Bocken and I. Boone, *Inleiding tot het schadevergoedingsrecht. Buitencontractueel aansprakelijkheidsrecht en andere schadevergoedingsstelsels*, Bruges, Die Keure, 2011, at 31.

for non-pecuniary damages in national law has a satisfactory function, in the sense that it has to offer a form of satisfaction for the irritations and anger that damaged people have felt.[246] Moreover, some national legal systems provide the possibility for judges to award a symbolic sum of €1 to compensate non-pecuniary damages. The difference between this approach and the approach of the ECtHR seems to be symbolic. Indeed, if a national judge only awards one symbolic euro, he implicitly seems to indicate that the finding of a violation in tort law suffices as just satisfaction.

3.4.1. Are Damages Necessary for Finding a Convention Violation?

Now that the use of declaratory judgments has been explained without devaluing the idea that the finding of a violation of the Convention in itself constitutes damages, the question arises as to why the Court in some cases argues that the existence of damages is not a condition to find a violation of the Convention. In order to untangle this contradiction, one has to put this jurisprudence into the right perspective. The Court has up until now only made this line of argument with regard to the criteria of applicability as enshrined in Art. 34 of the Convention. Moreover, the majority of the cases where the Court has made this line of argument had respect for procedural guarantees. Accordingly, it seems that one must take into account the principle of subsidiarity according to which the national legal system is the first protector of human rights and the Court only provides a secondary mechanism. Indeed, the cases where the Court argues that the existence of damages is not required to find a violation of the Convention have regard to situations where an applicant has not received a final judgment in the national legal order,[247] or where an applicant has won national procedures and claimed that his rights under Art. 6 had been violated.[248] What is more important is that the Court, in all the cases where it made this argument with regard to the criteria of applicability and where it found a violation of the Convention, awarded a sum of money under Art. 41 in all cases but those where it seemed to apply the *de minimis*

246 V. Karapanou and L. Visscher, 'Towards a Better Assessment of Pain and Suffering Damages', *JETL* 2010, p48 at 51.

247 E.g.: *Brumarescu v. Romania*, 23 January 2001 (just satisfaction) (Grand Chamber), appl. no. 28342/95, §50.

248 E.g.: *Shmalko v. Ukraine*, 20 July 2004, appl. no. 60750/00, §33; and *Romashov v. Ukraine*, 27 July 2004, appl. no. 67534/01, §26.

rule or where it did not find a causal link between the violation of the Convention and the alleged damages.[249]

What is more important in these cases is that the ECtHR in these cases encounters difficulties with defining non-pecuniary damages. It seems as if it uses the notion of damages in these cases in a meaning that only refers to pecuniary damages. This can be illustrated with *J.M. v. the United Kingdom*.[250] In this case the Court made the following observations:

> According to the Court's established case-law, the word 'victim' in the context of the Convention denotes the person directly affected by the act or omission in issue. The existence of a violation of the Convention is conceivable even in the absence of prejudice, which is relevant only in the context of just satisfaction [...] The Court considers that during the period at issue the applicant was directly affected by the MASC regulations and therefore has victim status within the meaning of Article 34 of the Convention. Although the financial consequences of the alleged discrimination were neutralised by the subsequent departure direction, the applicant's complaint is essentially one of principle, i.e. that the State discriminated against her on the basis of her sexual orientation by failing to recognise the relationship she entered into after her divorce when setting the level of child maintenance she was required to pay. The importance of this issue of principle is amply demonstrated by the care with which it was examined by four levels of jurisdiction. Moreover, as Sedley LJ stated in his judgment, the departure direction is a palliative but not a cure.[251]

249 Almost all of the exceptions to this rule can be explained by using other criteria that are discussed in the context of this book: (1) in *Eckle*, the Court found that the mere finding of a violation offered just satisfaction because the violation of the reasonable time requirement occurred in a very complicated fraud case where the applicants themselves had acted in a grave fraudulent manner: *Eckle v. Germany*, 21 June 1983 (just satisfaction), appl. no. 8130/78, §24; (2) in *Corigliano*, the Court found that a declaratory judgment offered enough satisfaction because it found that the exceeding of the reasonable time 'did not constitute one of his [the applicant] primary concerns': *Corigliano v. Italy*, 10 December 1982, appl. no. 8304/78, §53; (3) in *Amuur*, the Court quite easily argued that a declaratory judgment offered enough satisfaction: *Amuur v. France*, 25 June 1996, appl. no. 19776/92, §59; (4) in *Milatova*, the Court found that there was no causal link between the claimed damages and the violation of the Convention and argued that a declaratory judgment offered enough compensation for non-pecuniary damages: *Milatova et al. v. the Czech Republic*, 21 June 2005, appl. no. 61811/00, §§70–71; (5) in *Siliadin, Monnat, Voskuil* and *Nada*, the applicants did not claim damages: *Siliadin v. France*, 26 July 2005, appl. no. 73316/01, §151; *Monnat v. Switzerland*, 21 September 2006, appl. no. 73604/01, §§81–82; *Voskuil v. the Netherlands*, 22 November 2007, appl. no. 64752/01, §88; and *Nada v. Switzerland*, 12 September 2012 (Grand Chamber), appl. no. 10593/08, §239.

250 *J.M. v. the United Kingdom*, 28 September 2010, appl. no. 37060/06.

251 *J.M. v. the United Kingdom*, 28 September 2010, appl. no. 37060/06, §§27 and 63.

It is clear that the Court in these observations first and foremost refers to pecuniary damages. It does state that the financial consequences of the alleged violation were already neutralized but decided that the applicant still had a principle interest. What is also interesting in this case is that the Court found a violation of the Convention and awarded a sum of money as a just satisfaction for the suffered non-pecuniary damages. So, although the Court argues that the presence of prejudice is only relevant for Art. 41 and not for the criteria concerning the admissibility, it seems that the Court in the end found that the principal interest had constituted non-pecuniary damages.

It is also interesting to note that the Court, in the other way around, found that there is a direct link between the damages and the violation of the Convention if the statute of the applicant is clearly linked to damages. Take, for example, *Pankiewicz*.[252] This case concerned a detention that had been enforced in violation of Art. 5, but where the applicant had already received a satisfaction for both pecuniary and non-pecuniary damages at the national level. The defendant state consequently argued that the applicant had no interest in this case anymore. According to the defending state, the applicant could not be qualified as a victim anymore since he had already received compensation. The Court however found that this idea would have been correct if the applicant had received correct compensation. But the Court found that the national judges, when awarding compensation, had not taken into account the full length of the unlawful detention. Accordingly, it ruled that the applicant still had an interest, found a violation of the Convention and awarded an additional just satisfaction.

What these two cases illustrate, is that the Court will argue that an applicant has an interest if this interest consists of material damages, but that in cases where the interest is merely non-pecuniary, it sometimes argues that damages as such are not a necessary condition for the reason that it is not able to determine whether or not the applicant had suffered damages. Indeed, it is often hard to distinguish the problem of determining the existence of non-pecuniary damages from the *de minimis* rule. What is the difference between an annoying feeling and legally qualified non-pecuniary damage? Since both cannot be quantified, the judge will have to decide on both issues in the same way. The same cannot be said about pecuniary damages however. It is often clear that someone suffered

252 *Pankiewicz v. Poland*, 12 February 2008, appl. no. 34151/04.

pecuniary damages, but that one cannot estimate the precise size of the damages.

With the entry into force of the fourteenth protocol, things have changed. As seen in a previous chapter, this protocol has introduced a *de minimis* rule in the admissibility criteria. Since this rule is applicable to both pecuniary and non-pecuniary damages, the Court will now sometimes find that an applicant has no interest because his pecuniary damages are too low.

3.4.2. Does an Interest Have to be Legitimate?

In national tort law, damages are often not defined as an infringement of an interest, but as an infringement of a *legitimate* interest.[253] This raises the question of whether the ECtHR applies a similar concept and thus only awards just satisfactions for legitimate damages. In an interesting article, Ken Oliphant and Katarzyna Ludwichowska argue that the Court is competent to require damages to be legitimate in order to compensate them, because the text of Art. 41 states that the Court can award a just satisfaction 'if necessary'.[254] In the jurisprudence of the Court, observations on this topic cannot be traced. Thus, if the court would implicitly take into account the legitimacy of the infringed interests, it must be that it applies a very broad notion of what is legitimate. Indeed, the Court in the past has awarded just satisfaction for the loss of incomes that would have been generated by an unofficial job.[255] The Court has in one case also argued that the victims of a violation can generate evidence on the existence of damaged products that were bought on the black market.[256]

These cases clearly illustrate that if the Court considers the legitimate character of damages when it has to define them, it does apply a very broad concept of legitimacy. On the other hand, one can argue that the Convention in itself restricts the notion of legitimate interests. From the perspective of the Convention, it seems reasonable that the Court takes into account the guarantees of the Convention rights. The Convention has to be applied in a consistent and harmonious manner.[257] Because of this, it

---

253 C. Van Dam, *European Tort Law*, 2013, above n. 82, at 168–169.

254 K. Oliphant and K. Ludwichowska, 'Damage', 2011, above n. 3, p397 at 406.

255 *Velikova v. Bulgaria*, 18 May 2000, appl. no. 41488/98, §102.

256 *Baysayeva v. Russia*, 5 April 2007, appl. no. 74237/01, §§173–175.

257 D. Harris, M. O'Boyle, E. Bates and C. Buckley, *Law of the European Convention*, 2009, above n. 81, at 15.

seems obvious why the Court applies a broad definition of legitimacy: the substantive rights of the Convention by themselves offer a broad protection. For example, in Belgian tort law, the biggest problem that has existed regarding legitimate damages has regard to the question of whether people who have extramarital relations can suffer damages when one of them dies.[258] Belgian judges have argued in the past that the damages of these surviving relatives were not legitimate and thus could not be compensated. If the Court had to evaluate this national jurisprudence, it would find it to be in violation of the principle of equality read in conjunction with the right to a private life.[259] Although case law of the ECtHR on this topic does not exist, one must note that the Portuguese Constitutional Court in one case argued in this way with regard to the impossibility to receive compensation for non-pecuniary damages for the death of an extramarital partner.[260]

This example only illustrates how the Convention can be used to widen the notion of legitimate interests as applied in national law. It does not limit the Court's use of this concept. Nevertheless, it seems to be advisable for the Court to limit its notion of damages in this way for two reasons. Firstly, the Court has itself argued that a just satisfaction cannot illegitimately enrich an applicant.[261] Secondly, with regard to the application of the Convention in horizontal relationships, it seems evident that national judges, when awarding a satisfaction that fulfils the requirements of an effective remedy under Art. 13 of the Convention, takes into account the

---

258 E.g. Belgian Court of Cassation, 21 April 1958, *Pas.* 1958, I, 921.

259 In the past, the Court had already ruled that the unequal treatment of, for example, love children violates the principle of equality: *Merger and Cros v. France*, 22 December 2004, appl. no. 68864/01.

260 The Constitutional Court of Portugal made this decision on the ground of Art. 36/1 of the Portuguese Constitution. The provision declares that everyone has a right to family life that cannot be limited in a discriminatory manner: Tribunal Constitucional 24 July 2002, appl. no. 275/2002. For a discussion of this case, see: A. Dias Pereira, 'Portugal' in H. Koziol and B. Steininger (eds.), *European Tort Law* 2002, Vienna, Springer, p345 at 346–348. In a similar way, one could also question whether the right to life makes it impossible to qualify the birth of a child (in the context of wrongful birth or wrongful life cases) as damages. However, the Court up until now has always avoided this question: C. Herrmann and G. Kern, 'Wrongful life claims and the absolute value of human life: a contradiction' in G. Brüggemeier, A. Colombi Ciacchi and G. Commandé (eds.), *Fundamental Rights and Private Law in the European Union*, Cambridge, Cambridge University Press, 2010, p249 at 259.

261 *Varnava et al. v. Turkey*, 18 September 2009 (Grand Chamber), appl. nos. 16064/90, 16065/90, 16066/90, 16068/90, 16069/90, 16070/90, 16071/90, 16072/90 and 16073/90, §224*in fine*.

rights of the liable person. The judge will have to rule on whether the duty to pay compensation violates the Convention rights of the tortfeasor. If he does so, he will have to look at whether the infringement aims to fulfil a legitimate purpose. It seems obvious that compensating a damaged person is a legitimate purpose, but one cannot take for granted that compensating infringements of illegitimate interests will also be qualified as a legitimate purpose.

CHAPTER 8

FAULT AND BLAMEWORTHINESS

In tort law, the fault of the tortfeasor is one of the central elements of liability. This raises the question whether this notion also applies in the ECHR and if so, whether the Court applies it in a similar way as is done in national legal systems and whether both systems interact.[1] In order to answer these questions, this chapter makes a distinction between wrongfulness (objective fault) on the one hand and blameworthiness (subjective fault) on the other hand.[2]

1. BLAMEWORTHINESS

1.1. THE REQUIREMENT OF ACCOUNTABILITY

In order to be held liable in national tort law, a tortfeasor has to be blameworthy. Thus, if a tortfeasor is not accountable (for instance in cases where the tortfeasor is a very young child or is an adult with a mental disability), the damaged person might be unable to receive any compensation. In cases where a human right is violated, this might cause some friction with the requirements of Art. 13. Indeed, if a victim of a human rights violation is excluded from the possibility of receiving any compensation for his damages, one wonders whether the ECtHR would require the state to provide damages instead of the tortfeasor. Most legal systems have provided instruments to provide compensation in cases where damages are caused by someone who is not accountable for his behavior.

---

1 H. Koziol, 'Conclusions' in H. Koziol et al. (eds.), *Unification of Tort Law: Wrongfulness*, The Hague, Kluwer, 1998, p129 at 129.

2 However, this distinction is not made (very clearly) in every legal system: H. Koziol, 'Conclusions', 1998, above n. 1, p129 at 130; and P. Widmer, 'Comparative Report on Fault as a Basis of Liability and Criterion of Imputation (Attribution)' in P. Widmer et al. (eds.), *Unification of Tort Law: Fault*, The Hague, Kluwer, 2005, p331 at 347ff.

In Belgian law for instance, Art. 1386*bis* of the Civil Code provides the possibility for a judge to decide on the basis of equity, taking into account the financial situations of both tortfeasor and damaged person in order to decide whether the tortfeasor has to compensate the (full) damages that were caused by a tortfeasor with a mental disability. If damages are caused by young children, the Civil Code provides the possibility of holding the parents liable on the basis of a presumption of liability.

One can think about whether or not it is possible to introduce an objective liability scheme for damages caused by children and mentally disabled persons in combination with a liability scheme.[3] On the other hand, one can also wonder whether it is possible to abandon the requirement of blameworthiness in tort law at all. Indeed, if a fault is only interpreted in an objective way and not in a subjective way, victims of human rights abuses might be able to receive compensation in tort law regardless of the mental state of the tortfeasor. Such an approach might be reasonable from the perspective of the damaged person. A damaged person cannot choose by whom to be damaged, and these damages happen to people who would prefer not to be damaged at all. In French law the requirement of moral accountability has been put aside.[4] Concerning tortfeasors with a mental disability, in 1968 the lawmakers inserted Art. 489-2 into the Code Civil that enacted a guiltless and personal liability for mentally disabled persons.[5] The French Court of Cassation on the other hand introduced an objective principle of fault in the liability schemes for children and their parents.[6] Knowing that this is possible, the question arises whether the subjective element of the fault or the requirement that a tortfeasor must be morally accountable conflicts with the ECHR.

1.1.1. The Requirement of Accountability in General

It is not easy to know whether the Court requires tortfeasors to be blameworthy because the Court is only authorized to find violations of human rights that are caused by states. Since one can assume that states

3 This approach has been defended both in Belgium and in France: T. Vansweevelt and B. Weyts, *Handboek buitencontractueel aansprakelijkheidsrecht*, Antwerp, Intersentia, 2009, at 165–166; and G. Viney and P. Jourdain, *Les conditions de la responsabilité*, Paris, Librairie Générale de Droit et de Jurisprudence, 2006, at 599ff.

4 See: P. Brun, *Responsabilité civile extracontractuelle*, Paris, Lexisnexis, 2014, at 146ff.

5 See: G. Viney and P. Jourdain, *Les conditions de la responsabilité*, 2006, above n. 3, at 599ff.

6 French Court of Cassation, 9 May 1984, *J.C.P.* 1984, II, appl. no. 20255 *D.* 1984, at 529.

are always blameworthy for their actions, it seems that there is no way of finding out whether or not the Court uses the subjective element of the fault itself when applying Art. 41. Moreover, this provision does not mention the requirement of the fault as such, so why would it require a fault to be morally accountable to a tortfeasor.[7] Franz Bydlinski has argued that the lack of the criteria of fault in the text indicates that the Court does not require a fault under Art. 41.[8] He also finds that the Court has endorsed this opinion in the case of *Yöyler*.[9] This interpretation of the case of *Yöyler* is doubtful. It seems that the Court in this case only argued that one should not confuse the liability of a state under the Convention with the criminal accountability of the state or one of its bodies. The Court in *Yöyler* refers to a paragraph in *Avşar* that reads as follows:

> Where allegations are made under Articles 2 and 3 of the Convention however, the Court must apply a particularly thorough scrutiny (see, mutatis mutandis, the Ribitsch v. Austria judgment of 4 December 1995, Series A no. 336, p. 24, §32). When there have been criminal proceedings in the domestic court concerning those same allegations, it must be borne in mind that criminal law liability is distinct from international law responsibility under the Convention. The Court's competence is confined to the latter. Responsibility under the Convention is based on its own provisions which are to be interpreted and applied on the basis of the objectives of the Convention and in light of the relevant principles of international law. The responsibility of a State under the Convention, arising for the acts of its organs, agents and servants, is not to be confused with the domestic legal issues of individual criminal responsibility under examination in the national criminal courts. The Court is not concerned with reaching any findings as to guilt or innocence in that sense.[10]

What seems to be clear from these observations, is that the Court does not require states to be guilty of a violation of the Convention as is required in criminal law. This seems very reasonable. Convention rights can be violated if a state neglects to fulfil its positive obligations to protect persons under its jurisdiction against infringements of their human rights by other

7 B. Steininger and N. Wallner-Friedl, 'Wrongfulness and Fault' in A. Fenyves, E. Karner, H. Koziol and E. Steiner (eds.), *Tort Law in the Jurisprudence of the European Court of Human Rights*, Göttingen, De Gruyter, 2011, p501 at 501.

8 F. Bydlinski, 'Methodological Approaches to the Tort Law of the ECHR' in A. Fenyves, E. Karner, H. Koziol and E. Steiner (eds.), *Tort Law in the Jurisprudence of the European Court of Human Rights*, Göttingen, De Gruyter, 2011, p29 at 54.

9 *Yöyler v. Turkey*, 24 July 2003, appl. no. 26973/95.

10 *Avsar v. Turkey*, 10 July 2001, appl. no. 25657/94, §284.

private persons. A state can be held accountable under the Convention for not respecting its positive obligations as such. If a state in such cases can only be held accountable under the Convention if it would be found guilty in the sense of criminal law, then the Court would hardly ever find a violation of positive obligations. Indeed, to be held accountable in criminal law, one has to establish the fact that someone has intentionally acted in a criminal manner. Thus, if applicants before the Court have to prove that states intentionally refrained from protecting their human rights (against infringements of other private persons), one cannot imagine that the Court would find many violations of the Convention at all. In tort law, however, it is not required that someone intentionally causes damages. The notion of fault is less stringent in criminal law than it is in civil law. Mere negligence can suffice to establish civil liability. As a consequence, the argument of Bydlinski that the case of *Yöyler* illustrates that the Court does not apply the subjective element of fault similar to that in tort law, must be rejected. The case of *Yöyler* leaves the possibility open that the Court uses a notion of fault that is rather similar to that in national tort law.

The argument of Bydlinski does however also find support in a report made by the Commission of Human Rights made in *Ribbitsch*:

> The responsibility of a State under the Convention, arising for acts of all its organs, agents and servants, does not necessarily require any 'guilt' on behalf of the State, either in a moral, legal or political meaning.[11]

Barbara Steininger and Nora Wallner-Friedl argue that the Commission, by giving a very broad notion to the concept of guilt, does not require a subjective element of fault.[12] It does not seem to be necessary that someone be morally accountable to be held responsible under the Convention. Nevertheless, one might argue that the notion of guilt has only a criminal meaning or that the Commission made this observation in the context of finding a violation of the Convention, not in the application of Art. 41. Thus, it cannot be excluded that the Court, though it does not do so for finding a violation, requires that a violator of a human right must be morally accountable in order to compel him to pay damages to the human rights victim.

---

11 EComHR, *Ribitsch v. Austria*, Report of the Commission, 4 July 1994, appl. no. 18896/91, §110.

12 B. Steininger and N. Wallner-Friedl, 'Wrongfulness and Fault', 2011, above n. 7, p501 at 505.

Steininger and Wallner-Friedl also implicitly indicate this possibility. They do so by referring to the fact that the Court takes into account the intentions of a state that violates the Convention when it estimates the size of the damages.[13] In particular, in cases concerning the prohibition of torture and inhuman or degrading treatment of persons (Art. 3), where the Court finds a violation of the Convention although the state had not intended to torture people or to treat them in an inhuman or degrading way, the Court grants only limited just satisfactions under Art. 41.[14] Although this might give an indication that a kind of moral accountability is necessary, one should not jump to conclusions too easily. The wordings of Art. 3 suggest that this provision could only be violated intentionally.[15] From this point of view, one might think that Art. 3 can only be violated if the violator has criminal intentions, which is not the case. Thus, it seems that the practice of the Court to award more limited satisfactions when violations of Art. 3 were caused unintentionally, might be explained by the fact that the Court uses the moral damages in a dissuasive way in cases where violations are caused intentionally. The practice does not necessarily imply that the Court requires a form of moral accountability.

The foregoing illustrates that there is no real indication of whether or not the Court requires that violators of the Convention must be morally accountable in order to hold them liable for human rights violations. But this lack of indication is the logical consequence of the fact that only states can be convicted by the Court. Since it is hard to imagine that a state is or is not blameworthy because of a mental disease or young age, one must find a manner in which to investigate how the Court judges on private individuals that violate human rights. Although private persons cannot be sued before the ECtHR, it might be possible to look at the jurisprudence of the Court concerning the contributory fault of victims.[16] Indeed, the Court takes into account the fact that damages were caused partly by an act of a victim when it has to estimate the amount of damages. The Court has made

13 *Ibid.* at 506.

14 *V. v. the United Kingdom*, 16 December 1999 (Grand Chamber), appl. no. 24888/94, §71; *Kalashnikov v. Russia*, 15 July 2002, appl. no. 47095/99, §101; *Dankevich v. Ukraine*, 29 April 2003, appl. no. 40679/98, §142; *Wieser v. Austria*, 22 February 2007, appl. no. 2293/03, §36; and *A. et al. v. the United Kingdom*, 19 February 2009 (Grand Chamber), appl. no. 3455/05, §127.

15 B. Steininger and N. Wallner-Friedl, 'Wrongfulness and Fault', 2011, above n. 7, p501 at 512.

16 This argument can be nuanced. The question of whether the contributory fault of the victim must be dealt with in the same way as a normal fault might also be the subject of discussion in national tort law.

some interesting decisions in its jurisprudence concerning the violation of the reasonable time requirement. In *Skawinska* the Court attributed the exceeding of the reasonable time partly to an applicant's mental disability, and to the fact that the applicant had challenged some judges and had also refused to undergo psychological research.[17] In *Bähnk* the Court argued that a mentally ill person had not been able to estimate her claims,[18] and in *Jevremović* the Court investigated whether one could attribute the delay in the national procedures to the young age of the applicant.[19]

In all these cases the ECtHR seemed to accept the possibility that disabled persons or young children can be held responsible for a part of their damages.[20] Accordingly, it seems to be reasonable that the Court in the application of Art. 13 will require states to provide an effective remedy if a human rights violation is caused by mentally disabled persons or young children. Indeed, if a state would not provide any remedy at all in such a case, it seems likely that Art. 13 will be violated.

1.1.2. Grounds for Justification

The fact that the Court does not require tortfeasors to be to be morally accountable does not necessarily mean that the ECtHR does not recognize grounds of justification. It is possible that a fault cannot be imputed to a mentally disabled person, not because of his mental illness, but because he acted out of self-defense. For this reason, it is necessary to look at whether the Court in one way uses grounds of justification in its jurisprudence.

1.1.2.1. Force Majeure

The first ground for justification is the so-called force majeure. In legal doctrine, Dagmar Hinghofer-Szalkay and Bernhard Koch have argued that the cases of *Mykhaylenky* and *Sharenok*[21] illustrate that the ECtHR does not accept *force majeure* as a justification for a human rights violation. They argued that these cases illustrate that the Court does not accept

17 *Skawińska v. Poland*, 16 September 2003, appl. no. 42096/98, §69.

18 *Bähnk v. Germany*, 9 October 2008, appl. no. 10732/05, §37.

19 *Jevremović v. Serbia*, 17 July 2007, appl. no. 3150/05, §84.

20 The same argument has been made in: F. Bydlinski, 'Methodological Approaches', 2011, above n. 8, p29 at 61.

21 *Mykhaylenky et al. v. Ukraine*, 30 November 2004, appl. no. 35091/02 et al.; and *Sharenok v. Ukraine*, 22 February 2005, appl. no. 35087/02.

any defense as a ground for justification.[22] Both these cases concerned employees of state companies who sought recovery of salary in arrears against their former employers in national law. Their former employers were state-owned companies situated in Chernobyl that had to stop their activities following the nuclear disaster in 1986. The applicants had been successful in the national procedure against the companies, but they could not receive compensation because the judgment remained unenforced. The reason for this was that there were a large number of executing writs pending against the debtor company who could only pay its debts if its properties were attached. These properties, however, were all situated in Chernobyl. Because this area was contaminated by radiation, the attachment of property required special authorization from the Ministry of Emergencies that could not be granted. Consequently, the defending state invoked force majeure to defend itself against the claim that it had violated the right to property and the right of access to a judge (that contains the right to have a judgment executed) of the applicants. The Court did not agree with this defense and found a violation of both these Convention rights.

At first sight one might indeed agree with Dagmar Hinghofer-Szalkay and Bernhard Koch that these cases illustrate that the ECtHR does not accept any ground of justification and that it almost creates a kind of objective liability. But there are some elements in this case that might temper this conclusion. In one of these cases, the applicant claimed €688 for non-specified material damages under Art. 41. His salary arrears counted for €677. The defendant state argued that it could not be held responsible for the debts of state-owned companies that formed a separate legal entity. The court nevertheless argued that the company had been operating under contract of the state and that the state could thus be held responsible for the debts of the company. The Court consequently awarded €677 to the applicant.[23] This indicates that the Court probably did not pay any attention to the state's argument that the non-execution of the judgment was a case of force majeure because it found not only the specific company

[22] D. Hinghofer-Szalkay and B. Koch, 'No-Fault or Strict Liability' in A. Fenyves, E. Karner, H. Koziol, and E. Steiner (eds.), *Tort Law in the Jurisprudence of the European Court of Human Rights*, Göttingen, De Gruyter, 2011, pp567–577.

[23] Apart from the argument that the company was state-owned, the Court stressed that the company was active in the nuclear sector, a sector that requires intensive governmental surveillance: *Mykhaylenky et al. v. Ukraine*, 30 November 2004, appl. no. 35091/02 et al., §§43–46.

that was situated in the Chernobyl area, but the entire state of Ukraine responsible for the payment of the debts. Indeed, from that perspective there was no force majeure for the state had a lot of possessions outside of the radiated area.

Hinghofer-Szalkay and Koch also based their argument on the jurisprudence of the ECtHR concerning the violation of the reasonable time requirement.[24] They argued that in cases where a lawsuit has already dragged on for many years before a national court, the Court in these cases does not investigate whether the delay in the procedure could be blamed on the national states, but that the Court in these cases points to the delay in the procedures and requires the states to explain[25] or to justify[26] them. According to Dagmar Hinghofer-Szalkay and Bernhard Koch this illustrates that a principle of fault in general is not fundamental to finding a human rights violation. It is the opinion in this book that this line of argument does not hold up, and that what this jurisprudence illustrates is that the Court can reverse the burden of proof if it deems it necessary to do so in a specific case. Indeed, if the ECtHR finds that a procedure for a national tribunal has already lasted for a long time, it can assume that these procedures at first sight seem to be in violation with the reasonable time requirement, but that the government can still prove that this is not the case by illustrating that it has done everything that it was reasonably expected to do and could not handle the procedure in a shorter time because of the complexity of the case, the behavior of the parties or other reasons that are outside the control of the state.

Moreover, if the Court would not accept any limits on the capabilities of the state (if the Court would argue that a violation of the Convention could be found whether or not there was a case of force majeure), the Court would probably find a violation in almost every case. This line of reasoning is especially interesting if it is applied to positive obligations to protect human rights.[27] Indeed, if the Court finds a violation of a positive obligation, it must investigate whether the state neglected to adopt some

---

24 D. Hinghofer-Szalkay and B. Koch, 'No-Fault or Strict Liability', 2011, above n. 22, p567 at 573.

25 *Del Federico v. Italy*, 4 July 2002, appl. no. 35991/97, §21.

26 *Vodopyanovy v. Ukraine*, 17 January 2006, appl. no. 22214/02, §36.

27 Fenyves also argues that a faultless liability scheme cannot be reconciled with the notion of positive obligations: A. Fenyves, 'Concluding Remarks on Wrongfulness and Fault' in A. Fenyves, E. Karner, H. Koziol and E. Steiner (eds.), *Tort Law in the Jurisprudence of the European Court of Human Rights*, Göttingen, De Gruyter, 2011, p843 at 849.

measures. But in order to adopt measures, a government must be able to do so. If for example the state has to protect the right of life against infringements of private persons, it must be able to foresee possible threats to the right to life of its citizens. But in the context of the positive obligations of the state to protect human rights in horizontal relations, it has been demonstrated that a state cannot be held liable for a violation of human rights if it was materially impossible for the state to prevent the violation from occurring, for example because it was impossible for the state to have knowledge of the potential violation. Indeed, just as Jean-Luc Fagnart has noted in the context of tort law,[28] the pre-visibility is a fundamental aspect of the human rights control. Thus, if a state could not have had any knowledge of a human rights infringement by a private person, the Court cannot convict the state for a violation of the Convention. One might, for example, say that if someone without a criminal record suddenly, as a lonewolf, kills someone, the right to life of the victim was violated, but that the state could not be blamed for this because it had no power to prevent this violation from happening. As a consequence, one might argue that the Court implicitly applies the notion of force majeure.

Another interesting judgment is *Süssman*, a case concerning the reasonable time requirement in the wake of the German unification. The Court in this case found:

> In addition these appeals were filed at the same time as those brought by former civil servants of the German Democratic Republic to challenge a provision of the Treaty on German Unification terminating the employment contracts of around 300,000 persons (see paragraph 19 above). Admittedly, as the Commission pointed out, the amendments to the supplementary pensions scheme also concerned a large number of German civil servants. However, bearing in mind the unique political context of German reunification and the serious social implications of the disputes which concerned termination of employment contracts, the Federal Constitutional Court was entitled to decide that it should give priority to those cases.[29]

In this judgment the Court took into account the exceptionally heavy caseload of the judicial system in Germany caused by Germany's unification

---

[28] J.-L. Fagnart, 'Principe de précaution et responsabilité civile', *De Verzekering* 2011, p120 at 124.

[29] *Süssmann v. Germany*, 16 September 1996 (Grand Chamber), appl. no. 20024/92, §60. See also: *Gast and Popp v. Germany*, 25 February 2000, appl. no. 29357/95, §80; and *Trickovic v. Slovenia*, 12 June 2001, appl. no. 39914/98, §56ff.

when it had to judge on the supposed violation of the reasonable time requirement. By doing so, the Court applied the principle of force majeure in an implicit manner. Another example is *Varnava.*[30] This case concerned soldiers that had been missing since the war between Cyprus and Turkey. The Court found a violation of Arts 2 and 5 but refused to grant the applicants any compensation. The Court argued:

> The Court cannot but be sensitive to the fact that the present individual applications derive from a situation in which over 1,400 people were declared missing on the Greek-Cypriot side and some 500 claimed missing on the Turkish-Cypriot side. In the context of the inter-State case it must also take cognisance of the ongoing execution function being performed by the Committee of Ministers.[31]

A last example of judgments that seem rather similar to force majeure is the jurisprudence where the Court had to decide as to whether the lack of financial means could justify a violation of the Convention. Although the Court did not accept the lack of financial means as a justification for a violation, it reserved for itself the possibility to do so by arguing that the lack of budgetary means 'cannot in principle justify prison conditions which are so poor as to reach the threshold of treatment contrary to Art. 3.'[32] One could however argue that a lack of budgetary means cannot justify a violation that is caused by the bad conditions in prison but that it might only be used as an argument to postpone the compliance with the requirements of the Convention.[33]

1.1.2.2. Legitimate Self-Defense

Another ground for justification that the Court implicitly seems to apply is legitimate self-defense. The Court in some cases argues that the Convention had not been violated because the supposed violation had only been a legitimate reaction on an act of a private person. An example of this jurisprudence can be found in *Andronicou and Constantinou.*[34] A young

---

30 *Varnava et al. v. Turkey*, 10 January 2008, appl. no. 16064/90 et al.

31 *Ibid.*, §157. The consequences of this judgment cannot be overrated since the Grand Chamber in its sequel judgment awarded compensations: *Varnava et al. v. Turkey*, 18 September 2009 (Grand Chamber), appl. no. 16064/90 et al., §225.

32 *Dankevich v. Ukraine*, 29 April 2003, appl. no. 40679/98, §144. See also: *Kuznetsov v. Ukraine*, 29 April 2003, appl. no. 39042/97, §128.

33 See also: Concurring opinion of Judge Maluroni in *Amat-G Ltd and Mebaghishvili v. Georgia*, 27 September 2005, appl. no. 2507/03.

34 *Andronicou and Constantinou v. Cyprus*, 9 October 1997, appl. no. 25052/94.

man had taken his girlfriend hostage in an apartment. Since he threatened to kill her, a special police unit intervened and invaded the apartment. The young man started to fire at the police. The policemen fired back resulting in the killing of both the young man and his girlfriend. The families of these two people believed that their right to life was violated and filed a claim before the ECtHR. The Court, however, found no violation. It argued that the gunfire of the policemen was the direct result of the attempt of the young man to kill the policemen.[35]

The reasoning behind why the Court seems to accept a kind of self-defense on the grounds of a case probably lies in the fact that the Court has to balance the right to life of one person with the right to life of another person. Indeed, in the case of *Andronicou and Constantinou*, the state also had to act to protect the right to life of the hostage because the state has the positive obligation to protect the right to life of private persons against interference by other persons. This can be illustrated by the case of *McCann*.[36] This famous case concerned a police operation against three persons that were suspected of planning a terrorist attack in Gibraltar. The Court in this case found a violation of the right to life for the following reason:

> In sum, having regard to the decision not to prevent the suspects from travelling into Gibraltar, to the failure of the authorities to make sufficient allowances for the possibility that their intelligence assessments might, in some respects at least, be erroneous and to the automatic recourse to lethal force when the soldiers opened fire, the Court is not persuaded that the killing of the three terrorists constituted the use of force which was no more than absolutely necessary in defence of persons from unlawful violence within the meaning of Article 2 para. 2 (a) (Art. 2-2-a) of the Convention.[37]

By arguing that the Court was not persuaded that the killing of the three terrorists was no more than absolutely necessary in defending people from unlawful violence, the Court indicates that in some cases it might be necessary to use deadly violence to protect people's lives (as was the case in *Andronicou and Constantinou*). In that way, the Court interprets the protection of the right to life in a way that is very similar to legitimate self-defense.

---

35 *Andronicou and Constantinou v. Cyprus*, 9 October 1997, appl. no. 25052/94, §191.

36 *McCann et al. v. the United Kingdom*, 27 September 1995 (Grand Chamber), appl. no. 18984/91.

37 *Ibid.*, §213. See also: EComHR, *Kelly v. the United Kingdom*, 13 January 1993 (Decision), appl. no. 17579/90.

1.1.2.3. Insuperable Error

A last ground for justification that might, although with some creativity, be read in the jurisprudence of the ECtHR is justification because of an insuperable error. Indeed, if one looks at some judgments of the Court in highly sensitive matters where it found a violation of the Convention in a specific context for the first time, such as the *Marckx*,[38] *Osman*[39] or *McCann* cases,[40] one can wonder whether it is a coincidence that the Court did not award a just satisfaction in these cases. It seems that the Court found in these cases that because the Court had up until that judgment never made a decision in that sense, the states could have wondered about the precise requirements that are embedded in the ECHR.

1.2. HUMAN RIGHTS AS JUSTIFICATION GROUNDS

This book has argued that the positive obligation of the state to protect the right to life of a person can have an effect that is quite similar to legitimate self-defense. This raises the question of whether human rights can be qualified as a ground for justification in tort law. In other words, the question arises of whether an action that causes damages and that at first sight seems to be illegitimate, might be framed as legitimate if the tortfeasor was exercising his human rights.[41]

In this context it is important to know that the ECtHR in some cases has argued that the Convention can be violated if someone who exercises his right to free speech is held accountable in tort law and has to pay a very large amount of damages.[42] In the same way, it might be possible that the right to free speech is violated if someone who exercises his right to free speech is only sentenced to pay a limited amount in damages.[43]

---

38 *Marckx v. Belgium*, 13 June 1979 (Plenary), appl. no. 6833/74.

39 *Osman v. the United Kingdom*, 28 October 1998, appl. no. 23452/94.

40 *McCann et al. v. the United Kingdom*, 27 September 1995 (Grand Chamber), appl. no. 18984/91.

41 In the doctrine, this approach has been suggested in: W. Van Gerven and S. Covemaeker, *Verbintenissenrecht*, Leuven, Acco, 2010, at 345. Dirix is however of the opinion that human rights cannot constitute a ground for the justification of crimes: E. Dirix, 'Grondrechten en overeenkomsten' in K. Rimanque (ed.), *De toepasselijkheid van grondrechten in private verhoudingen*, Antwerp, Kluwer, 1982, p35 at 37.

42 *Steel and Morris v. the United Kingdom*, 15 February 2005, appl. no. 68416/01; and *Tolstoy Miloslavsky v. the United Kingdom*, 13 July 1995, appl. no. 18139/91.

43 E.g. *Mor v. France*, 15 December 2011, appl. no. 28198/09, §61ff.

In *Vides Aizsardzības Klubs* for example, the Court found a violation of Art. 10 even though the applicant had only been convicted by the civil court to publish the judgment of the civil court in its magazine and to pay a very limited amount as compensation.[44] In *John Anthony Mizzi* an applicant was convicted and had to pay €700 in damages. The ECtHR found that his right to free speech had been violated and awarded him €700 for material damages and an additional sum of €4,000 for moral damages.[45] A more interesting case is that of *Juppala*.[46] The applicant in this case had been told by a doctor that her grandson's injuries might have been caused by domestic violence. After the grandson had been visiting his father, the former son-in-law of the applicant, the applicant found that the behavior of her grandson had changed. This led to a criminal lawsuit where the former son-in-law was acquitted. The son-in-law consequently sued the applicant in a defamation case. The applicant was convicted in this lawsuit and forced to pay €3,600 in damages to her former son-in-law. After this case was brought before the ECtHR, the Court found that the liability for defamation in this case contradicted the right to free speech. The Court pointed to the possibility that threat of being obliged to pay compensation might deter people from reporting cases of sexual abuse. The Court thus granted the applicant compensation of €3,600 for her material damages and an additional compensation of €3,000.[47]

Looking at this jurisprudence, it should not come as a surprise to find similar applications of human rights in national law. One example is the judgment of the German *Bundesgerichtshof* on 4 November 1997.[48] The applicant in this case was a man who wanted to develop an industrial site in Eastern Germany after the fall of the Berlin wall. When his project developed, and some companies started to construct on the site, social protest began. Consequently, the construction work was temporarily halted. Since this caused damage to the companies, they wanted compensation

---

44 *Vides Aizsardzības Klubs v. Latvia*, 27 May 2004, appl. no. 57829/00. In this case, the Court awarded a higher compensation under Art. 41 as the applicants had paid in the national procedure.

45 *John Anthony Mizzi v. Malta*, 22 November 2012, appl. no. 17320/10, §49.

46 *Juppala v. Finland*, 2 December 2008, appl. no. 18620/03.

47 What is important here is that the Court takes into account whether or not the national judges did balance the human rights at stake (e.g.: the right to privacy with the right to free speech): *Dyundin v. Russia*, 14 October 2008, appl. no. 37406/03, §33; *Schüth v. Germany*, 28 June 2012 (just satisfaction), appl. no. 1620/03, §23; and *OOO IVPress et al. v. Russia, OOO IVPress et al. v. Russia*, 22 January 2013, appl. nos. 33501/04 et al., §71.

48 Bundesgerichtshof 4 November 1997.

from the developer, who in turn claimed damages from the protesters. The protesters then appealed to their right to free speech. The *Bundesgerichtshof* consequently found that an act that causes damages in principle might be undone if the unlawful character of a tortfeasor pertains the exercise of his human rights, but it found that the tortfeasors in this case exercised their human rights for the sole purpose of hindering the exercise of someone else's rights.

In England, some people had more success when they appealed an order to prevent liability for defamation based on the right to free speech.[49] An example can be found in *O'Shea v. MGN Ltd.*[50] At the origin of this case was an advertisement for a pornographic website in a magazine. The female model used in this advertisement looked very similar to a British woman. The woman thus found that people who knew her may think that she was the model in the advertisement for the pornographic website. She believed that her honor and reputation had been violated. She had a good chance of success when she filed an action in tort law because a violation of reputation via publications is regulated by a faultless liability scheme. It is not necessary that the person who publicized a defamatory publication had the intention of violating the reputation of the injured person.[51] Consequently, if these rules were to be applied to this specific case, the publisher would be held liable for defamation. Indeed, one could agree with the fact that the honor and reputation of the woman were violated. The judge, however, found that this liability would be contrary to the right to free speech of the publisher since he had not made an error. If publishers must also take into account the possibility that models have lookalikes, their right to free speech would be limited in an unproportionate way.

From this case it can be seen that human rights themselves can function as a ground for justification in national tort law. The case also illustrates that human rights do not have to be used as an interpretative framework for tort law but can also be used as autonomous legal figures that can trump national tort law.

---

49 K. Oliphant, 'Defamation' in D. Hoffman (ed.), *The Impact of the UK Human Rights Act on Private Law*, Cambridge, Cambridge University Press, 2011, p195 at 198ff.

50 England and Wales High Court (Queen's bench division), *O'Shea v. MGN Ltd*, 4 May 2001, *EMLR* 2001 943.

51 The victim only has to prove that there was a slanderous statement, that the defendant was responsible for the publication and that the publication can reasonably be connected with the victim: A. Mullis, 'The law of defamation – part 1' in K. Oliphant (ed.), *The Law of Tort*, Suffolk, LexisNexis Butterworths, 2007, p1279 at 1280; and D. Price and K. Duodu, *Defamation. Law, Procedure and Practice*, London, Sweet & Maxwell, 2004, at 4ff.

2. FAULT

Apart from the question of whether someone is blameworthy, the question also arises whether he behaved in a way that is consistent with the behavior of a normal and prudent person in the same situation. In a lot of legal systems, it is said that one has to compare the behavior of a person with the hypothetical behavior of the so-called *bonus pater familias*. This test must be described as the general standard of conduct.

2.1. THE GENERAL STANDARD OF CONDUCT AND HUMAN RIGHTS

2.1.1. The General Standard of Conduct of the State in the Jurisprudence of the ECtHR

When looking at the jurisprudence of the ECtHR, it cannot be ignored that the Court sometimes seems to refer to a standard of conduct. Take for example the following reasoning of the Court in the case of *McCann*:

> It considers that the use of force by agents of the State in pursuit of one of the aims delineated in paragraph 2 of Article 2 (Art. 2-2) of the Convention may be justified under this provision (Art. 2-2) where it is based on an honest belief which is perceived, for good reasons, to be valid at the time but which subsequently turns out to be mistaken. To hold otherwise would be to impose an unrealistic burden on the State and its law-enforcement personnel in the execution of their duty, perhaps to the detriment of their lives and those of others. It follows that, having regard to the dilemma confronting the authorities in the circumstances of the case, the actions of the soldiers do not, in themselves, give rise to a violation of this provision (Art. 2-2).[52]

The Court in this quote judges that the right to life as enshrined in Art. 2 of the Convention has not been violated by the policemen because they could have believed that the violence they had used was founded on a legitimate restriction of the right to life. This shows that the Court does take into account foreseeability as is also used in the general standard of conduct. But apart from that, it can also be argued more generally that the Court applies one of the most fundamental functions of the general standard of

---

52 *McCann et al. v. the United Kingdom*, 27 September 1995 (Grand Chamber), appl. no. 18984/91, §200.

conduct that exists in the limitation of liability. Indeed, the Court does point out that it should not impose an unrealistic burden on the state and its law-enforcement personnel. The state has no commitment to provide a result but only a commitment to make a reasonable effort. Indeed, in protecting the right to life, a state cannot be held accountable in every case when the right to life is violated but can only be held responsible if it did not take the necessary measures to provide for such violations in cases where it could reasonably foresee and prevent these violations.[53]

A similar approach can also be found in some cases where the ECtHR had to estimate the danger for society as a whole caused by the release of prisoners.[54] This problem arises in situations where a released prisoner commits a crime. In *Matromatteo* for instance, a released prisoner committed murder again shortly after he was released from prison. The family of the murdered person argued that the state had violated their right to life by releasing the prisoner (he had been released early due to mitigating circumstances). In this case the Court found that the right to life had not been violated because the government had taken enough measures to reintegrate the prisoner into society and because it could not have presumed that the release would pose a specific danger to certain persons.[55] In the similar case of *Maiorano*, the Court *a contrario* judged that there were specific indications from which the government could have presumed the danger that the release of the prisoner involved and thus found a violation of Art. 2 of the Convention.[56]

What these and other cases concerning the right to life illustrate[57] is that the Court takes into account the conduct of a state when it has to judge on the proportionality between the infringement of the right and the legitimate aim of the infringement. What is also interesting is that the Court developed a precautionary principle for activities that pose a great risk. For example, if a state applies medical tests on military personnel or plans to open an industrial site or a dump that emits toxic substances, it has to provide an effective regulation and control system to detect pollution.[58]

---

53 E.g. *Denizci et al. v. Cyprus*, 23 May 2001, appl. no. 25316/94 et al., §73.

54 In this context, Renucci used the words: '*L'imprudence ou la négligence de l'Etat*', J.-F. Renucci, *Droit européen des droits de l'homme*, Paris, Lextenso, 2012, 93.

55 *Mastromatteo v. Italy*, 24 October 2002 (Grand Chamber), appl. no. 37703/97.

56 *Maiorano et al. v. Italy*, 15 December 2009, appl. no. 28634/06, §121.

57 E.g.: *Güleç v. Turkey*, 27 July 1998, appl. no. 21593/93, §71; *Andronicou and Constantinou v. Cyprus*, 9 October 1997, appl. no. 25052/94, §183; and *Makaratzis v. Greece*, 20 December 2004 (Grand Chamber), appl. no. 50385/99, §69.

58 *L.C.B. v. the United Kingdom*, 9 June 1998, appl. no. 23413/94; *Guerra et al. v. Italy*, 19 February 1998 (Grand Chamber), appl. no. 14967/89; and *Öneryildiz v. Turkey*, 30 November 2004 (Grand Chamber), appl. no. 48939/99.

The same conclusion can also be drawn from the jurisprudence of the prohibition of torture and inhuman and degrading treatment. Barbara Steininger and Nora Wallner-Friedl refer in this context to the jurisprudence of the Court where it has to apply the proportionality test to investigate whether or not negligence can be qualified as inhuman or degrading treatment.[59] In cases where there was no doubt that someone was tortured, the ECtHR does not apply the proportionality test but immediately finds a violation of the Convention. It seems that it is obvious in those cases that the government did not act as a *bonus pater familias* would have acted. Indeed, a *bonus pater familias* does not torture. If, however, the Court must decide whether or not the negligence of the state in not providing good circumstances in prison can be qualified as inhuman treatment, it will have to check whether the state took the necessary measures to prevent the foreseeable inhuman situations to occur.[60] It thus seems that the Court has to refer to a general standard of conduct in applying Art. 3 of the Convention.

Now it has been demonstrated that the Court seems to refer to a general standard of conduct in the context of Arts 2 and 3, it seems reasonable that the Court also refers to this principle while applying other treaty rights. The right to life and the prohibition of torture are the most important rights in the Convention; thus, if the Court permits the limitations of the protection of these rights by making reference to a general standard of conduct, it seems logical that the Court also does so in relation to other Convention rights. Indeed, if one looks to the jurisprudence concerning the reasonable time requirement, the Court argues that the long duration of a national procedure cannot be qualified as a violation of Art. 6 of the Convention.[61] In *Klein*, the Court argues in this sense: 'a temporary backlog of court business does not entail a Contracting State's international liability if that State takes appropriate remedial action with the requisite promptness.'[62] The violation of the reasonable time requirement must be judged in the specific circumstances of the case.[63] The Court takes into

---

59 B. Steininger and N. Wallner-Friedl, 'Wrongfulness and Fault', 2011, above n. 7, p501 at 512.

60 *McGlinchey et al. v. the United Kingdom*, 29 April 2003, appl. no. 50390/99, §52ff.

61 B. Steininger and N. Wallner-Friedl, 'Wrongfulness and Fault', 2011, above n. 7, p501 at 525.

62 27 July 2000, appl. no. 33379/96, §43. See also: *Pammel v. Germany*, 1 July 1997, appl. no. 17820/91, §§69 and 71; *Trickovic v. Slovenia*, 12 June 2001, appl. no. 39914/98, §68; *Molnarova and Kochanova v. Slovakia*, 4 March 2003, appl. no. 44965/98, §32; and *Lickov v. the former Yugoslav Republic of Macedonia*, 28 September 2006, appl. no. 38202/02, §31.

63 *König v. Germany*, 28 June 1978 (Plenary), appl. no. 6232/73, §99; and *Buchholz v. Germany*, 6 May 1981, appl. no. 7759/77, §49.

account the complexity of the case, the behavior of both the government and the applicant[64] and the interests that were at stake. It thus seems that the Court in judging on the reasonable time requirement applies a method that entails strong similarities with the general rule of conduct.[65]

The Court in these cases also considers people's vulnerability. This was illustrated by *A. et al. v. Denmark*. In this case the Court found that the exceeding of the reasonable time could be blamed on the applicants, but it nevertheless found a violation of the reasonable time requirement in relation to eight out of ten applicants because it found that these applicants had serious diseases and that the government had to provide additional support for these applicants.[66]

An interesting case with regard to Art. 8 is *Worwa*.[67] The applicant in this case found that her right to privacy was violated because she had to undergo psychiatric examinations in the context of a criminal investigation. The ECtHR argued that a prosecutor can deem it necessary to order a psychiatric report to determine the mental state of a person charged with an offense. But when doing so the Court further argues that state authorities are required to make sure that these measures do not upset the fair balance that should be maintained between the individual's right to a private life and the concern of ensuring the proper administration in justice. Taking this into account, the Court found that this balance was not preserved in this case. The Court pointed to the fact that the applicant had to undergo these psychiatric examinations repeatedly and in short intervals. In addition, the Court pointed out that the applicant sometimes even had to travel far from home to learn upon arriving that no appointment had been made. The Court also noted that the prosecutor in one proceeding had forgotten that he had ordered two psychiatric examinations of the applicant. It thus found that, although there were some mitigating facts in the sense that the applicant had been involved in a large number of disputes, the judicial authorities had 'failed to act with due diligence.' Therefore, the Court concluded that the interference with the applicant's right to private life was unjustified.[68]

---

64 When applying these criteria, the Court only takes into account the exceeding of the reasonable period that is caused by the defended state: S. Jansen and D. Wenders, 'Een kroniek van de redelijke termijn', *NJCM-Bulletin* 2006, (1091) 1099ff.

65 V. Wilcox and O. Riss, 'Contributory Negligence' in A. Fenyves, E. Karner, H. Koziol and E. Steiner (eds.), *Tort Law in the Jurisprudence of the European Court of Human Rights*, Göttingen, De Gruyter, 2011, p771 at 775.

66 *A. et al. v. Denmark*, 8 February 1996, appl. no. 20826/92, §77ff.

67 *Worwa v. Poland*, 27 November 2003, appl. no. 26624/95.

68 *Ibid.*, §84.

By referring to the lack of 'due diligence' and by stating that the interference with the right to a private life was unjustified because of this lack of due diligence, one cannot but agree that the Court in this case referred to a general standard of conduct to which the state failed to adhere.[69] This is not an isolated case. The Court acted similarly in its jurisprudence with regard to Arts 3,[70] 5,[71] 6,[72] and 8[73] of the Convention

---

69 See also: *Cesnulevicius v. Lithuania*, 10 January 2012, appl. no. 13462/06, §85 ('the Court has to evaluate whether the officers in question displayed adequate diligence in protecting him, in so far as they knew or ought to have known about the threat'); and *Z. v. Poland*, 13 November 2012, appl. no. 46132/08, §105.

70 *Abdolkhani and Karimnia v. Turkey*, 22 September 2009, appl. no. 30471/08, §129; *Goloshvili v. Georgia*, 20 November 2012, appl. no. 45566/08, §41; *Janiashvili v. Georgia*, 27 November 2012, appl. no. 35887/05, §§75 and 79; *Irakli Mindadze v. Georgia*, 11 December 2012, appl. no. 17012/09, §40; *Jeladze v. Georgia*, 18 December 2012, appl. no. 1871/08, §42; *Uğur v. Turkey*, 13 January 2015, appl. no. 37308/05, §101; and *M.A. v. Slovenia*, 15 January 2015, appl. no. 3400/07, §51.

71 *Chahal v. the United Kingdom*, 15 November 1996 (Grand Chamber), appl. no. 22414/93, §123; *Novik v. Ukraine*, 18 December 2008, appl. no. 48068/06, §20; *Kevin O'Dowd v. the United Kingdom*, 21 September 2010, appl. no. 7390/07, §31; *Fedorenko v. Russia*, 20 September 2011, appl. no. 39602/05, §73; *Longa Yonkeu v. Lithuania*, 15 November 2011, appl. no. 57229/09, §153; *Rustamov v. Russia*, 3 July 2012, appl. no. 11209/10, §166; *Niyazov v. Russia*, 16 October 2012, appl. no. 27843/11, §117; *J.M. v. Denmark*, 13 November 2012, appl. no. 34421/09, §54; *Dirdizov v. Russia*, 27 November 2012, appl. no. 41461/10, §110; *Bakoyev v. Russia*, 5 February 2013, appl. no. 30225/11, §167; *Amie et al. v. Bulgaria*, 12 February 2013, appl. no. 58149/08, §79; *Yefimova v. Russia*, 19 February 2013, appl. no. 39786/09, §257; *Khomollo v. Ukraine*, 27 November 2014, appl. no. 47593/10, §52; *Petrov v. Slovakia*, 2 December 2014, appl. no. 64195/10, §55; and *H.S. et al. v. Cyprus*, 21 July 2015, appl. no. 41753/10, §311.

72 In one case where the Court had to judge on an alleged violation of Art. 5, §4, it made the following observation: 'Although it is not always necessary for an Article 5 §4 procedure to incorporate the same guarantees as required by Article 6 for criminal or civil litigation, it must have a judicial and adversarial character, ensure "equality of arms" between the parties, be conducted with due diligence, and be attended by other guarantees appropriate to the type of deprivation of liberty in question.' *Molotchko v. Ukraine*, 26 April 2012, appl. no. 12275/10, §149. There are, of course, also cases in which the Court found a violation of Art. 6 because the defendant state did not act with due diligence: *Frydlender v. France*, 27 July 2000 (Grand Chamber), appl. no. 30979/96, §45; *Nierojewska v. Poland*, 22 August 2006, appl. no. 77835/01, §33; *Dodov v. Bulgaria*, 17 January 2008, appl. no. 59548/00, §§107–109; *Nesterova v. Ukraine*, 28 May 2009, appl. no. 10792/04, §39; *Sobieccy v. Poland*, 19 January 2010, appl. no. 32594/03, §39; and *Wildgruber v. Germany (no.2)*, 21 January 2010, appl. nos. 42402/05 and 42423/05, §57ff.

73 'In my opinion, the Finnish courts have examined the applicant's case with due diligence': Partly dissenting opinion of Judge Wojtyczek in 29 January 2013, §3. See also: *Y.U. v. Russia*, 13 November 2012, appl. no. 41354/10, §108; *Van Colle v. the United Kingdom*, 13 November 2012, appl. no. 7678/09, §108; and *Manic v. Lithuania*, 13 January 2015, appl. no. 46600/11, §118.

and Art. 1 of the first protocol.[74] The Court in these cases refers to the diligence of the state in the same way: it requires in all these cases that a government acts with due diligence if it interferes with the Convention rights of its citizens. If the state does not act with due diligence when it interferes in someone's Convention rights, the Court finds a violation of the Convention. In this context, The Court moreover finds that a state must pursue its legitimate aims with the means that are the least harmful for the Convention rights of its citizens.[75]

What all this jurisprudence illustrates is that the Court adopts a standard of conduct in its application of the proportionality test: if an interference with a human right did not occur with due diligence, the interference cannot be found proportionate with the legitimate aim pursued by the state.

2.1.2. Do the Proportionality Test and the General Standard of Conduct Always Overlap?

The fact that the Court refers to the general standard of conduct does not prove that the principle of proportionality and the general standard of conduct always overlap. For this the question needs to be answered of whether a disproportionate interference with a human right will always be qualified as a violation of the general standard of conduct.

Steininger and Wallner-Friedl give some arguments that suggest that this is indeed the case.[76] They first argue, while referring to Art. 1 of the first protocol, that the finding of a violation always requires the Court to balance interests. They argue that 'such a weighing of interests, however, is the basis of any assessment of whether the required standard of conduct has been adhered to or not, in other words whether there has been a violation of a duty of care.'[77] This is an interesting point of view, but it does not provide an in-depth explanation. The authors do however refer

74 *Vassallo v. Malta*, 11 October 2011, appl. no. 57862/09, §46.

75 *Hatton et al. v. the United Kingdom*, 2 October 2001, appl. no. 36022/97, §97.

76 Apart from these arguments, these authors are somehow prudent since they only indicate that the general standard of conduct has a function in the context of the human rights test and then stress that it is hard to determine what this role is exactly: B. Steininger and N. Wallner-Friedl, 'Wrongfulness and Fault', 2011, above n. 7, p501 at 535.

77 *Ibid.*, p501 at 519.

to some interesting cases, one of which is *Broniowski*, a case where the Court argues:

> In assessing compliance with Article 1 of Protocol No. 1, the Court must make an overall examination of the various interests in issue, bearing in mind that the Convention is intended to safeguard rights that are 'practical and effective'. It must look behind appearances and investigate the realities of the situation complained of. That assessment may involve not only the relevant compensation terms – if the situation is akin to the taking of property – but also the conduct of the parties, including the means employed by the State and their implementation. In that context, it should be stressed that uncertainty – be it legislative, administrative or arising from practices applied by the authorities – is a factor to be taken into account in assessing the State's conduct. Indeed, where an issue in the general interest is at stake, it is incumbent on the public authorities to act in good time, in an appropriate and consistent manner.[78]

What is interesting here is that the Court not only makes a single reference to the due diligence of the state, but also really analyzes its practice in applying the proportionality test. Since the Court indicates that it does take into account the conduct of the parties when examining the interests in the context of the proportionality test, the Court seems to refer to a general rule of conduct. Indeed, one cannot imagine how the Court can take a specific conduct into account without referring to the hypothetical behavior that the *bonus pater familias* would have had.[79]

---

78 *Broniowski v. Poland*, 22 June 2004 (Grand Chamber), appl. no. 31443/96, §151. See also: *Vasilescu v. Romania*, 22 May 1998, appl. no. 27053/95, §51ff.; *Beyeler v. Italy*, 5 January 2000 (Grand Chamber), appl. no. 33202/96, §115ff; *Paduraru v. Romania*, 1 December 2005, appl. no. 63252/00, §92; *Hutten-Czapska v. Poland*, 19 June 2006 (Grand Chamber), appl. no. 35014/97, §168; *Fleri Soler and Camilleri v. Malta*, 26 September 2006, appl. no. 35349/05, §70; *Buczkiewicz v. Poland*, 26 February 2008, appl. no. 10446/03, §59; *Suljagic v. Bosnia and Herzegovina*, 3 November 2009, appl. no. 27912/02, §44; *Maria Atanasiu v. Romania*, 12 October 2010, appl. nos. 30767/05 and 33800/06, §168; *Tarnawczyk v. Poland*, 7 December 2010, appl. no. 27480/02, §103; *Potomska Potomski v. Poland*, 29 March 2011, appl. no. 33949/05, §66; *Lindheim et al. v. Norway*, 12 June 2012, appl. nos. 13221/08 and 2139/10, §119; *Manushaqe Puto et al. v. Albania*, 31 July 2012, appl. nos. 604/07, 34770/09, 43628/07 and 46684/07, §92; *Ališić et al. v. Bosnia-Herzegovina, Serbia, Slovenia and the former Yugoslav Republic of Macedonia*, 16 July 2014 (Grand Chamber), appl. no. 60642/08, §108; and *Sargsyan v. Azerbaijan*, 16 July 2015 (Grand Chamber), appl. no. 40167/06, §227. The Court makes similar observations in its jurisprudence on Art. 6: *Tudor Tudor v. Romania*, 24 March 2009, appl. no. 21911/03, §26; and *Ştefănică et al. v. Romania*, 2 November 2010, appl. no. 38155/02, §32.

79 Essentially, one can argue that judges, when applying a proportionality test or a criterion such as the *bonus pater familias* criterion, always has to balance rights or

But additional reasons must exist as to why the proportionality test will always lead to the same result as a test that is based on the general standard of conduct. One starting point can be found in the grounds for justification discussed earlier. This book has shown that the Court implicitly applied rules that were very similar to the grounds for justification. It has not however found a case where the Court explicitly referred to these grounds. The Court only applied these principles implicitly in the proportionality test. This is however interesting because one could argue that the grounds for justification can also be seen as applications of the general standard of conduct. Can force majeure not be described as a situation where the *bonus pater familias* would have been forced by external factors to act in a way that causes damages to other persons?[80] Some tort lawyers defined the grounds of justification as '*le négatif de la faute*.' (the opposite of the fault)[81] Indeed, if someone wants to appeal to force majeure, he will only have to illustrate that he acted as a *bonus pater familias*. He thus will have to illustrate that he did not commit a fault. And can one not make the same reasoning if one looks at the legitimate self-defense?

There might however be no difference between the general rule of conduct and the grounds for justification. This difference relates to the burden of proof: a justification ground has to be proved by the defendant, whereas the non-respect of the general standard of conduct has to be proved by the claimant. Normally, one will only refer to a ground for justification if the claimant has proved that the defendant had not acted as a *bonus pater familias*. The defendant can then try to refute this by appealing to a ground for justification by the fact that he did not possess free will. What is interesting with regard to human rights law is that

interests. The fact that judges make these balancing-exercices, is often criticized (see for an overview with regard to the ECtHR: S. Smet, 'Introduction – Conflicts of Rights in Theoretical and Comparative Perspective' in S. Smet and E. Brems, *When Human Rights Clash at the European Court of Human Rights*, Oxford, Oxford University Press, 2017, p1 at 11.

80 F. Baudoncq and T. Viaene, 'Schuldbekwaam maar niet aansprakelijk: speelbal van het lot? Inzichten in het overmachtsbegrip bij buitencontractuele foutaansprakelijkheid' in X. (ed.), *Vigilantibus ius scriptum. Feestbundel van Hugo Vandenberghe*, Bruges, Die Keure, 2007, p23 at 27.

81 L. Cornelis and P. Van Ommeslaghe, 'Les faits justificatifs dans le droit belge de la responsabilité aquilienne' in X. (ed.), *In memoriam Jean Limpens*, Antwerp, Kluwer, 1984, p265 at 272; and J. van Zuylen, 'Du fait justificatif à la force majeure: les visages contrastés de l'exonération de la responsabilité' in R. Capart and J. Bouckourt (eds.), *Liber Amicorum Nöel Simar: Evaluation du dommage, Responsabilité civile et Assurances*, Limal, Anthemis, 2013, p263 at 296.

the Court will sometimes easily change the burden of proof, as seen in the context of force majeure in cases concerning the reasonable time requirement. It seems that the Court in these cases presumes that the reasonable time requirement has been violated, but it grants the defendant states the possibility to defend themselves by proving that they acted with due diligence. The fact that the grounds for justification are essentially illustrations of the use of the standard of conduct by the ECtHR does not prove that the proportionality test and the general standard of conduct will always overlap. More arguments are needed.

A first argument can be found in the positive obligations of the state under the Convention. From the perspective of tort law, these positive obligations are very akin to negligence. Indeed, the Court will find a violation of a positive obligation if a state neglected to offer the required protection. On saying this, it becomes clear that the Court must always take into account the general standard of conduct. The Court in these types of cases has to consider what measures a *bonus pater familias* would have taken before it can argue that a government had neglected to take the necessary measures to protect the Convention rights. In this context, Dean Spielmann states that a positive obligation is always a commitment of effort and not a commitment to reach a specific result.[82] Thus, one must check whether a government has made the required efforts and one cannot merely investigate whether or not a government reached a certain goal because one has to check whether the actions taken were reasonable.

Secondly, it must be remembered that it has been shown before that the Court uses the same criteria in cases where it has to assess negative and positive obligations.

Apart from these jurisprudential arguments that plead for the concurrency of the proportionality test and the general standard of conduct, there is also a more theoretical argument. To make this argument, one must start from the most typical situation where the general standard of conduct in tort law is applied: a traffic accident. To start, the example shall be used of a situation where a driver passes another car (on a place where this is permitted) and hits a car that comes from the other direction. To check in tort law whether the driver committed a fault in the objective sense, one has to take into account the distance between the car of the driver, the car that he wanted to pass and the car that came from the

[82] D. Spielmann, 'The European Convention on Human Rights' in D. Oliver and J. Fëdtke (eds.), *Human Rights and the Private Sphere – A Comparative Study*, London, Routledge, 2007, p427 at 436.

opposite direction. If the car from the opposite direction was already close, a reasonable person or a *bonus pater familias* would not try to pass the car in front of him, just as he would not do this in a moment when he has bad visibility. But imagine the situation where a driver has a passenger who is in urgent need of a hospital (think for example of a pregnant women). In that case, it seems very likely that a judge will be less inclined to believe that the driver committed a fault by passing a slow car in front of him. Indeed, if a judge has to decide whether a reasonable person, if he were placed in the same situation would try to pass the car before him, the judge will take into account the necessity for the driver to balance interests that are at stake.[83] The driver will have to balance the risks of passing (and thus the interest of a potentially damaged person) with the interest of reaching his destination as soon as possible. Thus, a judge will probably be less severe when a driver causes an accident when he was bringing a very wounded person to a hospital than when the driver is heading to a local shopping mall and has plenty of time.

But even if one believes that a judge will not differentiate between these two situations, one can still argue that the proportionality test and the general standard of conduct overlap. The reason for this is the fact that the general standard of conduct in the context of traffic will always have to be placed within the context of safety and efficiency. If a judge has to define the general standard of conduct, he will definitely have to take this balancing exercise into account. But apart from the judge, the actors in the traffic situations also have to do this balancing exercise. A *bonus pater familias* is expected to assess dangerous situations and to take reasonable measures to prevent accidents from occurring. From this perspective, it seems impossible to find a general standard of conduct without taking into account the contrary interests of the tortfeasor and the damaged person. If, moreover, a judge also has to take into account the organizational and practical considerations of the tortfeasor, this argument becomes even stronger.

One could argue against this reasoning by pointing out possible situations where the general standard of conduct protects a less significant interest against a more significant interest. One can think about cases where a tortfeasor intentionally damages another person. Imagine the

83 From this perspective Koziol writes that establishing the general standard of conduct requires the balancing of interests of the person who needs protection on the one hand and those of the actor on the other. For this, the judge has to value the endangered interests and the significance of the threatening interference and the interests pursued by the actor: H. Koziol, 'Conclusions', above n. 1, 1998, p129 at 133–134.

situation where a tortfeasor endangers his life by trying to enter a house via the roof to steal a jewel and then falls. If the thief damages the house while falling, he would be held responsible for these damages even though he had put his life in danger. One could think that a proportionality test, which simply balances the interests, would in this case have a different result than an assessment based on the general standard of conduct. But one must be careful not to jump to conclusions. If the ECtHR applies the proportionality test, it will first ask whether the infringement of a human right is based on a legitimate aim. Because of this, the Court in this hypothetical case would not find a violation because it would argue that climbing on houses to steal from someone else is not a legitimate aim. On top of that, it must be pointed out that the ECtHR, when it has to balance the interests of two private persons, will look at whether a party exercising his rights has the possibility to do so in a way that is less damaging for other people.[84] If one has two possibilities to exercise a right that both have the same result, and if one is not damaging for other persons and the other is, one has to choose the non-damaging way. As a result, the balancing exercise will not always privilege the most significant interest.

It can thus be concluded that the ECtHR, though the Convention does not refer to the fault principle or to the general standard of conduct, implicitly refers to a general standard of conduct when it applies the proportionality test. As seen, this only holds true with regard to the objective element of the fault. The Court does not take into account the subjective element of the fault. For holding someone accountable for a human rights violation, it seems unnecessary to be morally accountable. The accountability of human rights violators cannot be limited by referencing the intentionality of the violation. On the contrary, as Ernst Karner notices, the Court makes considerable attempts to create liabilities out of risk by interpreting the criterion of pre-visibility very broadly.[85]

2.1.3. The Concretization of the General Standard of Conduct

Apart from the question of whether the ECtHR refers to the general standard of conduct, it must be investigated whether the Court concretizes

---

84 J. Velaers, 'De proliferatie van de zgn. klassieke "liberale" grondrechten in de XXIe eeuw' in X. (ed.), *De Grondwet in groothoekperspectief. Liber amicorum discipuloremque Karel Rimanque*, Antwerp, Intersentia, 2007, p99 at 147.

85 E. Karner, 'Concluding Remarks on No-Fault or Strict Liability' in A. Fenyves, E. Karner, H. Koziol and E. Steiner (eds.), *Tort Law in the Jurisprudence of the European Court of Human Rights*, Göttingen, De Gruyter, 2011, p857 at 859.

the general standard of conduct and whether or not the Court takes into account the physical or intellectual capabilities of a human rights violator. At first glance, it seems that the Court indeed does so. This at least, was the case in *Anguelova*.[86] It concerned a man who had died in prison because of medical reasons. Since the family of the deceased person claimed a violation of the right to life, the defendant government argued that the policemen were not medical experts and could not know that his life was in danger. The Court responded to this argument as follows:

> That argument is, however, irrelevant, as it is not disputed that at a certain point after 3 a.m. the police officers realised that Mr Zabchekov's condition was deteriorating. Even then, instead of calling for an ambulance, they contacted their colleagues who had arrested the boy. Those officers, who were on patrol duty, saw fit to abandon their patrolling tasks and drive back to the police station to verify the situation. Having seen Mr Zabchekov's condition, they took the time to drive to the hospital and then return, followed by an ambulance, instead of calling for one.[87]

Apart from the fact that this is a notable illustration of the ECtHR's use of the general standard of conduct, it is interesting that the Court noted that the policemen at a certain point were aware of the deterioration of the condition of the prisoner. By pointing to this fact, it seems that the Court would *a contrario* not find a violation of the Convention if the police officers had not been able to notice the deterioration in the prisoner's health. It seems that the Court then would apply the general standard of conduct more strictly in a similar situation in a hospital.

Another set of cases where the Court seems to consider the professional capabilities of a human rights violator can be found in the jurisprudence concerning the liability of the press (mainly in defamation). In these cases, the Court argues that journalists can only exercise their right to free speech if they act in good faith.[88] The requirement for the journalists to act in good faith is used in these cases to define the boundaries of what is acceptable according to the principle of proportionality.[89] This also stems

---

86 *Anguelova v. Bulgaria*, 13 June 2002, appl. no. 38361/97.

87 *Ibid.*, *Anguelova v. Bulgaria*, 13 June 2002, appl. no. 38361/97, §127. See also: *Gagiu v. Romania*, 24 February 2009, appl. no. 63258/00, §60.

88 *Bladet Tromso and Stensaas v. Norway*, 20 May 1999 (Grand Chamber), appl. no. 21980/93, §65; and *Bergens Tidende et al. v. Norway*, 2 May 2000, appl. no. 26132/95, §53.

89 Y. Galland, 'Les obligations des journalistes dans la jurisprudence de la Cour européenne des droits de l'homme', *Rev.Trim.D.H.* 2002, p853 at 855.

from *Michaud*, a case where the Court, in the context of a legal exception on the professional secrecy of attorneys to report suspected financial transactions, held:

> That the notion of 'suspicions' is a matter of common sense and that, an informed group such as lawyers can scarcely claim that they do not understand it in that, as the Government have explained, the Monetary and Financial Code gives certain specific indications. What is more, as the suspicions are to be reported to the chairman of the Bar, or the President of the Bar Council of the Conseil d'Etat and the Court of Cassation, any lawyer who has doubts about the existence of 'suspicions' in a given case can seek the advice of an informed and experienced colleague.[90]

2.1.4. The General Standard of Conduct of Private Persons in the Jurisprudence of the ECtHR

Since the ECtHR implicitly applies the standard of conduct, the question arises of whether the Court also requires individuals to take into account the general standard of conduct. At first glance, it seems impossible to answer this question since only states can be held accountable before the ECtHR, but there are some ways to get around this hindrance.

A first approach might be to refer to the idea that private citizens can abuse their rights. One can argue that if a private person (mainly an applicant) can abuse his rights under the Convention, then this points to a kind of general standard of conduct because this criterion requires the Court to judge how a person has to act so that he does not abuse these rights. In some systems of tort law, discussions exist as to whether or not the notion of abuse of rights is a special application of the general tort law provisions or not.[91] The differences that may exist according to these discussions are mainly situated in the remedies or the subjective element of the fault. Concerning the objective element of the fault, it is argued that these criteria must be seen as a balancing of interests which is, according to some authors, something different to an application of the general standard of conduct,[92] but this book cannot agree with this theory.

---

90 *Michaud v. France*, 6 December 2012, appl. no. 12323/11, §97.

91 This is the case in Belgian law. See: B. Dubuisson, V. Callewaert, B. De Coninck and G. Gathem, *La Responsabilité civile. Chronique de jurisprudence 1996–2007*, Part 1, *Le fait générateur et le lien causal*, Brussels, Larcier, 2009, at 51ff.

92 E.g.: L. Cornelis, 'Aansprakelijkheid in de ban van de goede trouw?' in M. Storme (ed.), *Recht halen uit aansprakelijkheid. XIXe postuniversitaire cyclus Willy Delva*, Gent, Mys and Breesch, 1993, (1) at 18 and 49.

Indeed, as seen in the previous chapter, one cannot apply the general standard of conduct without balancing the interests of the tortfeasor and the damaged person. As a result, it seems that if the Court applies the notion of abuse of rights towards private persons, it does so without explicitly referring to this concept.

From this perspective, it is interesting to note that the ECtHR sometimes applies the principle of abuse of rights with regard to the behavior of applicants in a procedure before the Court. The Court sometimes argues that an applicant can abuse his right to bring a case before it. For instance, this is the case when applicants intentionally write untruths in their application,[93] or when the applicant misleads the Court by not notifying some important events that occurred during the procedures.[94] The fact that the Court applies the notion of abuse of rights in the context of the procedure illustrates that it can apply a general standard of conduct on private persons, but it does not show that a general standard of conduct is used as an instrument to judge whether or not individuals have to respect each other's human rights.

A treaty provision that might apply the notion of abuse of rights in horizontal relationships is Art. 17, titled 'the prohibition of abuse of rights'. This provision stipulates that the treaty cannot be interpreted 'as implying for any State, group or person any right to engage in any activity or perform any act aimed at the destruction of any of the rights and freedoms set forth herein or at their limitation to a greater extent than is provided for in the Convention'. As such, this provision explicitly states that private persons cannot be permitted to violate or infringe the Convention rights of others.[95] The aim of this provision is to prohibit private persons from relying on their Convention rights with the aim of abolishing the Convention or the protection of its rights. It gives shape to a resilient democracy and is used against antidemocratic persons or groups.[96]

---

93 *Varbanov v. Bulgaria*, 5 October 2010, appl. no. 31365/96, §36; and *Centro Europa 7 S.R.L. and Di Stefano v. Italy*, 7 June 2012, appl. no. 38433/09, §97.

94 *Melnik v. Ukraine*, 28 March 2006, appl. no. 72286/01, §§58–60; *Nold v. Germany*, 29 June 2006, appl. no. 27250/02, §87; *Hadrabova v. The Czech Republic*, 25 September 2007 (Decision), appl. nos. 42165/02 and 466/03; *Predescu v. Romania*, 2 December 2008 (Decision), appl. no. 21447/03; and *Centro Europa 7 S.R.L. and Di Stefano v. Italy*, 7 June 2012, appl. no. 38433/09, §97.

95 A. Clapham, 'The "Drittwirkung" of the Convention' in R. Macdonald, F. Matscher and H. Petzold (eds.), *The European System for the Protection of Human Rights*, Dordrecht, Martinus Nijhoff Publishers, 1993, p163 at 167–169.

96 J. Vande Lanotte and Y. Haeck, *Handboek EVRM. Part 2, Artikelsgewijze Commentaar. Volume II*, Antwerp, Intersentia, 1995, at 246ff.

In some exceptional cases, the ECtHR has used Art. 17 as an interpretative tool when it had to deal with violations of other Convention rights.[97] The Court in these cases argues that an infringement of a Convention right with the legitimate aim of protecting the human rights of other individuals against the abuse of rights of the applicant was necessary and proportionate in a democratic society.[98] These cases are an interesting illustration of the ways in which the Court can apply human rights in horizontal relationships and of the use of the notion of an abuse of rights in horizontal relations. They are very rare, however. All the cases where the Court has applied Art. 17 concern Nazi, negationist or racist groups that oppose Democracy.[99] If Art. 17 is read literally, it seems possible to extend this approach to a broader set of cases, but such an approach would be contrary to the intentions of the drafters of the Convention and is thus not followed in the jurisprudence of the ECtHR.[100] Consequently, Art. 17 cannot in itself suffice as grounds to argue that private persons have to respect the general standard of conduct as related to the protection of the human rights of others and of a general application of the abuse of rights theory.

There are however more elements in the Convention that can imply the abuse of rights theory. One of these is the fault of an applicant. The Court takes into account the behavior of an applicant when judging on a violation of the Convention and on the compensation that an applicant can receive under Art. 41. As was pointed out before, the Court considers the behavior of an applicant who sued the government for the violation of the reasonable time requirement. The Court in different cases argued: 'although a party to civil proceedings cannot be blamed for using the avenues available to him under domestic law in order to protect his interests, he must accept

97 F. Jacobs, R. White and C. Ovey, *The European Convention on Human Rights*, Oxford, Oxford University Press, 2010, at 124.

98 For example, in the case of *Garaudy* the Court ruled that the criminal prosecution of someone who denied the Holocaust in a book did not violate Art. 10 since denying the Holocaust constitutes a violation of Art. 17: *Garaudy v. France*, 24 June 2003 (Decision), appl. no. 65831/01.

99 H. Cannie and D. Voorhoof, 'The abuse clause and freedom of expression in the European Human Rights Convention', *NQHR* 2011, p54 at 58ff; and D. Keane, 'Attacking hate speech under Article 17 of the European Convention on Human Rights', *NQHR* 2007, p641 at 641–651.

100 F. Jacobs, R. White and C. Ovey, *The European Convention*, 2010, above n. 97, at 125; and S. Van Drooghenbroeck, 'L'Article 17 de la convention européenne des droits de l'homme. Est-il indispensable?', *Rev.trim.D.H.* 2001, p540 at 544ff.

that such actions necessarily prolong the proceedings concerned.'[101] This citation does not show that the applicants have to protect human rights of other persons, but it does demonstrate that an applicant has to take into account a specific standard of conduct in the exercise of his rights. Indeed, as the case of *Proszak* illustrates, it is possible that an applicant involuntarily waves his rights because of his behavior:

> Although the lawyer had accepted the court's appointment of a fresh psychiatrist as an expert, Mrs Proszak did not attend on the day appointed for the examination. That was scarcely consistent with the diligence which must be shown by the plaintiff in civil proceedings.[102]

A similar principle can be found in the jurisprudence of the Court concerning the right to property in the case of *Beyeler.*[103] In 1977, a Swiss art dealer bought the painting 'Portrait of a Young Peasant,' that Van Gogh painted in Saint-Rémy-de-Provence, by using a middleman. In 1954, the Italian government had declared this painting to be a work of historical and artistic interest. The Swiss art dealer kept on hiding behind the middleman until he found an interested buyer in 1983. At that moment he informed the Italian government that he had owned the painting since 1977 and asked the government whether it would apply its pre-emption right. The Italian government did not respond to this request. Five years later, when the art dealer decided to sell the painting to the Peggy Guggenheim collection in Venice for $8.5 million, the Italian government exercised its pre-emption right and paid him the price that he had paid for the painting in 1977. Since this was a significantly smaller sum, the art dealer argued that his right to property had been violated. The Court found that the Italian government had violated Art. 1 of the first protocol for waiting too long to exercise its pre-emption right. For this reason, the Court awarded a sum of money to the art dealer for his damages. When considering the size of the damages,

---

101 *Dulskiy v. Ukraine*, 1 June 2006, appl. no. 61679/00, §81; *Belukha v. Poland*, 9 November 2006, appl. no. 33949/02, §64; *Ivanov v. Ukraine*, 7 December 2006, appl. no. 15007/02, §69; *Fandralyuk v. Ukraine*, 31 January 2008, appl. no. 22775/03, §24; *Pavlovska v. Ukraine*, 3 July 2008, appl. no. 36949/02, §38; *Voishchev v. Ukraine*, 19 February 2009, appl. no. 21263/04, §32; *Gutka v. Ukraine*, 8 April 2010, appl. no. 45846/05, §27; and *Kolomoyets v. Ukraine*, 15 July 2010, appl. no. 11208/03, §47.

102 *Proszak v. Poland*, 16 December 1997, appl. no. 25086/94. See also: *Humen v. Poland*, 15 October 1999 (Grand Chamber), appl. no. 26614/95, §66; *Boczon v. Poland*, 30 January 2007, appl. no. 66079/01, §51; and *Bunčič v. Slovenia*, 24 January 2008, appl. no. 42852/02, §59.

103 *Beyeler v. Italy*, 5 January 2000 (Grand Chamber), appl. no. 33202/96, §114.

the Court looked at the evolution of the worth of the painting but did not take into account the increase in value of the painting between 1977 and 1983 because it found that these damages were caused by the applicant's 'failure to act openly and honestly during that period.'[104]

This jurisprudence does not concern the question of whether the Court requires the application of a general standard of conduct in order to make private persons respect each other's Convention rights. To find jurisprudence that quite explicitly does this, one must look at the jurisprudence concerning the exercise of the free speech. Although *Tolstoy Miloslawsky* has shown that one's right to free speech can be violated if he has to pay compensation for the damages that were caused by the exercise of this right, this case also illustrates that the exercise of the right to free speech does not protect against all damage claims.[105] Indeed, the Court in this case did not find a violation for the reason that the applicant had to pay damages, but for the reason that there were no mechanisms to mitigate the size of the compensation that was too big. In essence, one could say that the treaty is only violated if rights are exercised in a way that is contrary to the general standard of conduct. This conclusion can also be derived from the wording of Art. 10, §2. This paragraph sums up what grounds can possibly legitimize an infringement on the right to free speech:

> The exercise of these freedoms, since it carries with it duties and responsibilities, may be subject to such formalities, conditions, restrictions or penalties as are prescribed by law and are necessary in a democratic society, in the interests of national security, territorial integrity or public safety, for the prevention of disorder or crime, for the protection of health or morals, for the protection of the reputation or rights of others, for preventing the disclosure of information received in confidence, or for maintaining the authority and impartiality of the judiciary.

Taking into account that the Convention itself refers to the duties and responsibilities of the people who exercise their right to free speech, it comes as no surprise that the ECtHR in its jurisprudence refers to these duties. Such is the case in *Fressoz and Roire*:

> It [Article 10 of the Convention] protects journalists' right to divulge information on issues of general interest provided that they are acting in good faith and on

104 *Beyeler v. Italy*, 28 May 2002 (just satisfaction) (Grand Chamber), appl. no. 33202/96, §23.
105 See also: W. Berka, 'Human Rights and Tort Law' in A. Fenyves, E. Karner, H. Koziol and E. Steiner (eds.), *Tort Law in the Jurisprudence of the European Court of Human Rights*, Göttingen, De Gruyter 2011, p237 at 247.

an accurate factual basis and provide 'reliable and precise' information in accordance with the ethics of journalism.[106]

By judging that Art. 10 protects journalists who act 'in good faith' and who provide 'reliable and precise' information that is based on an 'accurate factual basis,' the Court quite explicitly applies a general standard of conduct. From the viewpoint of a general standard of conduct, it is important that journalists do thoroughly research their publications. Thus, if the Court notices that a journalist who writes for a weekly magazine has more time than a journalist who writes for a newspaper that is published on a daily basis,[107] or argues that a journalist trusts the information provided by an official document,[108] one cannot but qualify this as an application of the general standard of conduct. Cannot one say that the Court in the case of *Fressoz and Roire* argued that a *bonus pater journalist* has to act in good faith and has to provide reliable and precise information on an accurate factual basis and in accordance with the ethics of journalism? The only thing that is missing is the notion that the journalist has to act 'with caution', as the Court required from a journalist in the case of *Godlevskiy*.[109]

Numerous other cases underpin this idea. Take for instance *Björk Eîsdóttir.* In this case the Court argued that a person who harms another person's reputation by insulting him must have the opportunity in a national procedure to prove that she has 'a real opportunity to absolve

106 *Fressoz and Roire v. France*, 21 January 1999 (Grand Chamber), appl. no. 29183/95, §54. See also: *Bladet Tromso and Stensaas v. Norway*, 20 May 1999 (Grand Chamber), appl. no. 21980/93, §65; *Bergens Tidende et al. v. Norway*, 2 May 2000, appl. no. 26132/95, §53; *McVicar v. the United Kingdom*, 7 May 2002, appl. no. 46311/99, §73; *Colombani v. France*, 25 June 2002, appl. no. 51279/99, §65; *Pedersen and Baadsgaard v. Denmark*, 19 June 2003, appl. no. 49017/99, §72; *Selisto v. Finland*, 16 November 2004, appl. no. 56767/00, §54; *Cumpana and Mazare v. Romania*, 17 December 2004 (Grand Chamber), appl. no. 33348/96, §102; *Savitchi v. Moldavia*, 11 October 2005, appl. no. 11039/02, §46; *Stoll v. Switzerland*, 25 April 2006, appl. no. 69698/01, §54; *Dupuis et al. v. France*, 7 June 2007, appl. no. 1914/02, §46; *Godlevskiy v. Russia*, 23 October 2008, appl. no. 14888/03, §42; *Eerikäinen et al. v. Finland*, 10 February 2009, appl. no. 3514/02, §60; *Fatullayev v. Azerbaijan*, 22 April 2010 (Grand Chamber), appl. no. 40984/07, §95; *Koprivica v. Montenegro*, 22 November 2011, appl. no. 41158/09, §64; *Axel Springer AG v. Germany*, 7 February 2012 (Grand Chamber), appl. no. 39954/08, §93; *Novaya Gazeta and Borodyanskiy v. Russia*, 28 March 2013, appl. no. 14087/08, §40; *Braun v. Poland*, 4 November 2014, appl. no. 30162/10, §46ff; and *Marian Marciejewski v. Poland*, 13 January 2015, appl. no. 34447/05, §84ff.

107 *Koprivica v. Montenegro*, 22 November 2011, appl. no. 41158/09, §69.

108 *Gorelishvili v. Georgia*, 5 June 2007, appl. no. 12979/04, §41.

109 *Godlevskiy v. Russia*, 23 October 2008, appl. no. 14888/03, §43.

herself of liability by establishing that she had acted in good faith.'[110] What the Court requires here is for someone's right to free speech not to be limited even if his insults were out of his control. The Court in this case had to judge whether a journalist could be condemned in a defamation case for the content of an interview that she published and where the interviewed person made insulting remarks. The Court in this case considered:

> that the disputed statements based on a first-hand account given by another person in an interview with the applicant, that the latter assessed the reliability of the said account and adduced evidence in support of the statements, the Court finds in the concrete circumstances of the present case that the applicant journalist cannot be criticised for having failed to ascertain the truth of the disputed allegations and is satisfied that she acted in good faith, consistently with the diligence expected of a responsible journalist reporting on a matter of public interest.[111]

This judgment not only illustrates that the Court takes into account the general standard of conduct, but also that the Court solidifies the general standard of conduct by taking into account the professional capacities of private persons.

A last example is *Selisto*.[112] The applicant here was a journalist who, in one of her articles, questioned the capabilities of a certain surgeon after some of his patients died. The journalist wrote that the mentioned surgeon sometimes came to the operation room drunk. She based these allegations on the testimonies of some nurses who were not present during the surgery of the people who afterwards died. As a consequence of these articles, the surgeon sued the journalist for defamation and the national courts commanded her to pay a limited compensation. The journalist believed that her right to free speech was violated. In its judgment, the ECtHR took into account that the relatives of the deceased persons had filed a criminal complaint that had not led to the prosecution of the surgeon. The defendant state argued that the journalist had not mentioned the decision of the prosecutor not to prosecute the surgeon in her article. The state argued that this proved that the journalist did not know the prosecutor's reasoning

110 *Björk Eîsdóttir v. Iceland*, 10 July 2012, appl. no. 46443/09, §76.

111 *Björk Eîsdóttir v. Iceland*, 10 July 2012, appl. no. 46443/09, §81. If the Court had ruled differently, it would have as a result that a journalist can be held responsible for of someone else's statements: *Erla Hlynsdóttir v. Iceland*, 10 July 2012, appl. no. 43380/10, §71.

112 *Selisto v. Finland*, 16 November 2004, appl. no. 56767/00.

for shelving the cases. The Court, however, did not take this defense into account, something that Judge Bratza criticized in his dissenting opinion:

> I find it difficult to see how the failure of the applicant to obtain a copy of the decision before publication of the two Articles may be said to be consistent with the diligence expected of a responsible journalist.[113]

This criticism proves that although the Court did not deal with the argument of the state in its judgment, it had taken this into account during its deliberation and that the Court had found that the failure to obtain a copy of the decision of the prosecutor did not contradict the general standard of conduct. What the Court did was point to the fact that a judge has to take into account a margin of appreciation when he reviews the acts of journalists:

> It is not for this Court, nor for the national courts for that matter, to substitute their own views for those of the press as to what technique of reporting should be adopted by journalists.[114]

2.2. THE VIOLATION OF A HUMAN RIGHT AS A FAULT IN ITSELF

2.2.1. *On Subjective Rights,* 'Troubles de Voisinage' *and Human Rights*

An interesting question is whether the violation of a human right, or a 'subjective right' as such must be qualified as a fault. Indeed, in some jurisdictions, the notion of a violation of a subjective right in itself is perceived as a fault. Thus, if a human right would be qualified as a subjective right in the national legal order, it would become the subject of a sort of faultless liability scheme. To illustrate this, it is best to examine national case-law.

---

113 Dissenting opinion of Judge Bratza in *Selisto v. Finland*, 16 November 2004, appl. no. 56767/00.

114 *Jersild v. Denmark*, 23 September 1994 (Grand Chamber), appl. no. 15890/89, §31. See also: *Bladet Tromsø and Stensaas v. Norway*, 20 May 1999 (Grand Chamber), appl. no. 21980/93, §63; *Bergens Tidende et al. v. Norway*, 2 May 2000, appl. no. 26132/95, §57; *Selisto v. Finland*, 16 November 2004, appl. no. 56767/00, §59; *Krone Verlags GMBH and CO KG v. Austria (no.4)*, 9 November 2006, appl. no. 72331/01, §34; *Tonsbergs Blad AS and Haukom v. Norway*, 1 March 2007, appl. no. 510/04, §94; *Eerikäinen et al. v. Finland*, 10 February 2009, appl. no. 3514/02, §65; *Bozhkov v. Bulgaria*, 19 April 2011, appl. no. 3316/04, §48; *Krone Verlag GMBH v. Austria*, 19 June 2012, appl. no. 27306/07, §47; *Björk Eîsdóttir v. Iceland*, 10 July 2012,

Take for instance the case on 31 March 2001 of the '*Hoge Raad*' of the Netherlands.[115] The facts that led to this judgment concern a house search by the police in a piggery of a farmer who was not a suspect in the criminal investigation. The police officers in charge of the search opened some doors in the piggery and left them open for quite a long time. This caused some distortions in the ventilation system. As a result of these distortions, some pigs became ill. The pig farmer had to hire a veterinarian and buy more expensive food for the pigs. He then sued the government for damages. The government argued that the search had been carried out in a legitimate way. This, according to the government, makes it clear that they had not committed a fault. The *Hoge Raad* did not agree with the government. The Court referred to the principle of equality and argued that this principle states that actions of governments should not have a disproportionate disadvantageous impact on a small number of persons. If a governmental act causes a disproportionate disadvantage, then the government must enact mechanisms to spread this disadvantage equally over the community as a whole (e.g. by compensating the disadvantage via taxes). The Court argued that the government already acted illegitimately by causing a disproportionate disadvantage to the pig farmer, whether or not the house search was carried out in accordance with the law.

Other illustrations can be found in cases with regard to the notion of '*troubles de voisinage*'. In Belgium this can be illustrated by two cases of 6 April 1960.[116] One case related to nuisance caused by public works whereas the other case concerned nuisance caused by the smoke that came out of a chimney owned by a private party. The Court of Cassation ruled in these cases that the owner of a property which disrupts the balance between the neighboring yards has to pay compensation to the owner of the disturbed yard, even if no fault was committed. Although these cases are not that interesting from a factual perspective, it is interesting to note that the Belgian Court of Cassation in these cases developed the notion of '*troubles de voisinage*' as a distinct faultless liability scheme and that the principle of equality as enshrined in the Belgian Constitution had an influence on this jurisprudential development.[117]

---

appl. no. 46443/09, §79; *Erla Hlynsdóttir v. Iceland*, 10 July 2012, appl. no. 43380/10, §70; *A.B. v. Switzerland*, 1 July 2014, appl. no. 56925/08, §57; *Murat Vural v. Turkey*, 21 October 2014, appl. no. 9540/07, §53; and *Armellini et al. v. Austria*, 16 April 2015, appl. no. 14134/07, §40.

115 Hoge Raad, 30 March 2001, *Rechtspraak van de week* 2001, at 71.

116 Belgian Court of Cassation, 6 April 1960, *Pasicresie* 1960, I, at 915.

117 N. Van Leuven, *Contracten en mensenrechten*, Antwerp, Intersentia, 2009, at 191.

A very different example can be found in the judgment of the Court of Appeal of Coimbra on 15 January 2002.[118] The applicant in this case complained that his right to private life under Art. 8 of the Convention was violated because of sounds that came from a pub near his house during the night. The Court of Appeal argued that this noise indeed infringed the right to private life of the applicant but stated that the owner of the pub also has fundamental rights, including the right to engage in economic activities. The Court had to balance these interests. The Court then remarked that a personality right in principle has a higher value than an economic right, but that personality rights are not absolute in nature and so can be limited. The Court ordered the pub owner to pay some compensation for the moral damages of the applicant and judged that for the future, the pub had to take into account a closing time. This case is not a unique one, similar cases have appeared in Spain[119] and in England.[120]

What these cases illustrate is that one can replace the application of the fault-principle in national tort law by a balancing test as appears in the jurisprudence of the ECtHR. This does not however mean that one enacts a faultless liability scheme. Indeed, the mere infringement of a human right cannot be qualified as a ground for liability. Liability can only be established after the proportionality test is applied. This seems to be reasonable because this book has shown that the exercise of human rights is not absolute but can be limited by the general standard of conduct.[121] It has also shown for instance that journalists have to act in good faith when they exercise their right to free speech. The reason for this is that the exercise of a human right can be limited by a law that has a legitimate aim or by the human rights of other persons.

As a result, it is hard to imagine that one can protect a human right as such by a faultless liability scheme. For example, if one wants to protect the right to property through tort law, one must take into account that

---

118 With regard to this topic, see: A. Dias Pereira, 'Portugal' in H. Koziol and B. Steininger (eds.), *European Tort Law 2002*, Vienna, Springer, p345 at 358–359.

119 J. Ribon, 'Spain' in H. Koziol and B. Steininger (eds.), *European Tort Law 2004*, Vienna, Springer, 2005, p538 at 544–545.

120 In English legal doctrine, is has been argued that the tort of nuisance has been developed on the basis of the proportionality test with regard to the right to property and the right to private life: D. Nolan, 'Nuisance' in D. Hoffman (ed.), *The Impact of the UK Human Rights Act on Private Law*, Cambridge, Cambridge University Press, 2011, p165 at 173–177. See also: C. Van Dam, *European Tort Law*, Oxford, Oxford University Press, 2013, at 582.

121 With regard to the negligence of the applicants to file a certain claim: *Katte Klitsche de la Grange v. Italy*, 27 October 1994, appl. no. 12539/86, §36; and *Pialopoulos et al. v. Greece*, 15 January 2001, appl. no. 37095/97, §§59 and 76.

the exercise of this right can conflict with the right to property of other persons and with other rights such as the right to free speech of another person. This book has provided examples that show that the ECtHR is very reluctant to find a fault in the acts of a journalist who exercises his right to free speech because the limitations on the right to free speech have to be interpreted very strictly.[122] In contrast, the Court grants the states a wide margin of appreciation to limit the right to property.[123] Thus, it seems hard to imagine that the right to property in general can be protected by an objective liability scheme since it is obvious that the rights to free speech, to freedom of religion, to privacy or to assembly of other persons cease to exist at the doorstep of private property. If this would be possible, employers or owners of private shopping centers would be able to exclude the fundamental rights of others from large parts of society.[124] This demonstrates that if the right to property in general is protected by a faultless liability scheme, this scheme will from time to time cause a violation of the rights of others. Indeed, by implementing such a scheme a better protection would be granted to some human rights (such as the right to property via concepts such as '*troubles de voisinage*')[125] than to others. By doing so the scheme would enact a hierarchy in the protection of human rights, something that, according to Jan Velaers, conflicts with the aims of the Convention.[126]

2.2.2. Colorizing the General Standard of Conduct with Human Rights

The previous chapter illustrated that tort law cannot grant better protection to some human rights than to others. This however seems a bit at odds

---

122 A. Van Rijn, 'Freedom of Expression (Article 10)' in P. Van Dijk, F. Van Hoof, A. Van Rijn and L. Zwaak (eds.), *Theory and Practice of the European Convention on Human Rights*, Antwerp, Intersentia, 2006, p773 at 793.

123 *Ibid.*, at 887–889.

124 To know more about the application of this principle in English law, see: K. Gray and S. Gray, 'Civil Rights, Civil Wrongs and Quasi-Public Space', *EHRLR* 1999, p46 at 69–70.

125 In legal doctrine, Stijns and Vuye have noted that it is strange that the right to property in Belgian private law is protected by a proportionality test whereas the same is not true for (other) human rights: S. Stijns and H. Vuye, 'Rechtsmisbruik en burenhinder: evenwichtsoefeningen op weg naar een evenwichtsleer' in *Liber Amicorum Walter van Gerven*, Deurne, Kluwer, 2000, p299 at 328.

126 According to this author, the lawmaker can develop a regulation to solve conflicts between human rights in a specific field in order to protect legal certainty but cannot stipulate that one human right will always prevail over another: J. Velaers, 'De proliferatie', 2007, above n. 84, p99 at 145–146.

with the jurisprudence of the *Hoge Raad* of the Netherlands and the Belgian Court of Cassation where these courts developed a stricter liability regime via the principle of equality. Indeed, it seems paradoxical that the principle of equality leads to stricter protection of the right to property when such a stricter protection seems at odds with the protection of other human rights.

One can untangle this paradox by looking at the rule that exists in Belgian tort law which states that the objective element of the fault cannot only exist from the violation of the general standard of conduct, but also from the violation of a specific behavior rule. A law that forbids people to drive a car when they are intoxicated can be qualified as a specific behavior rule because it clearly indicates what one has to do. Thus, if someone violates this rule, a judge will find a fault in the objective perspective and will not have to look at the general standard of conduct anymore. The mere fact of the violation of the specific behavior rule suffices.

It is interesting to note that although the notion of specific behavior rules was developed to simplify the finding of a fault, the rule causes its own interpretative problems. The problem appears when a judge is confronted with a legal norm and has to check whether this legal norm can be qualified as such a rule, in other words whether this legal norm enshrines an obligation of result or an obligation of endeavor. What is more interesting is the fact that this rule is essentially just an application of the general standard of conduct. Indeed, one could perceive the general standard of conduct and the specific behavior rule as two opposites on a scale between black and white and not as two separated criteria. One can say that the more precise a rule is the stronger the presumption will be that a violator of this rule commits acts in a way that is irreconcilable with the general standard of conduct. Indeed, if a legal norm only contains an obligation of endeavor, a judge will have to apply the general standard of conduct to check whether someone acted as he should have. If a rule on the other hand provides instructions that a person in a given situation is obliged to follow, one can expect that a reasonable person will adjust his behavior to these instructions. Everyone is considered to know the law and consequently everyone can be expected to adjust to the specific behavior rules in the law.

It can be argued that there is one difference between the specific behavior rule and the general standard of conduct. If one applies the general standard of conduct, the applicant in a lawsuit will have to prove that this standard is violated. If one however applies the specific behavior rule, the applicant will only have to prove that the defendant violated this rule. The defendant will then have the possibility of invoking force majeure and arguing that he acted as a *bonus pater familias* in the sense that every *bonus pater familias* would have violated the specific behavior rule in the given case because the acts were caused by factors out of his control such as in the case of legitimate self-defense or force majeure. The difference between the general standard of conduct and the specific behavior rule lies in the reversal of the onus of proof. When this rule can be applied, the claimant only has to prove the violation of the special behavior rule and then it is up to the defendant to prove that he acted as a *bonus pater familias* and that he cannot be held liable because the subjective element of the fault is not present because he can prove a ground for justification (such as force majeure). From this perspective, it is interesting to note that German tort law does not apply the specific behavior rule in the way described here. In German tort law, the violation of a legal norm only gives rise to a refutable presumption of liability, which can be rebutted by the tortfeasor proving that although he did not respect the legal norms, he acted as a reasonable and foreseeing person would have acted if he were in the same situation.[127] In the same way, the Principles of European Tort Law (PETL) do not qualify the violation of the specific behavior rule as a fault but only as an 'indication for fault'.[128]

This concept can be used to untangle the paradox that human rights on the one hand lead to a stricter protection of some human rights but on the other hand they cannot tolerate a better protection for some human rights against others. Indeed, taking into account the idea that the violation of a legal norm as such can constitute a fault or at least be an indication of fault, the question arises of whether a human right can be qualified as a specific behavior rule. At first sight this seems implausible, human rights are vague provisions that do not give guidance on how people or at least a government must act. Indeed, the ECtHR takes into account the principle of subsidiarity according to which states are better placed than the Court to decide how human rights can best be protected. Because of this principle, the Court grants the states a certain margin of appreciation. From this perspective, it seems impossible that a human right can be seen as a specific behavior

---

127 I. Claeys, 'Het foutbegrip bij overheidsaansprakelijkheid: zijn wetschending en fout nog één?' in X. (ed.), *Aansprakelijkheid, aansprakelijkheidsverzekering en andere schadevergoedingsmechanismen*, XXXIIIste Postuniversitaire cyclus Willy Delva, Mechelen, Kluwer, 2007, p193 at 200.

128 European Group on Tort Law, *Principles of European Tort Law. Text and commentaries*, Vienna, Springer, 2005, at 81.

rule. There is however some jurisprudence in Belgium where the Belgian Court of Cassation seems to apply human rights as a specific behavior rule. In a case of 28 September 2006, the Court of Cassation applied the requirement to provide a judgment within a reasonable time as a specific behavior rule.[129] According to Willem Verrijdt, the Court of Cassation found that the jurisprudence of the ECtHR illustrates that the reasonable time requirement is an obligation of result whereby the states have the freedom to choose the means through which it wants to reach this goal.[130]

What is interesting about this reasoning is that the author, just as the Court itself, refers to the jurisprudence of the ECtHR. Indeed, from the wording of Art. 6, one can only learn that everyone is 'entitled to a fair and public hearing within a reasonable time.' It is not mentioned in this provision how one must interpret the notion of a reasonable time or how a government should provide this. Thus, Art. 6 can hardly be seen as a specific behavior rule. One can say that the only clear rule that comes out of the Convention is the prohibition of torture. One argument for this is the fact that the ECtHR in its jurisprudence does not take into account the behavior of the victim of torture.[131] Take for instance *Gäfgen*. In this case the ECtHR argued that Germany had violated Art. 3 because the police had threatened a man with torture if he did not cooperate with the police to help them track down the child that this man kidnapped and whose life was in danger, even though the threat to torture the man could have saved the life of the child.[132] Thus, if such a grave fault by a victim of torture cannot justify the torture, it seems reasonable that there is no possible legitimation. It simply must be assumed that a *bonus pater familias* does not torture someone, regardless of the specific conditions.

But apart from Art. 3 of the Convention, all the provisions in the Convention are too vague to be qualified as a specific behavior rule. If, however, the way the ECtHR interprets a rule in specific situations is considered, it comes to mind that the Court sometimes develops specific jurisprudential rules by repeatedly making similar judgments. This in fact has nothing to do with the application of the Convention as a specific behavior rule and has more to do with granting authority to the

129 Belgian Court of Cassation, 1 June 2006, appl. no. AR C.05.0494.N.

130 W. Verrijdt, 'De plicht tot uitvoering van arresten van het Grondwettelijk Hof door de wetgever' in A. Alen and S. Sottiaux (eds.), *Leuvense Staatsrechtelijke Standpunten. Part 2*, Bruges, Die Keure, 2010, p305 at 328.

131 V. Wilcox and O. Riss, 'Contributory Negligence', 2011, above n. 65, p771 at 793.

132 *Gäfgen v. Germany*, 1 June 2010 (Grand Chamber), appl. no. 22978/05, §107.

jurisprudence of the ECtHR in a way that looks like the principle of *stare decisis*. Indeed, it is obvious from the jurisprudence of the ECtHR that the reasonable time requirement is violated if a case is pending in a national court for 20 years. One can apply this jurisprudential rule of the ECtHR as a specific behavior rule. This, of course, is a fictional example, but it has been seen here that the ECtHR does reverse the onus of proof when it is clear that a process has already lasted for a very long time. Taking this presumption into account, the application of the specific behavior rule in national law can be an instrument for implementing the protection that the ECtHR requires in situations where the Court itself would reverse the onus of proof.

Now that it has been shown how the specific behavior rule functions in general and in relation to human rights, one can start to untangle the paradox caused by the fact that human rights on the one hand seem to require a stricter protection of some human rights whereas on the other hand they seem to prohibit an absolute protection for some human rights (since that can lead to a violation of another human right). This paradox can be explained by the fact that the application of a human right in a specific situation leads to the formulation of jurisprudential rules that come very near to specific behavior rules. Thinking for example of situations of *troubles the voisinage*, where the right to property seems to be protected in a manner that seems to be faultless, this can be reframed by referring to the general standard of conduct. Indeed, a reasonable person is always aware of the fact that he has neighbors when he starts construction works on his land or when he plays loud music. As a result, he will have to take measures to prevent harming his neighbors. This of course is the purest example of the neighborhood principle. If one would, however, decide to develop the *troubles the voisinage* into a mechanism of strict liability that is based purely on the notion of risk, one has to take into account that this liability scheme might violate the human rights of others.

Because of all the foregoing reasons, it must be concluded that one cannot protect human rights by basing the objective element of the fault on the concept of subjective rights. An infringement of a human right cannot automatically lead to the finding of a fault. If one decides that the violation of a human right can be seen as a fault, after one has made the human rights test, including the proportionality test, the notion of a subjective right can be useful to protect human rights in national law. This, however, will not change much in comparison with general tort law provisions, since these provisions do apply a general standard of conduct in a similar way as the ECtHR does. But this does not mean that human rights have no influence on tort law. As Hugo Vandenberghe argued, tort law provisions such as Art. 1382 of the Belgian and French civil code are absorptive stipulations that reach a synthesis by involving all the relevant legal rules with the judgment of a case.[133] If a judge is confronted with a human right, he will take this into account in the sense that he will frame the general standard of conduct on the peculiarities of the involved human right. If a judge is confronted with a tortfeasor that exercised his freedom of speech, he will take into account other elements than if he will be confronted with a tortfeasor that exercises his right to property. As such, human rights can function as points of reference for a judge when he has to deal with a case in tort law.

The rights that are enshrined in the Convention thus carry the potential to color general liability rules in different shades. One could object that human rights are so vague that they cannot provide added value for private law disputes. Indeed, human rights are rather open provisions. Nevertheless, it must be admitted that they provide information about the protected interests. If tort law provisions do not do so, human rights can consequently provide information on the reasons for the limitation of a right or a freedom through the application of the open provision. In these types of cases, human rights can provide additional guidance in tort law disputes. They can serve as substantive criteria that can colorize the standard of care in tort law.

---

133 H. Vandenberghe, 'Over civielrechtelijke persaansprakelijkheid. Een stand van zaken' in M. Debaene and P. Soens (eds.), *Aansprakelijkheidsrecht. Actuele tendensen*, Brussels, De Boeck and Larcier, 2005, p109 at 110.

CHAPTER 9
CAUSALITY

If one wants to receive compensation for damages in national tort law, it is not only necessary to prove the presence of a fault and damages, one also has to prove the existence of a causal connection between the fault and actual damages. At first sight this requirement seems obvious: can one imagine that a person would be held liable to pay compensation for damages that were not caused by his fault? The requirement of causality does however raise a lot of problems. A fault rarely occurs alone. If one looks at a random event where damages were caused, different events that occur prior to or at the same time as the damages can be distinguished. To claim liability, one first has to look at which of these events can be qualified as faults. But since it is possible that more events can be qualified as someone's fault, it is also important to determine which of these faults caused the damages. For this reason, one can say that the principle of causality serves the purpose of finding the person who must pay compensation within the group of people who committed a fault.[1]

The appreciation of the principle of causality in most countries runs in two phases.[2] In the first phase, in order to define whether an act or an omission was a cause of the loss, one has to eliminate the act or omission mentally and has to consider whether or not the loss would still occur.[3] If the answer to this question is positive, the fault did not cause the damages. Indeed, if the damages would have occurred anyway, there does not seem to be any connection between fault and damages. If, however, the answer to this question is negative, the fault is a factual cause of the

---

1 M. Van Quickenborne, *Oorzakelijk verband tussen onrechtmatige daad en schade*, Mechelen, Kluwer, 2007, at 2.

2 J.H. Nieuwenhuis, 'Eurocausaliteit. Agenda voor het Europees debat over toerekening van schade', *Tijdschrift voor Privaatrecht* 2002, p1695 at 1698; W. Van Gerven, J. Lever and P. Larouche, *Cases, Materials and Texts on National, Supranational and International Tort Law*, Oxford, Hart Publishing, 2000, at 395ff; C. Van Dam, *European Tort Law*, Oxford, Oxford University Press, 2013, at 266–299.

3 J. Spier and O.A. Haazen, 'Comparative conclusions on Causation' in J. Spier et.al. (eds.), *Unification of Tort Law: Causation*, The Hague, Kluwer, 2000, p127 at 127.

damages. This test can be described as the factual causality or the criteria of the *conditio sine qua non*- or but-for test. But as we described, it will often occur that one can point to more faults that caused the damages. These different factual causations for the damages will probably not have the same impact on the manifestation of the damages. For this reason, most legal systems make a selection within the factual causations. They will then look to whether the causation is important enough to establish legal liability.[4] In this phase one will establish the legal causality.

This chapter will first discuss the application of the factual causality by the ECtHR and will then investigate whether or not the Court restricts the factual causality by legal causality. The chapter also looks into the notion of the loss of an opportunity in the jurisprudence of the Court.

1. FACTUAL CAUSALITY: THE BUT-FOR TEST

Although the text of Art. 41 does not mention the requirement of causality, there is no discussion that a causal link between the damages and the human rights violation is required. A clear causal link between the violation and the claimed damages must be established.[5] The Court argues that one cannot order a state to redress damages for which it is not responsible.[6] Thus, if an applicant before the ECtHR wants to obtain compensation for his damages, he will have to demonstrate that the damages are a necessary consequence of the violation of the Convention that the Court found.[7] If the applicant cannot demonstrate the causal

4 H. Koziol, *Basic Questions of Tort Law from a Germanic Perspective*, Vienna, Jan Sramek Verlag, 2012, at 269.

5 *Sargsyan v. Azerbaijan*, 12 December 2017 (Grand Chamber), appl. no. 40167/06; V. Wilcox, *A Company's Right to Damage for Non-Pecuniary Loss*, Cambridge, Cambridge University Press, 2016, at 57.

6 *Kingsley v. the United Kingdom*, 28 May 2002 (Grand Chamber), appl. no. 35605/97, §40; *Wilson, National Union of Journalists et al. v. the United Kingdom*, 2 July 2002, appl. nos. 30668/96, 30671/96 and 30678/96, §54; *Danilenkov et al. v. Russia*, 30 July 2009, appl. no. 67336/01, §142; and *F.G. v. Sweden*, 23 March 2016, appl. no. 43611/11, §163.

7 *NeuMayster v. Austria*, 7 May 1974 (just satisfaction), appl. no. 1936/63, §40; *Werner v. Poland*, 15 November 2001, appl. no. 26760/95, §38; *Mathew v. the Netherlands*, 29 September 2005, appl. no. 24919/03, §§223–224; *Vilnes et al. v. Norway*, 5 December 2013, appl. nos. 52806/09 and 22703/10, §269; *Lemo et al. v. Croatia*, 10 July 2014, appl. no. 3925/10 et al., §60; and *Magyar Keresztény Mennonita Egyház et al. v. Hungary*, 28 June 2016 (just satisfaction), appl. no. 70945/11 et al., §46. See also: M. Kellner and I. Durant, 'Causation' in A. Fenyves, E. Karner, H. Koziol and E. Steiner (eds.), *Tort Law in the Jurisprudence of the European Court of Human Rights, Göttingen*, De Gruyter, 2011, p449 at 464.

connection, the Court does not grant any compensation for the alleged damages.[8] This is also true if an applicant claimed damages on the basis of the violation of only one Convention right and the Court only finds a violation of another Convention right.[9] It must be stressed that the causal link between a Convention violation and immaterial damages must also be proved. This, according to Octavian Ichim, is self-evident: 'Moral suffering comes as an inherent consequence of a violation, the only problem is how to quantify it.'[10] Nevertheless, the Court will sometimes argue that there is no causal link between the claimed moral damages and the human rights violation. For instance, in *Halford*, the Court found that the stress that the applicant suffered was not caused by the violation of her right to privacy (because her telephone had been tapped by the police), but by her contact with the police in the context of other conflicts.[11]

The criterion of causality is probably the most difficult tort law element to research in the jurisprudence of the ECtHR.[12] In many cases, the Court makes only very limited or vague mentions of this criteria or does not inquire into this at all.[13] In some cases the Court does not even address

---

8 *Le Compte, Van Leuven and De Meyere v. Belgium*, 18 October 1982 (just satisfaction), appl. nos. 6878/75 and 7238/75, §15; *Bönisch v. Austria*, 2 July 1986 (just satisfaction), appl. no. 8658/79, §11; *Bricmont v. Belgium*, 7 July 1989, appl. no. 10857/84, §97; *Mats Jacobsson v. Sweden*, 28 June 1990, appl. no. 11309/84, §43; *Fredin v. Sweden*, 18 January 1991, appl. no. 12033/86, §65; *Fischer v. Austria*, 26 April 1995, appl. no. 16922/90, §§46–47; *Ahmed v. Austria*, 17 December 1996, appl. no. 25964/94, §50; *Müller v. Switzerland*, 5 November 2002, appl. no. 41202/98, §43; and *Busuioc v. Moldavia*, 21 December 2004, appl. no. 61513/00, §101.

9 *Trabajo Rueda v. Spain*, 30 May 2017, appl. no. 32600/12, §52.

10 O. Ichim, *Just Satisfaction under the European Convention on Human Rights*, Cambridge, Cambridge University Press, 2015, at 26. An argument for this interpretation can be found in the following ruling: 'As regards pecuniary loss, there must be a clear causal connection between the damage claimed and the violation of the Convention established': *O'Keeffe v. Ireland*, 28 January 2014 (Grand Chamber), appl. no. 35810/09, §201. Making use of an *a contrario* reasoning, one can prudently argue on the basis of this ruling that a direct causal link is required for the compensation of immaterial damages.

11 *Halford v. the United Kingdom*, 25 June 1997, appl. no. 20605/92, §76.

12 A. Garin, 'La perte de chance, un préjudice indemnisable: contribution à une problématique de l'indemnisation du dommage par la Cour européenne des droits de l'homme' in J.-F. Flauss and E. Lambert Abdelgawad (eds.), *La pratique d'indemnisation par la Cour européenne des droits de l'homme*, Brussels, Bruylant, 2011, p155 at 157.

13 For instance, Bydlinksi argues that there are some cases where the ruling on causality is incomprehensible: F. Bydlinski, 'Methodological Approaches to the Tort Law of the ECHR' in A. Fenyves, E. Karner, H. Koziol and E. Steiner (eds.), *Tort Law in the Jurisprudence of the European Court of Human Rights*, Göttingen, De Gruyter, 2011, p29 at 89–92.

the facts that are relevant to find a causal connection.[14] As a result it is very hard to develop a conclusive theory on the way the Court approaches causality. As Franz Bydlinski argued, the best possible solution is 'to find imprecise indications of a tangible reasoning.'[15] This incoherent application of the requirement of causality sometimes gives the impression that the Court uses this for reasons that have nothing to do with causality, such as considerations related to the existence or the proof of damages or considerations of equity. At least this jurisprudence illustrates that the Court does not sufficiently reflect on the principle of causality,[16] especially in those cases where applicants claim compensation for immaterial damages.[17]

One of the explanations of this problem can be found in the fact that the Court often has to judge on cases where applicants argue that a country violated the Convention due to procedural reasons such as the right to a fair trial as is enshrined in Art. 6 of the Convention. As Markus Kellner and Isabelle Durant argued, national tort law systems also encounter many problems in these type of cases.[18] If a procedural guarantee has been violated, it is hard to establish the legitimate alternative.[19] For instance, if a conviction in criminal law has been carried out in a procedure that violated Art. 6 because the accused person had no insight into some documents, it is hard to know whether the convicted person would also have been convicted if he had had the opportunity to look into the documents.

Because the Court frequently refuses to grant financial compensation for these types of cases, Dinah Shelton accuses the Court of using a standard that is too strict.[20] She argues that the Court cannot require an applicant to prove the causality between their damages and the disrespect for the procedural guarantees of the Convention. Indeed, how can one prove what a judgment would have been if the procedural guarantees were respected? According to Shelton, the Court in these cases does not

---

14 M. Kellner and I. Durant, 'Causation', 2011, above n. 7, p449 at 452.

15 F. Bydlinski, 'Methodological Approaches', 2011, above n. 13, p29 at 72.

16 *Ibid.*, at 72 and 92.

17 For instance, in the case of *Buzescu*, the Court found that it can award satisfaction based on the equity in cases where the causality between the violation of the Convention and the claimed damages and the possibility to estimate the damages precisely becomes uncertain due to the passing of time: *Buzescu v. Romania*, 24 May 2005, appl. no. 61302/00, §105. See also: *Lustig-Prean and Beckett v. the United Kingdom*, 25 July 2000 (just satisfaction), appl. nos. 31417/96 and 32377/96, §22; and *Stretch v. the United Kingdom*, 24 June 2003, appl. no. 44277/98, §47.

18 M. Kellner and I. Durant, 'Causation', 2011, above n. 7, p449 at 453.

19 A similar line of reasoning is made in: O. Ichim, *Just Satisfaction*, 2015, above n. 10, at 27.

20 D. Shelton, *Remedies in International Human Rights Law*, Oxford, Oxford University Press, 1999, at 235.

really take into account the requirement of causality, but in fact takes into account its sympathy for applicants and the idea of equity. To demonstrate this, she referred to *Delta*.[21] At the origin of this case lay a robbery of two French girls in the Paris metro. The police arrested a man of foreign origin. The man was condemned in a criminal procedure although he was not confronted by the girls (who did not even occur on the day of the trial) and the police had not found any evidence. The Court in this case found a violation of Art. 6 and granted a substantial amount of money as just satisfaction, although it could not speculate on the outcome of the procedure if Art. 6 had not been violated.

Apart from the cases where it is unclear whether or not the Court has applied the criteria of causality, it must also be pointed out that the Court in some cases reverses the onus of proof. An illustration can be found in *I. v. Finland*.[22] A woman who worked in a hospital was infected with HIV. She underwent treatment in the same hospital that she worked in. At a certain moment she discovered that her colleagues had knowledge of her medical records. She consequently found that her right to privacy had been violated. She filed a claim against the state before the national judge, but she could not receive any compensation because she could not prove the existence of a causal connection between the fact that her colleagues had knowledge of her medical records and the fact that the hospital did not have adequate regulations to protect the personal data of patients. The ECtHR in this case found that the requirement of causality was interpreted too strictly:

> The Court notes that the applicant lost her civil action because she was unable to prove on the facts a causal connection between the deficiencies in the access security rules and the dissemination of information about her medical condition. However, to place such a burden of proof on the applicant is to overlook the acknowledged deficiencies in the hospital's record keeping at the material time. It is plain that had the hospital provided a greater control over access to health records by restricting access to health professionals directly involved in the applicant's treatment or by maintaining a log of all persons who had accessed the applicant's medical file, the applicant would have been placed in a less disadvantaged position before the domestic courts. For the Court, what is decisive is that the records system in place in the hospital was clearly not in accordance with the legal requirements contained in section 26 of the Personal Files Act, a fact that was not given due weight by the domestic courts.[23]

---

21 *Delta v. France*, 19 December 1990, appl. no. 11444/85.
22 *I. v. Finland*, 17 July 2008, appl. no. 20511/03.
23 *Ibid.*, §44.

This case illustrates that the requirement to prove causality in national tort law can in some situations be found too strict, so that a person does not anymore dispose of an effective remedy to contest a human rights violation in national law. One could say that this jurisprudence requires states to find liability already in cases where it is very probable that a relation between a fault and damages exists. In those cases, a national judge can decide that it is up to the defendant to prove that he did not cause the alleged damages.

A similar conclusion can be drawn from *Lopes De Sousa Fernandes*.[24] The applicant in this case was a woman whose husband had died because of a hospital-acquired infection. She sued the government in national law for the medical negligence of a doctor in a state hospital, without success. The applicant argued that the procedural limb of Art. 2 was violated for two reasons: because the access to a court was not provided within reasonable time and because the state did not establish the cause of death of the said victim of a medical negligence. The Court agreed with both arguments of the applicant. With regard to the second argument, it found that where there is a *prima facie* arguable claim of a chain of events possibly triggered by an allegedly negligent act that may have contributed to the death of a patient, in particular if an allegation of a hospital-acquired infection is concerned, the authorities may be expected to conduct a thorough examination into the matter. The Court found that no such examination was conducted in the liability proceedings before the domestic courts. It argued that these courts, instead of carrying out an overall assessment, approached the chain of events as a succession of medical incidents, without paying particular attention to how they may have related to each other.

2. LEGAL CAUSALITY

2.1. THEORIES ON CAUSALITY

2.1.1. Equivalence

In most legal systems, the *conditio sine qua non* test is not a sufficient criterion to establish legal causality.[25] These legal systems add a second

---

[24] *Lopes De Sousa Fernandes v. Portugal*, 19 December 2017 (Grand Chamber), appl. no. 56080/13.

[25] J. Spier and O.A. Haazen, 'Comparative conclusions on Causation' in J. Spier et al. (eds.), *Unification of Tort Law: Causation*, The Hague, Kluwer, 2000, p127 at 127.

criterion in order to determine whether the causation is important enough.[26] The different factual causations of damages are not treated equally but for reasons of equity, one tries to distinguish the more important from the less important factual causations.[27] Only Belgian tort law does not limit factual causality by adding a second test.[28] In Belgian law, anyone who committed a fault that has a causal connection to the damages as they occurred,[29] can be held liable for the totality of the damages,[30] whether or not the fault contributed to the damages in a direct or indirect way.[31] They will then be able to claim regress from each other.[32]

It is important to note that this approach does not take into account the gravity of the fault. Someone who makes a very limited fault can be compelled to pay the totality of the damages as easily as someone who makes a very grave or even an intentional fault.[33] In the same way, it does not matter whether one makes a fault that directly or indirectly contributes to the damages.[34] Only when the damages would not have occurred if the

---

26 M. Kellner and I. Durant, 'Causation', 2011, above n. 7, p449 at 449.

27 T. Vansweevelt and B. Weyts, *Handboek buitencontractueel aansprakelijkheidsrecht*, Antwerp, Intersentia, 2009, at 764.

28 In principle, Austrian law also applies only one step in the evaluation of causation. However, this is so because Austrian law considers its second step not as a part of causation but as an independent doctrine: J. Spier and O.A. Haazen, 'Comparative conclusions on Causation', 2000, above n. 25, at 130.

29 An act that cannot be qualified as a fault can of course not be taken into account: Cass. 20 December 1996, AR C.95.0006.N and Cass. 19 September 2011, AR C.10.0680.N, Pas. 2011, 1994.

30 H. Bocken and I. Boone, *Inleiding tot het schadevergoedingsrecht. Buitencontractueel aansprakelijkheidsrecht en andere schadevergoedingsstelsels*, Bruges, Die Keure, 2011, at 72 and 83; B. Dubuisson, V. Callewaert, B. De Coninck and G. Gathem, *La Responsabilité civile. Chronique de jurisprudence 1996–2007*, Part 1, Le fait générateur et le lien causal, Brussels, Larcier, 2009, at 322.

31 B. Dubuisson, V. Callewaert, B. De Coninck and G. Gathem, *La Responsabilité civile. Chronique de jurisprudence 1996–2007*, Part 1, Le fait générateur et le lien causal, Brussels, Larcier, 2009, at 336; J.-L. Fagnart, 'La causalité. Volume 1' in J.-L. Fagnart (ed.), *Responsabilités – Traité théorique et pratique*, Mechelen, Kluwer, 2008, at 61.

32 H. Bocken and I. Boone, 'Causaliteit in het Belgisch recht', Tijdschrift voor privaatrecht 2002, p1625 at 1641; and B. De Coninck, 'Les recours après indemnisation en matière de responsabilité extracontractuelle: la condemnation in solidum et la contribution à la dette', *Journal des tribuneaux* 2010, 755–763.

33 E.g.: Belgian Court of Cassation, 6 February 2003, AR C.01.0426; Belgian Court of Cassation, 23 June 2005, AR C.03.0551.F; and Belgian Court of Cassation, 21 June 2007, AR C.06.0087.F.

34 M. Van Quickenborne, 'Overzicht van rechtspraak. Aansprakelijkheid uit onrechtmatige daad 2000–2007. Deel I Oorzakelijk Verband', *Tijdschrift voor Privaatrecht* 2010, p283 at 292. In EU law, there must however be a direct causal link between a fault and the damages: ECJ, *Brasserie du Pêcheur v. Germany*, 5 March 1996, C-46/93 and C-48/93, §51.

alleged fault had not occurred, as is required by the *conditio sine qua non*- or 'but-for' test, is there no causal effect.[35] We also have to stress that it is required that the fault led to the existence of the damages as they occurred *in concreto*. If for example a fault did not contribute to the manifestation of the initial damages but caused a deterioration of these damages, there is causality between the fault and the damages as they occurred *in concreto*.[36]

2.1.2. Adequacy

Most legal systems limit the potential liability of persons by adding to the requirement of factual causation a requirement of legal causation.[37] After applying the *conditio sine qua non* test, these legal systems apply a second test for reasons of equity. Indeed, as the German Bundesgerichtshof pointed out, the second test does not in the first place relate to considerations of causality but to 'die Suche nach einem Korrektiv, das den Kreis der rein logischen Folgen im Interesse billiger Ergebnisse auf die zurechenbaren Folgen einschränkt.'[38]

According to the doctrine of adequacy, as is applied in Germany, legal causation in tort law can only be established if the damages are the normal or reasonable consequence of the damage-causing act.[39] According to this approach, liability must be limited to persons on the basis of the foreseeability of the damages. This is a rather vague criterion that is similar to the general standard of conduct.[40] One might say that, according to this approach, a fault can only cause responsibility if a reasonable and foreseeable person could have expected that his act would be, taking into account the concrete situations, of a nature that could cause damages.[41]

---

35 See the jurisprudence in: M. Van Quickenborne, 'Overzicht van rechtspraak. Aansprakelijkheid uit onrechtmatige daad 2000–2007. Deel I Oorzakelijk Verband', *Tijdschrift voor Privaatrecht* 2010, p283 at 293ff.

36 M. Van Quickenborne, *Oorzakelijk verband tussen onrechtmatige daad en schade*, Mechelen, Kluwer, 2007, at 43–44.

37 C. Van Dam, *European Tort Law*, 2013, above n. 2, at 310ff.

38 BGH 23 October 1951, BGHZ 3, 267.

39 H. Koziol, *Basic Questions of Tort Law*, 2012, above n. 4, at 272; and P. Van Ommeslaghe, *De Page Traité de droit civil Belge, II, Les Obligations*, Vol. 2, Sources des obligations, Brussels, Bruylant, 2014, at 1611.

40 For this reason, it has been argued that the criterion of adequacy is not a pure causality criterion since it also encompasses normative arguments: J.-L. Fagnart, 'La causalité. Vol.1, 2008, above n. 31, at 35; H. Koziol, *Basic Questions of Tort Law*, 2012, above n. 4, at 272.

41 M. Van Quickenborne, *Oorzakelijk verband tussen onrechtmatige daad en schade*, Mechelen, Kluwer, 2007, at 19.

It has also been written that on the basis of this criteria, causation between a wrongful act and damages can only be established if:

> ... in general and not only under abnormal, completely improbable and in the ordinary course of things neglectable circumstances would have led to the occurance of the result that happened.[42]

2.1.3. Protective Purpose of the Norm

Another approach that can be used to limit factual causality is the protective purpose of the norm. According to this approach, tortfeasors can only be obliged to pay compensations if the violated rule of conduct was intended to protect the interests of the victim. This approach, which is used in Germany and Austria[43] in addition to the doctrine of adequacy,[44] is also described as the teachings of the '*Rechtswidrigkeitszusammenhang*' or the '*Schutzzweck der Norm*'. According to this approach, factual causality is limited because of three reasons, that Helmut Koziol describes as follows:

> Firstly, the wrongdoer has to compensate only the losses of those persons which the law is intended to protect; secondly, he has to indemnify only that damage which the violated rule is intended to avoid. One can add that, thirdly, the damaging party is only liable if he caused the damage in a way that is forbidden by law.[45]

On the basis of these criteria, it seems that factual causality is limited on the basis of the objectives of the violated rule. In order to grasp a better understanding of this, Cees Van Dam uses the example of the liability of governments for the condition of the roads. Although a government can be held accountable based on tort law if they do not protect the users of the road against damages, it cannot be obliged to reimburse the compensation

---

42 U. Magnus, 'Causation in German Tort Law' in J. Spier (ed.), *Unification of Tort Law: Causation*, Kluwer, The Hague, 2000, p63 at 65.

43 This doctrine was developed in the course of the twentieth century: C. Van Dam, *European Tort Law*, 2013, above n. 2, at 313.

44 In Swiss law it has been argued that the theories of adequacy and protective purpose are very close to one another, and thus cannot easily be detached from one another since 'both of them try to determine the extent of liability in accordance with the aim of the applicable norm': P. Widmer, 'Causation under Swiss Law' in J. Spier (ed.), *Unification of Tort Law: Causation*, Kluwer, Den Haag, 2000, p105 at 108.

45 H. Koziol, 'Causation under Austrian Law' in J. Spier (ed.), *Unification of Tort Law: Causation*, Kluwer, Den Haag, 2000, p11 at 12.

for pure economic losses that are caused by a traffic accident due to the poor state of the road. The reason for this is that 'the scope of the duty to take care of road safety does not include protection against pure economic loss.'[46]

2.2. CAUSALITY IN THE JURISPRUDENCE OF THE ECtHR

2.2.1. Indeterminacy of the Direct Causal Connection

Because most legal systems limit factual causality in a legal way, it seems likely that the ECtHR also does so. It would be likely that the ECtHR adds additional elements to the *conditio sine qua non* test.[47] Indeed, the Court in some cases indicates that a direct causal link between the violation of the Convention and the alleged damages is required to award damages.[48] By stating that the causal link has to be direct, it seems that the Court adds an additional requirement to the *conditio sine qua non* test. Since this jurisprudence has in the past been the subject of a study of Franz Bydlinski, his research will be used as a starting point in the next paragraphs.

Bydlinski starts his analysis with the judgment of *Çakıcı*.[49] The Court in this case found a violation of the right to life after a man died due to an operation by the security services. The Court in this case among others awarded compensation to the widow and to the children for the loss of income of the deceased person. The Court emphasized that there was a causal link at hand between the loss of income of the applicants and the violation of the right to life of the deceased person.[50] According to

---

46 C. Van Dam, *European Tort Law*, 2013, above n. 2, at 314.

47 E. Karner, 'Concluding Remarks on Causation' in A. Fenyves, E. Karner, H. Koziol and E. Steiner (eds.), *Tort Law in the Jurisprudence of the European Court of Human Rights*, Göttingen, De Gruyter, 2011, p835 at 838.

48 According to Jozon, the Court does not in fact differentiate direct and indirect consequences of a treaty violation so that both of these categories of damages have to be compensated: M. Jozon, 'Satisfaction by Finding a violation' in A. Fenyves, E. Karner, H. Koziol and E. Steiner (eds.), *Tort Law in the Jurisprudence of the European Court of Human Rights*, Göttingen, De Gruyter, 2011, p741 at 753.

49 F. Bydlinski, 'Methodological Approaches', 2011, above n. 13, p29 at 78.

50 *Çakici v. Turkey*, 8 July 1999 (Grand Chamber), appl. no. 23657/94, §127. See also: *Ertak v. Turkey*, 9 May 2000, appl. no. 20764/92, §150; *Salman v. Turkey*, 27 June 2000 (Grand Chamber), appl. no. 21986/93, §137; *Akkum et al. v. Turkey*, 24 March 2005 (Grand Chamber), appl. no. 21986/93, §285; *Estamirov et al. v. Russia*, 12 October 2006, appl. no. 60272/00, §129; *Imakayeva v. Russia*, 9 November 2006, appl. no. 7615/02, §213; *Akhmadova and Sadulayeva v. Russia*, 10 May 2007, appl. no. 40464/02, §143;

Bydlinski, the reference to the direct character of the causal link in this case is a bit confusing and cannot be taken literally.[51] He notes that the damages of the applicants in this case are typical reflected damages. The possibility of the applicants to receive a just satisfaction for these damages depends on their relationship with the direct victim of the human rights violation (in this case the deceased person) and of his contribution into the common household. According to Bydlinski, the use of the word 'direct' here is useless and might be an illustration of the fact that the reference to the necessity of a 'direct' causal link in general is meaningless.[52] To punctuate this thesis, he discusses more cases.

The first case that Bydlinski mentions in this context is *Rehbock*.[53] This case concerned a man who had been arrested and put in prison in a violent fashion. The Court found that Arts 3, 5 and 8 were violated. With relation to Art. 41 of the Convention, the applicants claimed that a just satisfaction would account for the loss of income that his wife suffered due to looking after her husband when he was injured instead of working, for the retention of his wife's car by the Slovenian authorities and for the depreciation of shares that he owned during his detention. The Court found that there was no direct causal link between the identified breaches of the Convention and the claimed pecuniary losses. The Court, however, did not give a reasoning. If the reason were to be that there was no reason to believe that the wife would have had a job if her husband would not have been in detention, that the retention of the car was legitimate whether or not

---

Sangariyeva et al. v. Russia, 29 May 2008, appl. no. 1839/04, §128; *Meshayeva et al. v. Russia*, 12 February 2009, appl. no. 27248/03, §139; *Khatuyeva v. Russia*, 22 April 2010, appl. no. 12463/05, §110; *Shokkarov et al. v. Russia*, 3 May 2011, appl. no. 41009/04, §140; *Vitayeva et al. v. Russia*, 7 June 2011, appl. no. 27459/07, §170; *Ilayeva et al. v. Russia*, 10 July 2012, appl. no. 27504/07, §113; *Umarova et al. v. Russia*, 31 July 2012, appl. no. 25654/08, §122; *Meryem Çelik et al. v. Turkey*, 16 April 2013, appl. no. 3598/03, §100; *Jelić v. Croatia*, 12 June 2014, appl. no. 57856/11, §121; *B. et al. v. Croatia*, 18 June 2015, appl. no. 71593/11, §89; and *Saydulkhanova v. Russia*, 25 June 2015, appl. no. 25521/10, §79. The Court also grants compensation for the loss of income in case a deceased person is unemployed. It suspects that all persons contribute to a household in one way or another. The granted compensation for loss of income in such cases is lower than when the deceased person had a job and is appraised equity: *Demiray v. Turkey*, 21 November 2000, appl. no. 27308/95, §67; and *Khadzilialiyev et al. v. Russia*, 6 November 2008, appl. no. 3013/04, §148.

51 F. Bydlinski, 'Methodological Approaches', 2011, above n. 13, p29 at 78.

52 The same is also true in the jurisprudence where the Court does not require the presence of a causal link, but requires that a cause is 'sufficient' or 'clear': M. Kellner and I. Durant, 'Causation', 2011, above n. 7, p449 at 453–457 and 467–470.

53 *Rehbock v. Slovenia*, 28 November 2000, appl. no. 29462/95.

the Convention rights were breached and that the Court did not believe that the detention of the applicant could possibly influence the value of his shares, it seems obvious that there was no causal link since these claims would not pass the *conditio sine qua non* test.

The second case Bydlinski refers to is *Edwards and Lewis.*[54] The applicants in this case had been sentenced in a criminal lawsuit for crimes that were, according to the applicants, provoked by undercover police officers. The Court found a violation of Art. 6 because the applicants had never been granted the possibility to look at the documents concerning the undercover operation. In relation to Art. 41, the applicants noted that the Court had awarded compensation for immaterial damages in other cases that were very similar, in the sense that the applicants in these cases had also been sentenced by a criminal court for a crime that was provoked by police officers and without them being able to examine all the relevant documents. The Court did not follow this line of reasoning. It argued that the violation of Art. 6 in this case did not directly cause the unlawful detention of the applicants.[55] Bydlinski notes that he could not find a reason why the Court did not grant a compensation for the stress and the frustrations that the applicants suffered during the criminal procedure.[56] But even if it could be assumed that the ECtHR was right in judging that the applicants were sentenced correctly, it is not obvious what the additional value of the requirement that the causal connection had to be 'direct' could be. The *conditio sine qua non* would have sufficed.

Moreover, if the Court indeed found that the applicants would have been sentenced whether or not Art. 6 was violated, it seems that the lack of an award for damages could probably be explained by other factors. This book has already shown that the Court takes into account the behavior of an applicant. In this sense, the Court sometimes refuses to grant financial compensation to applicants who committed a crime. Moreover, in one of the following sections the application of a *de minimis* rule by the Court will be examined. Taking these factors into account, it seems reasonable that the Court in this case took into account the contributory fault of the victim

---

54 *Edwards and Lewis v. the United Kingdom*, 22 July 2003, appl. nos. 39647/98 and 40461/98. This judgment has been confirmed by the Grand Chamber: *Edwards and Lewis v. the United Kingdom*, 27 October 2004 (Grand Chamber), appl. nos. 39647/98 and 40461/98.

55 *Edwards and Lewis v. the United Kingdom*, 22 July 2003, appl. nos. 39647/98 and 40461/98, §63.

56 F. Bydlinski, 'Methodological Approaches', above n. 13, p29 at 79.

and found that the limited moral damages that were caused, apart from this contributory fault, fell under the *de minimis* rule. Another explanation could be that the applicants in this case only claimed compensation for the fact that they had been condemned and not for the stress and frustrations that they had suffered during the procedures. Thus, if the Court had argued that the applicants would also have been condemned if the requirements of Art. 6 had been followed, the Court could not grant an award for the claimed damages.

The third case Bydlinski refers to is *Podkolzina*.[57] A woman participated in the parliamentary elections in Latvia for a party that aimed to protect the interests of the Russian-speaking minority in this country. In order to participate in the elections, she had to prove that she had mastered the Latvian language sufficiently. She was tested on this by examiners who visited her house without warning. Because these examiners found that she had not sufficiently mastered the Latvian language, she was not allowed to participate in the elections. She contested this decision in a Latvian Court, but she was not given another chance to demonstrate her knowledge of the Latvian language. As a consequence, the Court found that the active election rights of the applicant as enshrined in Art. 3 of the first protocol were violated. With regard to Art. 41, the applicant claimed compensation for the loss of income caused by the fact that she had resigned from her job because the violation of her honor and reputation had made continuing her job impossible. The government objected, arguing that she had resigned out of free will and so no causal link existed between the violation of Art. 3 of the first protocol and the loss of income that she suffered. The Court agreed that there was no direct causal link and rejected the request.[58] Although the Court did not explain its decision, it seems as if it followed the objections of the government. Accordingly, there is no obvious added value in the requirement of the 'direct' causal link, since it seems that the claim had not passed the *conditio sine que non* test anyway.

The fourth case Bydlinski refers to is *Balogh*.[59] The applicant was a gipsy of Roma origin who suffered hearing problems caused by the police. As a result, experts found that his chances of finding adequate work had been reduced by 50 percent.[60] The applicant consequently claimed an award of

57 *Podkolzina v. Latvia*, 9 April 2002, appl. no. 46726/99.
58 *Ibid.*, §49.
59 *Balogh v. Hungary*, 20 July 2004, appl. no. 47940/99.
60 *Ibid.*, §20.

just satisfaction for the fact that it was harder for him to find a job. The Court answered this request as follows:

> Although there is no direct causal link between the ill-treatment suffered and the loss of income claimed by the applicant on account of his impaired hearing, the Court accepts that the applicant must have suffered some pecuniary damage as a result of his condition and finds it equitable to award him 4,000 euros (EUR) under this head.[61]

Since the Court states that there is no causal link between the violation of the Convention and the alleged damages but does award a just satisfaction, Bydlinski correctly notes that the Court deprives every significance to the notion of a 'direct' causal link.[62] He argues that it would have been better if the Court had argued that the deterioration of the applicant's chances of finding a job was only partly caused by the violation of the Convention. This argument would have given solid ground to the award of a compensation. The Court would then have to estimate the degree to which the deterioration of the chances of the applicant to find a job were caused by the ill-treatment of the police.

The last case Bydlinski refers to is *Iglesias Gil*.[63] The applicant was a woman whose former husband had moved to the USA after their divorce with their common child, although the judge had forbidden the emigration of the child. The woman commenced different procedures to get her child back, but they all failed. She found that the government had failed to protect her right to family life by not providing appropriate measures for her to regain her child. The ECtHR followed this line of reasoning and found a violation of Art. 8 of the Convention. In the context of Art. 41, the applicant claimed damages for the loss of income for the fact that she had interrupted her job as a teacher for a year to go and find her child. The Court found that 'the causal link between the violation and the alleged pecuniary damage is too remote to justify an award of compensation under this head.'[64]

According to Bydlinski, these words prove that the Court found a causal connection between the violation of Art. 8 and the loss of income of the applicant but that this connection was *too remote*.[65] The Court, however,

---

61 *Ibid.*, §84.

62 F. Bydlinski, 'Methodological Approaches', 2011, above n. 13, p29 at 80.

63 *Iglesias Gil and A.U.I. v. Spain*, 29 April 2003, appl. no. 56673/00.

64 *Ibid.*, §70.

65 F. Bydlinski, 'Methodological Approaches', 2011, above n. 13, p29 at 80–81.

does not give any indication as to the reason why the causal connection was too remote. According to Bydlinski, it must be clear that a mother would interrupt her profession to find her child. The Court did however make a different decision. It awarded a sum of €20,000 for immaterial damages but did not award compensation for material damages.[66] It seems likely that the Court implicitly made an argument similar to that in *Podkolzina*, namely that the applicant had resigned from her job out of free will and thus that there was no causal connection between the violation of the Convention and the loss of income. Another explanation might be that the Court found that the damages were not primarily caused by the government not offering the appropriate measures, but by the father. In that case however, it seems that at least a part of the loss of income can be attributed to the violation of the Convention. Either way, what is clear is the fact that in these cases the requirement that the causal link must be direct does not seem to have any added value to factual causality.

2.2.2. Protective Purpose of the Norm

Another approach to the requirement of causation in the jurisprudence of the ECtHR has been elaborated by Jörg Fedtke. This author is of the opinion that the Court often uses the criteria of the purpose of the norm to limit factual causality.[67] According to Fedte, the Court has to establish the applicability of a Convention norm when it has to judge on the merits of a case. If the Court has to establish the scope of application of a substantial provision in the Convention, the Court in fact established the purpose of the provision. Because Art. 41 is only applicable if the Court finds a violation of the Convention, it seems reasonable to Fedtke that the Court takes into account the purpose of the norm (which of course is a treaty provision). At first glance, this approach seems to be very plausible. At least from a theoretical viewpoint, it seems reasonable that the Court will only find a causal link if the damages fall within the protective scope of the violated Convention right. It is regrettable that Fedtke does not explain the cases where the Court does not grant compensation due to the lack of a causal link. Thus, to make Fedtke's theory more convincing, his ideas must be demonstrated with further jurisprudence.

---

66 *Iglesias Gil and A.U.I. v. Spain*, 29 April 2003, appl. no. 56673/00, §67.

67 J. Fedtke, 'Protective Purpose of the Rule' in A. Fenyves, E. Karner, H. Koziol and E. Steiner (eds.), *Tort Law in the Jurisprudence of the European Court of Human Rights*, Göttingen, De Gruyter, 2011, p539 at 546ff.

The first type of case where the Court seems to apply the purpose of the norm concerns cases where it had to deal with the violation of a positive obligation to protect human rights in horizontal relations. Take for example *Inze*.[68] The applicant in this case had been excluded from the inheritance of a farm where he had worked his entire life. The reason for this was that Austrian law at that time prescribed that a farm had to be transmitted in its totality to one heir and that illegitimate children could not inherit the farm. The ECtHR in this case found a violation of the right to property and the principle of equality. Concerning the admissibility of this case, the Austrian government raised the objection that the applicant had already received three-eighths of the inheritance by concluding a settlement with his half-brother. The Court however found that:

> The word 'victim' in Article 25 refers to the person directly affected by the act or omission at issue; and the existence of a violation is conceivable even in the absence of prejudice, prejudice being relevant only for the purposes of Article 50. Therefore, the fact that a judicial settlement, concluded between private parties on their own, may have mitigated the disadvantage suffered by the applicant does not in principle deprive him of his status as 'victim'. The position might have been otherwise if, for instance, the national authorities had acknowledged either expressly or in substance, and then afforded redress for, the alleged breach of the Convention. In any event, the applicant's complaint was directed to the fact that, in the instant case, his illegitimate birth deprived him in law of any possibility of taking over his mother's farm in the partition of her estate. This situation remains unchanged and it is only its financial consequences which have been alleviated by the judicial settlement.[69]

The Court found a violation but did not grant an award for the loss of a part of the inheritance. It did however award a sum for the loss of an opportunity to inherit the farm in its totality. Thus, what is interesting in this case, is the fact that the Court did not take into account the settlement between the applicant and a private party. By doing so, it seems as if the Court makes a clear-cut distinction between those damages that are caused by the government and those damages that are caused by other private parties.

Another interesting judgment is *Bone*.[70] Despite the presence of warning signs and warnings of his friends, a 14-year-old boy stepped out of the wrong side of the train. He stepped on another rail instead of

---

68 *Inze v. Austria*, 28 October 1987, appl. no. 8695/79. See also: *Kozarov v. the former Yugoslav Republic of Macedonia*, 10 November 2005 (Decision), appl. no. 64229/01.

69 *Inze v. Austria*, 28 October 1987, appl. no. 8695/79, §32.

70 *Bone v. France*, 1 March 2005 (Decision), appl. no. 69869/01.

the train platform. Because a train was simultaneously arriving from the other direction, he stepped in front of the train causing his death. The parents of the boy found that the government had failed to comply with its positive obligation to protect the right to life of children by not making it impossible for passengers to open the doors of the train on the wrong side. The Court ruled that this could not be qualified as a violation of the Convention because the child had been imprudent himself:

> … c'est donc le comportement très imprudent du fils des requérants qui fut la cause déterminante du drame ayant conduit à son décès accidentel, et l'on ne saurait reprocher, dans les circonstances de la cause, aux autorités nationales de ne pas avoir pris des mesures qui auraient pu avoir pour effet de préserver la vie de celui-ci [it was the very reckless behavior of the applicants' son which was the decisive cause of the tragedy which led to his accidental death, and therefore the national authorities cannot be blamed, in the circumstances of the case, not to have taken measures that could have had the effect of preserving his life] (author's translation).[71]

What this case illustrates is the fact that the Court does not find a violation of the Convention if an infringement of a human right is caused by the behavior of a private person (in this case the victim himself). This shows that a state, at least in principle, cannot be held responsible for the acts of private persons. Here, this led to the fact that the Court could not find a violation, but this opens up the possibility that the Court will sometimes find a violation of the Convention but will not award all the claimed damages because a private person caused some of the damages. This happened in *Tahsin Acar.* The applicant in this case complained that his brother had been missing and that the government had not taken sufficient and appropriate measures to track him down.[72] The Court found a violation of the Convention, but it did not award compensation for the disappearance of the brother of the applicant because it found that there was no causal connection between the absence of an effective investigation and the disappearance of the applicant. It did, however, find that the absence of an effective investigation in itself constituted non-pecuniary damages for the relatives of the deceased person and awarded a sum of €10,000.

Another illustration can be found in *Lo Tufo.* The applicant in this case owned an apartment that was leased. Over the years, he had tried to end

71 *Ibid.*

72 *Tahsin Acar v. Turkey*, 8 April 2004 (Grand Chamber), appl. no. 26307/95.

the lease because the tenant had stopped paying his rent. Although he had once made an agreement signed by the tenant, he could not evict the tenant. Within a period of three years, a bailiff had made 16 attempts to evict the tenant, but each of these attempts failed. Moreover, the applicant never received police assistance to evict the tenant.[73] The ECtHR found a violation of the right to a peaceful enjoyment of property in this case because of the lack of assistance by the Italian state. The Court did not however award compensation for pecuniary damages because it found that:

> The damage, in the present case, actually stems from the unlawful conduct of the tenant, who, whether or not the State cooperated in the enforcement of the judicial eviction order, was bound to return the flat to its owners. The violation of the applicants' right to the peaceful enjoyment of their property is mainly the consequence of the tenant's unlawful conduct.[74]

Although the Court further noted that Italian law provided mechanisms to recover the damages from the tenants and granted the applicant a sum of money for the non-pecuniary damages, Judges Spielmann and Loucaïdes wrote a concurring opinion. They argued that there was a clear causal link in this case between the lack of enforcement from the government and that the loss of income was caused by the fact that the tenant did not pay his rent.[75] A similar conclusion can be drawn from the jurisprudence of the Court concerning the reasonable time requirement. This book has already shown that Under Art. 13 the ECtHR requires that states provide financial compensation if the reasonable time has already been exceeded. It seemed that there is a strong presumption that exceeding of the reasonable time caused non-pecuniary damages.

Interestingly, up until now the Court has almost never provided a just satisfaction for pecuniary damages in its jurisprudence concerning the reasonable time requirement. If an applicant claims compensation for pecuniary damages for exceeding the reasonable time, the Court most often does not find a causal link between the violation of Art. 6 and the pecuniary damages. Thereby, the Court acknowledges that it cannot speculate as to the outcome of a lawsuit in national law if the reasonable

---

73 *Lo Tufo v. Italy*, 21 April 2005, appl. no. 64663/01.

74 *Ibid.*, §§68–69.

75 Concurring opinion of Judges Spielmann and Loucaïdes in *Lo Tufo v. Italy*, 21 April 2005, appl. no. 64663/01.

time requirement had not been violated. An example of this jurisprudence can be found in *Glüsen*.[76] In this case the reasonable time requirement was violated in a tort law procedure where a man had claimed compensation for the injuries he had suffered from an act of violence. The applicant claimed compensation for the loss of income that was caused by the fact that he had been unable to exercise his job, which was prolonged because the national judges did not respect the reasonable time. The Court in this case found that there was no causal link between the alleged damages and the violation of the Convention and stressed that it could not speculate as to the outcome of the case. As will be seen further on, these wordings indicate that the Court was of the opinion that the theory of the loss of a chance might have been applicable.

It nevertheless seems that the question of whether or not the Court can speculate on the outcome of the national procedure is not relevant in the context of the reasonable time requirement. If Art. 6 is violated for the reason that a process was unfair, which was the judgment referred to by the Court in *Glüsen* when it had to deal with the application of Art. 41,[77] then it is relevant to know whether or not the procedure would have had different results if Art. 6 had not been violated. If a judge for example condemned someone in a case where one piece of evidence seems to have been obtained in a way that conflicts with the right to a fair trial, it would be interesting to know whether the judge would have made a different judgment if this piece of evidence were not used. The violation of the Convention could have caused harm in the sense that a judge punished someone. In such a case it is interesting to speculate on the outcome of a national case, and in case the Court cannot do this, one can expect the national courts to re-open the case. But if the Court has to award damages for the violation of the reasonable time requirement, one cannot apply the same line of reasoning. Indeed, the applicant in *Glüsen* only claimed pecuniary damages that were caused by the delay of the national procedure. That the Court did not grant compensation for the pecuniary damages can be explained by the fact that the national court at a point in the future will provide a judgment and thus will decide whether or not the applicant has a right to receive compensation for his damages.

What this demonstrates is that the Court in a case like *Glüsen* does not state that it cannot speculate as to the outcome of the national procedure

---

76 *Glüsen v. Germany*, 10 January 2008, appl. no. 1679/03.

77 These are: *Schmautzer v. Austria*, 23 October 1995, appl. no. 15523/89; and *Wettstein v. Switzerland*, 21 December 2000, appl. no. 33958/96.

in the same way as it does when there is a loss of a chance, but that the Court in this case actually indicates that it is up to the national court to decide on this issue.[78] A consequence of this is that when the violation of the reasonable time requirement occurs in a case where only private parties are involved, the other private party will be held responsible for the damages caused by the facts that lead to the national procedure. Thus, in these type of cases, it seems that the Court finds that a state can be held liable to pay the damages that are caused directly by exceeding the reasonable time but cannot be held liable to pay the damages that were the subject of the national procedure.[79]

At first sight this requirement seems obvious: why indeed, would a state be held responsible for the damages that are not directly caused by the human rights violation. But what is interesting is that the Court does limit factual causality by applying this criterion. In Belgian law, where there is no legal limitation of the damages, causation would have been established for all the damages. This book has shown that according to the theory of equivalence, one can be held responsible for damages if the damages would *in concreto* not have come into being in the same way if the fault had not been made. In such cases, everyone who made a fault that had influence on the manifestation of the damages individually can be held liable for the totality of the damages. Thus, if the criteria are applied on the jurisprudence of the violation of the reasonable time requirement, it seems obvious that in cases where the damages deteriorated because of the long procedures, the state made a fault that influenced the damages as they *in concreto* appeared. If indeed the judge in *Glüsen* would have provided his judgment within a reasonable time, the applicants would have suffered less

78 The same conclusion also stems from the similar case of *Sürmeli*. In this case the Court explicitly observed that it was of no interest whether the national judge had well considered his judgment: *Sürmeli v. Germany*, 8 June 2006 (Grand Chamber), appl. no. 75529/01, §144. Moreover, the case of *Burdov* can also be referred to, where the Court explicitly observed that although national judges are better able to determine the size of pecuniary damages, the same cannot be said about non-pecuniary damages: *Burdov v. Russia (no.2)*, 15 January 2009, appl. no. 33509/04, §100.

79 However, the Court sometimes observes that a causal link becomes more uncertain over the passing of time: *Sunday Times v. the United Kingdom*, 6 November 1980 (just satisfaction) (Plenary), appl. no. 6538/74, §15; *Smith and Grady v. the United Kingdom*, 25 July 2000 (just satisfaction), appl. nos. 33985/96 and 33986/96, §18; *Ramishvili and Kokhreidze v. Georgia*, 27 January 2009, appl. no. 1704/06, §147; *Schüth v. Germany*, 28 June 2012 (just satisfaction), appl. no. 1620/03, §19; and *Kurić et al. v. Slovenia*, 12 March 2014 (just satisfaction) (Grand Chamber), appl. no. 26828/06, §82. Nevertheless, it is unclear whether the Court adds a criterion in this way or merely indicates that a causal link is required.

loss of income. That the Court has never applied this approach in cases where this type of damages was claimed[80] is probably a consequence of the fact that the Court only awards a just satisfaction for the damages that fall within the scope of the purpose of the norm that is protected by the Convention.

One of the most important consequences of this jurisprudence has to do with the division of liability. Indeed, if one looks at the theory of equivalence in Belgian tort law, it is important to note that a damaged person only has to sue one tortfeasor. It is then up to this tortfeasor to claim compensation from the other tortfeasors so that in the end all tortfeasors will have to pay for the damages that they caused. Thus, the theory of equivalence protects the damaged person in two ways. The first way lies in the fact that he does not have to bring charges against all the tortfeasors but can choose to sue only one of them (although it is advisable to sue them all). The second and most important protection of the damaged person lies in the fact that the tortfeasors have to bear the risk that one of the tortfeasors is insolvent. Since the ECtHR limits its concept of liability, Art. 41 does not offer the same degree of protection to victims of human rights violations. This, however, is reasonable since the ECtHR has no authority as to decide on the way one tortfeasor (the state) would be able to claim a part of the paid just satisfaction from private parties.

This theory can also be found in *Ommer*, an exceptional case where the Court found pecuniary damages that were caused by the violation of the reasonable time requirement.[81] The applicant in this case was a manager of a real estate group who had been indicted for fraud. The criminal investigation lasted for more than ten years and was then stopped. He had never been accused officially before a criminal court. After the ECtHR found a violation of Art. 6, the applicant claimed pecuniary damages for the loss of income caused by the fact that he had lost clients because his reputation had been tarnished by the accusations of fraud. The Court in this case recognized these damages. This seems reasonable from the foregoing argument, in this case the pecuniary damages were directly caused by the government that had started the criminal proceedings.[82]

---

80 E.g.: *Herbst v. Germany*, 11 January 2007, appl. no. 20027/02, §89; *Bellut v. Germany*, 21 July 2011, appl. nos. 21965/09 and 21965/09, §45; *Mianowicz v. Germany*, 13 October 2011, appl. no. 37264/06, §43; and *Sedminek v. Slovenia*, 23 October 2013, appl. no. 9842/07, §71.

81 *Ommer v. Germany (no. 2)*, 13 November 2008, appl. no. 26073/03.

82 The Court did not award compensation for pecuniary damages in this case because it found that there was no clear evidence to estimate the size of the loss of income. On the other hand, it is striking that the Court awarded a remarkably high compensation

3. LOSS OF AN OPPORTUNITY

The loss of an opportunity or the loss of a chance concerns situations where someone has a real possibility but not a certainty to gain an advantage or to avoid a disadvantage and this possibility is hindered by the fault of a third person.[83] The damaged person in such cases cannot really argue that he has suffered damages, but he can argue that he has lost the chance to gain an advantage or to avoid a disadvantage. This type of situation often occurs in cases where procedural errors are made in a judicial or administrative procedure, in situations where an accident led to the failure to pass a year at school or in the context of medical liability where an error led to a diminished chance to recover or even to survive.[84]

The ECtHR in some cases awards just satisfaction for the loss of a chance, also as an additional compensation in case a national court had already granted a satisfaction.[85] The Court does not explicitly state the criteria that it uses to award damages for the loss of a chance. Thus, without a good explanation, one can only try to grasp the approach of the Court.[86] In what follows, the difference between the situation where the Court awards a just satisfaction for the loss of a chance in case a material aspect of a Convention right was violated and the situation where the Court finds a violation of a procedural aspect of a Convention right will be examined.

---

for non-pecuniary damages. By doing so, the Court gives the impression that it uses the compensation for non-pecuniary damages to compensate its inability to award compensation for the loss of income: *Ommer v. Germany (no. 2)*, 13 November 2008, appl. no. 26073/03, §81. See also: *Rumpf v. Germany*, 2 September 2010, appl. no. 46344/06, §79; and *Wienholtz v. Germany*, 21 December 2010, appl. no. 974/07, §§39–41.

83 H. Bocken, 'Geen kans verloren. Causale onzekerheid en de rechtspraak van het Hof van Cassatie over het verlies van een kans' in X. (ed.), *Aansprakelijkheid, aansprakelijkheidsverzekering en andere schadevergoedingsmechanismen, XXXIIIste Postuniversitaire cyclus Willy Delva*, Mechelen, Kluwer, 2007, p271 at 280.

84 E. Dirix, *Het begrip schade*, Antwerp, Maklu, 1984, at 85–90.

85 In the case of Bönisch, the Court, for example, found that the compensation that the Austrian judges had awarded to the applicant was insufficient. It found that the violation of Art. 6 constituted a loss of a chance for the applicant to prove his innocence, which had not been compensated by the Austrian judges: *Bönisch v. Austria*, 2 July 1986 (just satisfaction), appl. no. 8658/79, §§11–13.

86 A. Garin, 'La perte de chance, un préjudice indemnisable: contribution à une problématique de l'indemnisation du dommage par la Cour européenne des droits de l'homme' in J.-F. Flauss and E. Lambert Abdelgawad (eds.), *La pratique d'indemnisation par la Cour européenne des droits de l'homme*, Brussels, Bruylant, 2011, p155 at 159, 165 and 167.

3.1. VIOLATIONS OF MATERIAL ASPECTS OF CONVENTION RIGHTS

An interesting case where the ECtHR granted just satisfaction for the loss of a chance is *Sporrong and Lönnroth*. In this renowned case, the Court found a violation of the right to property because the Swedish government had granted the city of Stockholm permission to expropriate the lands of the applicants, but the city of Stockholm, after waiting for years, never used the permit.[87] In the context of Art. 41 of the Convention, the Court took into account the fact that for years the applicants had been unable to gain any added value on their property (for example by selling it or by renovating their houses) because the permit to expropriate the property always managed to undo these gains. The Court granted an award for the loss of an opportunity to gain added value.[88]

Another interesting case is *Campbell and Cosans*.[89] The case concerns corporal punishments in a Scottish school. The parents of Jeffrey Cosans found that the corporal punishment used in Scottish schools conflicted with their beliefs on education. They believed that their right to education as enshrined in Art. 2 of the first protocol was violated because their son had been suspended from school for almost the whole year because he had refused to receive corporal punishment. The ECtHR followed the reasoning of the applicants and found a violation of the Convention. The applicants then claimed compensation for the pecuniary damages that resulted from their son's loss of a chance to succeed in his education. Because he had been suspended from school for almost a year, they found that he had lost a chance to pass his exams and thus had lost a chance to find a good job and income. The Court responded to this claim:

> The extent to which Jeffrey suffered material damage is even more problematical. It is true that, in the normal course of events, an individual who has not had the full benefit of educational opportunities will be likely to encounter greater

---

87 *Sporrong and Lönnroth v. Sweden*, 18 December 1984 (just satisfaction) (Plenary), appl. nos. 7151/75 and 7152/75. See also: *Todorova et al. v. Bulgaria*, 24 April 2008 (just satisfaction), appl. nos. 48380/99, 51362/99, 60036/00 and 73465/01; *Guiso-Gallisay v. Italy*, 22 December 2009 (just satisfaction) (Grand Chamber), appl. no. 58858/00; *Schembri et al. v. Malta*, 28 September 2010, appl. no. 42583/06; and *Mullai et al. v. Albania*, 18 October 2011 (Decision), appl. no. 9074/07.

88 *Sporrong and Lönnroth v. Sweden*, 18 December 1984 (just satisfaction) (Plenary), appl. nos. 7151/75 and 7152/75, §25.

89 *Campbell and Cosans v. the United Kingdom*, 25 February 1982, appl. no. 7511/76 and 7743/76.

> difficulties in his future career than one who has. On the other hand, the evidence suggests that, even had the suspension not occurred, Jeffrey's schooling would probably have led to no more than a limited qualification. Moreover, the entire responsibility for his situation cannot be attributed to the respondent State: Jeffrey does not appear to have pursued to the full the possibility of undertaking further study and training, and he did not react to the suggestion made by the Government in this connection (see paragraph 24, sub-paragraph (b), above). Again, whilst he did make some attempts to earn a living on a self-employed basis, he remained for a considerable period unregistered with the local employment exchange. Finally, it has to be recognised that in the current economic situation even many of those who have completed their education and training experience problems in finding employment. The Court therefore concludes that, whilst the suspension may well have contributed to the material difficulties which Jeffrey encountered, it cannot be regarded as the principal cause thereof.[90]

The Court awarded a sum of £3,000 as just satisfaction. It seems that although the Court did not find that the suspension of the procedure was the principal cause of the difficulties of the applicant to find a job, it did contribute to a part of these difficulties. Although the Court did not explicitly refer to the proportion in which the violation of the Convention contributed to the loss of a chance, the fact must be highlighted that in other cases the Court explicitly found that it had to estimate the chances that an applicant had lost to find work in the future.[91] What is however interesting in *Campbell and Cosans* is that the Court had to estimate in what proportion the loss of a chance was caused by the negligence of the applicant himself.

Another illustration can be found in *Lingens*. The applicant was a newspaper that had been ordered by a national judge to publish the verdict of the judge. The ECtHR found that the national judge had violated the right to free speech. With regard to Art. 41 of the Convention it argued that the newspaper had lost a chance to gain more income out of an advertisement since it could have used the place in the newspaper where the verdict was published for advertisement.[92] Another interesting example in this context is the case of *Inze*, discussed previously.[93] The Court here

---

90 *Campbell and Cosans v. the United Kingdom*, 22 March 1983 (just satisfaction), appl. nos. 7511/76 and 7743/76, §26.

91 *Vogt v. Germany*, 26 September 1995, appl. no. 17851/91, §60; and *Lustig-Prean and Beckett v. the United Kingdom*, 25 July 2000 (just satisfaction), appl. nos. 31417/96 and 32377/96, §24ff.

92 *Lingens v. Austria*, 8 June 1986 (Plenary), appl. no. 9815/82, §51.

93 *Inze v. Austria*, 28 October 1987, appl. no. 8695/79.

found a violation of the principle of equality because illegitimate children were treated differently in inheritance law from children that were born out of a marriage because only the last were able to inherit a farm. Since the applicant had been excluded from this possibility, under Art. 41 the Court judged that the applicant had lost the opportunity to inherit the farm.[94]

In all these cases, the ECtHR ruled that it was impossible to calculate the precise size of the damages. It accordingly awarded a just satisfaction on an equitable basis, taking into account all the relevant elements.[95]

3.2. VIOLATIONS OF PROCEDURAL ASPECTS OF CONVENTION RIGHTS

The previous section showed that the ECtHR awards just satisfaction for the loss of a chance if a material aspect of a Convention right is violated. The Court, however, more often awards just satisfactions for the loss of a chance in cases where a procedural aspect of the Convention is violated. Most of these cases concern the requirements of a fair trial in civil or criminal law as enshrined in Art. 6.[96] The problem in these cases is that it is almost always uncertain whether the verdict of the national court would have been different if Art. 6 had been respected. The damages that

---

94 *Ibid.*, §47.

95 *Sporrong and Lönnroth v. Sweden*, 18 December 1984 (just satisfaction) (Plenary), appl. nos. 7151/75 and 7152/75, §27; *Lingens v. Austria*, 8 June 1986 (Plenary), appl. no. 9815/82, §51; and *Inze v. Austria*, 28 October 1987, appl. no. 8695/79, §51.

96 *Goddi v. Italy*, 9 April 1984, appl. no. 8966/80, §§35–36; *Colozza v. Italy*, 12 February 1985, appl. no. 9024/80; *Lechner and Hess v. Austria*, 23 April 1987, appl. no. 9316/81; *O. v. the United Kingdom*, 9 June 1988 (just satisfaction), appl. no. 9276/81; *Weeks v. the United Kingdom*, 5 October 1988 (just satisfaction) (Plenary), appl. no. 9787/82, §§13–15; *Martins Moreira v. Portugal*, 26 October 1988, appl. no. 11371/85; *Poitrimol v. France*, 23 November 1993, appl. no. 14032/88, §41; *Barberà, Messegué and Jabardo v. Spain*, 13 June 1994 (just satisfaction) (Plenary), appl. nos. 10588/83, 10589/83 and 10590/83, §16; *Bellet v. France*, 4 December 1995, appl. no. 23805/94, §43; *F.E. v. France*, 30 October 1998, appl. no. 38212/97, §61; *Zielinski, Pradal and Gonzalez et al. v. France*, 28 October 1999 (Grand Chamber), appl. no. 24846/94 et al., §79; *Khalfaoui v. France*, 14 December 1999, appl. no. 34791/97, §58; *Krčmář et al. v. the Czech Republic*, 3 March 2000, appl. no. 35376/97; *Georgiadis v. Cyprus*, 14 May 2002, appl. no. 50516/99, §53; *Markass Car Hire LTD v. Cyprus*, 2 July 2002, appl. no. 51591/99, §50; *Sara Lind Eggertsdottir v. Iceland*, 5 July 2007, appl. no. 31930/04, §59; *Paykar Yev Haghtanak LTD v. Armenia*, 20 December 2007, appl. no. 21638/03, §56; *Kambourov v. Bulgaria*, 14 February 2008, appl. no. 55350/00, §87; *Maggio et al. v. Italy*, 31 May 2011, appl. no. 46286/09 et al., §80; *Sabeh el Leil v. France*, 29 June 2011 (Grand Chamber), appl. no. 34869/05, §72; and *Arras et al. v. Italy*, 14 February 2012, appl. no. 17972/07.

the applicants suffer in these cases can thus be described as the loss of a chance to obtain a better result in a lawsuit. These damages have to be qualified as pecuniary damages. In almost all the cases where the Court awards damages for the loss of a chance for the violation of a procedural Convention right, a sum of money for non-pecuniary damages is also awarded.[97]

Also interesting is the fact that the Court in these cases requalifies the requests of the applicants. Indeed, in many cases the applicants do not claim the loss of a chance but claim that they have suffered damages because they did not win the national lawsuit. In situations like this, the Court first argues that there is no causal effect between the claimed damages and the violation of the Convention, and then implicitly requalifies the damages.[98] Afterwards, it observes that although the violation of the Convention did not cause the claimed damages, it did cause a loss of a chance. An illustration of this line of reasoning can be found in the case of *Krčmář*:

> The Court notes that the sums claimed in respect of pecuniary damage relate to the market value of the Company on 1 July 1991 and to the loss of profits from that date until 30 June 1999. The Court observes that thereby the applicants are in effect claiming compensation for a nationalization which, according to them, was unlawful. This, however, was not the complaint before the Court, which was only called upon to determine whether the applicants had a fair hearing within the meaning of Article 6 §1 of the Convention. Moreover, the Court cannot speculate as to the outcome of the hearing had the position been otherwise, but it does not find it unreasonable to regard the applicants as having suffered a loss of real opportunities.[99]

The fact that the Court requalifies a claim in this case seems to be at odds with the fact that it refused in other cases to grant just satisfaction for the loss of chance that applicants claimed because the applicants had not sufficiently demonstrated their damages.[100] The difference can likely be

97 The Court can, on the other hand, still award a compensation for non-pecuniary damages if it does not find a causal link between the violation of a procedural requirement of the Convention and the claimed damages: *Jelić v. Croatia*, 12 June 2014, appl. no. 57856/11, §§121 and 122; *B. et al. v. Croatia*, 18 June 2015, appl. no. 71593/11; and *Saydulkhanova v. Russia*, 25 June 2015, appl. no. 25521/10.

98 O. Ichim, *Just Satisfaction*, 2015, above n. 10, at 115.

99 *Krčmář et al. v. the Czech Republic*, 3 March 2000, appl. no. 35376/97, §50. Similar observations were also made in: *Bönisch v. Austria*, 2 June 1986 (just satisfaction), appl. no. 8658/79, §11.

100 *Gronus v. Poland*, 28 May 2002, appl. no. 29695/96, §42; *Feldbrugge v. the Netherlands*, 27 July 1987 (just satisfaction) (Plenary), appl. no. 8562/79, §10.

explained by the fact that the Court probably requires a minimal level of certainty that a chance is lost. Indeed, victims that claim a compensation for damages need to prove the existence of this damages, thus also the existence of a loss of an opportunity. More problematic is the fact that the Court in some cases argues that it cannot grant any compensation under Art. 41 because it cannot speculate on what the outcome of the national procedures might have been if the procedural right of the convention had been respected.[101] It is indeed paradoxical that the Court sometimes requalifies claimed damages to the loss of an opportunity and in other cases indicates that it cannot speculate on the outcome of the procedures.

A starting point to explain this difference can be found in *Boulois*. The applicant in this case explicitly claimed satisfaction for the loss of an opportunity. He alleged that, because he had not received a better regime in prison in a procedure that violated Art. 6, any progress towards a semi-custodial regime had been denied him until April 2009, and so he had been unable to engage in paid work prior to that date.[102] The Court however found that it could not calculate the outcome of the proceedings had the applicant had access to a court and thus found that there was no causal link between the violation of the treaty and the loss of an opportunity.[103] The problem with this judgment is that it seems to be an incorrect application of the loss of a chance. Since the applicant had not been granted access to a court, he lost the chance that the Court would annul an administrative decision taken by the governors of the prison. There is no obvious objection to finding a loss of opportunity in this case. This seems to indicate that the Court made this decision for other reasons. What probably happened was that the Court took into account the subsidiarity principle with regard to Art. 41.[104] Indeed, this book has shown that the

---

101 *Wloch v. Poland*, 19 October 2000, appl. no. 27785/95, §157; *Wettstein v. Switzerland*, 21 December 2000, appl. no. 33958/96, §53; *Celik (Bozkurt) v. Turkey*, 12 April 2011, appl. no. 34388/05, §43; *Neziraj v. Germany*, 8 November 2012, appl. no. 30804/07, §71; *Dimitar Krastev v. Bulgaria*, 12 February 2013, appl. no. 26524/04, §67; and *Papadakis v. the former Yugoslav Republic of Macedonia*, 26 February 2013, appl. no. 50254/07, §111.

102 *Boulois v. Luxemburg*, 14 December 2010, appl. no. 37575/04, §88. This case has been revised by the Grand Chamber, but not on the points that are referred to in this context: *Boulois v. Luxemburg*, 3 April 2012 (Grand Chamber), appl. no. 37575/04.

103 *Boulois v. Luxemburg*, 14 December 2010, appl. no. 37575/04, §90.

104 Karner is, in a similar way, of the opinion that the jurisprudence where the Court judges that it cannot speculate on the outcome of a case, is inspired by the will to respect the competences of the member states: E. Karner, 'Concluding Remarks on

Court in general is reluctant to apply the principle of subsidiarity in the context of Art. 41 but that it does so in cases where the national states are able to take measures through which they can as far as possible offer the applicants the *restitution in integrum*. This book has shown that the Court in this context grants precedence to the redress *in natura* before the financial compensation. The fact that the Court did make this type of reasoning can probably be deduced from the fact that the Court in its reasonings on the merits indicated that it required the state to re-open a judicial procedure in national law.[105]

This approach then can *mutatis mutandis* be applied in all the cases where the Court argues that it cannot speculate on the outcome of a national procedure.[106] Since the Court does award compensation for the loss of a chance to win a lawsuit, there seems to be no other plausible understanding of this jurisprudence. It is regrettable that the Court does not provide a better explanation for this jurisprudence. By stating that it cannot speculate on the outcome of the procedure, it does not only neglect to refer to the principle of subsidiarity, but it also makes statements that are confusing from the perspective of causality. Indeed, as Bydlinski notes, a court always has to speculate on the evolution of things if it has to decide whether or not a causal link is at hand in a given case.[107] To establish a causal link, a judge will always have to speculate on what would have happened if the violation of the Convention (or the wrongful act in tort law) had not occurred.

It might also be that the Court's reference to the impossibility to speculate on the outcome of a case can be explained by the fact that the Court in these cases finds that the applicants cannot prove that there was a minimal level of certainty that they had a real chance to win the procedure. Indeed, in national tort law systems it is required that there be at least a reasonable chance that the claimant would have had gained an advantage or would have avoided a disadvantage. This can be illustrated by *Milatova* where the Court explicitly referred to *Krčmář* to demonstrate that there

Causation' in A. Fenyves, E. Karner, H. Koziol and E. Steiner (eds.), *Tort Law in the Jurisprudence of the European Court of Human Rights*, Göttingen, De Gruyter, 2011, p835 at 839.

105 *Boulois v. Luxemburg*, 14 December 2010, appl. no. 37575/04, §§82–86.

106 See also: The Law Commission and the Scottish Law Commission, Damages under the Human Rights Act 1998. Report on a Reference under Section 3(1) (e) of the Law Commissions Act 1965, SE/2000/182, 2000, <https://www.scotlawcom.gov.uk/files/3012/7989/6877/rep180.pdf>, 78.

107 F. Bydlinski, 'Methodological Approaches', 2011, above n. 13, p29 at 84.

was no loss of an opportunity at this case.[108] Both of these cases concerned a procedure before the Czech Constitutional Court where the applicants had not been given the opportunity to comment on the documentary evidence that was produced by the national authorities at the request of the Constitutional Court. As already stated, the ECtHR granted compensation in *Krčmář* because of the following reasoning: 'the Court cannot speculate as to the outcome of the hearing had the position been otherwise, but it does not find it unreasonable to regard the applicants as having suffered a loss of real opportunities.'[109] In *Milatova* the Court pointed out that the Czech Constitutional Court in *Krčmář* had based its judgment on the documents that the applicants had not been able to comment on whereas in the case of *Milatova* it was not clear whether the Constitutional Court had based its judgment on the documents upon which the applicants had been unable to comment.[110] It thus seems that the ECtHR in *Milatova* did not award just satisfaction for the loss of an opportunity because it found the chance that the Czech Constitutional Court would have made a different judgment had the applicant been able to comment on the documents was very unlikely.[111]

Finally, the question arises as to whether the Court awards compensation for non-pecuniary damages under the heading of the loss of an opportunity. In *Vidal*, the Court did not award satisfaction for the claimed pecuniary damages because it found that it could not speculate on the outcome of the proceedings. It did, however, award a substantial amount of money for the non-pecuniary damages that resulted from the

---

108 *Milatova et al. v. the Czech Republic*, 21 June 2005, appl. no. 61811/00, §70.

109 *Krčmář et al. v. the Czech Republic*, 3 March 2000, appl. no. 35376/97, §50.

110 *Milatova et al. v. the Czech Republic*, 21 June 2005, appl. no. 61811/00, §63.

111 This interpretation is also in accordance with the observations made in the context of the loss of a chance and with the admissibility criteria according to which someone who has no chance that he would have won a procedure if the procedural rights of the Convention had been respected, does not suffer a significant disadvantage (with the result that his claim will be rejected): *Holub v. the Czech Republic*, 14 December 2010 (Decision), appl. no. 24880/05; *Bratři Zátkové v. the Czech Republic*, 8 February 2011 (Decision), appl. no. 20862/06; *Benet Praha, spol. s r.o. v. the Czech Republic*, 24 February 2011, appl. no. 33908/04 et al., §135; *Cavajda v. the Czech Republic*, 29 March 2011 (Decision), appl. no. 17696/07, §1; and *Liga Portuguesa de Futebol Professional v. Portugal*, 3 April 2012 (Decision), appl. no. 49639/09. When, in the opposite way, a violation of Art. 6 has influenced the result of a national procedure (for example when the judge used evidence that had not been the subject of a defended action), the Court finds that an applicant suffers a significant disadvantage: *Joos v. Switzerland*, 15 November 2012, appl. no. 43245/07.

loss of a chance to have a fair trial.[112] In *Feltbrugge*, the Court did not grant a sum of money for the loss of a chance, but awarded a considerable compensation for non-pecuniary damages without giving any explanation for this.[113] This unexplained jurisprudence of the Court seems to illustrate that the Court sometimes uses compensation for non-pecuniary damages to compensate the impossibility to find a loss of a chance,[114] or that it has problems in diverging the loss of an opportunity to receive redress for non-pecuniary damages and the non-pecuniary damages as such.[115]

3.3. CRITICISM

Although it is clear that the ECtHR accepts the loss of a chance, it is hard to figure out when it will do so. The jurisprudence of the Court gives almost nothing to go on. Nevertheless, the Court cannot be blamed for this. It is always hard to grasp the loss of a chance. To decide that a loss of a chance exists, it is necessary to determine the existence of the probability that the chance will be fulfilled. The boundary between the possibility that a chance will be fulfilled and the non-existence of the chance is always hard to draw, especially in a procedural context.[116] This difficult examination cannot be done *in abstracto*. It always requires a case-by-case analysis. It is thus no coincidence that national legal systems often struggle with the loss of a chance, and that a lot of them reject the concept in part or entirely.[117]

This does not mean that one cannot criticize the Court's approach in one way or another. Some authors find that the Court does not pay enough respect to the procedural guarantees in the Convention because it often

---

112 *Vidal v. Belgium*, 28 October 1992 (just satisfaction), appl. no. 12351/86, §9. See also: *Traore v. France*, 17 December 2002, appl. no. 48954/99, §31.

113 *Feldbrugge v. the Netherlands*, 27 July 1987 (just satisfaction) (Plenary), appl. no. 8562/79, §§10–13. See also: *Pini et al. v. Romania*, 22 June 2004, appl. nos. 78028/01 and 78030/01, §§201 and 205.

114 In this sense: Partly dissenting opinion of Judge Casadevall joined by Judges Bonello and Kovler in *Kingsley v. the United Kingdom*, 28 May 2002 (Grand Chamber), appl. no. 35605/97, §5.

115 E.g.: *Musial v. Poland*, 25 March 1999 (Grand Chamber), appl. no. 24557/94, §§55 and 58; and *Petur Thor Sigurdsson v. Iceland*, 10 April 2003, appl. no. 39731/98.

116 A. Garin, 'La perte de chance, un préjudice indemnisable: contribution à une problématique de l'indemnisation du dommage par la Cour européenne des droits de l'homme' in J.-F. Flauss and E. Lambert Abdelgawad (eds.), *La pratique d'indemnisation par la Cour européenne des droits de l'homme*, Brussels, Bruylant, 2011, p155 at 173.

117 C. Van Dam, *European Tort Law*, 2013, above n. 2, at 341–342.

argues that it cannot see as to how the result of national procedures would have been different if the guarantees of the Convention would have been respected.[118] These authors argue that the Court, by often making this kind of observation, seems to suggest that the procedural guarantees in the Convention are less relevant than the other provisions. They then conclude that it would be better if the Court would find a loss of a chance in these cases. Although this approach seems to be legitimate from the protective perspective, it cannot be accepted that easily. The first reason for this is that some of the cases where the Court refuses to award compensation for a loss of a chance, are actually inspired by the principle of subsidiarity. As was discussed before, the Court applies the principle of subsidiarity in situations where the national legal system can offer restitution in kind whereas the Court itself cannot. Thus, if it is possible to re-open a case in the national legal order, the Court will require states to do so.[119] In those cases the Court will not award a just satisfaction for the loss of a chance. Although it might be possible that the Court will award just satisfaction for moral damages that are partially inspired by the wish to compensate the loss of a chance, it would be more appropriate for the Court to make a clear distinction between the different categories of damages and to develop arguments on this issue. For this reason, the case-law where the Court awarded a satisfaction for the loss of a chance and the non-pecuniary damages that the applicant had already suffered while also ordering the case to be re-opened, must be welcomed.[120]

---

118 T. Thiede and E. Büyüksagis, 'Reduction of Damages' in A. Fenyves, E. Karner, H. Koziol and E. Steiner (eds.), *Tort Law in the Jurisprudence of the European Court of Human Rights*, Göttingen, De Gruyter, 2011, p803 at 818.

119 See: Partly dissenting opinion of Judge Zupancic in 18 February 1999; and A. Garin, 'La perte de chance', 2011, p155 at 179ff.

120 *Lawyer Partners A.S. v. Slovakia*, 16 June 2009, appl. no. 54252/07 et al., §§61–62; and *Idakiev v. Bulgaria*, 21 June 2011, appl. no. 33681/05, §§68–69.

CHAPTER 10
RESTITUTION

If someone proves he suffered damages that were caused by someone else's fault, national tort law will redress his damages. Restitution is the remedy in national tort law, whereas damages, fault and causality are the applicability criteria.[1] For this reason, damages and restitution, although they are entangled with one another, should be differentiated from one another.[2] There are two good reasons for this. The first reason is that it is necessary from a procedural perspective to separate the finding of the existence of damages from the assessing of the size of the damages.[3] The second reason is that there does not have to be a one-to-one relationship between the size of the damages and the size of the restitution. The law can depart from this idea.

1. THE PURPOSE OF RESTITUTION

When the ECtHR grants just satisfaction under Art. 41 of the Convention, it aims to put the human rights victim as far as possible in the situation in which he would have been if the Convention violation had not occurred.[4]

---

1 D. Simoens, *Buitencontractuele aansprakelijkheid, II, Schade en schadeloosstelling in Beginselen van Belgisch privaatrecht*, XI, Antwerp, Kluwer, 1999, at 3 and 20.

2 E. Dirix, *Het begrip schade*, Antwerp, Maklu, 1984, at 27.

3 E.g.: according to Belgian tort law, a judge has to award restitution for damages even if the amount cannot be proven: B. Kohl, 'Moment de l'Evaluation et variation du dommages' in B. Dubuisson and P. Jourdain (eds.), *Le dommage et sa réparation dans la responsabilité contractuelle et extracontractuelle. Etudes de droit comparé*, Brussels, Larcier, 2015, p237 at 361.

4 *Piersack v. Belgium*, 26 October 1984 (just satisfaction), appl. no. 8692/79, §12; *Scozzari and Giunta v. Italy*, 13 July 2000 (Grand Chamber), appl. nos. 39221/98 and 41963/98, §250; *Lustig-Prean and Beckett v. the United Kingdom*, 25 July 2000 (just satisfaction), appl. nos. 31417/96 and 32377/96, §22; *Kingsley v. the United Kingdom*, 28 May 2002 (Grand Chamber), appl. no. 35605/97, §40; *Former King of Greece et al. v. Greece*, 23 November 2002 (Grand Chamber), appl. no. 25701/94, §72; *Haase v. Germany*,

By doing so, the Court seems to apply restitution in the same way as is done in national tort law.[5] Nevertheless, there seems to be one difference. In national tort law, an injured party has a right to full compensation (the so-called *restitutio ad integrum*)[6] if all the criteria are met. The Court on the other hand argued in one case that applicants do not have a right to receive a just satisfaction under Art. 41.[7] In another recent case, it argued that it enjoys a certain discretion in its powers under Art. 41 so that it can, taking into account the particular features of a case, decide to award less than the value of the actual suffered damages.[8] It thus seems as if the Court can decide on a discretionary basis whether or not an applicant can receive just satisfaction. One can however question the existence and the legitimacy of such a discretionary power. Several arguments can be invoked against it.

First of all, under Art. 41 the Court requires full compensation: *restitution in integrum*.[9] Thus, if the Court, when awarding just satisfaction, starts from the need to provide full restitution,[10] it would be bizarre that it

---

8 April 2004, appl. no. 11057/02, §115; *Claes et al. v. Belgium*, 2 June 2005, appl. no. 46825/99 et al., §53; *Salduz v. Turkey*, 27 November 2008 (Grand Chamber), appl. no. 36391/02, §72; M. De Salvia, 'Le principe de l'octroi subsidiaire des dommages-intérêts: d'une morale des droits de l'homme à une morale simplement indemnitaire?' in J.-F. Flauss and E. Lambert Abdelgawad (eds.), *La pratique d'indemnisation par la Cour européenne des droits de l'homme*, Brussels, Bruylant, 2011, p9 at 10–11; E. Karner, 'Concluding Remarks on Damage' in A. Fenyves, E. Karner, H. Koziol and E. Steiner (eds.), *Tort Law in the Jurisprudence of the European Court of Human Rights*, Göttingen, De Gruyter, 2011, p829 at 830; H. Koziol, 'Concluding Remarks on Compensatory and Non-Compensatory Remedies' in A. Fenyves, E. Karner, H. Koziol and E. Steiner (eds.), *Tort Law in the Jurisprudence of the European Court of Human Rights*, Göttingen, De Gruyter, 2011, p863 at 864; and The Law Commission and the Scottish Law Commission, *Damages under the Human Rights Act 1998*, 2000, <https://www.scotlawcom.gov.uk/files/3012/7989/6877/rep180.pdf>, at 24–25 and 47–48.

5 Damages in national tort law also aim to restore the victim as far as possible to the status before the injury: U. Magnus, 'Comparative Report on the Law of Damages' in U. Magnus et al. (eds.), *Unification of Tort Law: Damages*, The Hague, Kluwer, 2001, p185 at 185.

6 *Ibid.*, at 188.

7 *Sunday Times v. the United Kingdom*, 6 November 1980 (Art. 41) (Plenary), appl. no. 6538/74, §15.

8 *B.K.M. Lojistik Tasimacilik Ticaret Ltd Sirketi v. Slovenia*, 17 January 2017, appl. no. 42079/12, §59.

9 This is a consequence of the fact that states have to provide an effective national remedy for human rights violations: K. Wolfram, 'Just Satisfaction in Art 41 ECHR and Public International Law – Issues of Interpretation and Review of International Materials' in A. Fenyves, E. Karner, H. Koziol and E. Steiner (eds.), *Tort Law in the Jurisprudence of the European Court of Human Rights*, Göttingen, De Gruyter, 2011, p345 at 355–356.

10 J. Hartshorne, 'The Human Rights Act 1998 and Damages for Non-Pecuniary Loss', *EHRLR* 2004, p660 at 662. See also: Dissenting opinion of Judge Spielmann in

does not grant the applicants a right to compensation. A previous chapter illustrated that the cases where the Court makes declaratory judgments can be explained by principles that are used in tort law. If it was argued that victims of human rights violations under Art. 41 have no right to compensation because the Court requires the existence of a causal link, applies a *de minimis* rule on non-pecuniary damages, gives priority to restitution in kind over financial compensation and refuses to award compensation for the damages that were caused by the fault of the victim, then it must also be argued that damaged individuals don't have a right to compensation in national tort law either.

A second reason why the Court cannot have discretionary power to decide on the compensation, has to do with the importance of legal certainty in the jurisprudence of the ECtHR. The court indeed attaches great importance to the principle of legal certainty. In *Marckx*, the Court found that the principle of legal certainty is included in the second part of the human rights test because an infringement of a human right has to be provided by the law.[11] Although the Court finds that jurisprudence can be qualified as a law in the context of the second part of the human rights test,[12] it sometimes happens that jurisprudence is so scattered and incoherent so that the Court argues that it cannot be conceived as a legal basis to infringe human rights. An interesting example thereof can be found in *RTBF*.[13] In this case the Court found that the Belgian jurisprudence with regard to defamation was so incoherent that it could not be perceived as a legitimate exception to the freedom of the press. Also interesting with regard to the principle of legal certainty is *Tolstoy Miloslawsky*.[14] The Court in this case found a violation of the right to free speech because the judges in a defamation case had not given enough incentives to the jury to define a proportionate compensation. It seemed as if the Court found it problematic that the jury had a discretionary power to decide the size of

Guiso-Gallisay v. Italy, 22 December 2009 (just satisfaction) (Grand Chamber), appl. no. 58858/00.

11 *Marckx v. Belgium*, 13 June 1979 (Plenary), appl. no. 6833/74, §58 *in fine*.

12 Jurisprudence can also be used as an instrument to make precise legal provisions that are not precise enough to be qualified as a legal basis in the context of the human rights test: *Handyside v. the United Kingdom*, 7 December 1976 (Grand Chamber), appl. no. 5493/72, §44; *Müller et al. v. Switzerland*, 24 May 1988, appl. no. 10737/84, §38; *De Haes and Gijsels v. Belgium*, 24 February 1997, appl. no. 19983/92, §33; and *Tammer v. Estland*, 6 February 2001, appl. no. 41205/98, §38.

13 *RTBF v. Belgium*, 29 March 2011, appl. no. 50084/06, §113.

14 *Tolstoy Miloslavsky v. the United Kingdom*, 13 July 1995, appl. no. 18139/91, §50.

the compensation in tort law.[15] Thus, if the Court requires national states to respect legal certainty when deciding on the existence and the size of compensations, one can wonder why the Court itself must not respect these same principles.

This argument is confirmed by the Court's practice to require states to provide compensations that are comparable to the just satisfactions that the Court awards in similar cases on the basis of Art. 13 (as was discussed before). Thus, if the Court on the one hand requires states to award satisfaction on a coherent basis and on the other hand requires national judges to take into account the satisfactions that the Court awards under Art. 41, one must conclude that the Court cannot decide on the presence and the size of satisfactions on a discretionary basis. Indeed, if the Court would act in a discretionary way, the national judges, in order to provide a satisfaction that is comparable to the satisfactions offered by the Court, must also act in a discretionary way.

Finally, it must be said that the Court does not stand above the law.

Thus, although the text of Art. 41 does not award a subjective right to compensation to victims of human right violations, it does so in fact. Indeed, the criteria that the Court developed in applying Art. 41 are jurisprudential rules from which the Court cannot easily depart. Since it has been shown that these jurisprudential rules are comparable with rules that exist in national tort law, one must conclude that Art. 41 offers a right to compensation in a similar manner as national tort law does.

2. THE CHOICE BETWEEN RESTITUTION IN KIND AND FINANCIAL COMPENSATION

Although the text of Art. 41 refers to a just satisfaction and does not permit the Court to annul legislation or to impose measures on member states, this book has shown that the ECtHR has judged that restitution in kind has priority over financial compensation. It has also been shown that the Court does so by reading Art. 41 in coherence with Art. 46. It is by the interplay between these two stipulations that the priority of restitution in kind emerges. If it is possible to award restitution in kind via Art. 46, the Court will only make a declaratory judgment under Art. 41. Since restitution in

15 W. Berka, 'Human Rights and Tort Law' in A. Fenyves, E. Karner, H. Koziol and E. Steiner (eds.), *Tort Law in the Jurisprudence of the European Court of Human Rights*, Göttingen, De Gruyter, 2011, p237 at 282.

kind is in many cases impossible or would pose a disproportionately heavy weight on the state compared with the additional value that it offers,[16] the Court in most cases awards a sum of money under Art. 41.[17] Octavian Ichim criticizes this approach.[18] He finds that the Court, by choosing to award financial compensation, makes it possible for states to buy off human rights violations. Nevertheless, it must be noted that the Court follows an approach that is quite uncommon in national legal systems since most tort law systems favor compensation in money over restitution in kind.[19]

The interesting question in this context is how the Convention can be used as an instrument to decide whether or not a restitution in kind is possible in national tort law. Since the Court applies this principle itself, it is reasonable that this principle, according to the Court, must at least be used towards the government. If a government violates a human right, restitution in kind must be possible in national law in those cases where the ECtHR itself would grant restitution in kind. If not, Art. 13 might be violated. One can however doubt whether the same line of reasoning can be expanded to tort law litigations between private persons. The reason for this is that tortfeasors have human rights and thus can appeal to these rights when they are asked by a national judge to award satisfaction. Because of the existence of positive obligations to protect human rights in horizontal relations, the judge will then have to take these arguments into account when judging on the form of compensation. He will then have to award a financial compensation if the duty to offer restitution in kind would violate the tortfeasor's human rights.

In one case of the Dutch High Court, this problem was explicitly raised. This was the so-called *Gedwongen Aidstest* case.[20] The claimant in this case was a woman that had been violently raped two times. The rapist used a gun to force her and did not use any contraceptives. The women thus claimed a court injunction to forbid the rapist from entering a certain area and also claimed a sum of money for non-pecuniary damages. The woman moreover argued that the rape had caused an unbearable uncertainty

---

16 *Verein gegen Tierfabriken Schweiz (VgT) v. Switzerland (no.2)*, 30 June 2009 (Grand Chamber), appl. no. 32772/02, §86. See also: *Savriddin Dzhurayev v. Russia*, 25 April 2013, appl. no. 71386/10, §248; and *Davydov v. Russia*, 30 October 2014, appl. no. 18967/07, §25.

17 See in the same sense: O. Ichim, *Just Satisfaction under the European Convention on Human Rights*, Cambridge, Cambridge University Press, 2015, at 38–39.

18 *Ibid.*, at 41–42.

19 U. Magnus, 'Comparative Report', 2001, above n. 5, p185 at 188.

20 High Court of the Netherlands 18 June 1993, *NJCM-Bulletin* 1993, at 786.

because the rapist had had many sexual contacts so that he had a high probability of being infected with HIV. After the rape, the woman had had a medical examination that indicated that she was not infected with HIV, but the doctors could only rule out the possibility that she had been infected after an incubation period of six months. Since the woman could not bear this uncertainty, she claimed that the rapist should undergo a medical examination. Because he did not want to have this examination, he appealed to his right to physical integrity as enshrined in Art. 8 of the Convention. The Dutch High Court in this case argued that the judge could force the rapist to have a medical examination because the right to physical integrity is not an absolute right, but a right that can be limited for the legitimate aim to compensate a damaged person.

Ten years later, the Dutch High Court had to decide on a similar issue in the framework of medical malpractice.[21] The claimant in this case was a man who needed a surgical operation to end his toothache. During this operation, the doctor had accidently cut his own finger with one of his instruments. Consequently, the blood of the doctor came into contact with the blood of the patient. Since one can be infected with HIV via blood contact, the patient requested that the doctor undergo a medical examination. The doctor refused this. The patient thus argued that this refusal of the doctor constituted a wrongful act in the meaning of tort law. The reason for this, according to the patient, was that the doctor, by having a medical examination, could easily avert a large risk. The doctor however found that an obligation to have a medical examination violated his physical integrity. The judge in appeal however found that the right to physical integrity could be limited by the law or law-based jurisprudence or regulation. Moreover, such a limitation can be found in the general rules of tort law and the principle of general conduct. The judge thus found that he had to apply the proportionality test in order to see whether the application of tort law in this case would violate the doctor's rights. He however found that the application was proportionate because the right to physical integrity of the doctor would only be infringed very slightly whereas for the patient there was more at stake.

Since the doctor did not agree with this case, he filed an appeal in cassation to the High Court and argued that the judge in appeal had granted too much importance to the interests of the patient and not enough to his own human rights. He moreover argued that his interests could be framed

21 High Court of the Netherlands, 12 December 2003, appl. no. C02/193.

as human rights and that the judge consequently had to be more reserved when deciding on a limitation of this right.

The Dutch High Court did not however agree with the doctor. The court only affirmed the judgment of the appeal court. The High Court did so without much observation, so it is hard to learn much of this case. There was however an interesting opinion delivered in this case by *procureur-generaal* Hartkamp. He started his opinion by pointing to the fact that it is vast jurisprudence of the Court that tort law and more precisely the general rule of conduct can interfere with the exercise of human rights in horizontal relations.[22] The reason that this is possible, he argues, is the fact that Convention rights can be limited by law. Hartkamp then continues with referring to the proportionality test. He notes that the application of this test in a case concerning horizontal relations must always be done with much attention to the specific circumstances of the case. He later notes that the judge then has to check whether the legitimate aim of the interference with the Convention rights can be reached in a manner that is less harmful for the infringed rights. If a less infringing measure would be possible, the more infringing measure violated the Convention. If it is however impossible to find a measure that would also reach the legitimate aim, then the judge will have to look at whether the infringement of the right and the legitimate aim are proportionate. To decide whether a proportionality exists, one has to take into account the nature of the infringed human right, the nature of the legal relationship between the private persons, the severity of the infringement and the importance of the legitimate aim.

In this specific case, Hartkamp found that there was no other measure by which one could receive certainty on the medical situation of the patient. The only way one could know whether the patient was infected with HIV was by doing a medical examination on the doctor. Consequently, the principle of proportionality had to be applied. With regard to this test, Hartkamp indicated the fact that the doctor had not contested that he was a member of a group of the population that has a higher risk to be HIV-infected. Thus, Hartkamp found that there was a concrete risk that the patient was infected with HIV. In other words, one can say that the patient had a real interest in knowing more about his medical situation. On the other hand, Hartkamp noted that the duty to have a medical investigation was an infringement of the doctor's human rights.

---

[22] With reference to: Hoge Raad, 5 June 1987 (*Goeroe I*); Hoge Raad, 2 February 1990 (*Goeroe II*); Hoge Raad, 18 June 1993 (*Gedwongen Aids-test*); and Hoge Raad, 2 May 2003 (*Storms v. Niessen*).

The infringement of this right was limited however. The doctor only had to undergo a blood test. This test did not pose any risk to the medical situation of the doctor. Moreover, Hartkamp argued that the results of this test would not be made public so that the test would not damage the reputation of the doctor. The applicant on the other hand had a great interest in getting more certainty on his medical situation, not only for psychological reasons, but also to start a medical treatment in due time if this was deemed to be necessary. Because the interests of the patient were far more severe than those of the doctor, Hartkamp found that the judges in appeal could oblige the doctor to undergo a blood test without violating his human rights.

What these cases illustrate, is how human rights can be used as criteria to decide whether or not restitution in kind can be applied in national law. If restitution in kind can be offered by a blood test on the tortfeasor, then the right to restitution of the harmed person will conflict with the right of physical integrity of the tortfeasor. Since human rights indicate these contradicting rights, it does create a framework to make a balancing exercise between these interests. But this does not mean that it will always push courts to grant restitution in kind. The contrary is truer. If the victim of the violation only suffers property damages, then his interest will not be as high as is the case with physical injuries. Accordingly, the proportionality test will not weigh that heavy towards the intention of the victim. Moreover, property damages can often be compensated by offering a sum of money to buy a new good or to hire someone to fix the damages.

3. THE ESTIMATION OF DAMAGES

3.1. A CONCRETE OR AN ABSTRACT ESTIMATION

Apart from the question of how damages are restituted, it is also important to know how they are estimated. Must damages be measured in a concrete or in an abstract manner? The first manner requires judges always to make a precise calculation of the damages. The second manner allows judges to indicate what size of damages are reasonably expected in cases where a specific damaging event occurs. When the judge estimates the damages in an abstract way, he can refer to systematized tables where all kind of damages are indicated, or he can judge on equity (*aequo et bono*).

Although one might expect that a concrete estimation of damages is necessary to determine the size of the restitution because the damages have to be compensated and not more than the damages, there are reasons that plea for an abstract estimation or an estimation *ex aequo et bono* in some cases.[23] A first reason has to do with efficiency. If judges do not have to estimate all the damages precisely but can use abstract criteria to estimate the damages, they will save a lot of time. The estimation of damages is often indeed a very technical, complex and thus expensive and time-consuming occupation for courts. Estimating the damages in an abstract or equitable manner will consequently benefit the overall output of the judiciary. A second argument for the abstract estimation of damages is the fact that it serves legal certainty. If there are clear indications as to what damages a specific type of wrongful act causes, people will know from the beginning how many damages they can be expected to pay or to receive. One can moreover argue that this also serves the equality between tortfeasors or damaged persons. The amount of money that they will have to pay or that they will receive will, because of the abstract estimation of the damages, not depend on factual issues or on the presence of convincing proof. On the other hand, it must be clear that an abstract estimation of damages can be perceived as unjust since it will certainly have as a result that some people will not receive compensation for all their damages. If, on the other hand, the abstract point of reference is too high, some people will receive money for harm that they never suffered. This might then result in more litigation for the Court since it stimulates people to try to gain money from accidents.

From the above paragraphs, it seems as if an abstract and a concrete manner to estimate damages must be opposed to one another. This is not the case. In general, both methods are used next to one another. Let us take Belgian tort law as an example. In this legal system, the Court of Cassation in principle requires a concrete estimation of the damages for the reason that only the damages must be compensated: nothing more (since that would lead to an unjust enrichment) and nothing less.[24] What is problematic is that the existence of damages is sometimes clear from the beginning, but that one cannot estimate their precise size. This is for instance the case with pecuniary damages that are difficult to estimate such as future loss of income of the damages that are caused by the loss of a chance, and is

23 E. Dirix, 'Abstracte en concrete schade', *Rechtskundig Weekblad* 2000–01, p1329 at 1329.

24 I. Durant, 'La réparation dite intégrale du dommage' in B. Dubuisson and P. Jourdain (eds.), *Le dommage et sa réparation dans la responsabilité contractuelle et extracontractuelle. Etudes de droit comparé*, Brussels, Larcier, 2015, p441 at 444.

always the case with non-pecuniary damages that, because of their nature, cannot be quantified.[25] Thus, according to the Belgian Court of Cassation, a judge can estimate the abstract if he knows that a victim suffered damages but where he cannot precisely estimate their size.[26] The reasoning behind this principle is that a victim has a right to compensation from the moment that he proves he suffered damages that are caused by a wrongful act. In other words, if the existence of damages, a wrongful act and a causal link between these two are proven, the victim has a right to restitution and the judge is obliged to offer it. The victim is only obliged to prove that he suffered damages but is not obliged to prove the exact size of it.

In the jurisprudence of the ECtHR, the same principle seems to apply. Victims of a human rights violation do not have to prove the precise size of their damages. This can be illustrated by *König*.[27] The applicant in this case was a plastic surgeon whose license to run a clinic and to exercise a medical profession was withdrawn by the authorities. He disputed this decision by filing a claim before the national courts, but the procedure kept on going without reaching a final decision. The surgeon thus found that his right to have a judicial decision within a reasonable time as is enshrined in Art. 6 was violated and filed a claim with the ECtHR. In its judgment on the merits, the Court found a violation of Art. 6 but argued with regard to Art. 41 that this issue was not yet ready for decision.[28] In the judgments on just satisfaction, the applicant argued that he had suffered damages because of the defamation and the loss of income that resulted from his inability to continue his business. He also supplied some information on the incomes that he could have earned if he had not been forced to end his business. However, since he could not estimate his damages precisely, he requested that the Court estimate the damages.[29]

The Court observed that the absence of proof of the precise size of the damages could not hinder the award of just satisfaction. It further

---

25 R. Kruithof, 'La réparation du dommage extrapatrimonial en cas de mort ou d'atteinte à l'intégrité physique' in *Rapports belges au XIe Congres de l'Académie International de droit comparé*, Antwerp, Kluwer, 1982, p283 at 295.

26 D. de Callataÿ, 'Choix des modes de réparation (capital, rente ou forfait) et barémisation des indemnités' in B. Dubuisson and P. Jourdain (eds.), *Le dommage et sa réparation dans la responsabilité contractuelle et extracontractuelle. Etudes de droit comparé*, Brussels, Larcier, 2015, p669 at 671.

27 *König v. Germany*, 28 June 1978 (Plenary), appl. no. 6232/73 and *König v. Germany*, 10 March 1980 (just satisfaction) (Plenary), appl. no. 6232/73.

28 *König v. Germany*, 28 June 1978 (Plenary), appl. no. 6232/73, §§111 and 113–114.

29 *König v. Germany*, 10 March 1980 (just satisfaction) (Plenary), appl. no. 6232/73, §11.

explained that although it normally requires applicants to prove the size of the damages, it cannot require this in this particular case:

> it is in fact an extremely difficult matter to identify with precision the prejudice suffered as a result of the undue length of the domestic proceedings. Although applicants should as a rule quantify their claims, the Court would be failing to pay proper regard to the principle of equity imposed by Article 50 (Art. 50) were it not to take into consideration the problems confronting Dr. König in this respect. Accordingly, the Court did not deem it appropriate to have Dr. König called on to plead the exact amount of reparation he was claiming.[30]

With these observations, the Court made clear that it normally estimates the damages in a concrete manner but that it – for reasons of equity – will use an abstract manner of estimating damages in case it is (because of the nature of the damages) impossible to prove the precise size of the damages. For an applicant, it is consequently not necessary to make a precise calculation of the damages in order to receive compensation.[31] If the applicant can prove that he had suffered damages but is not able to prove the exact size of the damages, the Court will award a satisfaction by using an abstract manner to estimate the size of the damages. This also stems from *Yöyler*:

> In view of its finding that the applicant's home and possessions were destroyed by the security forces, the Court considers that it is necessary to award compensation for pecuniary damage. However, as the applicant has not substantiated his claims as to the quantity and value of his lost property with any documentary or other evidence, the Court will make its assessment of the amounts on an equitable basis.[32]

From a theoretical point of view, this is a very reasonable approach. Indeed, the Court in principle respects the idea that only the damages and not more

---

30 *Ibid.*, §19.

31 *Başkaya and Okçuoğlu v. Turkey*, 8 July 1999 (Grand Chamber), appl. nos. 23536/94 and 24408/94, §88; *Fener Rum Erkek Lisesi Vakfı v. Turkey*, 9 January 2007, appl. no. 34478/97, §§74–75; *Timpul Info-Magazin and Anghel v. Moldavia*, 27 November 2007, appl. no. 42864/05, §§45–46; *Varnava et al. v. Turkey*, 18 September 2009 (Grand Chamber), appl. no. 16064/90 et al., §224; O. Ichim, *Just satisfaction*, 2015, above n. 17, at 50 and 107; and D. Scorey and T. Eicke, *Human Rights Damages. Principles and Practices*, London, Sweet & Maxwell, at A2-47–48.

32 *Yöyler v. Turkey*, 24 July 2003, appl. no. 26973/95, §106.

than the damages must be compensated and in theory only exceptionally deviates from this rule. It thus applies a principle that is exactly the same as in some national legal systems. The problem however is that in practice the exception almost becomes the rule. This is so because human rights violations often cause non-pecuniary damages and that non-pecuniary damages by their nature do not allow a precise calculation.[33] The same holds true for future damages since the assessment of future losses involves a large number of imponderables.[34] Consequently, the Court often has no choice but to estimate the size of the damages in an abstract manner. If the Court however can estimate the damages more precisely, it will do so in most cases.[35] In some cases, however, the Court does not require a precise calculation of the pecuniary damages[36] and even of the procedural costs.[37] Pecuniary damages are also often hard to estimate.[38] Thus, the Court not

---

33 In this type of case, the Court for instance observes that 'the nature of the violation found does not allow for restitutio in integrum': *Salah v. the Netherlands*, 6 July 2006, appl. no. 8196/02, §75; *Baybasin v. the Netherlands*, 7 June 2007, appl. no. 13600/02, §77; and C. Kissling and D. Kelliher, 'Compensation for Pecuniary and Non-Pecuniary Loss' in A. Fenyves, E. Karner, H. Koziol and E. Steiner (eds.), *Tort Law in the Jurisprudence of the European Court of Human Rights*, Göttingen, De Gruyter, 2011, p579 at 624ff.

34 *Buzescu v. Romania*, 24 May 2005, appl. no. 61302/00, §105; and *Magyar Keresztény Mennonita Egyház et al. v. Hungary*, 28 June 2016 (just satisfaction), appl. no. 70945/11 et al., §47.

35 Judge Myer argues that the requirement to estimate damages in a concrete manner explains why the Court in general awards higher just satisfactions for pecuniary damages as for non-pecuniary damages: E. Myjer, 'Article 1 protocol 1 and the entitlement of just satisfaction' in H. Vandenberghe (ed.), *Propriété et droits de l'homme*, Bruges, Die Keure, 2006, p99 at 101.

36 It has been argued that this results from the fact that the ECtHR has less means to gather evidence than national courts: The Law Commission and the Scottish Law Commission, Damages under the Human Rights Act 1998. Report on a Reference under Section 3(1) (e) of the Law Commissions Act 1965, SE/2000/182, 2000, <https://www.scotlawcom.gov.uk/files/3012/7989/6877/rep180.pdf>, 68.

37 This happens in cases where the applicants complain about the violation of several articles and the Court only finds a violation of one of them: *X and Y v. the Netherlands*, 26 March 1985 (Grand Chamber), appl. no. 8978/80, §40; and *Johnston et al. v. Ireland*, 18 December 1986 (Plenary), appl. no. 9697/82, §86.

38 *Sporrong and Lönnroth v. Sweden*, 18 December 1984 (just satisfaction) (Plenary), appl. nos. 7151/75 and 7152/75, §§31–32; *Baggetta v. Italy*, 25 June 1987, appl. no. 10256/83, §29; *Martins Moreira v. Portugal*, 26 October 1988, appl. no. 11371/85, §§65–67; *Union Alimentaria Sanders SA v. Spain*, 7 July 1989, appl. no. 11681/85, §45; *Comingersoll S.A. v. Portugal*, 6 April 2000 (Grand Chamber), appl. no. 35382/97, §29; *Ernestina Zullo v. Italy*, 10 November 2004, appl. no. 64897/01, §25; *Öneryildiz v. Turkey*, 30 November 2004 (Grand Chamber), appl. no. 48939/99, §166; *Musci v. Italy*, 10 November 2004, appl. no. 64699/01, §26; *Strain et al. v. Romania*, 21 July 2005, appl. no. 57001/00, §79;

only takes into account the nature of the damages, but also takes into consideration that it is sometimes almost impossible for the victims of human rights violations to produce the required evidence.[39]

What is important however is that the Court is stricter with regard to pecuniary damages than it is with regard to non-pecuniary damages. With regard to pecuniary damages, the Court – as in *König* – in principle only makes an abstract evaluation of the damages if there is a beginning of proof.[40] An illustration can be found in the jurisprudence concerning the loss of an income due to the death of a relative. In *Ogur* for example, the Court did not award a just satisfaction for the claimed loss of income because the applicants could not demonstrate that their deceased son had an income and contributed to the household.[41] In *Cakici* on the other hand, the Court awarded just satisfaction to a woman and her children for the death of their respective husband or father because they were able to give a precise description of the income that they had lost.[42] In some cases, the Court is nevertheless quite flexible with regard to the loss of an income due to the death of a relative. Take for example *Velikova*. The Court in this case argued that the applicants must have suffered damages due to the death of their relative, although the deceased relative had no official income and the applicants could not prove what kind of income he

Lupsa v. Romania, 8 July 2006, appl. no. 10337/04, §70; *Beshiri et al. v. Albania*, 22 August 2006, appl. no. 7352/03, §112; *Rusu et al. v. Romania*, 19 July 2007, appl. no. 4198/04, §33; *Driza v. Albania*, 1 November 2007, appl. no. 33771/02, §131; *Suciu Werle v. Romania*, 13 December 2007, appl. no. 26521/05, §28; *Marini v. Albania*, 18 December 2007, appl. no. 3738/02, §185; *Kambourov v. Bulgaria*, 14 February 2008, appl. no. 55350/00, §87; *Todorova et al. v. Bulgaria*, 24 April 2008 (just satisfaction), appl. no. 48380/99 et al., §7; *Kushoglu v. Bulgaria*, 3 July 2008 (just satisfaction), appl. no. 48191/99, §9; EctHR *Kanala v. Slovakia*, 14 October 2008, appl. no. 57239/00, §16; *Skibinscy v. Poland*, 21 October 2008, appl. no. 52589/99, §18; *Teodorescu Olimpia-Maria v. Romania*, 4 November 2008, appl. no. 43774/02, §33; *Dumbrava v. Romania*, 17 February 2009, appl. no. 25234/03, §40; *Ursan v. Romania*, 6 April 2010, appl. no. 35852/04, §43; *Perdigao v. Portugal*, 16 November 2010 (Grand Chamber), appl. no. 24768/06, §85; *Denisova and Moiseyeva v. Russia*, 14 June 2011, appl. no. 16903/03, §12; *Albergas and Arlauskas v. Lithuania*, 27 May 2014, appl. no. 17978/05, §81; *S.B. v. Romania*, 23 September 2014, appl. no. 24453/04, §94; and *Zaieţ v. Romania*, 24 March 2015, appl. no. 44958/05, §67.

39 *Paratheristikos Oikodomikos Synetairismos Stegaseos Ypallilon Trapezis Tis Ellados v. Greece*, 29 January 2013 (just satisfaction), appl. no. 2998/08, §26.

40 If the Court does not find enough indications to determine the size of the damages on an equitable basis, it does not award compensation: *Vilnes et al. v. Norway*, 5 December 2013, appl. nos. 52806/09 and 22703/10, §270.

41 *Ogur v. Turkey*, 20 May 1999 (Grand Chamber), appl. no. 21594/93, §98.

42 *Çakici v. Turkey*, 8 July 1999 (Grand Chamber), appl. no. 23657/94, §127.

had earned from unofficial work.[43] Another case that is interesting in this respect is *Öneryildiz*. Here the Court argued that although the applicants could not precisely describe the contribution of their deceased adult relatives, it could judge that 'each member of the household must, in one way or another, have provided a contribution, if only an accessory one, to the sustenance of all.'[44] The same line of reasoning did not however apply to minors that had died. It seems as if the Court in this case argues on an abstract basis that the death of minor children does not cause a loss of income whereas the death of an adult child does cause a loss of income. These last cases illustrate that the Court is not only willing to accept an abstract approach to estimate the size of the damages but sometimes also towards the existence of damages. This, of course, is quite far-going. But it seems as if the Court sometimes goes even further in deviating from the principle that the damages have to be estimated precisely. This stems from an exceptional interpretative judgment. The Commission had requested the Court to motivate as to why it had granted just satisfaction in a particular case. In its interpretative judgment, the Court explicitly stated that it was not obliged to make a motivation on the reasons as to why it awards a specific just satisfaction. The Court moreover found that it was not obliged to make a difference for the compensation of pecuniary and non-pecuniary damages.[45] Some judges went even further and argued in a partially dissenting opinion that a satisfaction for a specific type of damages could at the same time also serve as a satisfaction for another type of damages.[46]

---

43 *Velikova v. Bulgaria*, 18 May 1999 (decision), appl. no. 41488/98, §102. See also: *Salman v. Turkey*, 27 June 2000 (Grand Chamber), appl. no. 21986/93, §137.

44 *Öneryildiz v. Turkey*, 30 November 2004 (Grand Chamber), appl. no. 48939/99, §168. See also: *Hornsby v. Greece*, 1 April 1998 (just satisfaction), appl. no. 18357/91, §18; *Lustig-Prean and Beckett v. the United Kingdom*, 25 July 2000 (just satisfaction), appl. nos. 31417/96 and 32377/96, §22; *Smith and Grady v. the United Kingdom*, 25 July 2000 (just satisfaction), appl. nos. 33985/96 and 33986/96, §18; *Tanli v. Turkey*, 10 April 2001, appl. no. 26129/95, §182; *Z. et al. v. the United Kingdom*, 10 May 2005 (Grand Chamber), appl. no. 29392/95, §120; *Orhan v. Turkey*, 18 June 2002, appl. no. 25656/94, §431; *Aktaş v. Turkey*, 24 April 2003, appl. no. 24351/94, §353; *Nachova et al. v. Bulgaria*, 26 February 2004, appl. nos. 43577/98 and 43579/98, §183; *Buzescu v. Romania*, 24 May 2005, appl. no. 61302/00, §105; *Denis Vasilyev v. Russia*, 17 December 2009, appl. no. 32704/04, §166; and *Basarba Ood v. Bulgaria*, 20 January 2011 (just satisfaction), appl. no. 77660/01, §20.

45 *Allenet de Ribemont v. France*, 7 August 1997 (interpretative), appl. no. 15175/89, §§22–23.

46 Partly dissenting opinion of Judges Casadevall, Bonello and Kovler in *Kingsley v. the United Kingdom*, 28 May 2002 (Grand Chamber), appl. no. 35605/97.

This benevolent approach towards the abstract estimation of damages must not be seen too easily as safe conduct for national courts. In exceptional situations, the Court might take the reasoning of national judges into account, as was illustrated in *Carvalho Pinto De Sousa Morais*.[47] The applicant underwent a surgical procedure to remove the left and right Barthlin glands of the vagina. Since the left pudental nerve had been injured during the operation, she began to experience intense pain and loss of sense in the vagina, suffered from urinary incontinence, had difficulty sitting and walking and could not have sexual relations. For this reason, the applicant filed claims in national tort law and was granted compensation for her damages. The first instance court in Portugal awarded her €80,000 in respect of non-pecuniary damages. The Supreme Administrative Court of Portugal however limited the compensation to €50,000. The court made two arguments for limiting this compensation. First, it argued that the medical fault did not cause the damages but only aggravated them. Secondly, the court relied on the fact that the applicant was 'already fifty years old at the time of the surgery and had two children, that is an age when sexuality [is] not as important as in younger years, its significance diminishing with age'. Moreover, the Supreme Administrative Court of Portugal also reduced the claimed costs for a maid that the court of first instance had awarded on the grounds that the applicant probably did not need a full-time maid because, considering the age of her children, she 'probably only needed to take care of her husband.' The ECtHR found a violation of the principle of equality in this case, because the Portuguese Supreme Court clearly based its estimation of damages on the assumption that sexuality is not as important for a 50-year-old woman and mother of two children as for someone of younger age and thus on the assumption of female sexuality as being essentially linked to child-bearing purposes. This case illustrates that national judges cannot base their estimation of damages on assumptions that violate a Convention right.

From the foregoing it must be concluded that the use of an abstract or equitable estimation of the size of the damages is often used in the jurisprudence of the ECtHR and that the Court is flexible in deviating from the principle that the damages have to be estimated on a precise manner.[48] According to Franz Bydlinski, this freedom explains why Art. 41 uses the

---

47 *Carvalho Pinto De Sousa Morais v. Portugal*, 25 July 2017, appl. no. 17484/15.

48 D. Shelton, *Remedies in International Human Rights Law*, Oxford, Oxford University Press, 1999, at 224.

phrase 'just satisfaction'.[49] Gerhard Danneman on the other hand argues that the Court sometimes uses this possibility to conceal the conflicting opinions of the judges within the Court.[50] Although the suggestion of Danneman might be true in some cases, the interpretation of Bydlinski seems to be more important.

But although there are similarities between the approach of the Court and the approach in national tort law, it must be stressed that the Court rarely motivates its practices. It thus comes as no surprise that the practice of the Court to award damages without referring to the different categories, is the subject of criticism. Take for example *Prodan*:

> In my opinion, in the present case there is no single piece of evidence which would prove the fact that the applicant actually suffered any pecuniary damage in the form claimed by her and her lawyers (...) In order to be compensated, pecuniary damage must have been established by the Court at the level of a proven 'fact' and not at the level of a 'supposition'. I regret very much that the Chamber failed to make this distinction and took a 'supposition' for a clearly established and proven legal 'fact'. Moreover, speaking about damage in this particular case the Chamber failed to indicate what kind of damages it had granted. Both civil law and the law of tort recognise different types of damages: general damages, special damages, compensatory damages, punitive damages, nominal damages etc. All of them are of a pecuniary nature. What kind of damages are we speaking about in this particular case?[51]

This particular case concerned a violation of the right to property as is protected by Art. 1 of the first protocol. The violation was caused by the fact that the government had hindered owners from disposing of their property. After the Court had found this violation, they claimed satisfaction for the suffered material damages that were caused by the fact that they had not been able to sell or rent their property. Judge Pavlovschi did however refer to the inability of the applicants to prove that they had the intent to sell

---

49 F. Bydlinski, 'Methodological Approaches to the Tort Law of the ECHR' in A. Fenyves, E. Karner, H. Koziol and E. Steiner (eds.), *Tort Law in the Jurisprudence of the European Court of Human Rights*, Göttingen, De Gruyter, 2011, p29 at 105.

50 G. Danneman, *Schadensersatz bei Verletzung der Europaïscher Menschenrechtskonvention*, PhD, Freiburg, Keulen, 1994, at 69.

51 Partly dissenting opinion of Judge Pavlovschi in *Prodan v. Moldavia*, 18 May 2004, appl. no. 49806/99. See also: Joint partly dissenting opinion of Judges Sajo, Karakas and Tsotsoria that has been joined by Judge Steiner in *Centro Europa 7 S.R.L. and Di Stefano v. Italy*, 7 June 2012, appl. no. 38433/09.

or rent their property or that they would have been able to find buyers or tenants within due time.[52]

This criticism illustrates the lack of a clear approach towards the estimation of pecuniary damages. Although one can blame this fact on the manifold use of the abstract estimation of damages, this cannot explain the entire problem. Indeed, it is one thing to know whether one estimates the damages precisely or in an abstract manner, but it is another thing to know how precisely the Court uses the abstract manner of calculation. At the start of this chapter it was shown that one can do this by referring to tables where all kind of damages are indicated or on an equitable basis. So, since different modes of abstract calculation exist, one must look to the Court's approach. Due to a lack of motivation the jurisprudence of the Court does not however give much indication as to the used approach. The only thing that seems to be true is that the Court more and more often bases the size of just satisfactions on its older jurisprudence.[53] It has even been argued that the Court internally uses tables that are unknown to the outside world.[54]

3.2. SHARED RESPONSIBILITY OF TORTFEASOR AND VICTIM

3.2.1. The Contributory Fault of the Victim Leads to Shared Liability

The question that arises now is whether the Court takes into account the fault of the victim when it determines the size of the just satisfaction as is done in several national legal systems. Article 2 of the Practice Direction

---

52 The criticism of Judge Pavlovschi nonetheless contradicts other jurisprudence of the Court where it finds that applicants would probably have rented the houses: *Popov v. Moldavia*, 17 January 2006 (just satisfaction), appl. no. 74153/01, §11; and *Ermicev v. Moldavia*, 8 August 2006, appl. no. 42288/02. It seems that the Court will only accept that an applicant does not have an intention to rent a property if he lives in it: *Calvo v. Italy*, 11 March 2004, appl. no. 59636/00.

53 *Ilhan v. Turkey*, 27 June 2000 (Grand Chamber), appl. no. 22277/93, §112; *Özgür Gündem v. Turkey*, 16 March 2000, appl. no. 23144/93, §84; and *A. et al. v. the United Kingdom*, 19 February 2009 (Grand Chamber), appl. no. 3455/05.

54 O. Ichim, *Just Satisfaction*, 2015, above n. 17, at 121. This also stems from *Holomiov* where Judge Pavlovschi in his dissenting opinion criticized the size of the awarded satisfaction for non-pecuniary damages for the reason that they were not in line with the satisfaction that the Court had granted in earlier cases: Partly concurring, partly dissenting opinion of Judge Pavlovschi in *Holomiov v. Moldova*, 7 November 2006, appl. no. 30649/05.

concerning Just Satisfaction Claims stipulates that the ECtHR can award a just satisfaction that is smaller in size than the suffered damages for reasons of equity. The stipulation then explicitly states that the Court might do so if the victim himself made a fault. From this stipulation, it seems that the Court applies a form of shared responsibility if the victim makes a fault himself.

An interesting line of jurisprudence with regard to this topic is the jurisprudence where the Court finds a violation of the requirement to make a judgment within a reasonable time as is required by Art. 6.[55] In this jurisprudence, the Court does not only look at the own fault as an element in the context of Art. 41, but also in its reasoning on the merits.[56] Indeed, in order to determine whether or not a state violated the reasonable time requirement, the Court has to take into account the complexity of the national case, the behavior of the state and the behavior of the applicant.[57] The Court for example considers whether the applicant had often requested a suspension of the case,[58] whether the applicant was present at the hearings in the national case,[59] whether the applicants informed the national courts adequately on what they were doing,[60] and whether the applicant had used all the procedural means so as to speed up his procedure.[61] The Court does not however only take the behavior of the applicant into account as to decide on the merits of the case, it even does so as to judge whether an applicant has an interest in filing a case (as is required for a case to be admissible). In *Shefer*, the Court for instance argues that the applicant had no interest in filing a case for the reason that he had not taken any procedural steps for a long time.[62] The Court found that the negligence of the applicant to take actions in a long time illustrated that he was not really interested in the progress of the case.

Since this book showed earlier that there is a strong connection between the notion of an interest as a condition of admissibility and the

---

55 M.L. Van Emmerik, *Schadevergoeding bij schending van mensenrechten. De rechtspraktijk onder het EVRM vergeleken met die in Nederland*, Stichting NJCM-Boekerij, Leiden, 1997, at 180.

56 With regard to this topic, see: V. Wilcox and O. Riss, 'Contributory Negligence' in A. Fenyves, E. Karner, H. Koziol and E. Steiner (eds.), *Tort Law in the Jurisprudence of the European Court of Human Rights*, Göttingen, De Gruyter, 2011, p771 at 776–779.

57 *Zimmermann and Steiner v. Switzerland*, 13 July 1983, appl. no. 8737/79, §24.

58 *Pedersen and Baadsgaard v. Denmark*, 19 June 2003, appl. no. 49017/99, §44.

59 *Smirnova v. Russia*, 24 July 2003, appl. nos. 46133/99 and 48183/99, §86.

60 *Klamecki v. Poland*, 28 March 2002, appl. no. 25415/94, §93.

61 *Union Alimentaria Sanders SA v. Spain*, 7 July 1989, appl. no. 11681/85, §35.

62 *Shefer v. Russia*, 13 March 2012 (Decision), appl. no. 45175/04, §§25–27.

notion of damages under Art. 41, it seems logical that this approach is also extended to the application of the last provision. In this sense it was demonstrated that the finding of a violation in itself might suffice as a just satisfaction (a so-called declaratory judgment) if the victim himself made a fault. In the same way it is also possible that the Court finds that the state still has to pay an – although more limited – amount of damages.[63] The applicants in these cases only had the right to the reparation of a part of the damages he suffered.

Another illustration of the application of the principle of the own fault can be found in *Pressos Compania Naviera*.[64] This case has already been discussed in the first part of this book in the context of the subsidiarity of Art. 41, because the Court in this case only awarded a just satisfaction to one of the applicants and judged that the other applicants had a case pending before a national court and had a good chance of receiving full compensation of their damages via these procedures. Thus, the party that received a just satisfaction from the Court was – as all the other applicants – a shipping company that had suffered damages due to a shipping accident where a state-employed shipping pilot had been involved. The company had sued the government for damages in a Belgian Court but had lost the case because the Belgian lawmaker had, after the case had been brought before the Court, passed a law that stipulated that the Belgian state could not be held responsible for the damages caused by the negligence of its shipping pilots. This law entered into force retroactively. When this case was brought before the Court, it judged that retroactivity of the law violated the applicant's right to property as enshrined in Art. 1 of the first protocol. The applicant then claimed one million Belgian francs as compensation for the material damages. This was the amount of money that the applicant in a national procedure had been ordered to pay to the owner of another ship that had been damaged by the ship of the applicant (on which the state-employed shipping pilot was present) increased with interest.

The defending government however argued that it was not sure that had the retroactive law not been applicable and had the national judge judged on the merits of the case, he would have found the state liable. Indeed, it had been possible that the accident could have been attributed to both the captain of the ship who was employed by the applicant and the

---

63 *Luberti v. Italy*, 23 February 1984, appl. no. 9019/80, §41; *Capuano v. Italy*, 25 June 1987, appl. no. 9381/81, §§28–29; and *A. et al. v. Denmark*, 8 February 1996, appl. no. 20826/92, §86.

64 *Pressos Compania Naviera S.A. et al. v. Belgium*, 20 November 1995 (just satisfaction), appl. no. 17849/91.

state-employed shipping pilot. The government, in other words, pointed to the applicant's responsibility for at least a part of the damages. Although the Court in this case did not explicitly deal with the arguments of the defending government, it seems that it took them into account. It judged that the 'apportionment of liability' was unsure and ruled that it was equitable to award half of the damages to the applicant.[65]

Another situation in which the Court attributes a part of the damages to the applicant, is when the applicant committed a crime. As was discussed before, the Court regularly makes declaratory judgments. But it sometimes just offers a more limited compensation. Franz Bydlinski for example mentions that the Court in *Doran* awarded a remarkably small amount of damages because the applicants, whose right to a fair trial had been violated, had committed serious crimes.[66] Dinah Shelton notes in the same way that the Court in *Ribbitsch*[67]curiously granted a lower amount of damages than the applicant had claimed and against which claim the government had not filed a protest.[68] She argues that this deviation from the principle that the Court normally awards a sum of money if the defendant state does not make objections, must be ascribed to the fact that the applicant had sold heroin and had caused the deaths of two persons. The same is true in *Makaratzis*. The Court awarded the applicant in this case only a limited satisfaction after the state had noted that the applicant had put the life of other people in danger.[69]

It is not clear on the basis of which principles the Court divides the damages between the applicant and the state. The Court never indicates whether it bases the division of responsibility on the criteria of faultiness or on the criteria of causality.[70] Different arguments can be made. On the one hand, it seems that the Court takes into account the gravity of the fault since this might explain why it sometimes does not award any compensation at all in cases where applicants committed crimes. It would also be hard to see how the crime would have contributed in a causal way to, for example, the exceeding of the reasonable time. On the other

---

65 *Ibid.*, §20.

66 *Doran v. Ireland*, 31 July 2003, appl. no. 50389/99 and F. Bydlinski, 'Methodological Approaches', 2011, above n. 49, p29 at 97.

67 *Ribitsch v. Austria*, 4 July 1994, appl. no. 18896/91.

68 D. Shelton, *Remedies*, 1999, above n. 48, at 227.

69 *Makaratzis v. Greece*, 20 December 2004 (Grand Chamber), appl. no. 50385/99, §§91–93.

70 Moreover, the Court is not obliged to indicate the amount of damages it would have granted to the applicants if they had not made a contributory fault: V. Wilcox and O. Riss, 'Contributory Negligence', 2011, above n. 56, p771 at 784–785.

hand, one might argue that the Court – as seen before – does not take into account whether or not an applicant is mentally ill. This raises the question of how one can attribute a part of the damages on the basis of fault to someone who has no sense of guilt. It seems as if there are no clear criteria in the jurisprudence of the Court.

What is also interesting to know is whether the Court imputes the fault of the direct victim to its relatives. A previous chapter showed that the relatives of a deceased person can claim compensation for their moral damages. As far as is known, there is however no jurisprudence where the Court awards a satisfaction to the relatives of a deceased person that made a fault. The only jurisprudence that can be referred to is that where the Court made a declaratory judgment when the deceased person had committed a crime.[71] Although this jurisprudence seems to indicate that the Court will adhere the fault of the deceased victim to the relatives, this is open to doubt. Because these judgments all relate to non-pecuniary damages, one can moreover question whether this hypothesis can be extended to pecuniary damages as well.

3.2.2. Predetermination of the Victim

If the ECtHR has to judge on the existence of a human rights violation, it often takes into account the age of the victim. For example, the Court will more easily find a violation of Art. 2 of the Convention if a victim is very old[72] or very young.[73] It thus comes as no surprise that the Court also takes the age of the victim into account when judging on Art. 41. In *Hutten-Czapska*, the Court for example took into account that the victim was very old and in bad health for settling the amount of moral damages for the violation of the requirement to make a judgment within a reasonable time.[74] In the cases of *Anguelova* and *Dolgova*, the Court made a similar line of reasoning with regard to Art. 5 of the Convention.[75]

---

71 *McKerr v. the United Kingdom*, 4 May 2001, appl. no. 28883/95, §181.

72 *Dushka v. Ukraine*, 3 February 2011, appl. no. 29175/04, §53. See also: *Lungu v. Moldavia*, 9 May 2006, appl. no. 3021/02, §23.

73 *Z. et al. v. the United Kingdom*, 10 May 2005 (Grand Chamber), appl. no. 29392/95; *Mubilanzila, Mayeka and Kaniki Mitunga v. Belgium*, 12 October 2006, appl. no. 13178/03, §69; and *Corsacov v. Moldavia*, 4 April 2006, appl. no. 18944/02, §§86–87.

74 *Hutten-Czapska v. Poland*, 19 June 2006 (Grand Chamber), appl. no. 35014/97, §248. See also: *Kostovska v. the former Yugoslav Republic of Macedonia*, 15 June 2006, appl. no. 44353/02, §58.

75 *Anguelova v. Bulgaria*, 13 June 2002, appl. no. 38361/97, §173; and *Dolgova v. Russia*, 2 March 2006, appl. no. 11886/05, §59.

In the case of *Anguelova* this was most clear. The Court in this case awarded a satisfaction of €19,500 for the harm that the minor victim had suffered from an unlawful detention. This amount of money was over five times the amount that an applicant in the similar case of *Velikova* had received, but which applicant was an adult person and not a minor as in *Anguelova*.[76] These cases suggest that a human rights violator must take the applicant as he is. It seems as if the Court takes into account the concrete characteristics of the damaged person in order to determine the size of the damages by judging that the violation of the reasonable time is more harmful for an old person in bad health as for a normal adult person or by judging that minors suffer more from an unlawful detention than normal adults.

The question now arises of whether the Court considers the fact that victims are predetermined to suffer some type of damages. There are no cases known where the Court had to judge on the size of the damages in a situation where the damaged person would have suffered the damages anyway. Situations that might be thought of with this regard are the death of a person with a deadly disease or the injury of a person that was determined to suffer from this specific handicap. In national tort law, it is sometimes argued that liable persons in those cases do not have to compensate the death or handicap of the victim but only have to compensate for the fact that the death or injury was caused earlier. Since the ECtHR has no jurisprudence where it directly deals with this issue, it is uncertain whether this approach in national tort law can be justified by the Convention. Nevertheless, there are arguments that support this claim. With regard to causality, the Court takes into account the protective purpose of the rule in the context of legal causality. The Court only awards satisfactions for the damages that were directly and reasonably caused by the human rights violation. It thus seems reasonable, especially when one takes into account the margin of appreciation of states, that the Court would accept the application of this criterion with regard to the predetermination of the damages.

3.3. THE VICTIM'S DUTY TO MITIGATE DAMAGES

In most legal systems, victims of a tort have a duty to mitigate their damages. If, for example, their car is damaged, and they need a car to go

---

76 In this case, the Court granted 8,000 Bulgarian Lev (about €4,000) to the applicants: *Velikova v. Bulgaria*, 18 May 1999 (decision), appl. no. 41488/98, §102.

to work, they are supposed to hire a not too expensive car so that they can continue their work and do not suffer a loss of income. If a victim suffers from a health problem because of a tort, he is expected to go to a doctor and take the appropriate steps to limit the damages. The *ratio legis* of this principle is to limit the costs of torts on society as a whole. The question however arises whether this principle can be reconciled with human rights. Indeed, cannot a victim appeal to his right to privacy and a personal life when he decides as to how he will deal with his damages. Take for example the situation where a person suffers aesthetic damages because of a wound to his face. It might be possible to limit this damage by undergoing aesthetic-surgery. But can one force a victim to have surgery if he fears the treatment? Or can one force a Jehovah's witness to have a blood transfusion even though his religious views forbid it? Thus, if a lawyer is confronted with such a situation, he will have to take into account the human rights of the victim.

A first indication as to whether the duty to mitigate damages can be reconciled with the ECHR, can be found in the jurisprudence of the Court with regard to Art. 41. The Court does consider this principle itself when it awards just satisfactions under Art. 41.[77] A first case that illustrates this is *Campbell and Cosans.*[78] The Court in this case found a violation of the right to education as is enshrined in Art. 2 of the first protocol. The Court then had to judge whether the applicant could receive an award for material damages that resulted from the lesser chances on the job market due to his suspension from school. The Court in this case observed that the applicant had not contributed to the coming into being of the damages. Indeed, the suspension from his school had to be ascribed to the school. The Court noted that Jeffrey Cosans had breached the disciplinary rules of his school, but it argued that his suspension from school was both out of proportion to the disciplinary offence committed and in violation of Art. 2 of the first protocol to the Convention. The Court then argued that the schooling of Jeffrey would probably have led to no more than a limited qualification. But although limited, it still is a qualification that has

77 Apart from damages, the procedural costs of the parties also have to be proportionate to the alleged violation: *Pridatchenko et al. v. Russia*, 21 June 2007, appl. nos. 2191/03, 3104/03, 16094/03 and 24486/03, §69. See also: F. Bydlinski, 'Methodological Approaches', 2011, above n. 49, p29 at 46.

78 *Campbell and Cosans v. the United Kingdom*, 25 February 1982, appl. nos. 7511/76 and 7743/76.

been lost and thus has to be compensated. The Court however made the following observations:

> The entire responsibility for his situation cannot be attributed to the respondent State: Jeffrey does not appear to have pursued to the full the possibility of undertaking further study and training, and he did not react to the suggestion made by the Government in this connection (see paragraph 24, sub-paragraph (b), above). Again, whilst he did make some attempts to earn a living on a self-employed basis, he remained for a considerable period unregistered with the local employment exchange. Finally, it has to be recognised that in the current economic situation even many of those who have completed their education and training experience problems in finding employment. The Court therefore concludes that, whilst the suspension may well have contributed to the material difficulties which Jeffrey encountered, it cannot be regarded as the principal cause thereof.[79]

A similar conclusion can be drawn from *Baggetta*.[80] The applicant in this case had been employed by a railway company. When he was charged in a criminal procedure, he was found to be unable to continue exercising his job. Since the procedure had exceeded the reasonable time as required by Art. 6, the applicant claimed just satisfaction for the protracted impossibility to exercise his job. The Court however found that there was no reason to assume that 'Mr. Baggetta was unable to take up other paid work and thus mitigate his material loss.'[81] The Court's refusal to award just satisfaction for material damages was thus clearly based on the duty of the applicant to limit his damages. Another case where the Court referred to the duty to reduce damages in a case concerning the reasonable length of procedure, is *Rehbock*. In this case the Court did not award a just satisfaction for physical damages for the following reason:

> the Court must take into account the fact that the applicant had not been willing to undergo the appropriate treatment for his injury in Slovenia notwithstanding the view of medical specialists that surgery was necessary.[82]

These cases illustrate that the ECtHR itself finds that applicants have a duty to mitigate their damages. In *Humen*, the Court moreover found that

---

79 *Campbell and Cosans v. the United Kingdom*, 22 March 1983 (just satisfaction), appl. nos. 7511/76 and 7743/76, §26.

80 *Baggetta v. Italy*, 25 June 1987, appl. no. 10256/83.

81 *Ibid.*, §28.

82 *Rehbock v. Slovenia*, 28 November 2000, appl. no. 29462/95, §108.

the difficulties that national judges encounter when tort victims do not mitigate their damages, can justify the exceeding of the requirement to provide a judgment within due time. The applicant in this case had been wounded in prison. In order to receive compensation for the damages that resulted from his wounds, he had sued the government in national tort law. Because the national procedures kept on going, he sued the state in the ECtHR for the violation of Art. 6 of the Convention. The Court did not however find such a violation. It found that the excessive length of the procedures was partly caused by the applicant himself who had refused to undergo a brain scan that could have been useful to determine the existence and the size of the damages.[83] Thus, because the applicant had made it difficult for the judges to determine the existence and the size of the damages, the Court found no violation of Art. 6 of the Convention.

Apart from the jurisprudence of the ECtHR, there are also some national cases that are interesting with regard to this issue. Take for example the cases of the Dutch high court concerning blood transfusions that were discussed before. In these cases, a tortfeasor had been ordered to undergo a blood test to determine whether a victim had been infected with HIV. These cases clearly illustrate how human rights influence the possibility to order a tortfeasor to award restitution in kind. Although these cases concern the human rights of tortfeasors, the Dutch High Court did refer to the victim's duty to mitigate damages. This case has already been discussed in this book. The case concerned a situation where the blood of a doctor was intermingled with that of a patient and where the doctor invoked his right to private life under Art. 8 of the Convention to refuse a blood investigation. A previous chapter illustrated that the Dutch High Court in this case has argued that the rights of the doctor under Art. 8 were not violated. What is interesting in this case is that the Court noted that the duty of the doctor to undergo a blood examination cannot be perceived as problematic because the law in the same way expects from victims to mitigate their damages.[84] It thus seems that the Dutch High Court finds that the criteria under which it has to decide whether restitution in kind is possible, is comparable to the criteria that have to be used to judge whether a victim has a duty to mitigate its damages.

But although the Dutch High Court correctly stressed that the application of human rights on the duty to provide *restitutio in integrum* is

83 *Humen v. Poland*, 15 October 1999 (Grand Chamber), appl. no. 26614/95, §66.
84 High Court of the Netherlands, 12 December 2003, C02/193, §3.4.2.

comparable with the application of human rights on the duty to mitigate the damages, it must be stressed that these two things are not one and the same. Indeed, with regard to the duty to provide *restitutio in integrum*, one has to look at whether the human rights of the tortfeasor are violated whereas the duty to mitigate the damages concerns the human rights of the victim. As a result, there is a shift in perspective and thus also in interests. A previous chapter showed that the rights of the tortfeasor in most cases will prevent the restitution in kind and will make the judge award a financial compensation instead. This has as a consequence that in most tort cases the victim will receive a sum of money as compensation. Thus, where the interest of the tortfeasor with regard to the form of restitution lies in the fact that he does not want to be obliged to make some handling or to undergo a treatment, the interest of the victim with regard to the obligation to mitigate damages lies in the amount of money that he will receive as compensation for his damages. Thus, if the victim does not mitigate his damages as is required, he will only be compensated for the amount of damages that are reasonable. The difference between the obligation of the tortfeasor to award restitution in kind and the obligation of the victim to mitigate his damages, thus differs in the respect that the victim cannot be forced by this principle to act in a similar way, whereas the tortfeasor can be forced to act in a similar way. Consequently, from a human rights perspective, there is much more at stake for a tortfeasor who is obliged to act in a specific way than for a victim that is free to act in a way it deems necessary, but that has to bear the financial consequences thereof. Indeed, if a victim refuses to undergo a medical treatment, his interest does not directly lie in the protection of Art. 8 (as is the case of the tortfeasor that is confronted with an obligation to award restitution in kind), but in the amount of money that he can possibly receive.[85]

To evaluate these ideas more precisely, it is interesting to look at a case that was judged by the '*kantonrechter*' of Amsterdam in the field of labor law.[86] A bus driver that suffered from diabetes mellitutis had been declared incompetent to continue his job but still received compensation from his employer. This incompetency had to be examined on a regular

[85] In cases where the violation had been caused by a forced medical treatment, the Court would presumably have found a violation of the Convention. This is so because the Convention does not allow forced medical treatment: N. Moreham, 'The Right to Respect for Private Life in the European Convention on Human Rights: A Re-examination', *European Human Rights Law Review*, 2008, p44 at 50.

[86] Sector Kanton Rechtbank Amsterdam, 9 August 2012.

basis. On one of these examinations, the doctor that was hired by the employer had found that the employee should be able to continue his job in the near future if he underwent the right medical treatment. The employee however refused to follow the said treatment. Instead he used alternative approaches by going to the gym on a regular basis and by taking tablets of Surinamese herbs. Accordingly, the employer stopped paying the compensation to the employee from the moment that the employee, according to the doctor, would have been healthy if he had used the indicated treatment. The employee however found that this action of the employer violated his right to private life as enshrined in Art. 8 of the Convention. The judge who had to deal with this case argued that the employee is indeed free to choose the medical treatment he wants to follow, and that this freedom is based on the horizontal application of human rights. The judge however continued to argue that these rights can be limited. He consequently applied the proportionality test on this case and argued that the interest of the employee was not that great since it only existed in the limitation of the compensation that was paid by the employer for the delay in the healing process.

Another interesting judgment is one of the Austrian High Court, the *Oberste Gerichtshof*, from 22 June 2011.[87] The applicant in this case was a Jehovah's witness who had been the victim of a car accident and who had refused to undergo a blood transfusion. The Austrian High Court in this case argued that the freedom of religion and conscience cannot have as a result that when one makes a decision with adverse consequences, one does not have to bear these consequences. If this were the case, then Jehovah's witnesses would receive preferential treatment. This, according to the Court, would violate the principle of equality. Barbara Steininger criticized this judgment by arguing that the case violates the principle that a tortfeasor has to take his victim the way he is.[88] She compares this case with the situation where a victim is in bad health. In such cases, the tortfeasor must pay compensation for all damages, whether or not another victim in good health would have suffered lesser damages. He cannot claim that he was unable to know that the victim was of bad health and would suffer a lot of damages. This comparison does not seem to be correct. The obligation to mitigate damages and the rule that the tortfeasor has to take the concrete victim as he is, have different conditions

87 Oberste Gerichtshof 22 June 2011, 2 Ob 219/10k.

88 B. Steininger, 'Austria' in K. Oliphant and B. Steininger (eds.), *European Tort Law 2011*, Berlin, De Gruytrer, 2012, p37 at 57.

of application. The duty to mitigate damages is applicable in cases where a victim has to choose how to deal with his damages after the damages occurred. The rule that the tortfeasor has to take the concrete victim as he is, is applicable in situations where a victim has a specific characteristic that was already there and did not occur as a result of a decision after the damage occurred. The difference between these two principles lies in the presence or absence of the victim's possibility to act freely. Consequently, the two situations that Steiniger compares are based on an objective criterion of differentiation.

3.4. THE ACCEPTANCE OF A RISK

Another interesting question is whether the size of the compensation can be influenced by the fact that a victim took a large risk.[89] If someone for example participates in sport games or exercises a dangerous job, one can wonder whether he did not accept the chance to be a victim of damages. Although this situation seems to give rise to specific questions, tort law can conceive this problem as a specific application of the own fault of the victim.[90] The specific situation however gives rise to a specific question. By referring to the acceptance of a risk, it seems as if it is possible to willingly renounce from the possibility to claim compensations if a tort would occur. This raises the question of whether this approach can be reconciled with human rights.

At first sight it seems as if the notion of the acceptance of a risk does not necessarily conflict with the ECHR. According to the Court people can waive their Convention rights. The waiver can however only be established in an unequivocal manner and if there are minimal guarantees that are proportionate to the interest of the right that is waived.[91] Both of these

---

89 B. Dubuisson, V. Callewaert, B. De Coninck and G. Gathem, *La Responsabilité civile. Chronique de jurisprudence 1996–2007*, Part 1, Le fait générateur et le lien causal, Brussels, Larcier, 2009, at 355.

90 B. Weyts, *De fout van het slachtoffer in het buitencontractueel aansprakelijkheidsrecht*, Antwerp, Intersentia, 2003, at 181.

91 In *Deweer*, the Court for instance observed that the applicant could in principle waive his right to have access to a judge in order to make a settlement but judged that in the concrete case the applicant had not waived this right as a free man: *Deweer v. Belgium*, 27 February 1980, appl. no. 6903/75, §49ff. See also: *Barbera, Messegué and Jabardo v. Spain*, 6 December 1988 (Plenary), appl. nos. 10588/83, 10589/83 and 10590/83, §82; *Oberschlick v. Austria*, 23 May 1991 (Plenary), appl. no. 11662/85, §51; *Pfeifer and Plankl v. Austria*, 25 February 1992, appl. no. 10802/84, §37; and *Hermi v. Italy*, 18 October 2006 (Grand Chamber), appl. no. 18114/02, §73.

criteria have to be respected. It is possible for example that the Court finds that one can waive his rights because the minimal guarantees are provided, but that it finds that the applicant did not unequivocally waive his rights.[92] This is possible when the Court finds that the applicant was somehow forced to waive his rights[93] or when the Court judges that an applicant was unable to assess the implications of his waiver of rights for the reason that he was unable to have the required knowledge.[94] But although the waiver of rights has to be established in an unequivocal manner, it is not required that this waiver is made in an explicit manner.[95] The Court in one case even ruled that an implicit waiver of rights can be found in a situation where victims must have known that a procedure should have been followed (because it was prescribed by the law) and where they did not object to the fact that it was not followed.[96]

Because a waiver of rights can be done in a tacit manner, the Convention in theory must accept that victims do not receive a (part of their) compensation if they accept a risk. The acceptance of a risk can be perceived as an implicit waiver of their rights. It should not however be forgotten that the ECtHR requires minimal guarantees and takes into account the principle of proportionality. For this reason, it is clear that the Court does not permit a waiver of rights that it deems to be very fundamental.[97] One can for example not waive his right not to be tortured.[98] Neither is a waiver of rights possible when it relates to very important public interests.[99] In *Konstantin Markin* the Court for example found that gender equality

---

92 *NeuMayster v. Austria*, 7 May 1974 (just satisfaction), appl. no. 1936/63, §36; *Albert and Le Compte v. Belgium*, 10 February 1983 (Plenary), appl. nos. 7299/75 and 7496/76, §35; and *Colozza v. Italy*, 12 February 1985, appl. no. 9024/80, §28.

93 *Deweer v. Belgium*, 27 February 1980, appl. no. 6903/75, §49.

94 In the case of *Pfeifer and Plankl* the Court judged that a waiver of a right to have access to a judge was illegitimate because the applicants, who lacked judicial support from an attorney, were unable to estimate the implications of this waiver: *Pfeifer and Plankl v. Austria*, 25 February 1992, appl. no. 10802/84, §§38–39. See also: *D.H. et al. v. the Czech Republic*, 13 November 2007 (Grand Chamber), appl. no. 57325/00, §202.

95 *Le Compte, Van Leuven and De Meyere v. Belgium*, 23 June 1981 (Plenary), appl. nos. 6878/75 and 7238/75, §59.

96 *Hakansson and Sturesson v. Sweden*, 21 February 1990, appl. no. 11855/85, §67.

97 M. Busstra, 'Eigen verantwoordelijkheid bij mensenrechten: een verkenning binnen het EVRM-systeem', *NJCM-Bulletin* 2008, p345 at 353.

98 *Chahal v. the United Kingdom*, 15 November 1996 (Grand Chamber), appl. no. 22414/93, §80; *Egmez v. Cyprus*, 21 December 2000, appl. no. 30873/96, §§76–77; and *Gäfgen v. Germany*, 1 June 2010 (Grand Chamber), appl. no. 22978/05, §87.

99 *Hakansson and Sturesson v. Sweden*, 21 February 1990, appl. no. 11855/85, §66; *Sejdovic v. Turkey*, 1 March 2006 (Grand Chamber), appl. no. 56581/00, §86; and *Hermi v. Italy*, 18 October 2006 (Grand Chamber), appl. no. 18114/02, §73.

is so fundamental that one cannot waive from this right.[100] This case concerned a male soldier who was unable to go on parental relief whereas his female colleagues were able to do this. The defending government in this case argued that the applicant had waived his right to equal treatment by signing his contract with the military. The Court did not however agree with this line of reasoning and pointed out that the right not to be discriminated against on the basis of gender cannot be waived, just as it is impossible to waive from the right not to be discriminated against on the basis of race.

With respect to the acceptance of a risk, the question will generally be raised whether one can waive his right to restitution as is guaranteed by Art. 1 of the first protocol. Jurisprudence on this topic lacks, but it seems reasonable that the right to receive restitution is not as fundamental for public interest as the principle of non-discrimination on account of sex or race. Indeed, the previous sections illustrated that the Court takes into account the own fault of the victim when awarding restitution and that the acceptance of a risk can be qualified as such an acceptance.[101] Moreover, the Court does not only take into account faults of the applicant when awarding just satisfaction, it also takes into account neutral acts that influence the size of the damages. A neutral act cannot only result in a limitation of the just satisfaction, but can also have as a result that the Court will not find a violation of the Convention at all.[102] Indeed, the Court has in some cases argued that people who choose to be a public personality such as politicians and celebrities, enjoy a more limited protection of their right to privacy then ordinary citizens. Since they entered public life, they can reasonably expect to become a topic of public interest.[103] If one enters the public sphere as a public figure, one waives a part of his right to privacy, which does not however mean that one waives all his privacy rights. Also, public figures have a right to privacy that must be protected. The audience is, in other words, not entitled to know everything about the private life of public figures.[104] It cannot be accepted that someone, by entering the public sphere, waives all key aspects of his right to privacy.

---

100 *Konstantin Markin v. Russia*, 22 March 2012 (Grand Chamber), appl. no. 30078/06, §150.

101 C. Van Dam, *European Tort Law*, Oxford, Oxford University Press, 2013, at 375–376.

102 M. Busstra, 'Eigen verantwoordelijkheid', 2008, above n. 97, p345 at 354.

103 *Lingens v. Austria*, 8 June 1986 (Plenary), appl. no. 9815/82, §43; *Tammer v. Estland*, 6 February 2001, appl. no. 41205/98, §68; and *Dichand et al. v. Austria*, 26 February 2002, appl. no. 29271/95, §37ff.

104 *Von Hannover v. Germany*, 24 June 2004, appl. no. 59320/00, §67ff.

4. DETERRENCE AND THE SIZE OF RESTITUTION

A last topic of interest is the influence of deterrence on the size of the restitution. Since the first chapters of this book argued that the lawmaker can use tort law as an instrument to effectively protect human rights in private relations and that tort law in this context sometimes needs to have a deterrent effect, the question arises whether the ECtHR can stimulate the deterrent function of tort law.

4.1. PUNITIVE DAMAGES

4.1.1. English Law

A first question with regard to this topic is whether the ECtHR stimulates the use of punitive damages. Punitive damages have their origin in English tort law.[105] They can be explained as a sum of money that a liable person has to pay on top of the compensation of the damages as a way to repay the injustice that one has done and as a way to deter future tortfeasors.[106] The most important aim is to teach tortfeasors that torts don't reward.[107] They also have a regulatory function. Punitive damages make the proceedings rewarding for injured parties. As a consequence, people who suffer damages will start procedures more easily and by doing so will contribute to the maintenance of law and order.[108]

105 This function of damages is also recognized in French, Austrian and US law: U. Magnus, 'Comparative Report', 2001, above n. 5, p185 at 186.

106 However, one must remember that tort law originally pursued punitive goals. In the oldest codifications in history, tort law and criminal law were one field of law. As such, it aimed to bring private revenge in line with the talio principle: P. Lucas, 'Pourrait-on évaluer le cas Noël Simar?' in R. Capart and J. Bouckourt (eds.), *Liber Amicorum Nöel Simar: Evaluation du dommage, Responsabilité civile et Assurances*, Limal, Anthemis, 2013, p21 at 23ff. Also, in Roman law torts aimed revenge via a private punishment and were not primarily aimed at compensation: D. Deroussin, *Histoire du droit des obligations*, Paris, Economica, 2007, at 643. It was only due to the influence of canon law and medieval urban law that tort law and criminal law separated, and that tort law became primarily concerned with the compensation of damages: J. Hallebeek, 'Buitencontractuele aansprakelijkheid aan de vooravond van de moderne samenleving' in B. Debaenst and B. Delbecke (eds.), *Vangnet of springplank? Het buitencontractuele aansprakelijkheidsrecht in een moderne samenleving (1804-heden)*, Bruges, Die Keure, 2014, p15 at 22–23.

107 U. Magnus, 'Why is US Tort Law so Different?', *JETL* 2010, p102 at 105.

108 This element is important in the United States: I. Englard, *The Philosophy of Tort Law*, Dartmouth, Publishing Company, 1993, at 147.

In England, the possibility to award punitive damages was limited by the case of *Rookes v. Barnard.*[109] The Supreme Court in this case ruled that judges can only award punitive damages if a public servant acted in an arbitrary or unconstitutional manner or if someone committed a tort with the aim of gaining profit. Since then, the English Law Commission has proposed up to two times to re-extend the field of application of punitive damages. In 1993 and 1997, the English Law Commission proposed to introduce punitive damages in general tort law.[110] The idea was that it should only become possible to award punitive damages in case a tortfeasor, when committing a tort, illustrated a 'deliberate and outrageous disregard of the plaintiff's rights' and, if other remedies were insufficient, to deter the tortfeasor. This would not be the case if, for example, the tortfeasor had already been convicted in criminal law. If these conditions were met, so argued the English Law Commission, a judge has a discretionary competence to award punitive damages. He should however take into account the presence of other (non-criminal) sanctions.

4.1.2. The European Convention on Human Rights

In order to know whether punitive damages can be reconciled with the European Convention on Human Rights, it is necessary to look at whether the Court itself awards punitive damages under Art. 41. The text of Art. 41 is however a bit ambiguous with regard to this topic. On the one hand, the Convention grants the Court a wide margin of appreciation as to choose whether it awards a just satisfaction to the applicants. According to Jean-Luc Flauss, this wide margin of appreciation makes it possible for the Court to use the just satisfaction as a way to teach states that they have to respect the treaty in a practical and not merely in a theoretical manner.[111] On the other hand, Art. 41 only allows the Court to award a just satisfaction to applicants if national law does not provide full

---

109 House of Lords, *Rooks v. Barnard* (1964) AC 1129 and (1964) 1 A11 ER 367. See also: V. Wilcox, 'Punitive Damages in England' in H. Koziol and V. Wilcox (eds.), *Punitive Damages: Common Law and Civil Law Perspectives*, Vienna, Springer, 2009, p7 at 8ff; and U. Magnus, 'Why is US Tort Law so Different?', 2010, above n. 107, p102 at 105.

110 Law Commission, Consultation Paper No. 132: aggravated, examples and restitutionary damages, <https://s3-eu-west-2.amazonaws.com/lawcom-prod-storage-11jsxou24uy7q/uploads/2016/08/No.132-Aggravated-Exemplary-and-Restitutionary-Damages-A-Consultation-Paper.pdf>; Law Commission, Report No. 247, 6; recommendation 18 and draft bill 3 at 6.

111 J.-F. Flauss, 'La banalisation du contentieux indemnitaire devant la Cour européenne des droits de l'homme', *Rev.Trim.D.H.* 1996, p93 at 96.

restitution. Because of this rule the Court can in principle only award a just satisfaction if the national member states do not provide *restitutio in integrum*, which indicates that the satisfaction cannot be larger in size than the damages.[112] Paragraph 9 of the *Practice Direction on Just Satisfaction* moreover stipulates that just satisfactions under Art. 41 are not aimed to punish states.[113] It thus seems that more arguments can be found in the text of Art. 41 that plea against the use of punitive damages than that there are textual arguments that plea for punitive damages. It consequently comes as no surprise that the European Court of Human Rights in its jurisprudence on Art. 41 does not award punitive damages. In some cases, the applicants have requested that the Court award punitive damages. The Court never supported these requests. In some cases, the Court did not even make any arguments as to the reasons why it did not award punitive damages.[114] In other cases the Court just noted that in the specific case punitive damages did not have to be addressed.[115]

An interesting case with regard to this topic, is the second *Olsson* case.[116] In the first *Olsson* case, a husband and his wife had brought a case before the Court because their children had been taken into public care.[117] They found that the taking into public care of their children, amongst others, violated their right to family life as is protected by Art. 8. The Court in this case found

112 F. Bydlinski, 'Methodological Approaches', 2011, above n. 49, p29 at 40.
113 Practice Direction on Just Satisfaction, 28 March 2007.
114 *Aydin v. Turkey*, 25 September 1997 (Grand Chamber), appl. no. 23178/94; *Akdivar et al. v. Turkey*, 1 April 1998 (Grand Chamber) (just satisfaction), appl. no. 21893/93; *Mentes et al. v. Turkey*, 24 July 1998 (just satisfaction), appl. no. 23186/94; *McElhinney v. Ireland*, 21 November 2001 (Grand Chamber), appl. no. 31253/96; *Price and Low v. the United Kingdom*, 29 July 2003, appl. nos. 43185/98 and 43186/98, §27ff; *B.B. v. the United Kingdom*, 10 February 2004, appl. no. 53760/00; *A. and E. Riis v. Norway* 31 May 2007, appl. no. 9042/04; *Crabtree v. The Czech Republic*, 25 February 2010, appl. no. 41116/04, §§58–60; and *Orphanides v. Turkey*, 22 June 2010, appl. no. 36705/97.
115 *W. v. the United Kingdom*, 9 June 1988 (just satisfaction) (Plenary), appl. no. 9749/82; *Yagci and Sargin v. Turkey*, 8 June 1995, appl. nos. 16419/90 and 16426/90; *Ribitsch v. Austria*, 4 December 1995, appl. no. 18896/91; *Selçuk and Asker v. Turkey*, 24 April 1998, appl. nos. 23184/94 and 23185/94, §119; *Cable et al. v. the United Kingdom*, 18 February 1999, appl. nos. 24436/94, 24582/94, 24583, 94, 24584/94, 24895/94, 25937/94, 25939/94 25940/94, 25940/94, 25941/94, 26271/95, 26525/95, 27341/95, 27342/95, 27346/95, 27357/95, 27389/95, 27409/95, 27760/95, 27762/95, 27772/95, 28009/95, 28790/95, 30236/96, 30239/96, 30276/96, 30277/96, 30460/96, 30461/96, 30462/96, 31399/96, 31400/96, 31434/96, 31899/96 and 32024/96, §§29–30; and *Ludescher v. Austria*, 20 December 2001, appl. no. 35019/97, §30.
116 *Olsson v. Sweden (no.2)*, 27 November 1992, appl. no. 13441/87.
117 *Olsson v. Sweden (no.1)*, 24 March 1988 (Plenary), appl. no. 10465/83, §51.

that the government in the specific situation had correctly decided that the children could be taken into public care, but that the government had not respected the involvement of the parents enough as to decide the specific conditions of the public care. The Court found that the children had been transferred to places that were too distant to the parents' house so that the taking into care of the children made it in fact almost impossible for the parents to keep in touch with their children.[118] With regard to Art. 41, the Court observed that the violation of Art. 8 caused the applicants considerable inconvenience and above all substantial anxiety and distress. The Court noted that 'regular and frequent contacts with the children were greatly impeded and the possibility for the whole family to meet together were minimal. And the situation, with its deleterious effects on the applicants' family life, endured for some seven years.'[119] The Court consequently awarded a just satisfaction of 200,000 Swedish Crown.

Afterwards, the Swedish government did not take any action as to make sure that the applicants would be able to see their children more often. The Olsson family thus brought a new case before the Court. The Court ruled that Art. 8 was violated for the same reasons as in the first *Olsson* case and now also found a violation of the right of access to a court as is enshrined in Art. 6. It did however only find a violation of a small number of the alleged violations of the Convention. Under the heading of Art. 41, the applicants in this case petitioned the Court to award an extra-large just satisfaction (*in casu* 5 million Swedish Crown) for the reason that the Swedish government had not complied with the judgment in the first *Olsson* case.[120] The Court did not go along with this request. It observed that only a part of the alleged violations had been found correct and awarded a sum of 50,000 Swedish Crown as a just satisfaction for the suffered non-pecuniary damages.[121]

This case clearly illustrates that the ECtHR is not willing to award a satisfaction to punish states, even if the states had not respected older judgments of the Court. It does not however give us a clue as to the reasons why the Court does not award punitive damages. The first argument that the Court made as to refuse a petition for punitive damages was that the Court had never done so before.[122] It was only in *Varnava* that the Court

118 *Ibid.*, §§82–83.

119 *Ibid.*, §102.

120 *Ibid.*, §110.

121 *Ibid.*, §111.

122 *Orhan v. Turkey*, 18 June 2002, appl. no. 25656/94, §448. See also: *Tepe v. Turkey*, 9 May 2003, appl. no. 27244/95, §218; *Ikincisoy v. Turkey*, 27 July 2004, appl. no. 26144/95, §149;

lifted up this veil of ignorance. The applicants in this case petitioned the Court under Art. 46 to impose daily fines on the government so that it would comply with the judgment and they also claimed a large sum of money as a just satisfaction for non-pecuniary damages. With regard to Art. 46, the Court however made the following argument:

> In so far as the applicants suggested that daily fines be imposed on the respondent Government until they finally comply with the Court's judgments, the Court has consistently rejected claims for punitive damages (see Akdivar and Others, cited above, §38, and Orhan v. Turkey, no. 25656/94, §448, 18 June 2002). It considers there to be little, if any, scope under the Convention for directing governments to pay penalties to applicants which are unconnected with damage shown to be actually incurred in respect of past violations of the Convention; in so far as such sums would purport to compensate for future suffering of the applicants, this would be speculative in the extreme.[123]

With regard to the request to award a large sum of money to compensate the non-pecuniary damages, the Court observed that the just satisfactions are not intended to give financial comfort or sympathetic enrichment to human right victims at the expense of the condemned government.[124]

4.2. THE DISSUASIVE USE OF NON-PECUNIARY DAMAGES

What is interesting about *Varnava* is that the applicants in this case did not explicitly petition the Court to award punitive damages, but that they required the Court to award a larger sum of money for non-pecuniary damages for dissuasive reasons. And although the Court in the case of *Varnava* clearly rejected this petition by stating that the satisfactions are not intended to give financial comfort or sympathetic enrichment to the human rights victims, one can wonder whether the Court sometimes does

---

Efendiyeva v. Azerbaijan, 11 December 2008, appl. no. 31556/03, §23; *Mikayil Mammadov v. Azerbaijan*, 17 December 2009, appl. no. 4762/05, §149; *Stefanou v. Greece*, 22 April 2010, appl. no. 2954/07, §82; *Greens and M.T. v. the United Kingdom*, 23 November 2010, appl. nos. 60041/08 and 60054/08, §97; and *Hadzhiev v. Bulgaria*, 23 October 2012, appl. no. 22373/04, §65.

123 *Varnava et al. v. Turkey*, 18 September 2009 (Grand Chamber), appl. nos. 16064/90, 16065/90, 16066/90, 16068/90, 16069/90, 16070/90, 16071/90, 16072/90 and 16073/90, §223.

124 *Ibid.*, §224 *in fine*.

not use the satisfaction for non-pecuniary damages as an instrument to dissuade states from violating the Convention again.[125] Indeed, one can wonder whether the Court does for example take into account the fact that a violation was caused intentionally or not.[126] This might not even be in contradiction with the fact that satisfactions are not intended to enrich human rights victims. The reason for this is that one can argue that victims of human rights violations suffer more non-pecuniary damages if their rights were violated intentionally as if they were not violated intentionally.[127] With regard to this question, one must be aware of the fact that non-pecuniary damages by their nature cannot be estimated and thus that they always have to be estimated in an abstract manner. Moreover, it must be remembered that the Court is not reluctant to measure material damages in an abstract manner either.[128] It thus does not seem to be impossible for the Court to use this abstract manner of estimation to strengthen the dissuasive function of just satisfactions. This seemed to be the case in *Scordino* where the Court ruled that the right to have a judgment within a reasonable time was violated and granted a just satisfaction:

> Thus the Court, like the Commission, after years of examining the reasons for the delays attributable to the parties under the Italian procedural rules, has had to resolve to standardize its judgments and decisions. This has allowed it to adopt more than 1,000 judgments against Italy since 1999 in civil length-of-proceedings cases. That approach has made it necessary to establish scales on equitable principles for awards in respect of non-pecuniary damage under Article 41, in order to arrive at equivalent results in similar cases.
>
> All this has led the Court to award higher levels of damages than those awarded by the Convention institutions prior to 1999, and which may differ from those

---

125 It also noteworthy that a lot of national legal systems accept that the threat of damages in tort law can force potential wrongdoers to behave more cautiously so that future damages are prevented: U. Magnus, 'Comparative Report', 2001, above n. 5, p185 at 185.

126 F. Bydlinski, 'Methodological Approaches', 2011, above n. 49, p29 at 41; and J.-F. Flauss, 'Conclusion générale' in J.-F. Flauss and E. Lambert Abdelgawad (eds.), *La pratique d'indemnisation par la Cour européenne des droits de l'homme*, Brussels, Bruylant, 2011, p329 at 336.

127 See: C. Cauffman, 'Naar een punitief Europees verbintenissenrecht? Een rechtsvergelijkende studie naar de draagwijdte, de grondwettigheid en de wenselijkheid van het bestraffend karakter van het verbintenissenrecht', *Tijdschrift voor Privaatrecht* 2007, (799) at 823.

128 Which is often criticized, e.g.: Partially dissenting opinion of Judge Matscher in *Gaygusuz v. Austria*, 16 September 1996, appl. no. 17371/90.

> applied in the event of a finding of other violations. This increase, far from being a punitive measure, was intended to serve two purposes. On the one hand it encouraged States to find their own, universally accessible, solution to the problem, and on the other hand it allowed applicants to avoid being penalized for the lack of domestic remedies.[129]

These observations illustrate that although the Court does not award punitive damages, it sometimes uses compensation for non-pecuniary damages for dissuasive goals.[130] It thus comes as no surprise that different authors argue that the Court, when it has to award a just satisfaction for non-pecuniary damages, takes into account the severity of the human rights violation. By doing so, the Court uses an approach that has similarities with the 'aggravated damages' in English tort law.[131] Aggravated damages are damages that have to be compensated in full in cases where the tortfeasor harmed the victim intentionally or on an offensive or lucrative manner. Moreover, Octavian Ichim observes that some judges in their dissenting or occurring opinions indicated that the majority awarded moral damages for dissuasive reasons or that the satisfactions are, for unknown reasons, much higher than in similar cases.[132] Judges Bonello and Maruste in a dissenting opinion once explicitly stated that the just satisfactions do not only serve as a means to restitute the damages but also serve as 'a concrete warning to erring governments'.[133] It thus seems reasonable that the Court uses Art. 41 as a dissuasive instrument. Nevertheless, this hypothesis requires more research into the criteria that the Court uses to estimate the size of non-pecuniary damages.

---

129 *Scordino v. Italy (no.1)*, 29 March 2006 (Grand Chamber), appl. no. 36813/97, §176.

130 See also: C. Kissling and D. Kelliher, 'Compensation', 2011, above n. 33, p579 at 678; and V. Wilcox, *A Company's Right to Damage for Non-Pecuniary Loss*, Cambridge, Cambridge University Press, 2016, at 75.

131 The Law Commission and the Scottish Law Commission, *Damages under the Human Rights Act 1998*, 2000, <https://www.scotlawcom.gov.uk/files/3012/7989/6877/rep180.pdf>, at 36 and 71; V. Wilcox, 'Punitive and Nominal Damages' in A. Fenyves, E. Karner, H. Koziol and E. Steiner (eds.), *Tort Law in the Jurisprudence of the European Court of Human Rights*, Göttingen, De Gruyter, 2011, p725 at 729.

132 O. Ichim, *Just Satisfaction*, 2015, above n. 17, at 166–167. See also: Partly dissenting opinion of Judge Matscher in *Gaygusuz v. Austria*, 16 September 1996, appl. no. 17371/90; Partly dissenting opinion of Judge Gölcüklü in *Aktaş v. Turkey*, 24 April 2003, appl. no. 24351/94; and Separate opinion of Judges Sajo and Pinto de Albuquerque in *Silva Pontes v. Portugal*, 23 March 1994, appl. no. 14940/89.

133 Partly dissenting opinion of Judge Bonello, joined by Judge Maruste in *Nikolova v. Bulgaria*, 25 March 1999, appl. no. 31195/96.

4.2.1. *Awarding Just Satisfaction under Article 41 of the Convention*

With regard to the size of the satisfaction for non-pecuniary damages, the Court has indicated that it can use the compensations that are granted in national legal systems as a source of inspiration, but that it is not bound by national practice.[134] The main source of inspiration is found in the jurisprudence of the Court itself. The Court tries to take into account the satisfactions that it has awarded in older cases. Ichim even stated that the Court uses tables as guidelines to determine the size of non-pecuniary damages.[135] The Court can of course only take its own jurisprudence as a source of inspiration if there is older jurisprudence at hand that deals with similar situations. If the Court is confronted for the first time with a specific situation, it will by definition estimate the satisfaction in a discretionary way.[136]

According to Christa Kissling and Denis Kelliher, the Court takes into account the following four criteria to determine the size of the satisfaction for non-pecuniary damages: the character and the gravity of the human rights violation, the length and the seriousness of the infringement and the standard of living in the country where the applicant lives.[137] Another criterion that the Court seems to take into account when awarding a satisfaction for non-pecuniary damages is the number of people that claim a satisfaction for non-pecuniary damages. The following paragraphs will deal with these criteria and will try to answer the question of whether these criteria somehow have a punitive goal.

4.2.1.1. The Character and the Seriousness of the Human Rights Violation

A previous chapter illustrated that a violation of Arts 2 and 3 of the Convention cannot be compensated by a mere declaratory judgment. With regard to this jurisprudence, the Court argues that these are the most fundamental rights that are enshrined in the Convention. It should thus not come as a surprise that it has been argued in doctrine that the nature of the violated Convention right and the seriousness of the violation have an influence on the size of the just satisfactions that the Court awards for

---

134 *Z. v. Finland*, 25 February 1997, appl. no. 22009/93, §122; *Osman v. the United Kingdom*, 28 October 1998, appl. no. 23452/94, §164; and *Z. et al. v. the United Kingdom*, 10 May 2005 (Grand Chamber), appl. no. 29392/95, §131.

135 O. Ichim, *Just Satisfaction*, 2015, above n. 17, at 121.

136 F. Bydlinski, 'Methodological Approaches', 2011, above n. 49, p29 at 111.

137 C. Kissling and D. Kelliher, 'Compensation', 2011, above n. 33, p579 at 626ff.

non-pecuniary damages.[138] At first hand this seems to be a reasonable approach as the more serious a Convention right is violated, the more severe the consequences of this violation will be for the victim. It seems logical that the damages will be larger if a right is more severely infringed upon, which in turn will influence the amount of satisfaction that has to be paid.[139] Indeed, in the doctrine it has been proposed that the Court takes into account the offensive behavior in which a state has violated the Convention rights as a reason to award a higher amount of compensation for non-pecuniary damages.[140] It is for this reason that the Court sometimes argues that a declaratory judgment cannot suffice as a means to compensate the damages if there is a grave human right violation at hand.[141] On top of that, this criterion seems to be in line with the *de minimis* rule.

On the other hand, there cannot be a clear-cut line between the violated Convention right and the size of the just satisfaction.[142] The only thing that – according to these authors – seems to be true, is that the Court is willing to award a bigger just satisfaction for non-pecuniary damages if more than one treaty provision is violated. A case that is referred to in this context is *Shamayev* where the Court awarded different amounts of just satisfaction for non-pecuniary damages to the different applicants depending on the amount of their Convention rights that were violated.[143] This case does however only illustrate that the compensation for non-pecuniary damages is influenced by the seriousness and the length of the Convention violation. Since the applicants in this case all complained about facts that were similar but that had no connection with one another, it seems more plausible that the Court looked into the concrete situations where the fundamental

---

138 F. Bydlinski, 'Methodological Approaches', above n. 49, 2011, p29 at 95; C. Kissling and D. Kelliher, 'Compensation', 2011, above n. 33, p579 at 628; D. Scorey and T. Eicke, *Human Rights Damages*, above n. 31, at A2-35; D. Shelton, *Remedies*, 1999, above n. 48, at 230.

139 F. Bydlinski, 'Methodological Approaches', 2011, above n. 49, p29 at 104.

140 The Law Commission and the Scottish Law Commission, *Damages under the Human Rights Act*, 2000, <https://www.scotlawcom.gov.uk/files/3012/7989/6877/rep180.pdf>, at 37.

141 E.g.: *El-Masri v. The former Yugoslav Republic of Macedonia*, 13 December 2012, appl. no. 39630/09, §269.

142 C. Kissling and D. Kelliher, 'Compensation', 2011, above n. 33, p579 at 628. Similarly, but with regard to Art. 3: E. Lambert Abdelgawad, 'Comment chifrer la réparation des traitements inhumains/dégradants et de la torture' in J.-F. Flauss and E. Lambert Abdelgawad (eds.), *La pratique d'indemnisation par la Cour européenne des droits de l'homme*, Brussels, Bruylant, 2011, p189 at 217ff.

143 *Shamayev et al. v. Georgia and Russia*, 12 April 2005, appl. no. 36378/02, §525.

rights of all these applicants were violated, than to the qualification of these violations in the Convention. Such an interpretation is also more in line with the fact that the Court in other cases does not take into account the number of Convention provisions that were violated when awarding a satisfaction for non-pecuniary damages.

This can be illustrated with the cases of *Lanteri* and *Paratheristikos Oikodomikos*.[144] In both these judgments that were made on the same date, the Court ruled that the right to property was violated. In the first case the violation was caused by an unlawful expropriation and in the second case the violation was caused by the fact that a state had given too small a compensation for the establishing of a public lease. In both these cases, the Court awarded substantial compensation for the material damages. In *Lanteri*, the Court also awarded compensation for the non-pecuniary damages that resulted from the frustrations that the applicants had suffered because of the expropriation. In *Paratheristikos Oikodomikos*, the Court however ruled that the violation of the right to property was compensated by the mere declaratory judgment. The Court in this case nevertheless awarded a satisfaction for non-pecuniary damages for the violation of Art. 6, §1, because the applicants had suffered for the fact that they did not have adequate access to national legal remedies.

What is interesting about these cases is that in both of them the Court awarded a satisfaction for non-pecuniary damages although in one case only the right to property was violated whereas in the other case both the right to property and the right of access to a Court were violated. It seems plausible that the Court in these cases either looked at the specific context of the case, and not to the number of Convention rights that were violated, or in *Paratheristikos Oikodomikos* did not award a satisfaction for the non-pecuniary damages that were caused by the violation of the right to property since it already awarded a satisfaction for the violation of the right of access to a Court. Although this last interpretation seems at odds with the idea that the Court has to take into account the suffered damages, it finds support in *Curmi*.[145] In this case, the Court found a violation of both the right to property and the right to have access to a court as it did in *Paratheristikos Oikodomikos*. The Court also awarded a sum of €10,000 for non-pecuniary damages but did not specify whether this sum of money was

144 *Paratheristikos Oikodomikos Synetairismos Stegaseos Ypallilon Trapezis Tis Ellados v. Greece*, 29 January 2013 (just satisfaction), appl. no. 2998/08; and *Lanteri v. Italy*, 29 January 2013 (just satisfaction), appl. no. 56578/00.

145 *Curmi v. Malta*, 9 July 2013 (just satisfaction), appl. no. 2243/10.

intended to compensate the non-pecuniary damages that the applicants had suffered by the violation of the right to property or by the violation of the right to have access to a court. What is interesting, however, is that the Court in *Lanteri*, also awarded a sum of €10,000 for non-pecuniary damages. This is interesting because the Court in this case only found a violation of the right to property. Thus, in both these cases in which the Court found an expropriation to be in violation with Art. 1 of the first protocol, the Court awarded the same amount of money, although in one of these cases it had also found a violation of the right of access to a court. In *Paratheristikos Oikodomikos*, the Court however only awarded €3,000 for non-pecuniary damages. This can probably be explained by the fact that this case had no regard to an expropriation but to the establishment of a public lease that was not sufficiently compensated.[146] Thus, what these cases illustrate is that the amount of satisfaction for non-pecuniary damages is not determined by the number of Convention rights that are violated, but by the gravity of the violations in the specific case.

This raises the question of whether the Court takes into account dissuasive elements when it estimates the size of the compensation on the basis of the character and the seriousness of the violation. One can indeed argue that this criterion is only determined by the moral damages that human rights victims suffer. It must however be noted that this reasoning only offers a partial explanation of the Court's jurisprudence. It has been illustrated in previous sections that the Court is sometimes willing to award a larger amount of money if a country repeatedly violates the same right in the same way. This cannot be explained but by referring to the dissuasive aims of the compensation for non-pecuniary damages. Moreover, even if this would be so, dissuasion can also be enacted if one argues that non-pecuniary damages are larger when violations were made intentionally. That the Court does so is illustrated in *Bozano*:

> In the Court's view, such a sum is far from being commensurate with the seriousness of the breach of Article 5 §1 (Art. 5-1) which, in its judgment of 18 December 1986, it held had been committed. This was a violation of the right to liberty and to security of person, a disguised form of extradition designed to circumvent a negative ruling by the appropriate French court, and an abuse of deportation procedure for objects and purposes other than its normal ones.

146 However, in the similar case *Hagiescu*, the Court awarded €4,700 for the violation of the right to property read in conjunction with the right to have access to a judge: *Hagiescu et al. v. Romania*, 18 March 2014 (just satisfaction), appl. no. 7901/02, §12.

> The attendant circumstances inevitably caused the applicant substantial non-pecuniary damage.[147]

A last case that suggests the dissuasive use of the satisfaction for non-pecuniary damages, is the case of *Trévalec*.[148] At the origin of this case lay an operation of the police to catch some suspected criminals. At this operation, police officers had shot some of the suspects in the legs. When this case was brought before the ECtHR, the Court found that the right to life as enshrined in Art. 2 had been violated because it found that the police had not prepared its operation with the required caution.[149] This case was however only brought before the ECtHR after the victims had received an amount of money from a fund that compensated the disability to work for both pecuniary and non-pecuniary damages. Since the ECtHR in this case awarded a just satisfaction under the heading of Art. 41, some judges remarked in their dissenting opinion that the Court had used the satisfaction for non-pecuniary damages in a punitive way. They were of the opinion that the national fund had already awarded a satisfaction for the total of non-pecuniary damages.[150] Thus, if the dissenters in this case must be believed, the Court did award a just satisfaction for dissuasive reasons.

4.2.1.2. The Length and the Gravity of the Damages

Among scholars it is generally accepted that the ECtHR takes into account the length and the gravity of the damages when estimating the size of the non-pecuniary damages.[151] This stems from the fact that the Court often states that the size of the just satisfaction is inspired by the presence of a

---

147 *Bozano v. France*, 2 December 1987 (just satisfaction), appl. no. 9990/82, §8. In this context, Shelton also refers to *Bock*. In this case the Court awarded a large compensation after it ruled that the violation of the Convention 'represented a serious encroachment on human dignity'. However, it is the opinion in this book that the Court does not refer to the culpability of the defendant state but to the size of the damages as such: *Bock v. Germany*, 29 March 1989, appl. no. 11118/84, §46.

148 *Trévalec v. Belgium*, 23 September 2013 (just satisfaction), appl. no. 30812/07.

149 *Trévalec v. Belgium*, 14 June 2011, appl. no. 30812/07.

150 In this sense, see the dissenting opinions in this case and: O. Sabard, 'Le principe de réparation intégrale menacé par la satisfaction équitable', *Revue générale des assurances et des responsabilités* 2014, no. 15060; and C. Quézal-Ambrunaz, 'Des dommages et intérêts octroyés par la Cour européenne des droits de l'homme', *Revue des droits et libertés fondamentaux* 2014, chron. No.5.

151 H. McGregor, *McGregor on Damages*, London, Sweet & Maxwell, 2009, 1745; C. Kissling and D. Kelliher, 'Compensation', 2011, above n. 33, p579 at 628; A. Weber, 'Le droit à indemnisation dans les affaires relatives à des violations systématiques

'serious interference'[152] in the rights of the applicant, or that it had found '(extreme) grave violations',[153] or 'a combination of serious violations of the applicant's fundamental human rights',[154] or that the Court argues that the violation had a 'serious effect'[155] on the wellbeing of the applicants.

Together with the gravity of the damages, the Court also considers the length of the violation. The Court clearly indicates this in some judgments with regard to the exceeding of the requirement to deliver a judgment within a reasonable time[156] and in its jurisprudence where it finds a detention to be in violation of Art. 3.[157] In these cases the Court takes into account the length of the exceeding of the reasonable time or the length of the detention as to estimate the amount of non-pecuniary damages.

4.2.1.3. The Number of Human Rights Victims

Another criterion that might influence the amount of non-pecuniary damages is the number of human rights victims.[158] If the Court would consider the presence of more human rights victims when estimating the non-pecuniary damages, it must be that it takes into account elements that have nothing to do with the way the human rights victims suffer non-pecuniary damages but that are more violator-oriented.

The judgment that indicates that the Court takes into account the presence of more human rights victims is *Arvanitaki-Roboti*.[159] In this exceptional case, the Court had to estimate the damages of 91 victims for the exceeding of the reasonable time requirement in a collective case before the Greek courts. After the Court found a violation of Art. 6, §1, the Court made the following observation with regard to the request to award a satisfaction for non-pecuniary damages:

> It also takes into consideration the number of applicants, the nature of the violation found and the need to determine the amount in such a way that the

---

d'indemnisation des victims' in J.-F. Flauss and E. Lambert Abdelgawad (eds.), *La pratique d'indemnisation par la Cour européenne des droits de l'homme*, Brussels, Bruylant, 2011, p259 at 274.

152 *Beshiri et al. v. Albania*, 22 August 2006, appl. no. 7352/03, §114.

153 *Ilascu et al. v. Moldavia and Russia*, 8 July 2004 (Grand Chamber), appl. no. 48787/99, §489; and *Popov v. Russia*, 13 July 2006, appl. no. 26853/04, §264.

154 *Moiseyev v. Russia*, 9 October 2008, appl. no. 62936/00, §272.

155 *G.B. and R.B. v. Moldova*, 18 December 2012, appl. no. 16761/09, §39.

156 *Scordino v. Italy (no.1)*, 29 March 2006 (Grand Chamber), appl. no. 36813/97, §267ff.

157 *Mathew v. the Netherlands*, 29 September 2005, appl. no. 24919/03, §228.

158 See also: V. Wilcox, *A Company's Right to Damage*, 2016, above n. 130, at 72.

159 *Arvanitaki-Roboti et al. v. Greece*, 15 February 2008 (Grand Chamber), appl. no. 27278/03.

overall sum is compatible with the relevant case-law and is reasonable in the light of what was at stake in the proceedings in question.[160]

The Court granted all the victims a satisfaction of €3,500 for non-pecuniary damages. Judges Zupancic and Zagrebelsky in their partly dissenting opinion heavily criticized this approach.[161] They argued that the majority of the Court had not raised any argument in their judgment as to determine to what degree the compensation had to be limited, but that their approach had resulted in a 'substantial reduction of the compensation in comparison to the Court's general practice.' According to these dissenters, there is no psychological or other argument that can explain why people in a large group would suffer less non-pecuniary damages because of an exceeding of the reasonable time requirement. They argue that Art. 41 requires that every victim has to be compensated as good as possible on an individual basis: 'whatever the number of victims, each of them must be compensated, "if necessary", for the consequences which he or she must have suffered as a result of the violation in question.' The dissenters moreover found that it is understandable that the Court wanted to reduce the total amount of damages that the state would have to pay, but they found that this could not be done by reducing the amount of damages in this case, but that the Court in general had to award smaller amounts of money as to compensate the non-pecuniary damages that result from the violation of the reasonable time requirement. Although the Court in later cases did not lower the sums of money that it awards to compensate the violations of Art. 6, it did follow the arguments of the dissenters with regard to the fact that it cannot limit the size of the compensation when more applicants are present:

Le nombre des requérants ne doit pas être pris en compte et entraîner une réduction du montant à allouer dans la mesure où en l'espèce les intéressés n'étaient pas, sauf dans le cadre de la procédure de redressement et liquidation judiciaire, parties à une procédure commune, mais avaient mené des procédures judiciaires et d'exécution distinctes. [The number of applicants does not need to be taken into account and result in a reduction in the amount to be allocated, insofar as in the present case, the persons concerned were not, except in the context of the redress and court ordered liquidation, parties to joint

160 *Ibid.*, §36.

161 Partly dissenting opinion of Judges Zupancic and Zagrebelsky in *Arvanitaki-Roboti et al. v. Greece*, 15 February 2008 (Grand Chamber), appl. no. 27278/03.

proceedings, but had conducted separate judicial and enforcement proceedings] (author's translation).[162]

If this new approach is to be continued in the future, it might be possible that the Court will never again judge that the number of applicants has an influence on the size of the compensation for non-pecuniary damages. Nevertheless, the case of *Arvanitaki-Roboti* illustrates that the Court, at least in the past, took into account violator-focused arguments as to determine the size of the compensation for non-pecuniary damages. By limiting the compensation of many victims to a similar amount as the total compensation would have been as if the human rights violation had only had one victim, the Court illustrates that it bases its compensation on violator-focused elements. By doing so, the Court actually indicates that the obligation to pay all the victims together a similar amount as it would award to one victim is not proportionate with regard to the fault of the state. The Court thus implicitly used the compensation for non-pecuniary damages as an instrument to dissuade states from violating the Convention rights again.

4.2.1.4. The Behavior of the Parties in the Procedure

One of the main principles of the Convention is the principle of subsidiarity. This means that the protection that the Convention offers is only secondary towards the protection that is offered by national law. The Court in the same way also grants a primary role to the will of the parties that stand before the Court. Thus, if an applicant and a state find an agreement to settle the dispute, the Court will strike out the case.[163] In a similar manner, the Court awards the compensation that an applicant claims if the defending state does not dispute the size of the compensation.[164] Different authors have found that the Court is often willing to award a claimed compensation for

---

162 *Belev et al. v. Bulgaria*, 2 April 2009, appl. nos. 16354/02, 16485/02, 16878/02, 16885/02, 16886/02, 16889/02, 17333/02, 17340/02, 17344/02, 17613/02, 17725/02, 17726/02, 18410/02, 18413/02, 18414/02, 18416/02, 21023/02, 21024/02, 21027/02, 21029/02, 21030/02, 21033/02, 21038/02, 21052/02, 21071/02, 21284/02, 21378/02, 21800/02, 22430/02, 22433/02, 26478/02, 26498/02, 31049/02, 31333/02, 31518/02, 37816/02, 42567/02, 43529/02, 758/03, 3461/03 and 11219/03, §112.

163 For a thorough analysis see: M.L. Van Emmerik, *Schadevergoeding*, 1997, above n. 55, at 72.

164 E.g.: *Ilhan v. Turkey*, 27 June 2000 (Grand Chamber), appl. no. 22277/93, §109.

non-pecuniary damages if the compensation is reasonable.[165] This respect to the will and the behavior of the parties can however also work the other way around. Indeed, the Court has already ruled that the behavior of an applicant shows that he does not really suffer non-pecuniary damages, or even that the behavior illustrates that an applicant has no interest in bringing a case before the Court so that it declares a case inadmissible.[166]

Also interesting is that the importance to the free will of the parties in theory also result in the notion that the Court in principle does not grant more damages then the applicant has claimed.[167] But this principle is not very clear-cut. Earlier it was demonstrated that the Court sometimes awards a just satisfaction under Art. 41 out of its own motion. Consequently, the Court in a similar way has also awarded a higher amount of damages for non-pecuniary damages as were claimed in *Stradovnik*.[168] Since the Court did not make any observation as to the reasons of the higher compensation, it seems as if the Court would have done so for dissuasive reasons.

4.2.1.5. Earlier Convictions of a Member State

In *Scordino*, the Court referred to the number of violations of Art. 6 of the Convention as an argument to award a higher compensation for non-pecuniary damages. It thus seems clear that the Court awards higher amounts of damages when a state has already been condemned several times for the same Convention violation. This has been remarked in the literature by David Scorey and Tim Eicke.[169] The only reason for which the Court would use this approach must be found in its dissuasive intentions.

---

165 In this sense, see: C. Pettiti, 'Stratégie de la partie requérante face à la perspective d'octroi de dommages et intérêts par la cour Européenne des droits de l'homme' in J.-F. Flauss and E. Lambert Abdelgawad (eds.), *La pratique d'indemnisation par la Cour européenne des droits de l'homme*, Brussels, Bruylant, 2011, p56 at 70; E. Lambert Abdelgawad, 'Comment chifrer la réparation', 2011, above n. 142, p189 at 211. In the opposite way, it has also been argued that defendant states often abide by the wisdom of the Court when it is clear that an applicant will receive compensation and the claimed damages are not disproportionate: M. Sirinelli 'La stratégie des parties face à la perspective d'octroi de dommages-intérêts par la Cour – côté etat défendeur' in J.-F. Flauss and E. Lambert Abdelgawad (eds.), *La pratique d'indemnisation par la Cour européenne des droits de l'homme*, Brussels, Bruylant, 2011, p75 at 82.

166 *Heather Moor & EDGECOMB LTD v. the United Kingdom*, 26 June 2012, appl. no. 30802/11, §25.

167 See: *Ernestina Zullo v. Italy*, 10 November 2004, appl. no. 64897/01, §32.

168 *Stradovnik v. Slovenia*, 13 April 2006, appl. no. 24784/02, §§23–25.

169 D. Scorey and T. Eicke, *Human Rights Damages*, above n. 31, at A2-38–39.

4.2.1.6. The Standard of Living in the Country Where the Applicant Lives

A last element that influences the size of the compensation for non-pecuniary damages is the standard of living of the country where the applicant lives. If a country has a higher standard of living, the Court will award a higher amount of damages.[170] This element does of course not teach anything about the dissuasive use of compensation for non-pecuniary damages, but it is necessary to know this when one is comparing the amount of damages that the Court awarded in different judgments.

4.2.1.7. Conclusion

From the above paragraphs, it must be concluded that the ECtHR uses the compensation for non-pecuniary damages sometimes for dissuasive purposes. As pointed out earlier, this seems to be at odds with the idea that only the damages must be compensated and thus that the size of the compensation can only be influenced by victim-focused elements and not by violator-focused elements. However, it has been shown that the gravity of the intentional character of a violation can have an influence on the suffering of a victim. As a consequence, the dissuasive use of compensation for non-pecuniary damages can somehow be reconciled with the idea that only the size of the damages can determine the size of the compensation. Because national legal systems, in order to award an effective remedy to protect human rights as is required by Art. 13 have to award compensations that are similar to those that the Court awards in similar cases, it seems that the Court stimulates the dissuasive use of the compensation of moral damages in national law. This however, is in the first place only true with regard to state responsibility for human rights violations. Indeed, only governments can be sued before the Court. It can however be argued that if the Court influences the rules on compensation that apply in the field of state liability, the principle of equality requires a similar compensation if a similar violation has been made by a private individual.[171] This compensation, as illustrated in this book, might be granted by the state itself, but such an approach would put a heavy burden on the state budget. Consequently, it seems reasonable that the national

---

170 On this topic: C. Kissling and D. Kelliher, 'Compensation', 2011, above n. 33, p579 at 633–634.

171 See: S. Somers, 'Special liability regimes and human rights under Belgian law and the European Convention on Human rights', *Journal of European Tort Law* 2014, 310–338.

tort law systems will have to award more dissuasive damages. Nevertheless, it must be remembered that a lot of cases where the Court used the compensation for non-pecuniary damages, have to do with human rights violations that can only be done by states. Indeed, it is hard to imagine a case where a private individual violates another private person's right to have a judgment within a reasonable time.

4.2.2. Punitive Damages and the Right to an Effective Remedy

Apart from the appeal to the principle of equality as an instrument that might push national tort law in a more dissuasive direction, one might also appeal to the right to provide an effective remedy. From this perspective, one can wonder whether the obligation to pay a higher amount of damages cannot provide an effective remedy as to protect human rights in horizontal relationships. This idea was one raised by the Belgian scholar Karel Rimanque.[172] He found that judges in Belgian tort law would have to award larger sums for non-pecuniary damages when human rights are violated as a mean to deter tortfeasors from violating human rights in the future again. A similar line of reasoning was used by the Belgian Constitutional Court.[173] In this case the Court had to answer the question of whether the anti-discrimination laws did not violate the principle of equality by installing a mechanism that provides fixed compensations for non-pecuniary damages that are larger than the tortfeasor in general tort law usually have to pay. The Belgian Constitutional Court did not find a violation of the principle of equality because it observed that judges in general tort law often only provide very small amounts of compensation for non-pecuniary damages. Because of the seriousness of the anti-discrimination law, the Court ruled that the lawmaker could provide relatively high fixed compensations in this particular field.

The question then arises of whether this approach also stems from the European Convention on Human Rights. To answer this question, it is interesting to look back to the cases *X and Y v. the Netherlands* and *Vo.* Earlier chapters illustrated that the Court in these cases found that the possibility to sue a private person who violated someone else's rights in tort law can be qualified as an effective remedy in the meaning of Art. 13 if the tortfeasor violated the victim's rights in an unintentional and not in

172 K. Rimanque, 'Nationale bescherming van grondrechten', *Tijdschrift voor Bestuurswetenschappen en Publiekrecht* 1981, p33 at 41.

173 Constitutional Court of Belgium 12 February 2009, appl. no. 17/2009, §B.26.10.

an intentional manner. If the tortfeasors in these cases violate the rights of the victims intentionally, the Court requires the states to provide a criminal remedy as a way to deter private persons from violating each other's human rights. The Court thus makes a difference between criminal and civil liability on the basis of the degree of dissuasion. To deter people from committing intentional human rights violations, more dissuasion is required than when people only commit unintentional human rights violation. It thus seems reasonable that damages are used in a dissuasive way in cases where human rights are violated intentionally but where the violator did not commit a crime. By strengthening the dissuasive effect of tort law, one can correct the lack in protection of criminal law.

Although there are reasons that argue for a dissuasive effect of horizontal tort law, up until now the Court has never required states to provide punitive damages in tort law under Art. 13 of the Convention. It is quite the opposite. In *Perez*, the Court found with regard to the right to have access to a court under Art. 6 that private persons have no right to *private revenge*.[174] The court, *Öneryildiz*, also confirmed this idea in the context of Art. 13 of the Convention.[175]

However, the cases of *Armonienė* and *Biriuk*,[176] two cases that have almost identical facts, illustrate that the Court can require national states to provide larger compensation for non-pecuniary damages. These cases did not concern Art. 13 but Art. 8. The applicants in these cases complained that their right to privacy under Art. 8 was violated because the national judges had only awarded a limited amount of compensation for the non-pecuniary damages that they suffered in a defamation case. In both cases, the applicants had received about 10,000 Lithuanian Litas, which is less than €3,000. This was the maximum amount of money that Lithuanian judges at that time could grant in a defamation case because the law capped

174 *Perez v. France*, 12 February 2004 (Grand Chamber), appl. no. 47287/99, §70. See also: *Biszta v. Poland*, 12 September 2006, appl. no. 4922/02, §4; *Kositsina v. Ukraine*, 15 January 2008 (Decision), appl. no. 35157/02; *Rachwalski and Ferenc v. Poland*, 21 October 2008 (Decision), appl. no. 47709/99; *Khaylo v. Ukraine*, 13 November 2008, appl. no. 39964/02, §89; *Mihova v. Italy*, 30 March 2010 (Decision), appl. no. 25000/07; *Lysaya v. Ukraine*, 1 February 2011, appl. no. 11408/02, §42; and *Janowiec et al. v. Russia*, 5 July 2011, appl. nos. 55508/07 and 29520/09, §116.

175 *Öneryildiz v. Turkey*, 30 November 2004 (Grand Chamber), appl. no. 48939/99, §14. See also: *Budayeva et al. v. Russia*, 20 March 2008, appl. nos. 15339/02, 11673/02, 15343/02, 20058/02 and 21166/02, §191; and *Volchkov v. Russia*, 14 October 2010, appl. no. 45196/04, §40.

176 *Armonienė v. Lithuania*, 25 November 2008, appl. no. 36919/02; and *Biriuk v. Lithuania*, 25 November 2008, appl. no. 23373/03.

these compensations. The ECtHR ruled that the legal cap was too low to protect the right to privacy of the applicants if one considered the serious nature of the infringements on the applicant's rights. The Court thus judged that Art. 8 was violated and awarded the applicants an additional compensation of €6,500 for non-pecuniary damages.[177] This jurisprudence cannot come as a surprise since the first part of this book showed in Chapter 3 that the Court requires from national tort law that it has a certain deterrent effect.

It can thus be concluded that the Court does not require states to introduce punitive damages but that it can implicitly require states to use compensations in a dissuasive manner. Nevertheless, the influence of the ECtHR on the dissuasive character of compensation will be rather limited. This is especially true because of two reasons. On the one hand it is so that the size of the compensation that the ECtHR awards for non-pecuniary damages is rather small in comparison with the amount of damages that are awarded in national legal systems.[178] On the other hand there seems to be a tendency within national legal systems throughout Europe to award higher sums of money to compensate non-pecuniary damages.[179] The impact of the Court on this existing evolution might be limited.

4.3. LIMITING THE *RESTITUTIO IN INTEGRUM* BY APPEALING TO HUMAN RIGHTS

4.3.1. A Tendency Towards Material Equality in Tort Law

Apart from a push towards a more dissuasive use of compensation, it must also be examined whether the Convention can have a contrary

---

177 *Armonienė v. Lithuania*, 25 November 2008, appl. no. 36919/02, §52; and *Biriuk v. Lithuania*, 25 November 2008, appl. no. 23373/03, §51. In his dissenting opinion, Judge Zagrebelsky argued that the Court had infringed the margin of appreciation of the member states because the compensation that the applicants had received in national law was, in his opinion, not disproportionate: Dissenting opinion of Judge Zagrebelsky in *Armonienė v. Lithuania*, 25 November 2008, appl. no. 36919/02, §4; and Dissenting opinion of Judge Zagrebelsky in *Biriuk v. Lithuania*, 25 November 2008, appl. no. 23373/03, §4.

178 On the comparison with the amount of compensations that are awarded in English tort law, see: D. Nolan, 'Government liability' in K. Oliphant (ed.), *The Law of Tort*, Suffolk, LexisNexis Butterworths, 2007, p885 at 941.

179 This was already noted in the doctrine in 2001: B. Koch, 'Comparative Remarks' in H. Koziol and B. Steininger (eds.), *European Tort Law 2002*, Vienna, Springer, 2003, p512 at 515–523.

influence on tort law. In other words, one must examine whether human rights can limit the compensation that tortfeasors have to pay. At first sight this question seems to be a bit bizarre because one is inclined to link human rights with the protection of victims. But as seen in the context of the character of the restitution, it is also possible for a tortfeasor to appeal to his human rights. Moreover, it has been illustrated that a national judge sometimes violates the Convention by obliging a tortfeasor to redress damages.

This was first and foremost illustrated by *Tolstoj Miloslawksy.*[180] This case, that was discussed before, concerned an English journalist of Yugoslavian origin who had been condemned for defamation for the reason that he had harmed the honor and reputation of a school principal by accusing him of being responsible for the death of thousands of Yugoslavians during the Second World War. But with regard to the current question, a more interesting case is *Steel and Morris*, the case concerning the Greenpeace activists that were condemned for defamation because they distributed pamphlets in London where they criticized the workings of McDonalds. After the Court in this case referred to *Tolstoj Miloslawksy*, it found that the compensation for non-pecuniary damages that the applicants had to pay were disproportionately high with regard to the aimed goal.[181]

At first sight this conclusion seems to be a bit bizarre. The compensations that Steel and Morris had to pay were remarkably lower than the compensation that Tolstoy Miloslawksy had to pay. The Court however observed that it does not have to estimate the proportionality of a compensation in an abstract manner by referring to the character and the seriousness of the damaging act on the one hand and the size of the compensation on the other. The Court is of the opinion that the disputed compensation in *Steel and Morris* 'although relatively moderate by contemporary standards in defamation cases in England and Wales, were very substantial when compared to the modest incomes and resources of the two applicants.' The Court moreover noted that the libel that Steel and Morris had caused was serious but that the victims of this libel were 'large and powerful corporate entities' that, according to English law, were not obliged to indicate that they had suffered financial loss because of the pamphlets. The Court thus found that the right to free speech of Steel and Morris had been violated and granted them respectively €20,000

180 *Tolstoy Miloslavsky v. the United Kingdom*, 13 July 1995, appl. no. 18139/91.
181 *Steel and Morris v. the United Kingdom*, 15 February 2005, appl. no. 68416/01, §98.

and €15,000 for non-pecuniary damages.[182] The Court did not award compensation for pecuniary damages for the large compensation that the applicants had to pay to McDonald's because 'McDonald's would need the leave of the court before it could proceed to enforce the award.'[183] The fact that the Court takes into account the financial situation of the tortfeasors, is somehow remarkable. By taking into account the financial situation of the tortfeasors, the Court bears in mind that an obligation to restitute damages somehow has a punitive character. This is something that is completely absent in national tort law systems. By doing so the Court moreover takes far-reaching decisions into the sovereignty of the national judges as to decide the size of the compensation. By judging that an obligation to pay a large amount of money for non-pecuniary damages can be qualified as a human rights violation of a tortfeasor, the Court in fact tops these compensations in national tort law. The fact that the Court has repeated this principle in the cases of *Lepojić* and *Koprivica* shows that *Steel and Morris* is not a flash in the pan.[184] Indeed, in *Olafsson*, another case regarding the award of high compensation in a defamation case, the Court made this possibility very clear:

> Although the compensation was not a criminal sanction, and the amount may not appear harsh, the Court reiterates that in the context of assessing proportionality, irrespective of whether or not the sanction imposed was a minor one, what matters is the very fact of judgment being made against the person concerned, even where such a ruling is solely civil in nature. Any undue restriction on freedom of expression effectively entails a risk of obstructing or paralysing future media coverage of similar questions[185]

The duty to pay a compensation in tort law can also be in violation of other Convention rights than the right to free speech. This is illustrated by *Mamidakis* with regard to the right to property as is enshrined in Art. 1 of the first protocol. The ECtHR in this case ruled that a fine for evading taxes can be so high that it is in fact a confiscation in violation

---

182 *Ibid.*, §109.

183 *Ibid*, §105.

184 The Court took into account the income of the tortfeasors and the average income in the country where he lived: *Lepojic v. Serbia*, 6 November 2007, appl. no. 13909/05, §77; and *Koprivica v. Montenegro*, 22 November 2011, appl. no. 41158/09, §73. In this last case the Court noted that the compensation amounted to 25 times the monthly pension of the liable person.

185 *Ólafsson v. Iceland*, 16 March 2017, appl. no. 58493/13, §61. See also: *Traustason et al. v. Iceland*, 4 May 2017, appl. no. 44081/13, §54.

of the right to property.[186] Of course, this case was situated in criminal law. It must be stressed that a tort claim in itself can be qualified as a possession in the sense of Art. 1 of the first protocol.[187] For this reason, it seems reasonable that the Court might in the future apply the same criteria in tort law cases.

The impact of this jurisprudence might be that in the future tort law will have to leave its formal notion of equality of the parties for a substantial equality of the parties. Today, tort law takes as a point of reference the formal equality between parties. What this means can be illustrated by an example given by Jessy Emaus.[188] As an example, assume that a tort has occurred between a rich merchant and a vagabond. If one of these parties injures the other, tort law does not accept that a judge takes into account the financial situation of these two persons. The restitution of the damages is defined by the damages and not by any other criteria. Thus, it might be that the vagabond will have to pay more damages when he injures the rich merchant as the rich merchant will have to pay for injuring the poor vagabond because the vagabond will have to pay the loss of income of the merchants whose income is substantially higher than the income of the vagabond. This principle might however be contested if the tortfeasor in an exceptional case can appeal to a Convention right.

4.3.2. A Minimal Protection of Substantial Equality between the Parties

The question now arises as to how far this tendency towards material equality can go. Indeed, it is one thing to say that the ECtHR sometimes argues that an obligation to pay compensation for non-pecuniary damages violates a human right of the tortfeasor and another to replace the formal equality of the parties by a substantial equality for all tort cases. One can doubt that the Court will ever push for such a landslide in national tort law. Especially considering the fact that the Court itself does not normally

---

186 *Mamidakis v. Greece*, 11 January 2007, appl. no. 35533/04. For a similar approach with regard to fiscal sanctions: *Buffalo S.R.L. IN Liquidation v. Italy*, 3 July 2003, appl. no. 38746/97, §32; and *S.C. Complex Herta Import Export S.R.L. Lipova v. Romania*, 18 June 2013, appl. no. 17118/04, §38.

187 *Pressos Compania Naviera S.A. et al. v. Belgium*, 20 November 1995, appl. no. 17849/91, §31; *Depalle v. France*, 29 March 2010 (Grand Chamber), appl. no. 34044/02, §63; and *Centro Europa 7 S.R.L. and Di Stefano v. Italy*, 7 June 2012, appl. no. 38433/09, §173.

188 J.M. Emaus, *Handhaving van EVRM-rechten via het aansprakelijkheidsrecht. Over de inpassing van de fundamentele rechtsschending in het Nederlandse burgerlijk recht*, Den Haag, Boom juridische Uitgevers 2013, at 64–65.

take into account the financial situations of the parties and the fact that the Court acknowledges that the member states are in principle better placed to protect human rights and to estimate (especially pecuniary) damages. Because of these two reasons, it seems likely that the Court will not replace the formal notion of equality of the parties by a substantial notion of equality but that it will only draw a marginal boundary.

One can object to this conclusion that the Court in *Steel and Morris* ruled that Art. 8 was violated although the compensation that the applicants in national tort had to pay were rather limited. But these were only compensations for non-pecuniary damages that, by their nature, cannot be estimated precisely. It is far more acceptable that courts take into account the financial situation of the parties with regard to non-pecuniary damages as with regard to pecuniary damages. Indeed, with regard to non-pecuniary damages, one can note that the Greek Court of Cassation, the *Areoios Pagos*, and the Lithuanian High Court have already taken into account the financial situation of the applicants.[189] Similar judgments cannot be found in cases where pecuniary damages had to be compensated. So, for pecuniary damages, it seems plausible that the right to an integral restitution of damages can only be limited in very exceptional situations.

The question arises then how these exceptional situations can be defined, how one can draw a marginal boundary for the application of the substantial equality of the parties instead of the formal equality of the parties. At what point can we decide that the human rights of a tortfeasor can triple formal equality in tort law? An interesting approach can be found in the *Bürgschaft* case of the German *Bundesverfassungsgericht.*[190] A daughter had provided sureties for the debts of her father. The father was an estate agent who could only receive a credit of €25,000 with the bank. To double this amount of money, the bank required the daughter to provide sureties for the debts of her father. This daughter however, had had no education or regular job. Two years after the loan had been established, the father left his job as an estate agent and created a shipping company. To do this, he borrowed €660,000 to buy a ship. His plans did not succeed however. After a while, he had about €1.2 million's worth of debt

189 On this topic, see: E. Dacaronia, 'Greece' in H. Koziol and B. Steininger (eds.), *European Tort Law 2006*, Vienna, Springer, 2007, p237 at 249–251; and S. Selelionyte-Drukteiniene and L. Saltinyte, 'Lithuania' in K. Oliphant and B. Steininger (eds.), *European Tort Law 2011*, Berlin, De Gruyter, 2012, p386 at 392.

190 BVerfG 19 October 1993.

with the bank. At that point the bank decided to appeal the sureties of the daughter. Since the daughter had only very limited financial means, she could not pay the debts of her father. She then disputed the validity of the contract in which she had provided the sureties. Before the normal judges, the case was focused on the question of whether the bank had fulfilled its pre-contractual information duties. The *Bundesgerichtshof* decided that the bank had not sufficiently stressed the long-term risks of a surety, but found that it was up to the daughter to overlook the financial situation of her father. The daughter was thus held liable to pay the debts of her father.

The daughter did not stop there however. She filed a constitutional complaint with the *Bundesverfassungsgericht* and claimed that both her right to self-determination as enshrined in Art. 2(1) of the German Constitution and the principle of the social state as enshrined in Arts 20(1) and 28(1) of the German Constitution were violated. She argued that the size of the debts she had to compensate, deprived her of every change to acquire property in the future, which according to her constituted a violation of her right to self-determination. Thus the question arose that if the civil judges, by giving effect to the surety and by not attaching much weight to the precontractual information duty of the bank, violated the right to self-determination of the daughter. The *Bundesverfassungsgericht* noted in its judgment that the lawmaker had the task of protecting the right to self-determination in the relationships between private persons and had to pay special attention to situations where one of the parties is in position of power. If one of the parties in a contractual relationship is in a position of power that is able to impose its conditions unilaterally on the other country, the Court finds that one cannot accept that the other party voluntarily concluded the contract anymore. In such cases, the German Constitutional Court argued, civil law has to provide remedies.

The Court acknowledged that the lawmaker cannot provide remedies for all disproportionate power balances between private parties. It is hard for a lawmaker to foresee future power concentrations on the one hand and it would be problematic if courts could overrule the principle of *pacta sunt servanda* in every possible contract. From the perspective of legal certainty, one cannot accept that the validity of every single contract can be doubted based on an impaired power balance. If there does exist a structural inequality between two parties and if the results of a contract are extremely detrimental to one of the parties, private law has to provide a remedy to protect the right to self-determination of that person.

Applied to this case, the *Bundesverfassungsgericht* observed that the sureties were raised for an extremely high risk. The Court moreover found that the bank could reasonably have known that the daughter would not be able to pay her debts within her lifetime. The fact that the daughter was an adult at the time that she concluded the surety contract did not hinder the Court from this conclusion. The Court also found that for an adult person it was extremely difficult to know for what risk one can be appealed to. It moreover found that a professional merchant would not be able to foresee the extremely high risk that went with this surety contract. The *Bundesverfassungsgericht* thus ruled that the *Bundesgerichtshof* had had to interpret the pre-contractual information duty in such a way that it would have protected the right to self-determination in an appropriate way. Although this judgment was somehow criticized in the literature, the *Bundesverfassungsgericht* confirmed this approach later on.[191]

This judgment was decided based on the social state and the right to self-determination as is protected by the German constitution. The Convention does not contain these rights. This does not however mean that one cannot apply this approach in an analogous way in the context of the right to property or the right to a private life,[192] as enshrined in Art. 1 of the first protocol and Art. 8 of the Convention. Another obstacle could be found in the fact that this case had regard to a surety contract and not to tort law. It nevertheless seems possible to apply these same principles in tort law as well. The first reason for this lies in the fact that the case also had respect to the pre-contractual information duty, a topic that in some countries is regulated by tort law. Moreover, the German scholar Claus-Wilhelm Canaris has argued for the application of this jurisprudence in the context of tort law.[193] He argued that in cases where a victim is not dependent on compensation for his damages whereas the tortfeasor would be confronted with the impossibility of building a future, the compensation should be limited in favor of the tortfeasor. In one case, the civil tribunal of Dessau has already applied this principle in a case where children were held liable via a faultless liability scheme.[194] The Austrian scholar Franz Bydlinski also argued that this principle had to be applied

191 O. Cherednychenko, 'The harmonisation of contract law in Europe by means of the horizontal effect of fundamental rights?', *Erasmus Law Review* 2007, p37 at 42.

192 For a similar line of reasoning, but without referring to *Burgerschaft*, see: W. Berka, 'Human Rights and Tort Law', 2011, above n. 15, p237 at 285–286.

193 C.-W. Canaris, 'Verstöße gegen das verfassungsrechtliche Übermaßverbot im Recht der Gëschäftsfähigkeit und im Schadensersatzrecht', *Juristen Zeitung* 1987, p993 at 995–996.

194 See also: N. Ferreira, 'Fundamental Rights, Constitutional Principles, and the Law of Torts: Tortfeasors v. Tort Victims' in A. Colombi Ciacchi, C. Godt, P. Rott and L. Smith (eds.), *Liber Amicorum Gert Brüggemeier. Liability in the Third Millenium*, Baden-Baden, Nomos, 2009, p49 at 58.

in civil law as a general principle of proportionality.[195] He argued that it is sometimes reasonable to mitigate the compensation for damages because a lot of factors that influence the size of the damages are often the result of coincidental or at least unpredictable elements.[196] Helmut Koziol also argued that such an approach would provide an added value to the rules of insolvency law because insolvency law only guarantees a subsistence level of protection, whereas tort law could provide a broader protection to tortfeasors.[197]

---

195 F. Bydlinski, *System und Prinzipien des Privatrechts*, Vienna, Springer, 1996, 225–233.

196 *Ibid.*, 228.

197 H. Koziol, *Basic Questions of Tort Law from a Germanic Perspective*, Vienna, Jan Sramek Verlag, 2012, at 305.

CONCLUSION

When confronted with a car accident, a professional accident or a case of medical liability, one does not immediately think that it might be useful to appeal to human rights. At first sight it seems unlikely that human rights have any relevance in such a case for the simple reason that tort law and human rights traditionally belonged to different spheres of the law. This book has illustrated that both fields of law are growing towards one another and have become entangled. The reason for this is that the ECHR more and more influences national tort law, both on the level of governmental liability and with regard to the horizontal application of tort law. Accordingly, human rights may be of use in cases of medical negligence, traffic accidents or professional liabilities. The fact that tort law provides a remedy for the violation of material or moral interests of persons, can at least partially be explained by human rights for the reason that a government should ensure that remedies in national law exist when the fundamental rights of people are infringed. Tort law often offers such a remedy. It is not the only system in national law that can provide it, but it is an indispensable one. Tort law has both a compensatory and a deterrent function. Human rights require that national remedies have both these functions. Of course, this does not have to be done via tort law. But tort law is flexible and has a broad field of application. It can provide a remedy when new societal evolutions appear, and human rights require an effective remedy, even when the lawmaker has not yet had the chance to provide an effective remedy. Tort law is not restricted by the principle of legality in the same way as criminal law or social security law. Consequently, it can be used as a deterrent instrument when the ECHR requires so and when no other national legal instrument is at hand.

This book did not only intend to illustrate how human rights can influence tort law. The influence of human rights on tort law is only one side of the book. The book has a dual aim: to investigate how national tort law can be influenced by the ECHR and to assess how human rights can be perceived as tort law. In order to do so, the book showed that the ECHR can be used as a compensatory instrument. One can appeal to the Convention in order to challenge national tort law to provide compensation that is effective in the meaning of Art. 13 of the Convention and one can appeal to the Court in order to receive compensation on the basis of Art. 41 of the Convention. Both methods are also connected. Compensation in national tort law is considered effective in the sense of Art. 13 when it is more or less in line with the compensation that the Court itself grants on the basis of Art. 41 of the Convention.

Accordingly, it was shown that the Court in its jurisprudence uses notions that are very similar to those used in national tort law systems, although it does so while applying a different terminology. First of all, national tort law and Art. 41 have the same goal in mind with regard to restitution of damages. Both systems aim to repair the damages of the injured party by putting him as far as possible in the situation he would find himself in if the human rights violation of the event giving rise to the damage had never occurred. Moreover, both systems give precedence to restoration in kind over compensation by equivalent. Indeed, both tort law and the Convention assume that recovery in kind must be offered, except if this is impossible for factual or legal reasons. With this regard, it has been shown that the protection of the Convention rights of the liable person can be used as a criterion in national tort law. Thirdly, both systems try to assess the damage in a concrete manner but appeal to an abstract assessment of damages if it is impossible to assess the actual damages precisely. However, the ECtHR seems to assess damages more often in an abstract manner. This can be attributed to the intangible nature of many human rights violations and the inability to estimate immaterial damage in a concrete manner.

These similarities between tort law and Art. 41 of the Convention in the context of restitution illustrate that the ECtHR develops a compensatory practice that shares many similarities with national tort law. At first sight however, there seems to be one big difference between the practice of the Court and tort law. In its application of Art. 41, the Court often uses declaratory judgments. This means that it does not award financial compensation to the victims of a Convention violation but declares that the mere finding of a violation of the Convention in itself grants sufficient satisfaction to the victim of the Convention violation and that further financial compensation is therefore unnecessary. Where the *restitutio in integrum* is the basic goal of Art. 41, declaratory judgments are the main exception. It is unfortunate that the Court in its jurisprudence poorly motivates why it awards only declaratory judgments, but this book has illustrated that most of these judgments can be explained by referring to principles of national tort law. Indeed, the Court seems to make declaratory judgments when no causal link could be established between the Convention violation and the claimed damages, when the human rights victim made a decisive contributory fault, when the Court at the same time required the state to take measures under Art. 46 to compensate the damages, when the suffered loss was very minimal, etc.

The only reason that seems to be at odds with national tort law, is the *de minimis* rule. Of course, this rule also exists (at least implicitly) in some national legal systems, but there is one major difference between its application in national law and in the framework of Art. 41. When the *de minimis* rule is applied in the context of Art. 41, the Court will still find a violation of the Convention. In national tort law, a judge will probably reject the claim. This raises the question of whether judges in national law must also be able to make declaratory judgments. From the perspective of Art. 13 of the Convention, this might be required in order to provide an effective remedy in national law. This does not however have as a result that the application of declaratory judgments must be generalized in national law, as a kind of remedy for subjective rights violations. Article 13 only applies to Convention rights and not to other rights that citizens derive from national law. If a national state provides the possibility to file a claim in national law directly on the basis of the Convention, and if this can result in the finding of a violation even without compensation if it is not required under Art. 41, the state fulfils its obligations under Art. 13 of the Convention. On the other hand, states can also choose to apply general rules of liability law and grant one symbolic euro as compensation for a human rights violation.

The focus on declaratory judgments might not give the impression that the ECtHR cannot have an effect on the level of damages in national law. Indeed, it has been illustrated that the interaction between Arts 13 and 41 of the Convention can have an impact on the amounts of damages that must be awarded under national law. For example, in cases where the right to life or the prohibition of torture is violated, the Court requires states to provide a real financial compensation for moral damages and sometimes even awards such compensation out of its own motion. With regard to the assessment of compensation for moral damages, the Court might have a real impact on national tort law. This is especially true for the reason that the Court shows less constraint when it has to award compensation for moral damages. With regard to material damages, the Court regularly ruled that national judges are better placed to estimate their size. With regard to non-pecuniary damages, it rules that this is not so. Thus, the practice of the Court under Art. 41 can have a relevant impact on this issue in national tort law. The impact of the Court on the compensation of non-pecuniary damages can be influenced both by the need of the Court to grant human rights victims redress or by the will to deter private citizens and governments to violate human rights.

The requirement to provide an effective remedy might also have other implications for tort law. Take for instance the situations where an unknown person who is certainly part of a defined group, but who cannot be identified, harms a human right of another citizen. One can think about the situation where an employee worked for different employers in the asbestos industry and is hit by a cancer that is caused by exposure to asbestos. This person under some legal systems will be unable to claim damages in torts, because he will not be able to establish a causal link between his disease and the exposure to asbestos while working for one specific factory. Taken from the perspective of the Convention, this might be a problem. The ECtHR requires states to provide an effective remedy, in principle including compensation for moral damages, in order to protect the right to life. In case the right to life is violated and no remedy is offered for the strict application of the principle of causality, a violation of the Convention can be found.

With this in mind, it must be remembered that the Court uses a very broad notion of causality. Indeed, at first sight it seemed that the Court did not limit the factual causality, the causal link as is established by the *conditio sine qua non* test, by a notion of legal causality. Although there are some indications that the Court applies the theory of the protective purpose of the norm, the only real limitation of causality in the Court's approach comes from its competence. Indeed, it seems that the protective purpose of the norm is applied in a way so that states only have to compensate damages that fall under the purpose of their Convention obligations. If the harm that is caused by a Convention violation is simultaneously caused by an act of a third private citizen, the state can only be held liable for that part of the damages that is caused due to the Convention violation of the state, and not for the rest.

This book has also looked into the use by the Court of a principle of fault and blameworthiness. With regard to the blameworthiness of a tortfeasor, it was argued that the Court takes into account the own faults of mentally disabled persons and children with regard to the estimation of damages. Thus, it was argued that the Court does not take the blameworthiness into account much and will require states to provide effective remedies if human rights are violated by persons that are not blameworthy. It was also argued that the Court takes into account notions such as force majeure, legitimate self-defense and insuperable error. Moreover, it has also argued that the human rights of a tortfeasor might also be perceived as a justification ground in national tort law. With regard to the fault, it was argued that the Court somehow takes the general standard of conduct into account when applying the human rights test. Indeed, in both legal systems one can only be held liable if a certain behavior can be blamed on someone. In the context of human rights, a proportionality test is used and not the general standard of conduct, but the similarities between the two tests can hardly be ignored. The due diligence test always involves a weighing of interests. If one behaves with due diligence, he will always have to make a proper balance between his own interests and those of a potential injured party. A consequence of this is that it is hard to protect a human right by a general faultless liability scheme. Only when the protection of a human right can be protected with a faultless liability regime that applies in a very specific situation, can it be accepted that the mere violation of this regime leads to liability.

The fact that there are large similarities between the general standard of conduct and the human rights test does not have as a consequence that the Convention cannot influence this element of national tort law. Quite the opposite is true. Although human rights may not lead to the introduction of a lot of faultless liability schemes, they do present a catalog of interests that must be protected by tort law. One might say that human rights express the underlying principles of fault in the factual and concrete circumstances of its application. Human rights do not differ that much from the general standard of conduct, but they do offer substantive instruments on which the judge can support his considerations. The interaction between human rights and liability law therefore seems to be supported, not only on the grounds that the criteria of liability law are implicitly included in the human rights test, but also on the fact that liability law internalizes human rights. One of the aspects of Art. 1382 in the Code Civil is that it forces the judge to include a whole branch of other legal provisions in the assessment of a case. In a similar way, the substantive criteria that human rights law provides can be used to apply the general standard of conduct in a more concrete way. Indeed, the jurisprudence of the ECtHR concerning, for example, the reasonable time requirement or the exercise of the freedom of expression, might influence jurisprudence in continental liability law systems so that it will develop more concrete criteria in all these types of cases, based upon human rights principles. It might be that the practice of tort law or liability law in some legal systems will become more fragmented into different branches, based upon the different human rights.

Whether the Convention will have as an effect that national liability law will become more fragmented is still an open question. What is certain is that the Convention influences national liability law on several manners more and more. The Convention can influence all the different elements of liability, both in a way that is protective for the tortfeasor as for the victim. In exceptional cases, notions of damages and fault in national law might be corrected by the Convention. For this reason, it is important that the Convention becomes a part of the research on comparative, European and national tort law. Such an approach will not only be benevolent for national law, but also for human rights law. A comparative approach towards tort law that includes the study of the Convention must make human rights lawyers more aware of the relevance of a tort-law perspective on the Convention and the jurisprudence of the Court. Indeed, if one reads the jurisprudence of the Court from a tort-law perspective, it seems that the Court can still learn a lot from the national legal orders, especially when dealing with Art. 41 of the Convention.

BIBLIOGRAPHY

ABEL, R., 'Torts' in D. KAIRYS (ed.), *The politics of law. A progressive critique*, New York, Basic Books, 1998, 445–470.

AHSMANN, M., 'Van "delictum" tot "delict": De gemeenschappelijke wortels van strafrecht en privaatrecht' in A. HOL and C. STOLKER (eds.), *Over de grenzen van strafrecht en burgerlijk recht*, Deventer, Kluwer, 1995, 11–23.

AMRANI MEKKI, S., 'Les causes de suspension et d'interpretation de la prescription' in P. JOURDAIN and P. WERY (eds.), *La prescription extinctive. Etudes de droit comparé*, Brussels, Bruylant, 2010, 474–505.

ANG, F., and BERGHMANS, E., 'Friendly settlements and striking out of applications' in P. LEMMENS and W. VANDENHOLE (eds.), *Protocol No. 14 and the Reform of the European Court of Human Rights*, Antwerp, Intersentia, 2005, 89–104.

ANTHONY, G., 'Positive Obligations and Policing in the House of Lords', *EHRLR* 2009, 538–551.

ARAI, Y., 'The System of Restrictions' in P. VAN DIJK, F. VAN HOOF, A. VAN RIJN and L. ZWAAK (eds.), *Theory and Practice of the European Convention on Human Rights*, Antwerp, Intersentia, 2006, 333–350.

——, 'Right to an effective Remedy before a National Authority (Article 13)' in P. VAN DIJK, F. VAN HOOF, A. VAN RIJN and L. ZWAAK (eds.), *Theory and Practice of the European Convention on Human Rights*, Antwerp, Intersentia, 2006, 997–1026.

BACACHE-GIBEILI, M., *Traité de Droit Civil, Tome 5, Les obligations: La responsabilité civile extracontractuelle*, Paris, Economica, 2012, 968p.

BAGINSKA, E., 'Poland' in H. KOZIOL and B. STEININGER (eds.), *European Tort Law 2004*, Vienna, Springer, 2005, 462–478.

BAGINSKA, E., (ed.), *Damages for Violations of Human Rights. A Comparative Study of Domestic Legal Systems*, Heidelberg, Springer, 2016, 486p.

BAGSHAW, R., 'Tort design and human rights thinking' in D. HOFFMAN (ed.), *The Impact of the UK Human Rights Act on Private Law*, Cambridge, Cambridge University Press, 2011, 110–135.

BARAK, A., 'Constitutional Human Rights and Private Law', *Review of Constitutional Studies* 1996, 218–281.

——, 'Constitutional Human Rights in Private Law' in D. FRIEDMAN and D. BARAK-ERERTZ (eds.), *Human Rights in Private Law*, Oxford, Hart Publishing, 2003, 13–34.

BARGELLI, E., 'Italy' in H. KOZIOL and B. STEININGER (eds.), *European Tort Law 2003*, Vienna, Springer, 2004, 266–277.

——, 'Italy' in H. Koziol and B. Steininger (eds.), *European Tort Law 2006*, Vienna, Springer, 2007, 299–310.

Barkhuysen, T., 'EHRM, *Kudla v Poland*, 26 oktober 2000, Appl.nr. 30210/96', *NJCM-Bulletin* 2001, 71–88.

Barkhuysen, T., Van Emmerik, M. and Loof, J., '50 jaar EVRM en het Nederlandse staats- en bestuursrecht - ontwikkelingen en overzichten', *NJCM-Bulletin* 2000, 327–408.

Barkhuysen, T. and Van Emmerik, M., 'Constitutionalisation of Private Law: The European Convention on Human Rights Perspective' in T. Barkhuysen and S.D. Lindenbergh, *Constitutionalization of Private Law*, Leiden, Martinus Nijhoff Publishers, 2006, 43–57.

Barkhuysen, T. and Van Emmerik, M., 'Rechtsherstel bij schending van het EVRM in Nederland en Straatsburg', *NJCM-Bulletin* 2006, 39–64.

Beever, A., 'Our most fundamental rights' in D. Nolan and A. Robertson, *Rights and Private Law*, Oxford, Hart Publishing, 2012, 63–87.

Bell, J., 'The Development of tort Law' in H. Koziol and B. Steininger (eds.), *European Tort Law* 2007, Vienna, Springer, 2008, 2–23.

Berka, W., 'Human Rights and Tort Law' in A. Fenyves, E. Karner, H. Koziol and E. Steiner (eds.), *Tort Law in the Jurisprudence of the European Court of Human Rights*, Göttingen, De Gruyter, 2011, 237–288.

Bernhardt, R., 'The Convention and Domestic Law' in R. Macdonald, F. Matscher and H. Petzold (eds.), *The European System for the Protection of Human Rights*, Dordrecht, Martinus Nijhoff Publishers, 1993, 25–40.

Besson, S., 'Human Rights in Relation. A Critical Reading of the ECtHR's Approach to Conflicts of Rights' in S. Smet and E. Brems, *When Human Rights Clash at the European Court of Human Rights*, Oxford, Oxford University Press, 2017, 24–37.

Birsan, C., 'Les aspects nouveaux de l'application des Articles 41 et 46 de la convention dans la jurisprudence de la cour européenne des droits de l'homme' in H. Hartig (ed.), *Trente ans de droit européen des droits de l'homme. Etudes à la mémoire de Wolfgan Strasser*, Brussels, Bruylant, 2007, 19–44.

Bitans, A., 'Latvia' in K. Oliphant and B. Steininger (eds.), *European Tort Law 2011*, Berlin, De Gruyter, 2012, 364–385.

Bocken, H. and Boone, I., 'Causaliteit in het Belgische recht', *TPR* 2002, 1625–1685.

Bocken H., Boone, I., and Kruithof, M., *Inleiding tot het schadevergoedingsrecht. Buitencontractueel aansprakelijkheidsrecht en andere schadevergoedingsstelsels*, Bruges, Die Keure, 2014, 270p.

Boerefijn, I., 'Billijker genoegdoening', *NJCM-Bulletin* 2004, 920–923.

Borghetti, J.-S., 'Punitive Damages in France' in H. Koziol and V. Wilcox (eds.), *Punitive Damages: Common Law and Civil Law Perspectives*, Vienna, Springer, 2009, 55–73.

Bowers, J. and Lewis, J., 'Whistleblowing: Freedom of Expression in the Workplace', *European Human Rights Law Review* 1996, 637–648.

BREMS, E., 'The Margin of Appreciation Doctrine of the European Court of Human Rights; Accommodating Diversity within Europe' in D. FORSYTHE and P. MCMAHON (eds.), *Human Rights and Diversity; Area Studies Revisited*, Lincoln and London University of Nebraska Press, 2003, 81–110.

——, 'Evans v. UK. Three Grounds for Ruling Differently' in S. SMET and E. BREMS, *When Human Rights Clash at the European Court of Human Rights*, Oxford, Oxford University Press, 2017, 75–94.

BRINKTRINE, R., 'The Horizontal Effect of Human Rights in German Constitutional Law: The British debate on horizontality and the possible role model of the German doctrine of mittelbare Drittwirkung der Grundrechte', *European Human Rights Law Review* 2001, 421–432.

BRÜGGEMEIER, G., 'Constitutionalization of Private Law, The German Perspective' in T. BARKHUYSEN and S.D. LINDENBERGH, *Constitutionalization of Private Law*, Leiden, Martinus Nijhoff Publishers, 2006, 59–82.

——, 'Protection of personality rights in the law of delict/torts in Europe: mapping out paradigms' in G. BRÜGGEMEIER, A. COLOMBO CIACCHI and P. O'CALLAGHAN (eds.), *Personality Rights in European Tort Law*, Cambridge, Cambridge University Press, 2010, 5–37.

——, 'European Civil Liability Law outside Europe. The Example of the Big Three: China, Brazilo, Russia', *Journal of European Tort Law* 2011, 1–22.

BRUN, P., *Responsabilité civile extracontractuelle*, Paris, Lexisnexis, 2014, 642p.

BUKSPAN, E., 'A new home for human rights and social responsibility', *Intercultural Human Rights Law Review* 2012, 329–388.

BURGESS, G., *Absolute Monarchy and the Stuart Constitution*, New Haven, Yale University Press, 1996, 240p.

BUSSTRA, M., 'Eigen verantwoordelijkheid bij mensenrechten: een verkenning binnen het EVRM-systeem', *NJCM-Bulletin* 2008, 345–363.

BYDLINSKI, F., *System und Prinzipien des Privatrechts*, Vienna, Springer, 1996, 777p.

——, 'Methodological Approaches to the Tort Law of the ECHR' in A. FENYVES, E. KARNER, H. KOZIOL and E. STEINER (eds.), *Tort Law in the Jurisprudence of the European Court of Human Rights*, Göttingen, De Gruyter, 2011, 29–127.

CANARIS, C.-W., 'Verstöße gegen das verfassungsrechtliche Übermaßverbot im Recht der Gëschäftsfähigkeit und im Schadensersatzrecht', *Juristen Zeitung* 1987, 993–1004.

CANIVET, J., 'De la réparation du préjudice des victimes par ricochet', *JT* 1963, 597–603.

CANNIE, H. and VOORHOOF, D., 'The abuse clause and freedom of expression in the European Human Rights Convention', *Netherlands Quarterly of Human Rights* 2011, 54–83.

CARUANA-DEMAJO, G., QUINTANO, L. and ZAMMIT, D., 'Malta' in H. KOZIOL and B. STEININGER, *European Tort Law 2009*, Vienna, Springer, 2010, 392–425.

CASSESE, A., 'Prohibition of Torture and Inhuman or Degrading Treatment or Punishment' in R. MACDONALD, F. MATSCHER and H. PETZOLD (eds.),

The European System for the Protection of Human Rights, Dordrecht, Martinus Nijhoff Publishers, 1993, 225–261.

Cauffman, C., 'Naar een punitief Verbintenissenrecht? Een rechtsvergelijkende studie naar de draagwijdte, de grondwettigheid en de wenselijkheid van het bestraffend karakter van het verbintenissenrecht', *TPR* 2007, 799–865.

Cherednychenko, O., 'Towards the control of private acts by the European Court of Human Rights?', *Maastricht Journal of European and Comparative Law* 2006, 195–218.

——, 'The harmonisation of contract law in Europe by means of the horizontal effect of fundamental rights?', *Erasmus Law Review* 2007, 37–57.

Christoffersen, J., 'Denmark: Drittwsirkung and Conflicting Rights – Viewed from National and International Perspectives' in D. Oliver and J. Fëdtke (eds.), *Human Rights and the Private Sphere – A Comparative Study*, London, Routledge, 2007, 27–62.

Clapham, A., *Human Rights in the Private Sphere*, Oxford, Clarendon Press, 1993, 385p.

——, 'The "Drittwirkung" of the Convention' in R. Macdonald, F. Matscher and H. Petzold (eds.), *The European System for the Protection of Human Rights*, Dordrecht, Martinus Nijhoff Publishers, 1993, 163–206.

——, 'Opinion: The Privatisation of Human Rights', *European Human Rights Law Review* 1996, 20–32.

Cohen-Jonathan, G., 'Respect for Private and Family Life' in R. Macdonald, F. Matscher and H. Petzold (eds.), *The European System for the Protection of Human Rights*, Dordrecht, Martinus Nijhoff Publishers, 1993, 405–444.

Cornhill, Lord Bingham of, 'The Uses of Tort', *Journal of European Tort Law* 2010, 1–15.

Costa, J.-P., 'The provision of compensation under Article 41 of the European Convention on Human Rights' in D. Fairgrieve, M. Adenas and J. Bell (eds.), *Tort Liability of Public Authorities in Comparative Perspective*, London, The British Institute of International and Comparative Law, 2002, 3–16.

——, 'Concepts juridiques dans la jurisprudence de la Cour européenne des droits de l'homme: de l'influence de différentes traditions nationales', *Rev.Trim.D.H.* 2004, 101–110.

Cousy, H., 'Over aansprakelijkheidsrecht en verzekering: living apart together?' in *Liber Amicorum Walter Van Gerven*, Antwerp, Kluwer, 2000, 203–222.

Cremer, H.-J., *Human Rights and the Protection of Privacy in Tort Law. A Comparison between English and German law*, London, Routledge, 2001, 277p.

Dawn, O., 'Constitutional Guarantees in the Light of Privatization' in M. Andenas, S. Diaz Alabart, B. Markesinis, H. Micklitz and N. Pasquini (eds.), *Liber Amicorum Guido Alpha. Private Law beyond the National Systems*, London, British Institute of International and Comparative Law, 2007, 328–344.

De Beco, G., 'Le protocole no 12 à la convention européenne des droits de l'homme', *Rev.trim.dr.h.* 2010, 591–615.

DE CALLATAŸ, D. and ESTIENNE, N., *La responsabilité civile: chronique de jurisprudence 1996–2007: le Dommage*, Brussels, Larcier, 2009, 605p.

DE CALLATAŸ, D., 'Choix des modes de réparation (capital, rente ou forfait) et barémisation des indemnités' in B. DUBUISSON and P. JOURDAIN (eds.), *Le dommage et sa réparation dans la responsabilité contractuelle et extracontractuelle. Etudes de droit comparé*, Brussels, Larcier, 2015, 669–683.

DEDEK, H., 'Of rights superstructural, inchoate and triangular: the role of rights in Blackstone's Commentaries' in D. NOLAN and A. ROBERTSON, *Rights and Private Law*, Oxford, Hart Publishing, 2012, 183–220.

DE GAAY FORTMAN, B., 'Human Rights as *Regulae Iuris*: An Inquiry into the Dialectics of Legality versus Legitimacy', *European Review of Private Law* 2012, 409–424.

DE HERT, P. and SOMERS, S., 'Principles of national constitutionalism limiting individual claims in human rights law. Constitutionalism and the balance between national and international legal reform', *Vienna Journal on International Constitutional Law* 2013, 5–28.

DEJEMEPPE, B., 'Pouvoir judiciaire et responsabilités', *JT* 1987, 278–279.

DEROUSSIN, D., *Histoire du droit des obligations*, Paris, Economica, 2007, 916p.

DE SALVIA, M., 'La satisfaction equitable au titre des mesures individuelles et la pratique des organs de la convention européenne des droits de l'homme: qu'en est-il du principe de sécurité juridique?' in H. HARTIG (ed.), *Trente ans de droit européen des droits de l'homme. Etudes à la mémoire de Wolfgan Strasser*, Brussels, Bruylant, 2007, 45–53.

——, 'Can the Reparation Awarded to Victims of Violations under the ECHR be Considered a Real "Just" Satisfaction' in A. FENYVES, E. KARNER, H. KOZIOL and E. STEINER (eds.), *Tort Law in the Jurisprudence of the European Court of Human Rights*, Göttingen, De Gruyter, 2011, 387–393.

——, 'Le principe de l'octroi subsidiaire des dommages-intérêts: d'une morale des droits de l'homme à une morale simplement indemnitaire?' in J.-F. FLAUSS and E. LAMBERT ABDELGAWAD (eds.), *La pratique d'indemnisation par la Cour européenne des droits de l'homme*, Brussels, Bruylant, 2011, 9–26.

DE SCHUTTER, O., 'Reasonable Accommodations and Positive Obligations in the European Convention on Human Rights' in A. LAWSON and C. GOODING (eds.), *Disability Rights in Europe: From Theory to Practice*, Oxford, Hart Publishing, 2005, 35–64.

DE VOS, B.J., *Horizontale werking van grondrechten. Een kritiek*, Apeldoorn-Antwerp, Maklu, 2010, 416p.

DIAS PEREIRA, A., 'Portugal' in H. KOZIOL and B. STEININGER (eds.), *European Tort Law 2002*, Vienna, Springer, 2003, 345–363.

DIRIX, E., *Het begrip schade*, 2de ongewijzigde druk, Antwerp, Maklu, 1998, 150p.

——, 'Abstracte en concrete schade', *RW* 2000-01, 1329–1335.

——, 'Verkenningen op de grenzen van privaat- en publiekrecht' in A. ALEN, V. JOOSTEN, B. LEYSEN and W. VERRIJDT (eds.), *Liberae cogitationes. Liber Amicorum Marc Bossuyt*, Antwerp, Intersentia, 2013, 253–265.

Drzemczewski, A., 'The European Human Rights Convention and Relations between Private Parties', *Netherlands International Law Review* 1979, 163–181.

Drzemczewski, A. and Giakoumopoulos, C., 'Article 13' in L.E. Pettitti, E. Decaux and P.-H. Imbert (eds.), *La Convention Européenne des droits de l'homme. Commentaire Article par Article*, Paris, Economica, 1999, 455–474.

Dubuisson, B., 'De la légèreté de la faute au poids du hasard. Réflexions sur l'évolution du droit de la responsabilité civile', *RGAR* 2005, nr. 14.009.

——, 'Responsabilité contractuelle et responsabilité aquillienne. Comparaison n'est pas raison' in S. Stijns and P. Wery (eds.), *De raakvlakken tussen de contractuele en de buitencontractuele aansprakelijkheid*, Bruges, Die Keure, 2010, 1–51.

Dubuisson, B., Callewaert, V., De Coninck, B. and Gathem, G., *La Responsabilité civile. Chronique de jurisprudence 1996–2007*, Part 1, Le fait générateur et le lien causal, Brussels, Larcier, 2009, 1074p.

Dubuisson, B., Callewaert, V., De Coninck, B. and Gathem, G., *La Responsabilité civile. Chronique de jurisprudence 1996–2007*, Part 2, *Le dommage*, Brussels, Larcier, 2009, 605p.

Dufwa, B., 'Horizontal effect of the European Convention: Swedish Case Law' in A. Colombi Ciacchi, C. Godt, P. Rott and L. Smith (eds.), *Liber Amicorum Gert Brüggemeier. Liability in the Third Millenium*, Baden-Baden, Nomos, 2009, 85–109.

du Plessis, M. and Ford, J., 'Developing the Common Law Progressively – Horizontality, the Human Rights Act and the South African Experience', *EHRLR* 2004, 286–313.

Edel, F., 'L'indemnisation par la Cour européenne des droits de l'homme des victimes de violations de la liberté d'expression' in J.-F. Flauss and E. Lambert Abdelgawad (eds.), *La pratique d'indemnisation par la Cour européenne des droits de l'homme*, Brussels, Bruylant, 2011, 229–257.

Eissen, M.-A., 'The Principle of Proportionality in the Case-Law of the European Court of Human Rights' in R. Macdonald, F. Matscher and H. Petzold (eds.), *The European System for the Protection of Human Rights*, Dordrecht, Martinus Nijhoff Publishers, 1993, 125–146.

Emaus, J.-M., 'Verkenningen in en rondom the borderland between private and public acts. Enkele opmerkingen bij het door Engelhard besprokene' in L. Besselink and R. Nehmelman (eds.), *De aangesproken staat. Staatsrechtconferentie 2009 Universiteit van Utrecht*, Wolf Legal Publishers, Nijmegen, 2010, 59–69.

——, *Handhaving van EVRM-rechten via het aansprakelijkheidsrecht. Over de inpassing van de fundamentele rechtsschending in het Nederlandse burgerlijk recht*, Den Haag, Boom juridische Uitgevers, 2013, 427p.

Engelhard, E., '(Staats)aansprakelijkheid bij de schending van EVRM-rechten in het "grijze" gebied' in L. Besselink and R. Nehmelman (eds.), *De aangesproken staat. Staatsrechtconferentie 2009 Universiteit van Utrecht*, Wolf Legal Publishers, Nijmegen, 2010, 10–57.

Englard, I., *The Philosophy of Tort Law*, London, Dartmouth Publishing Company, 1993, 254.

Fagnart, J.-L., 'La compensation du dommage: Entre le droit de nuire et la réparation de l'irréparable' in R. Capart and J. Bouckourt (eds.), *Liber Amicorum Nöel Simar: Evaluation du dommage, Responsabilité civile et Assurances*, Limal, Anthemis, 2013, 225–249.

——, 'La peine privée: une réalité qui dérange?' in X. (ed.), *Liber Amicorum François Glansdorff et Pierre Legros*, Brussels, Bruylant, 2014, 133–167.

Faure, M., 'Vergoeding van immateriële schade vanuit rechtseconomisch perspectief' in P. Kottenhagen-Edzes (ed.), *Immateriële schade: tendensen en wensen*, Groningen, Intersentia, 2000, 107–123.

——, 'Liability for Omissions in Tort Law: Economic Analysis', *Journal of European Tort Law* 2011, 184–208.

Faure, M. and Van Den Bergh, R., 'Efficiënties van het foutcriterium in het Belgisch aansprakelijkheidsrecht', *Rechtskundig Weekblad* 1987–88, 1105–1119.

Faure M. and Hartlief, T., 'The Netherlands' in H. Koziol and B. Steininger (eds.), *European Tort Law 2006*, Vienna, Springer, 2007, 338–360.

Favilli, C. and Fusaro, C., 'Italy: The Protection of Constitutional Rights in the Private Sphere' in D. Oliver and J. Fëdtke (eds.), *Human Rights and the Private Sphere - A Comparative Study*, London, Routledge, 2007, 276–311.

Fëdtke, J., 'Germany' in H. Koziol and B. Steiniger (eds.), *European Tort Law 2001*, Vienna, Springer, 2002, 229–268.

——, 'Germany' in H. Koziol and B. Steininger (eds.), *European Tort Law 2005*, Vienna, Springer, 2006, 281–305.

——, 'Protective Purpose of the Rule' in A. Fenyves, E. Karner, H. Koziol and E. Steiner (eds.), *Tort Law in the Jurisprudence of the European Court of Human Rights*, Göttingen, De Gruyter, 2011, 539–566.

Feldman, D., 'Remedies for Violations of Convention Rights under the Human Rights Act', *European Human Rights Law Review* 1998, 691–711.

Fenet, P.A., *Receuil complet des travaux préparatoires du Code civil*, Vol. XIII, Paris, 1827, 832p.

Fenwick, H., Masterman, R. and Philippson, G., 'The Human Rights Act in contemporary context' in H. Fenwick, G. Philippson and R. Masterman (eds.), *Judicial reasoning under the UK Human Rights Act*, Cambridge, Cambridge University Press, 2007, 1–21.

Fenyves, A., 'Concluding Remarks on Wrongfulness and Fault' in A. Fenyves, E. Karner, H. Koziol and E. Steiner (eds.), *Tort Law in the Jurisprudence of the European Court of Human Rights*, Göttingen, De Gruyter, 2011, 843–850.

Ferreira, N., 'Fundamental Rights, Constitutional Principles, and the Law of Torts: Tortfeasers v. Tort Victims' in A. Colombi Ciacchi, C. Godt, P. Rott and L. Smith (eds.), *Liber Amicorum Gert Brüggemeier. Liability in the Third Millenium*, Baden-Baden, Nomos, 2009, 49–84.

Ferreira, N., Krzeminska-Vamvaka, J. and Russo, T., 'The horizontal effect of fundamental rights and freedoms in European Union Law' in G. Brüggemeier, A. Colombi Ciacchi and G. Commandé (eds.), *Fundamental Rights and Private Law in the European Union*, Vol. I, *A Comparative Overview*, Cambridge, Cambridge University Press, 2010, 8–39.

Flauss, J.-F., 'L'abus de droit dans le cadre de la Convention Européenne des droits de l'homme', *R.F.D.A.* 1992, 1026–1031.

——, 'La banalisation du contentieux indemnitaire devant la Cour européenne des droits de l'homme', *Rev.Trim.D.H.* 1996, 93–100.

——, 'Le droit à un recours effectif au secours de la règle du délai raisonnable: un revirement de la jurisprudence historique', *Rev.Trim.D.H.* 2002, 179–201.

——, 'Conclusion générale' in J.-F. Flauss and E. Lambert Abdelgawad (eds.), *La pratique d'indemnisation par la Cour européenne des droits de l'homme*, Brussels, Bruylant, 2011, 329–340.

Fletcher, G., *Tort Liability for Human Rights Abuses*, Oxford, Oregon, 2008, 214p.

Fontana, B., 'Damage awards for human rights violations in the European and the Inter-American courts of human rights', *Santa Clara Law Review* 1991, 1127–1169.

Foqué, R., 'De rechter is het sprekende recht' in F. Evers and P. Lefranc (eds.), *Kiezen tussen recht en rechtvaardigheid*, Bruges, Die Keure, 2009, 79–91.

Gabartas, H. and Lauciene, M., 'Lithuania' in H. Koziol and B. Steininger (eds.), *European Tort Law 2004*, Vienna, Springer, 2005, 405–419.

Gabartas, H. and Saltinyte, L., 'Lithuania' in H. Koziol and B. Steininger (eds.), *European Tort Law 2010*, Berlin, De Gruyter, 2011, 353–383.

Galland, Y., 'Les obligations des journalistes dans la jurisprudence de la Cour européenne des droits de l'homme', *Rev.Trim.D.H.* 2002, 853–874.

Ganshof van der Meersch, 'L'ordre public et les droits de l'homme', *JT* 1968, 658–663.

Garin, A., 'La perte de chance, un préjudice indemnisable: contribution à une problématique de l'indemnisation du dommage par la Cour européenne des droits de l'homme' in J.-F. Flauss and E. Lambert Abdelgawad (eds.), *La pratique d'indemnisation par la Cour européenne des droits de l'homme*, Brussels, Bruylant, 2011, 155–185.

Garlicki, L., 'Relations between Private Actors and the European Convention on Human Rights' in A. Sajo and R. Uitz (eds.), *The Constitution in Private Relations: Expanding Constitutionalism*, Utrecht, Eleven, 2005, 129–143.

Gerards, J., 'Rechtsvinding door het Europees Hof voor de Rechten van de mens', *NJCM-Bulletin* 2006, 93–122.

Gerkens, J.-F., 'De l'origine criminelle des obligations' in X. (ed.), *Une criminologie de la tradition à l'innovation. Hommage à Georges Kellens*, Brussels, Larcier, 2006, 131–139.

Gerry, A., 'Öneryildiz t. Turkije', *European Human Rights Law Review* 2005, 203–212.

Gerstenberg, O., 'What constitutions do (but courts sometimes don't): property, speech, and the influence of constitutional norms on private law', *Canadian Journal of Law and Jurisprudence* 2004, 61–81.

——, 'Private law, constitutionalism and the limits of the judicial role' in C. Scott (ed.), *Torture as Tort. Comparative Perspectives on the Development of Transnational Human Rights Litigation*, Oxford, Hart Publishing, 2001, 687–703.

Girard, B., *Responsabilité civile extracontractuelle et droits fondamentaux*, Paris, LGDJ, 2015, 405p.

Glansdorff, F., 'Les conditions de la responsabilité extracontractuelle' in E. Van den Haute (ed.), *Le droit des obligations dans les jurisprudences français et belge*, Brussels, Bruylant, 2013, 103–122.

Goldberg, J., 'Introduction: pragmatism and private law', *Harvard Law Review* 2012, 1640–1663.

Golsong, H., 'Quelques réflexions a propos du pouvoir de la Cour Européenne des Droits de l'homme d'accorder une satisfaction équitable' in *René Cassin. Amicorum Discipulorumque*, Boek I., *Problèmes de protection internationale des droits de l'homme*, Paris, 1969, 89–94.

Goossens, C., 'Droits civils et droits politiques: constantes et variantes dans la jurisprudence; nature du droit à réparation en cas de lésion d'un droit politique', *RCJB* 1969, 308–339.

Gray, C., *Judicial Remedies in International Law*, Oxford, Clarendon Press, 1987, 250p.

Gray, K. and Gray, S., 'Civil Rights, Civil Wrongs and Quasi-Public Space', *European Human Rights Law Review*, 46–102.

Graziadei, M., 'What went wrong? Tort law, personal responsibility, expectations of proper care and compensation' in H. Koziol and B. Steininger (eds.), *European Tort Law 2008*, Vienna, Springer, 2009, 2–24.

Griffin, J., *On Human Rights*, Oxford, Oxford University Press, 2008, 339p.

Grundmann, S., 'On the Unity of Private Law from a Formal to a Substance-Based Concept of Private Law', *European Review of Private Law* 2010, 1055–1078.

Haeck, Y., *Procederen voor het Europees Hof voor de Rechten van de Mens*, Antwerp, Intersentia, 2009, 427p.

Hakalehto-Wainio, S., 'Finland' in H. Koziol and B. Steininger (eds.), *European Tort Law 2010*, Berlin, De Gruyter, 2011, 169–174.

Harby, C., 'The Changing Nature of Interim Measures before the European Court of Human Rights', *European Human Rights Law Review* 2010, 73–84.

Harpwood, V., 'Negligence: breach of duty' in K. Oliphant (ed.), *The Law of Tort*, Suffolk, LexisNexis Butterworths, 2007, 731–782.

Harris, D., O'Boyle, M., Bates, E. and Buckley, C., *Law of the European Convention on Human Rights*, Oxford, Oxford University Press, 2009, 902p.

Hartkamp, A., 'Europese mensenrechten en national dwingend recht – De Nederlandse rechter en het EVRM', *NJCM-Bulletin* 2000, 23–35.

Hartlief, T., 'Geld zetten op aansprakelijkheidsrecht', *TPR* 2009, 565–580.

Hartshorne, J., 'The Human Rights Act 1998 and Damages for Non-Pecuniary Loss', *European Human Rights Law Review* 2004, 660–671.

HERRMANN, C. and KERN, G., '"Wrongful life" claims and the absolute value of human life: a contradiction' in G. BRÜGGEMEIER, A. COLOMBI CIACCHI and G. COMMANDÉ (eds.), *Fundamental Rights and Private Law in the European Union*, Cambridge, Cambridge University Press, 2010, 249–278.

HINGHOFER-SZALKAY, D. and KOCH, B., 'No-Fault or Strict Liability' in A. FENYVES, E. KARNER, H. KOZIOL and E. STEINER (eds.), *Tort Law in the Jurisprudence of the European Court of Human Rights*, Göttingen, De Gruyter, 2011, 567–577.

HIRSCH, W., *Law and Economics. An introductory Analysis*, San Diego, Academic Press, 1999, 358.

HOUBBEN, M., 'Le devoir pour la victime de minimiser son dommage' in B. DUBUISSON and P. JOURDAIN, *Le dommage et sa réparation dans la responsabilité contractuelle et extracontractuelle. Etudes de droit comparé*, Brussels, Larcier, 2015, 513–566.

HRADEK, J., 'Czech Republic' in H. KOZIOL and B. STEININGER (eds.), *European Tort Law 2002*, Vienna, Springer, 2003, 119–135.

——, 'Czech Republic' in H. KOZIOL and B. STEININGER (eds.), *European Tort Law 2006*, Vienna, Springer, 2007, 123–145.

ICHIM, O., *Just Satisfaction under the European Convention on Human Rights*, Cambridge, Cambridge University Press, 2015, 376p.

JACOBS, F., WHITE, R. and OVEY, C., *The European Convention on Human Rights*, Oxford, Oxford University Press, 2010, 644.

JAK, N. and VERMONT, J., 'De Nederlandse rechter en de margin of appreciation. De rol van de margin of appreciation in de interne horizontale relatie tussen de rechtery, de wetgever en het bestuur', *NJCM-Bulletin* 2007, 125–140.

JANCZUK, A. and VELOSO GOMES, M., 'Claims for non-pecuniary losses by "third persons" upon death or injury' in G. BRÜGGEMEIER, A. COLOMBI CIACCHI and G. COMMANDÉ (eds.), *Fundamental Rights and Private Law in the European Union*, Cambridge, Cambridge University Press, 2010, 200–248.

JANSEN, N., and RADEMACHER, L., 'Punitive Damages in Germany' in H. KOZIOL and V. WILCOX (eds.), *Punitive Damages: Common Law and Civil Law Perspectives*, Vienna, Springer, 2009, 75–86.

JANSEN, S., 'The Defect of Consent Deceit, Information Duties and Discrimination Legislation: The Thor Steinar Cases Applied in Belgian Law', *European Review of Private Law* 2011, 371–393.

JEFFRIES, J., 'A comment on the constitutionality of punitive damages', *Virginia Law Review* 1986, 139–158.

JOZON, M., 'Satisfaction by Finding a Violation' in A. FENYVES, E. KARNER, H. KOZIOL and E. STEINER (eds.), *Tort Law in the Jurisprudence of the European Court of Human Rights*, Göttingen, De Gruyter, 2011, 741–770.

KARAPANOU, V. and VISSCHER, L., 'Towards a Better Assessment of Pain and Suffering Damages', *Journal of European Tort Law* 2010, 48–74.

KARNER, E., 'Concluding Remarks on Damage' in A. FENYVES, E. KARNER, H. KOZIOL and E. STEINER (eds.), *Tort Law in the Jurisprudence of the European Court of Human Rights*, Göttingen, De Gruyter, 2011, 829–834.

——, 'Concluding Remarks on Causation' in A. Fenyves, E. Karner, H. Koziol and E. Steiner (eds.), *Tort Law in the Jurisprudence of the European Court of Human Rights*, Göttingen, De Gruyter, 2011, 835–841.

——, 'Concluding Remarks on No-Fault or Strict Liability' in A. Fenyves, E. Karner, H. Koziol and E. Steiner (eds.), *Tort Law in the Jurisprudence of the European Court of Human Rights*, Göttingen, De Gruyter, 2011, 857–861.

Kay, R., 'The European Convention on Human Rights and the Control of Private Law', *European Human Rights Law Review* 2005, 466–479.

Keane, D., 'Attacking hate speech under Article 17 of the European Convention on Human Rights', *Netherlands Quarterly of Human Rights* 2007, 641–663.

Keirse, A., 'EVRMering van (letselschade)recht', *Letsel & Schade* 2011, afl. 1, 5–7.

Keller, H. and Garin, A., 'Câmpeanu: quo vadis? – Le recours individual en péril' *Revue Trimestrielle des Droits de l'Homme* 2017, 485–509.

Kellner, M. and Durant, I., 'Causation' in A. Fenyves, E. Karner, H. Koziol and E. Steiner (eds.), *Tort Law in the Jurisprudence of the European Court of Human Rights*, Göttingen, De Gruyter, 2011, 449–500.

Kenna, P., 'Housing Rights: Positive Duties and Enforceable Rights at the European Court of Human Rights', *European Human Rights Law Review* 2008, 193–208.

Kenny, J., 'European Convention on Human Rights and Social Welfare', *European Human Rights Law Review* 2010, 495–503.

Kissling, C. and Kelliher, D., 'Compensation for Pecuniary and Non-Pecuniary Loss' in A. Fenyves, E. Karner, H. Koziol and E. Steiner (eds.), *Tort Law in the Jurisprudence of the European Court of Human Rights*, Göttingen, De Gruyter, 2011, 579–723.

Kloth, M., *Immunities and the Right of Access to Court under Article 6 of the European Convention on Human Rights*, Leiden, Martinus Nijhof, 2010, 220p.

Koch, B., 'Comparative Remarks' in H. Koziol and B. Steininger (eds.), *European Tort Law 2002*, Vienna, Springer, 2003, 512–528.

——, 'Comparative Overview' in H. Koziol and B. Steininger (eds.), *European Tort Law 2005*, Vienna, Springer, 2006, 602–612.

Kohl, B., 'Moment de l'Evaluation et variation du dommages' in B. Dubuisson and P. Jourdain, *Le dommage et sa réparation dans la responsabilité contractuelle et extracontractuelle. Etudes de droit comparé*, Brussels, Larcier, 2015, 237–402.

Kortmann, J., 'The Tort Law Industry', *European Review of Private Law* 2009, 789–811.

Koziol, H., 'Conclusions' in H. Koziol et al. (eds.), *Unification of Tort Law: Wrongfulness*, The Hague, Kluwer, 1998, 129–135.

——, 'Concluding Remarks regarding the Methods of Interpreting Art. 41 ECHR' in A. Fenyves, E. Karner, H. Koziol and E. Steiner (eds.), *Tort Law in the Jurisprudence of the European Court of Human Rights*, Göttingen, De Gruyter, 2011, 825–828.

——, 'Causation under Austrian Law' in J. Spier (ed.), *Unification of Tort Law: Causation*, Kluwer, Den Haag, 2000, 11–21.

——, 'Liability for Omissions. Basic Questions', *Journal of European Tort Law* 2011, 127–134.

——, 'Concluding Remarks on Compensatory and Non-Compensatory Remedies' in A. Fenyves, E. Karner, H. Koziol and E. Steiner (eds.), *Tort Law in the Jurisprudence of the European Court of Human Rights*, Göttingen, De Gruyter, 2011, 863–875.

——, *Basic Questions of Tort Law from a Germanic Perspective*, Vienna, Jan Sramek Verlag, 2012, 380p.

Krenc, F., 'De l'obligation d'agir préalablement contre l'Etat belge devand les juridictions nationales en cas de dépassement du délai raisonnable', *JT* 2007, 722–724.

Krüger, H. and Norgaard, C., 'The Right of Application' in R. Macdonald, F. Matscher and H. Petzold (eds.), *The European System for the Protection of Human Rights*, Dordrecht, Martinus Nijhoff Publishers, 1993, 657–675.

Kruithof, R., 'La réparation du dommage extra-patrimonial en cas de mort ou d'atteinte à l'intégrité physique' in *Rapports belges au XIe congrès de l'Académie internationale de droit comparé*, Brussels, Bruylant, 1982, 283–311.

Krzeminska-Vamvaka, J. and O'Callaghan, P., 'Mapping out a right of privacy in tort law' in G. Brüggemeier, A. Colombi Ciacchi and G. Comandé (eds.), *Fundamental Rights and Private Law in the European Union*, Vol. II, *Comparative analyses of selected case patterns*, Cambridge, Cambridge University Press, 2010, 111–163.

Kumm, M., 'Who is Afraid of the Total Constitution? Constitutional Rights as Principles and the Constitutionalization of Private Law', *German Law Journal* 2006, 341–370.

Kuty, F., 'La satisfaction équitable et l'autorité de chose jugée des arrêts de la Cour européenne des droits de l'homme', *JLMB* 2000, 1571–1579.

Lahe, J., and Kull, I., 'Estonia' in H. Koziol and B. Steininger (eds.), *European Tort Law 2006*, Vienna, Springer, 2007, 178–190.

——, 'Punitive Damages in Estonian Tort Law?', *Journal of European Tort Law* 2011, 280–293.

Lambert Abdelgawad, E., 'La pratique récente de reparation des violations de la convention européenne de sauvegarde des droits de l'homme et des libertés fondamentales: plaidoyer pour la preservation d'un acquis remarquable', *Rev. Trim.D.H.* 2000, 199–227.

——, 'Introduction générale' in J.-F. Flauss and E. Lambert Abdelgawad (eds.), *La pratique d'indemnisation par la Cour européenne des droits de l'homme*, Brussels, Bruylant, 2011, 1–5.

——, 'Comment chifrer la réparation des traitements inhumains/dégradants et de la torture' in J.-F. Flauss and E. Lambert Abdelgawad (eds.), *La pratique d'indemnisation par la Cour européenne des droits de l'homme, Brussels*, Bruylant, 2011, 189–228.

Lampe, R., 'Slovenia' in H. Koziol and B. Steininger (eds.), *European Tort Law 2006*, Vienna, Springer, 2007, 417–428.

LAVENDER, N., 'The Problem of the Margin of Appreciation', *European Human Rights Law Review* 1997, 380–390.

LAVRANOS, N., 'Hierarchy in multilevel regulation' in A. FOLLESDAL, R.A. WESSEL and J. WOUTERS (eds.), *Multilevel regulation and the EU. The Interplay between Global, European and National Normative Processes*, Leiden, Martinus Nijhoff, 2008, 367–375.

LAVRYSEN, L., 'Human Rights in a Positive State: Rethinking the Relationship between Positive and Negative Obligations Under the European Convention on Human Rights', Ghent University Dissertation, 2016, 413p.

LAWSON, R., 'Positieve verplichtingen onder het EVRM: opkomst en ondergang van de "fair balance" test – Deel 1', *NJCM-Bulletin* 1995, 558–573.

——, 'Positieve verplichtingen onder het EVRM: opkomst en ondergang van de "fair balance" test – Deel 2', *NJCM-Bulletin* 1995, 727–750.

——, annotation under ECtHR, *Muso v Italy*, 14 December 1999, *NJCM-Bulletin* 2000, 693–697.

LEACH, P., 'Beyond the Bug River – A New Dawn for Redress Before the European Court of Human Rights', *European Human Rights Law Review* 2005, 148–164.

——, *Taking a Case to the European Court of Human Rights*, Oxford, Oxford University Press, 2011, 619p.

LEACH, P., PARASKEVA, C., and UZELAC, G., 'Human rights fact-finding. The European Court of Human Rights at a crossroads', *Netherlands Quarterly of Human Rights* 2010, 41–77.

LEIGH, I., 'The standard of judicial review after the Human Rights Act' in H. FENWICK, G. PHILIPPSON and R. MASTERMAN (eds.), *Judicial reasoning under the UK Human Rights Act*, Cambridge, Cambridge University Press, 2007, 174–205.

LÉONARD, T., *Conflits entre droits subjectifs, libertés civiles et intérêts légitimes*, Brussels, Larcier, 2005, 894p.

LIVINGSTONE, S., 'Article 14 and the Prevention of Discrimination in the European Convention on Human Rights', *European Human Rights Law Review* 1997, 25–34.

LONDONO, P., 'Positive Obligations, Criminal Procedure and Rape Cases', *European Human Rights Law Review* 2007, 158–171.

LOUCAIDES, L., 'Reparation for Violations of Human Rights under the European Convention and Restitutio in Integrum', *European Human Rights Law Review* 2008, 182–192.

LOVELAND, I., 'Rethinking the Rule in Hammersmith v. Monk from a Human Rights Perspective', *EHRLR* 2002, 327–342.

LUCAS, O., 'La Convention européenne des droits de l'homme et les fondements de la responsabilité civile', *La Semaine Juridique Edition Générale* 6 February 2002, 8p.

LUCAS, P., 'Pourrait-on évaluer le cas Noël Simar?' in R. CAPART and J. BOUCKOURT (eds.), *Liber Amicorum Nöel Simar: Evaluation du dommage, Responsabilité civile et Assurances*, Limal, Anthemis, 2013, 21–55.

LUNNEY, M., 'Trespass to Land' in K. OLIPHANT (ed.), *The Law of Tort*, Suffolk, LexisNexis Butterworths, 2007, 485–534.

MACDONALD, R., 'The Margin of Appreciation' in R. MACDONALD, F. MATSCHER and H. PETZOLD (eds.), *The European System for the Protection of Human Rights*, Dordrecht, Martinus Nijhoff Publishers, 1993, 83–124.

MACQUEEN, H., 'Delict, contract and the bill of rights: a perspective from the United Kingdom', *The South African Law Journal* 2004, 359–394.

MADDEN, M., 'Tort law through time and culture: themes of economic efficiency' in M. MADDEN (ed.), *Exploring Tort Law*, Cambridge, Cambridge University Press, 2005, 11–51.

MAGNUS, U., 'Causation in German Tort Law' in J. SPIER (ed.), *Unification of Tort Law: Causation*, Kluwer, Den Haag, 2000, 63–73.

——, 'Comparative Report on the Law of Damages' in U. MAGNUS et al. (eds.), *Unification of Tort Law: Damages*, The Hague, Kluwer, 2001, 185–217.

——, 'Why is US Tort Law so Different?', *Journal of European Tort Law* 2010, 102–124.

MAHIEU, M. and VAN DROOGHENBROECK, S., 'La responsabilité de l'état législateur', *JT* 1998, 825–846.

MAK, C., *Fundamental Rights in European Contract Law. A Comparison of the Impact of Fundamental Rights on Contractual Relationships in Germany, the Netherlands, Italy and England*, Alphen aan den Rijn, Kluwer, 2008, 365p.

MALINVAUD, P., FENOUILLET, D. and MEKKI, M., *Droit des obligations*, Paris, Lexisnexis, 2014, 802p.

MALINVERNI, G., 'Variations sur un thème encore méconnu: l'Article 13 de la Convention européenne des droits de l'homme', *Rev.Trim.D.H.* 1998, 647–657.

MARSHALL, J., 'A Rights to Personal Autonomy at the European Court of Human Rights', *European Human Rights Law Review* 2008, 337–356.

MAS, M.E., 'Right to Compensation under Article 50' in R. MACDONALD, F. MATSCHER and H. PETZOLD (eds.), *The European System for the Protection of Human Rights*, Dordrecht, Martinus Nijhoff Publishers, 1993, 775–790.

MASTERMAN, R., 'Aspiration or foundation? The status of the Strasbourg jurisprudence and the "Convention rights" in domestic law' in H. FENWICK, G. PHILIPPSON and R. MASTERMAN (eds.), *Judicial reasoning under the UK Human Rights Act*, Cambridge, Cambridge University Press, 2007, 57–86.

MATSCHER, F., 'Methods of Interpretation of the Convention' in R. MACDONALD, F. MATSCHER and H. PETZOLD (eds.), *The European System for the Protection of Human Rights*, Dordrecht, Martinus Nijhoff Publishers, 1993, 63–81.

MCBRIDE, J., 'Redress for human rights violations' in G. HAND and J. MCBRIDE (eds.), *Essays in honour of L. Neville Brown*, Oxford Monographs in International Law, Oxford, Oxford University Press, 1991, 161–174.

MCBRIDE, N. and BAGSHAW, R., *Tort Law*, Harlow, Pearson, 2012, 934p.

MCGREGOR, H., *McGregor on Damages*, London, Sweet & Maxwell, 2009, 1981p.

MCMANUS, F., 'Noise Pollution and Human Rights', *European Human Rights Law Review* 2005, 575–587.

MENYHARD, A., 'Hungary' in H. KOZIOL and B. STEININGER (eds.), *European Tort Law 2003*, Vienna, Springer, 2004, 231–244.

MERILLS, J., *The Development of International Law by the European Court of Human Rights*, Manchester, Manchester University Press, 1988, 235p.

MONTERO, E. and GOFFAUX, B., 'La référence au paradigme du "bon père de famille" en responsabilité extracontractuelle', *Forum de l'assurance Anthemis* 2014, no.140, 1–15.

MOREHAM, N., 'The Right to Respect for Private Life in the European Convention on Human Rights: A Re-examination', *European Human Rights Law Review* 2008, 44–79.

MOWBRAY, A., *The Development of Positive Obligations Under the European Convention on Human Rights by the European Court of Human Rights*, Oxford, Hart Publishing, 2004, 239p.

MULLIS, A., 'The law of defamation – part I' in K. OLIPHANT (ed.), *The Law of Tort*, Suffolk, LexisNexis Butterworths, 2007, 1279–1359.

——, 'The law of defamation – part II' in K. OLIPHANT (ed.), *The Law of Tort*, Suffolk, LexisNexis Butterworths, 2007, 1361–1504.

MURPHY, C., 'The Principle of Legality in Criminal Law under the European Convention on Human Rights', *European Human Rights Law Review* 2010, 192–207.

MYJER, E., 'Article 1 protocol 1 and the entitlement of just satisfaction' in H. VANDENBERGHE (ed.), *Propriété et droits de l'homme*, Bruges, Die Keure, 2006, 99–128.

NAVARRETTA, E. and BARGELLI, E., 'Italy' in H. KOZIOL and B. STEINIGER (eds.), *European Tort Law 2001*, Vienna, Springer, 2002, 335–352.

NAVARRETTA, E. and BARGELLI, E., 'Italy' in H. KOZIOL and B. STEININGER (eds.), *European Tort Law 2004*, Vienna, Springer, 2005, 382–394.

NEHMELMAN, R., 'Private vrijheid! Over de werking van grondrechten in het privaatrecht', *Letsel & Schade* 2011, afl. 1, 18–27.

NICOLAOU, G., 'The New Perspective of the European Court of Human Rights on the Effectiveness of its judgments', *Human Rights Law Journal* 2011, 269–275.

NIEUWENHUIS, J.H., 'Fundamental Rights Talk. An Enrichment of legal discourse in private law?' in T. BARKHUYSEN and S.D. LINDENBERGH, *Constitutionalization of Private Law*, Leiden, Martinus Nijhoff Publishers, 2006, 1–8.

NOLAN, D., 'Government liability' in K. OLIPHANT (ed.), *The Law of Tort*, Suffolk, LexisNexis Butterworths, 2007, 885–943.

——, 'Nuisance' in K. OLIPHANT (ed.), *The Law of Tort*, Suffolk, LexisNexis Butterworths, 2007, (1101) 1107.

——, 'Nuisance' in D. HOFFMAN (ed.), *The Impact of the UK Human Rights Act on Private Law*, Cambridge, Cambridge University Press, 2011, 165–194.

OF LAIRG, I., 'Activism and Restraint: Human Rights and the Interpretative Process', *European Human Rights Law Review* 1999, 350–372.

OLINGA, A.-D. and PICHERAL, C., 'La théorie de la marge d'appreciation dans la jurisprudence récente de la Cour européenne des droits de l'homme', *Rev.Trim.D.H.* 1995, 567–604.

Oliphant, K., 'England and Wales' in H. Koziol and B. Steiniger (eds.), *European Tort Law 2001*, Vienna, Springer, 2002, 131–175.

——, 'Comparative Remarks' in H. Koziol and B. Steininger (eds.), *European Tort Law 2008*, Vienna, Springer, 2009, 658–675.

——, 'Defamation' in D. Hoffman (ed.), *The Impact of the UK Human Rights Act on Private Law*, Cambridge, Cambridge University Press, 2011, 195–205.

——, 'Cultures of Tort Law in Europe', *Journal of European Tort Law*, 2012, 147–157.

Oliphant, K. and Ludwichowska, K., 'Damage' in A. Fenyves, E. Karner, H. Koziol and E. Steiner (eds.), *Tort Law in the Jurisprudence of the European Court of Human Rights*, Göttingen, De Gruyter, 2011, 397–447.

Oliver, D., 'England and Wales: The Human Rights Act and the Private Sphere' in D. Oliver and J. Fëdtke (eds.), *Human Rights and the Private Sphere – A Comparative Study*, London, Routledge, 2007, 63–97.

Opsahl, T., 'The Right to Life' in R. Macdonald, F. Matscher and H. Petzold (eds.), *The European System for the Protection of Human Rights*, Dordrecht, Martinus Nijhoff Publishers, 1993, 207–223.

Osborne, C., 'Does the End Justify the Means? Retrospectivity, Article 7, and the Marital Rape Exemption', *European Human Rights Law Review* 1996, 406–416.

Osiatynski, W., *Human Rights and Their Limits*, Cambridge, Cambridge University Press, 2009, 241p.

Palmer, V., 'May God protect Us from the Equity of Parliaments. Comparative perspectives on English and French Equity Power', *Tulane Law Review* 1998–99, 1287–1308.

Papier, H.-J., 'Execution and Effects of the Judgments of the European Court of Human Rights from the Perspective of German National Courts', *Human Rights Law Journal* 2006, 1–4.

Pasquino, P., 'Prolegomena to a theory of judicial power: the concept of judicial independence in theory and history', *The Law and Practice of International Courts and Tribunals* 2003, 11–25.

Pattinson, S. and Beyleveld, D., 'Horizontal applicability and horizontal effect', *Law Quarterly Review* 2002, 623–664.

Pettiti, C., 'Stratégie de la partie requérante face à la perspective d'octroi de dommages et intérêts par la cour Européenne des droits de l'homme' in J.-F. Flauss and E. Lambert Abdelgawad (eds.), *La pratique d'indemnisation par la Cour européenne des droits de l'homme*, Brussels, Bruylant, 2011, 56–74.

Petzold, H., 'The Convention and the Principle of Subsidiarity' in R. Macdonald, F. Matscher and H. Petzold (eds.), *The European System for the Protection of Human Rights*, Dordrecht, Martinus Nijhoff Publishers, 1993, 41–62.

Phillipson, G., 'Clarity postponed: horizontal effect after Campbell' in H. Fenwick, G. Philippson and R. Masterman (eds.), *Judicial reasoning under the UK Human Rights Act*, Cambridge, Cambridge University Press, 2007, 143–173.

——, 'Privacy: the development of breach of confidence – the clearest case of horizontal effect?' in D. Hoffman (ed.), *The Impact of the UK Human Rights Act on Private Law*, Cambridge, Cambridge University Press, 2011, 136–164.

PHILIPSON, G. and WILLIAMS, A., 'Horizontal Effect and the Constitutional Constraint', *The Modern Law Review* 2011, 878–910.

PINTO SOARES, P., 'Tangling Human Rights and international criminal law: the practice of international tribunals and the call for rationalized legal pluralism', *Criminal Law Forum* 2012, 161–191.

POLAK, J., 'Het EVRM en de vordering op grond van onrechtmatige overheidsdaad' in T. BARKHUYSEN, M. VAN EMMERIK and J. LOOF (eds.), *Geschakeld recht. Verdere studies over Europese grondrechten ter gelegenheid van de 70'ste verjaardag van prof. mr. E.A. Alkema*, Deventer, Kluwer, 2009, 425–439.

PRICE, D. and DUODU, K., *Defamation. Law, Procedure and Practice*, London, Sweet & Maxwell, 2004, 626p.

QUÉZAL-AMBRUNAZ, C., 'Fault, Damage and the Equivalence Principle in French Law', *Journal of European Tort Law* 2012, 21–43.

——, 'Des dommages et intérêts octroyés par la Cour européenne des droits de l'homme' *RDLF* 2014, chron. no.5.

QUILL, E., 'Ireland' in H. KOZIOL and B. STEININGER (eds.), *European Tort Law 2003*, Vienna, Springer, 2004, 245–265.

——, 'Affirmative Duties of Care in the Common Law', *Journal of European Tort Law* 2011, 151–183.

RADÉ, C., 'Réflexions sur les fondements de la responsabilité civile', *Dalloz.* 1999, 313–327.

——, 'Plaidoyer en faveur d'une réforme de la responsabilité civile', *Dalloz* 2003, 2247–2255.

RADULETU, I., 'Romania' in H. KOZIOL and B. STEININGER (eds.), *European Tort Law 2006*, Vienna, Springer, 2007, 516–546.

RAINEY, B., WICKS, E. and OVEY, C., *Jacobs, White and Ovey: The European Convention on Human Rights*, Oxford, Oxford University Press, 2017, 768p.

RIMANQUE, K. and PEETERS, P., 'De toepasselijkheid van grondrechten in de betrekkingen tussen private personen. Algemene probleemstelling' in K. RIMANQUE (ed.), *De toepasselijkheid van grondrechten in de betrekkingen tussen private personen*, Antwerp, Kluwer, 1982, 1–33.

REID, K., *A Practitioner's Guide to the European Convention on Human Rights*, London, Thomson, 2008, 709p.

REMY, P. and BORGHETTI, J.-S., 'Présentation du projet de réforme de la responsabilité délictuelle' in F. TERRÉ (ed.), *Pour une réforme du droit de la responsabilité civile*, Paris, Dalloz, 2011, 60–86.

RENUCCI, J.-F., *Droit européen des droits de l'homme*, Paris, Lextenso, 2012, 1297p.

RESS, G., 'The Effects of Judgments and Decisions in Domestic Law' in R. MACDONALD, F. MATSCHER and H. PETZOLD (eds.), *The European System for the Protection of Human Rights*, Dordrecht, Martinus Nijhoff Publishers, 1993, 801–850.

RIBON, J., 'Spain' in H. KOZIOL and B. STEININGER (eds.), *European Tort Law 2004*, Vienna, Springer, 2005, 538–567.

Rigaux, F., 'Les fondements philosophiques des droits de l'homme', *Rev.Trim.D.H.* 2007, 307–349.

Rimanque, K., 'Nationale bescherming van grondrechten', *TBP* 1981, 33–42.

Rizzo, A., 'Les incertitudes du juge face au concours de droits fondamentaux', *Rev.b.dr.const.* 2012, 115–159.

Rogers, W., 'Tort Law and Human Rights: A new experience?' in H. Koziol and B. Steininger (eds.), *European Tort Law 2002*, Vienna, Springer, 2003, 35–64.

Ronse, J., *Aanspraak op schadeloosstelling uit onrechtmatige daad*, Brussels, Larcier, 1954, 499p.

Ruedin, X.-B., 'De minimis non curat the European Court of Human Rights: The Introduction of a New Admissibility Criterion (Article 12 of Protocol No. 14)', *European Human Rights Law Review* 2008, 80–105.

Ruiz Fabri, H., 'The Use of International Judicial Precedents by the European Court of Human Rights: On the Trail of Judicial Policy', *European Journal of Human Rights* 2017, 231–248.

Sabard, O., 'Le principe de réparation intégrale menacé par la satisfaction équitable', *RGAR* 2014, nr. 15060.

Schamps, G., 'La prévisibilité du dommage en responsabilité civile. De son incidence sur la faute, et sur le rapport de causalité', *RDP* 1994, 375–395.

Schultz, M., 'Rights Through Torts: The Rise of a Rights Discourse in Swedish Tort Law', *European Review of Private Law* 2009, 305–333.

Scorey, D. and Eicke, T., *Human Rights Damages. Principles and Practices*, London, Sweet & Maxwell, looseleaf.

Sebok, A., 'Punitive damages in the United States' in H. Koziol and V. Wilcox (eds.), *Punitive Damages: Common Law and Civil Law Perspectives*, Springer, Vienna, 2009, 155–196.

Selelionyte-Drukteiniene, S., and Saltinyte, L., 'Lithuania' in K. Oliphant and B. Steininger (eds.), *European Tort Law* 2011, Berlin, De Gruyter, 2012, 386–419.

Sevinc, I., 'La pratique par la Turquie des règlements amiables et de leur composante indemnitaire' in J.-F. Flauss and E. Lambert Abdelgawad (eds.), *La pratique d'indemnisation par la Cour européenne des droits de l'homme*, Brussels, Bruylant, 2011, 85–110.

Sharpe, J., 'Article 50' in L.E. Pettitti, E. Decaux and P.-H. Imbert (eds.), *La Convention Européenne des droits de l'homme. Commentaire Article par Article*, Paris, Economica, 1999, 809–842.

Shelton, D., *Remedies in International Human Rights Law*, Oxford, Oxford University Press, 1999, 387p.

Shelton, D., 'Subsidiarity and Human Rights Law', *Human Rights Law Journal* 2006, 4–11.

——, *Buitencontractuele aansprakelijkheid*, II, *Schade en schadeloosstelling* in *Beginselen van Belgisch privaatrecht*, XI, Antwerp, Kluwer, 1999, 433p.

Simonart, H., 'L'obligation de légiférer adéquatement' in X. (ed.), *En homage à Francis Delpérée. Itinéraires d'un constitutionaliste*, Brussels, Bruylant, 2007, 1429–1439.

SING, R., *The Future of Human Rights in the United Kingdom: Essays on Law and Practice*, Oxford, Hart Publishing, 1997, 150p.

SIRINELLI, M., 'La stratégie des parties face à la perspective d'octroi de dommages-intérêts par la Cour – côté etat défendeur' in J.-F. FLAUSS and E. LAMBERT ABDELGAWAD (eds.), *La pratique d'indemnisation par la Cour européenne des droits de l'homme*, Brussels, Bruylant, 2011, 75–84.

SLOAN, A. and CHEPKE, M., *Medical Malpractice*, Cambridge Massachusetts, The Massachusetts Institute of Technology Press, 2008, 458p.

SMET, S., 'Introduction – Conflicts of Rights in Theoretical and Comparative Perspective' in S. SMET and E. BREMS, *When Human Rights Clash at the European Court of Human Rights*, Oxford, Oxford University Press, 2017, 1–20.

SMIS, S., JANSSENS, C., MIRGAUX, S. and VAN LAETHEM, K., *Handboek mensenrechten. De internationale bescherming van de rechten van de mens*, Antwerp, Intersentia, 2011.

SMITH, H., 'Non-Tracing Cases of Culpable Ignorance', *Criminal Law and Philosophy*, 2011, 115–146.

SMITH, M., 'The Adjudicatory Fact-finding Tools of the European Court of Human Rights', *European Human Rights Law Review* 2009, 206–228.

SMITS, J., 'Private Law and Fundamental Rights: a Sceptical View' in T. BARKHUYSEN and S.D. LINDENBERGH, *Constitutionalization of Private Law*, Leiden, Martinus Nijhoff Publishers, 2006, 9–22.

——, 'Constitutionalisering van het vermogensrecht' in X. (ed.), *Preadviezen uitgebracht voor de Nederlandse Vereniging voor Rechtsvergelijking*, Deventer, Kluwer, 2003, 1–163.

SOMERS, S., *Aansprakelijkheidsrecht en mensenrechten: Kruisbestuiving in een meergelaagde* rechtsorde, Antwerp, Intersentia, 2016, 787p.

——, 'Declaratory judgments and the right to compensation in the jurisprudence of the European Court of Human Rights: Does Art. 41 ECHR grants human right victims a right to financial compensation?', *European Journal of Human Rights* 2016, 57–82.

SPIELMANN, D., 'Obligations Positives et Effet Horizontal des Dispositions de la Convention' in F. SUDRE (red.), *L'interprétation de la Convention des droits de l'homme*, Brussels, Bruylant, 1998, 133–156.

——, 'Du principe de proportionalité dans la mise en oeuvre de la responsabilité du journaliste', *Rev.Trim.D.H.* 2002, 210–222.

——, 'The European Convention on Human Rights' in D. OLIVER and J. FËDTKE (eds.), *Human Rights and the Private Sphere – A Comparative Study*, London, Routledge, 2007, 427–464.

SPIER, J. and HAAZEN, O.A., 'Comparative conclusions on Causation' in J. SPIER et al. (eds.), *Unification of Tort Law: Causation*, The Hague, Kluwer, 2000, 127–154.

STEINER, E., 'Just Satisfaction under Art. 41 ECHR: A compromise in 1950 – Problematic Now' in A. FENYVES, E. KARNER, H. KOZIOL and E. STEINER (eds.), *Tort Law in the Jurisprudence of the European Court of Human Rights*, Göttingen, De Gruyter, 2011, 3–26.

Steininger, B., 'Wrongful Birth and Wrongful Life: Basic Questions', *Journal of European Tort Law* 2010, 125–155.

——, 'Austria' in K. Oliphant and B. Steininger (eds.), *European Tort Law 2011*, Berlin, De Gruytrer, 2012, 37–63.

Steininger, B. and Wallner-Friedl, N., 'Wrongfulness and Fault' in A. Fenyves, E. Karner, H. Koziol and E. Steiner (eds.), *Tort Law in the Jurisprudence of the European Court of Human Rights*, Göttingen, De Gruyter, 2011, 501–537.

Sudre, F., 'Les "Obligatons Positives" dans la jurisprudence europeénne des droits de l'homme', *Rev. Trim. Dr. H.*, 1995, 363–384.

Sundberg, F., 'Le principe de l'octroi subsidiaire des dommages-intérêts – coté comité des ministres' in J.-F. Flauss and E. Lambert Abdelgawad (eds.), *La pratique d'indemnisation par la Cour européenne des droits de l'homme*, Brussels, Bruylant, 2011, 27–51.

Supperstone, M. and Coppel, J., 'Judicial Review after the Human Rights Act', *European Human Rights Law Review* 1999, 301–329.

Szyczak, D., 'Le droit à indemnisation dans le cadre des procedures pilotes' in J.-F. Flauss and E. Lambert Abdelgawad (eds.), *La pratique d'indemnisation par la Cour européenne des droits de l'homme*, Brussels, Bruylant, 2011, 275–295.

The Law Commission and the Scottish Law Commission, *Damages under the Human Rights Act 1998. Report on a Reference under Section 3(1) (e) of the Law Commissions Act 1965*, SE/2000/182, <http://www.lawcom.gov.uk>, 188p.

Thiede, T. and Büyüksagis, E., 'Reduction of Damages' in A. Fenyves, E. Karner, H. Koziol and E. Steiner (eds.), *Tort Law in the Jurisprudence of the European Court of Human Rights*, Göttingen, De Gruyter, 2011, 803–821.

Thorgeisdottir, H., 'Journalism worthy of the name: an affirmative reading of Article 10 of the ECHR', *Netherlands Quarterly of Human Rights* 2004, 601–622.

Thunis, X., and Fosséprez, B., 'Caractère indemnitaire ou punitif des dommages et intérêts' in B. Dubuisson and P. Jourdain, *Le dommage et sa réparation dans la responsabilité contractuelle et extracontractuelle. Etudes de droit comparé*, Brussels, Larcier, 2015, 237–310.

Tichy, L., 'Czech Republic' in H. Koziol and B. Steiniger (eds.), *European Tort Law 2001*, Vienna, Springer, 2002, 105–130.

Touzé, S., 'Les limites de l'indemnisation devant la Cour européenne des droits de l'homme: le constat de violation comme satisfaction équitable suffisante' in J.-F. Flauss and E. Lambert Abdelgawad (eds.), *La pratique d'indemnisation par la Cour européenne des droits de l'homme*, Brussels, Bruylant, 2011, 127–153.

Troper, M., 'Who Needs a Third Party Effect Doctrine? The Case of France' in A. Sajo and R. Uitz (eds.), *The Constitution in Private Relations: Expanding Constitutionalism*, Utrecht, Eleven, 2005, 115–128.

Tulkens, F. and Van Kerckhove, M., 'La nature et les contours de la peine. Regards croisés sur la jurisprudence interne et internationale' in X. (ed.), *Une criminologie de la tradition à l'innovation. Hommage à Georges Kellens*, Brussels, Larcier, 2006, 453–474.

Turgis, S., 'La recours aux expertises' in J.-F. Flauss and E. Lambert Abdelgawad (eds.), *La pratique d'indemnisation par la Cour européenne des droits de l'homme*, Brussels, Bruylant, 2011, 113–125.

Uhl, R.-J., 'Vrijheid van meningsuiting en eigendomsrecht', *NJCM-Bulletin* 2005, 416–426.

Van, A., 'Recente ontwikkelingen op het gebied van de vergoeding van immateriële schade in de praktijk' in P. Kottenhagen-Edzes (ed.), *Immateriële schade: tendensen en wensen*, Groningen, Intersentia, 2000, 19–35.

Van Brustem, M., 'Mérule et insalubrité publique: l'autorité communale se voit imposer un devoir d'information des riverains', *JLMB* 2009, 1317–1321.

Van Dam, C., *European Tort Law*, Oxford, Oxford University Press, 2013, 601p.

——, 'Tort Law and Human Rights: Brothers in Arms. On the Role of Tort Law in the Area of Business and Human Rights', *Journal of European Tort Law* 2011, 221–254.

Van Drooghenbroeck, S., 'L'Article 17 de la convention européenne des droits de l'homme. Est-il indispensable?', *Rev.trim.D.H.* 2001, 540–566.

Van der Sloot, B., 'Where is the Harm in a Privacy Violation? Calculating the Damages Afforded in Privacy Cases by the European Court of Human Rights' *J.Intell.Prop.Info.Tech.&Elec.Com.L.* 2017, 322–351.

Van Eeckhoutte, D. and Vandaele, A., *Doorwerking van internationale normen in de Belgische rechtsorde*, Katholieke Universiteit Leuven, Instituut voor Internationaal Recht, Working Paper nr. 33, 2002, <http://www.law.kuleuven.be/iir/nl/onderzoek/wp/WP33n.pdf>, 31p.

Van de Heyning, C., 'Grondwettelijke Conversaties: een meerwaarde voor de bescherming van fundamentele rechten? De interpretatie en toepassing van fundamentele rechten in een complexe context van gelaagde bescherming', *TBP* 2012, 395–419.

Vande Lanotte, J. and Haeck, Y., *Handboek EVRM. Artikelsgewijze Commentaar.* Vol. II, Antwerp, Intersentia, 1995, 762p.

Vande Lanotte, J. and Haeck, Y., *Handboek EVRM. Algemene beginselen*, Vol. I, Antwerp, Intersentia, 2005, 949p.

Van Dijk, P., 'Access to Court' in R. Macdonald, F. Matscher and H. Petzold (eds.), *The European System for the Protection of Human Rights*, Dordrecht, Martinus Nijhoff Publishers, 1993, 345–379.

Van Emmerik, M.L., *Schadevergoeding bij schending van mensenrechten. De rechtspraktijk onder het EVRM vergeleken met die in Nederland*, Stichting NJCM-Boekerij, Leiden, 1997, 442p.

——, 'Verplichtingen voor de wetgever na Straatsburgse uitspraken op grond van het EVRM', *Preadvies Staatsrechtconferentie vol. 12: Wetgever en grondrechten*, Nijmegen, 2008, 129–160.

Van Gerven, W., *Beginselen van Belgisch Privaatrecht*, Vol. I, *Algemeen deel*, Brussels, E-story-scientia, 1987, 519p.

——, 'Principe de proportionallité, abus de droits et droits fondamentaux', *J.T.* 1992, 305–309.

——, 'Remedies for Infringements of Fundamental Rights', *European Public Law* 2004, 261–284.

Van Gerven, W., Lever, J. and Larouche, P., *Cases, Materials and Text on National, Supranational and International Tort Law*, Oxford, Hart Publishing, 2006, 969p.

Van Gerven, W. and Covemaeker, S., *Verbintenissenrecht*, Leuven, Acco, 2010, 719p.

Van Gerven, W. and Lierman, S., *Algemeen deel. Veertig jaar later. Privaat- en publiekrecht in een meergelaagd kader van regelgeving, rechtsvorming en rechtstoepassing*, Kluwer, Mechelen, 2010, 606p.

Van Grunderbeeck, D. and Seiburgh, C., 'Privaatrecht en grondrechten', *TPR* 2014, 643–688.

Van Leuven, N., *Contracten en mensenrechten*, Antwerp, Intersentia, 2009, 582p.

Van Leuven, N. and Vancrayebeek, L., 'L'effet horizontal des droits et libertés' in S. Van Drooghenbroeck (ed.), *Le droit international et européen des droits de l'homme devant le juge national*, Brussels, Larcier, 2014, 261–272.

Vanneste, F., 'A new inadmissibility ground' in P. Lemmens and W. Vandenhole (eds.), *Protocol No. 14 and the Reform of the European Court of Human Rights*, Antwerp, Intersentia, 2005, 69–88.

Van Rijn, A., 'Freedom of Expression (Article 10)' in P. Van Dijk, F. Van Hoof, A. Van Rijn and L. Zwaak (eds.), *Theory and Practice of the European Convention on Human Rights*, Antwerp, Intersentia, 2006, 773–816.

——, 'Right to the peaceful enjoyment of one's possessions (Article 1 of Protocol No. 1)' in P. Van Dijk, F. Van Hoof, A. Van Rijn and L. Zwaak (eds.), *Theory and Practice of the European Convention on Human Rights*, Antwerp, Intersentia, 2006, 863–893.

Vansweevelt, T. and Weyts, B., *Handboek Buitencontractueel Aansprakelijkheidsrecht*, Antwerp, Intersentia, 2009, 935p.

Van Zuylen, J., 'Du fait justificatif à la force majeure: les visages contrastés de l'exonération de la responsabilité' in R. Capart and J. Bouckourt (eds.), *Liber Amicorum Nöel Simar: Evaluation du dommage, Responsabilité civile et Assurances*, Limal, Anthemis, 2013, 263–298.

Varahus, J., 'Damages: private law and the HRA – never the twain shall meet?' in D. Hoffman (ed.), *The Impact of the UK Human Rights Act on Private Law*, Cambridge, Cambridge University Press, 2011, 223–248.

Velaers, J., 'De proliferatie van de zgn. klassieke "liberale" grondrechten in de XXIe eeuw' in X. (ed.), *De Grondwet in groothoekperspectief. Liber amicorum discipuloremque Karel Rimanque*, Antwerp, Intersentia, 2007, 99–159.

Vermeulen, B., 'Freedom from torture and other inhuman or degrading treatment or punishment' in P. Van Dijk, F. Van Hoof, A. Van Rijn and L. Zwaak (eds.), *Theory and Practice of the European Convention on Human Rights*, Antwerp, Intersentia, 2006, 405–441.

Viney, G., *Introduction à la responsabilité*, Paris, Librairie Générale de Droit et de Jurisprudence, 2008, 693p.

VINEY, G. and JOURDAIN, P., *Les conditions de la responsabilité*, Paris, Librairie Générale de Droit et de Jurisprudence, 2006, 1,397p.

——, 'Réparation en nature, cessation de l'illicite et mesures purement préventives. Rapport français' in B. DUBUISSON and P. JOURDAIN, *Le dommage et sa réparation dans la responsabilité contractuelle et extracontractuelle. Etudes de droit comparé*, Brussels, Larcier, 2015, 7–58.

VINEY, G. and JOURDAIN, P., *Les effets de la responsabilité*, Paris, Librairie Générale de Droit et de Jurisprudence, 2011, 936p.

VOERMANS, W., 'Applicability of Fundamental Rights in Private Law: What is the Legislature to do? An Intermezzo from a Constitutional Point of View' in T. BARKHUYSEN and S.D. LINDENBERGH, *Constitutionalization of Private Law*, Leiden, Martinus Nijhoff Publishers, 2006, 33–41.

VON BAR, C., *Principles of European Law. Non-Contractual Liability Arising out of Damage Caused to Another*, München, European Law Publishers, 2009, 1384p.

WALDRON, J., 'John Locke: Social contract versus political anthropology' in D. BOUCHER and P. KELLY (eds.), *The Social Contract from Hobbes to Rawls*, London, Routledge, 1994, 51–72.

——, 'Are Sovereigns Entitled to the benefit of the International Rule of Law?', *European Journal of International Law* 2011, 315–343.

WALTER, R., 'Gleichheitsgrundsatz und Schadenersatzrecht', *Zeitschrift für Verkehrsrecht* 1979, 33–43.

WARBRICK, C., 'The European Convention on Human Rights and the Human Rights Act: the view from outside' in H. FENWICK, G. PHILIPPSON and R. MASTERMAN (eds.), *Judicial reasoning under the UK Human Rights Act*, Cambridge, Cambridge University Press, 2007, 25–56.

WATERS, C., 'Loutchansky v. Times Newspapers: the impact of the UK's Human Rights Act on private law and a comparison with the Canadian approach', *Alberta Law Review* 2003, 761–769.

WESTER-OUISSE, V. and THIEDE, T., 'Punitive Damages in France: A new Deal?', *Journal of European Tort Law* 2012, 115–122.

WHEELER, M., 'The Constitutional Case for Reforming Punitive Damages Procedures', *Virginia Law Review* 1983, 269–351.

WIDMER, P., 'Causation under Swiss Law' in J. SPIER (ed.), *Unification of Tort Law: Causation*, Kluwer, Den Haag, 2000, 105–122.

WIDMER, P., 'Comparative Report on Fault as a Basis of Liability and Criterion of Imputation (Attribution)' in P. WIDMER et al. (eds.), *Unification of Tort Law: Fault*, The Hague, Kluwer, 2005, 331–367.

WILCOX, V., 'Punitive Damages in England' in H. KOZIOL and V. WILCOX (eds.), *Punitive Damages: Common Law and Civil Law Perspectives*, Vienna, Springer, 2009, 7–53.

——, 'Punitive and Nominal Damages' in A. FENYVES, E. KARNER, H. KOZIOL and E. STEINER (eds.), *Tort Law in the Jurisprudence of the European Court of Human Rights*, Göttingen, De Gruyter, 2011, 725–740.

——, *A Company's Right to Damage for Non-Pecuniary Loss*, Cambridge, Cambridge University Press, 2016, 192p.

Wilcox, V. and Riss, O., 'Contributory Negligence' in A. Fenyves, E. Karner, H. Koziol and E. Steiner (eds.), *Tort Law in the Jurisprudence of the European Court of Human Rights*, Göttingen, De Gruyter, 2011, 771–802.

Williams, A., 'Public authorities: what is a hybrid public authority under the HRA?' in D. Hoffman (ed.), *The Impact of the UK Human Rights Act on Private Law*, Cambridge, Cambridge University Press, 2011, 48–65.

Winiger, B., 'Strict liability: what about fault?' in H. Koziol and B. Steiniger (eds.), *European Tort Law 2001*, Vienna, Springer, 2002, 2–17.

Wintemute, R., 'Filling the Article 14 "Gap": Government Ratification and Judicial Control of Protocol No. 12 ECHR', *European Human Rights Law Review* 2004, 485–499.

Witt, J., 'The long history of state constitutions and American tort law', *Rutgers Law Journal* 2005, 1158–1199.

Wolfram, K., 'Just Satisfaction in Art 41 ECHR and Public International Law – Issues of Interpretation and Review of International Materials' in A. Fenyves, E. Karner, H. Koziol and E. Steiner (eds.), *Tort Law in the Jurisprudence of the European Court of Human Rights*, Göttingen, De Gruyter, 2011, 345–386.

Wright, J., *Tort Law and Human Rights*, Oxford, Hart Publishing, 2001, 206p.

——, *Tort Law and Human Rights*, Oxford, Hart Publishing, 2017, 312p.

Wünsch, S., and Panetti, F., 'Non-pecuniary damages: how fundamental rights shake traditional barriers' in G. Brüggemeier, A. Colombi Ciacchi and G. Comandé (eds.), *Fundamental Rights and Private Law in the European Union*, Vol. II, *Comparative analyses of selected case patterns*, Cambridge, Cambridge University Press, 2010, 165–199.

Xenos, D., *The Positive Obligations of the State under the European Convention of Human Rights*, New York, Routledge, 2012, 231p.

Young, A., 'Mapping horizontal effect' in D. Hoffman (ed.), *The Impact of the UK Human Rights Act on Private Law*, Cambridge, Cambridge University Press, 2011, 16–47.

Zwaak, L., 'General Survey of the European Convention' in P. Van Dijk, F. Van Hoof, A. Van Rijn and L. Zwaak (eds.), *Theory and Practice of the European Convention on Human Rights*, Antwerp, Intersentia, 2006, 1–93.

——, 'The Procedure before the European Court of Human rights' in P. Van Dijk, F. Van Hoof, A. Van Rijn and L. Zwaak (eds.), *Theory and Practice of the European Convention on Human Rights*, Antwerp, Intersentia, 2006, 95–290.

ABOUT THE AUTHOR

Dr Stefan Somers is a professor at the Free University of Brussels (VUB) where he lectures on the law of obligations. He is also a trainee judge and prosecutor at the Court of First Instance and the Commercial Court, Antwerp. He obtained Bachelor's degrees in both law and history at the University of Antwerp and Master's degrees in both law and political sciences at the Catholic University of Leuven (KU Leuven). During his PhD studies, he undertook research at Oxford University, Leiden University, Paris II Panthéon-Assas and the Institute for European Tort Law Vienna. In 2015–16 Stefan worked as an attorney at the Antwerp Bar Association. In 2016–17 he was a post-doctoral BAEF fellow at Columbia Law School.

www.ingramcontent.com/pod-product-compliance
Ingram Content Group UK Ltd.
Pitfield, Milton Keynes, MK11 3LW, UK
UKHW021827100926
8556IPUK00003B/194

9 781780 68683

